"Much has been written (and considerably more said!) on the practical challenges confronting the church, on the need for the church to interact more effectively with contemporary culture and on practical strategies for addressing the problems it faces. Ross Hastings has the theological depth and insight to penetrate beyond commonplace admonitions and advice to offer a penetrating analysis of the triune mission of God and how this encourages us to conceive and reconceive the mission that defines the church. The result is inspired and inspiring! Moreover, the integrated vision of the church that unfolds is not only encouraging and uplifting, it serves to address in original and profound ways precisely those 'practical' concerns which so easily confuse and mislead us. This should be obligatory reading not only for ministers and students but for all those who have thought to ask what it is to be the church."

Alan J. Torrance, professor of systematic theology, University of St. Andrews

"Ross Hastings—pastor, theologian, scientist, lover of people—has written what can only be called a 'game changer.' With Spirit-infused passion, insight, precision and grace, Ross has engaged all the major players in the missional conversation and has significantly moved the conversation forward. Massively forward! Working with the Easter evening story of the resurrected Jesus in John 20, Ross relentlessly and joyfully draws us deeper and deeper into a thrilling vision of the inner life of the triune missional God. As a result we can face the challenges before us out of renewed intimacy and 'intoxication' with the Great Missionary. This is the book we will return to again and again!"

Darrell Johnson, pastor, First Baptist Church, Vancouver, BC

"Ross Hastings has written a masterful work that, while taking a step back in order to look at the sad state of much of the Western church, offers hope based on deep theological truths and a renewed understanding of what we as a community of believers are called to embrace. Looking at missional concepts from a communal context, Ross sounds a clarion call for the church to become what it was intended to be, a community of shalom, healing and forgiveness in a hostile land."

Andy Harrington, executive director, Greater Vancouver Youth for Christ

D1554120

"Drawing on theological conversation partners throughout the history of the church, and more importantly, the text of Scripture, Ross Hastings has crafted the definitive work on the missional church. Hastings brings into a dynamic synthesis years of pastoral experience and academic research and teaching. This is theology at its best: grounded in the Word of God, immensely practical and founded supremely on the beautiful reality of the missional triune God. After a careful analysis of our societal and ecclesial reality, Hastings takes us on an inspiring tour of trinitarian theology, Christian humanism, the kingdom of God and a deep ecclesiology. The end result of God's mission, he argues, is the inbreaking of the kingdom, shalom in the world, and a fully human existence for people inside and outside the church. Thus the missional church would be both wide and deep. Would that this book were read and applied by every church leader."

R. Paul Stevens, professor emeritus of marketplace theology, Regent College, Vancouver, and author, *The Other Six Days and Doing God's Business*

Missional God, Missional Church

HOPE FOR RE-EVANGELIZING THE WEST

...

ROSS HASTINGS

IVP Academic

An imprint of InterVarsity Press
Downers Grove, Illinois

InterVarsity Press
P.O. Box 1400, Downers Grove, IL 60515-1426
World Wide Web: www.ivpress.com
E-mail: email@ivpress.com

InterVarsity Press® is the book-publishing division of InterVarsity Christian Fellowship/USA®, a movement of
students and faculty active on campus at hundreds of universities, colleges and schools of nursing in the United States
of America, and a member movement of the International Fellowship of Evangelical Students. For information
about local and regional activities, write Public Relations Dept., InterVarsity Christian Fellowship/USA, 6400
Schroeder Rd., P.O. Box 7895, Madison, WI 53707-7895, or visit the IVCF website at <www.intervarsity.org>.

All Scripture quotations, unless otherwise indicated, are taken from the Holy Bible, Today's New International
Version™ Copyright © 2001 by International Bible Society. All rights reserved.

Cover design: Cindy Kiple
Images: commuters: ©René Mansi/iStockphoto
        stained glass: © Leah-Anne Thompson/iStockphoto
Interior design: Beth Hagenberg

ISBN 978-0-8308-3955-1

Printed in the United States of America ∞

Library of Congress Cataloging-in-Publication Data

Hastings, Ross, 1956-
  Missional God, missional church : hope for re-evangelizing the West /
Ross Hastings.
      p. cm.
  Includes bibliographical references (p.   ) and index.
  ISBN 978-0-8308-3955-1 (pbk. : alk. paper)
  1. Missions—Theory. 2. Church 3. Trinity. I. Title.
  BV2063.H35 2012
  266—dc23

                                                                                    2012027654

| P | 20 | 19 | 18 | 17 | 16 | 15 | 14 | 13 | 12 | 11 | 10 | 9 | 8 | 7 | 6 | 5 | 4 | 3 | 2 | 1 |
| Y | 29 | 28 | 27 | 26 | 25 | 24 | 23 | 22 | 21 | 20 | 19 | 18 | 17 | 16 | 15 | 14 | 13 | 12 |

to my late wife Sharon,

beloved of God

Contents

Preface 11

Acknowledgments 17

1 THE GREATEST COMMISSION 19

    Outlines of John 20:19-23 and of This Book 22

    Matters of Interpretation 28

    Defiant Optimism 31

    The State of the Western Church 33

**2 BREAKING FREE THROUGH DISCERNING
INCULTURATION** 37

    Inculturation Without Enculturation 38

    Cultural Disconnection of Western Churches
    and Breaking Free 39

**3 BREAKING FREE OF THE ENTRAPMENT OF
INDISCRIMINATE ENCULTURATION** 59

    Indiscriminate Enculturation of the
    Western Churches 62

    Despair Leading to Isolation 69

    Despair Within Even the Radical Emergent 71

    The Despair Undergirding Radical Orthodoxy 74

    Hope in the Christocentric, Trinitarian Church 77

4 GREATEST CO-MISSION: THE MISSIONAL TRINITY 80

    What Does It Mean to Be Trinitarian? 83

    The Trinity and the Power of Relationality 84

    The Trinity and the Dignity of Personhood 93

    The Trinity and Coinherence 99

    The Immanent and the Economic Trinities
    (Two Trinities or One?) 100

    The Trinity and Creation 106

    The Trinity and Election 108

    The Trinity and the Church: *Unity with Diversity*. . . . 112

PART ONE: DISCOVERING SHALOM 119

5 COMMUNITIES OF CHRIST'S RISEN PRESENCE. 121

    Church as Christocentric Community. 122

    Church as Celebratory Community 125

    Church as a Community of Shalom 126

    Church as a Missional, Open Community:
    A Community of Hospitality. 128

    Church as Essential Community 131

    Church as the One Catholic Community 135

    Church as Community That Is Both Lively and Old . . 136

    Church as a Missional Community 140

    Church as a Catechetical Community 144

6 MISSION OF INCARNATION AND RESURRECTION 147

The Incarnation-Resurrection Dynamic Reaffirms
God's Creation and Confirms the Church's Mission
as a Creational Mission 149

The Incarnation-Resurrection Dynamic Affirms That
Christian Mission Is a New Creational Mission 169

7 COMMUNITIES OF CHRIST'S CRUCIFIED PRESENCE:
BEAUTIFUL SCARS 190

Communities of Christ's Crucified Presence:
Joy Generated by Beautiful Scars 192

Communities of Christ's Crucified Presence:
Through Christocentric, Cruciform Worship,
Teaching and Community Life 198

8 MISSION ABOUT THE CROSS, MISSION UNDER
THE CROSS: HIS COMPLETED REDEMPTION 219

Mission About the Cross 222

Mission Under the Cross 230

PART TWO: DISSEMINATING SHALOM 241

9 COMMUNITIES OF THE TRIUNE MISSIONAL GOD:
MISSION THE MOTHER OF THEOLOGY,
THEOLOGY THE MOTHER OF MISSION 243

Biblical Evidence of God as Missional 246

Theological Considerations of God as Missional 249

The Nature of the Missional Church 265

10 MISSION AS THEOSIS 268

    Participation in the Son's Sentness *by the Spirit* 271

    Participation in the *Son's Sentness* by the Spirit 276

    Implications of Incarnational and Pneumatic
    Theosis for the Church's Mission 285

11 COMMUNITIES OF THE SPIRIT:
GATHERED AND SCATTERED 293

    The Spirit in the Missional Church Gathered. 295

    The Spirit in Missional Church Moral Formation . . . 301

    The Spirit in the Missional Church Scattered. 304

12 COMMUNITIES OF FORGIVENESS:
MISSION OF ABSOLUTION AND FREEDOM 307

    Remission at the Heart of the Gospel 308

    Remission Expressed in Participation
    with Christ by the Spirit. 310

    Remission as an Initial and Permanent Saving Act
    and as an Ongoing Relational Practice 313

    Remission and Reconciliation as a
    Sign of the Kingdom. 318

Bibliography. 323

Name and Subject Index 327

Scripture Index 331

Preface

■ ■ ■

CONFLICT BETWEEN THE SO-CALLED traditional evangelical church and various strands of the emerging church is now well-documented. A middle way described as the *deep church* has been proposed by two sets of authors. In *Remembering Our Future: Explorations in Deep Church* (Andrew Walker and Luke Bretherton, eds.), a group of mostly British scholars, rather than directly assailing either the traditional or the emerging wings of the church, drive all parties back to the roots and into the depths of what it means to be the one, holy, catholic and apostolic church of Christ. They suggest that severance from these roots threatens the long-term viability of the emerging churches, who in their championing of relevance to the emerging culture may neglect the depth of the tradition. They also implicitly challenge any tendencies of the traditional church to ignore culture and state that "to be a deep church means to stand on the cusp or the breaking point of both the Christian tradition and the emerging culture, deeply rooted in the former while fully engaged in the latter."[1] Depth is defined in terms of catholicity, liturgy, catechesis, community and so on. By contrast, Jim Belcher's work *Deep Church* majors on the concerns and deficits of the emerging church, offering similarly deep understandings and practices.[2]

---

[1]Andrew Walker and Luke Bretherton, eds., *Remembering Our Future: Explorations in Deep Church* (London: Paternoster Press, 2007), p. xviii.
[2]Like the British authors, Belcher borrows the term "deep church" from C. S. Lewis. Surprisingly, he interacts very little with their work.

Neither of these books on the deep church challenges the contention that the nature of the church is missional. Rather, they support it. My contribution to this important ongoing discussion of the nature of the besieged church in the twenty-first century is to express affirmation of the so-called deep approach but to re-emphasize the *missional* nature of the deep church, and therefore to suggest that missional may in fact be a better term to describe the kind of ecclesiology necessary for such a time as this (at all times, actually, but especially necessary when the church is in decline and captivity, as it is in the West in our day). My principal concern is to make explicit what may be implicit in the deep church approach, that the deep church is in fact the *wide* church also. It is to contend that *missional church* is a term that, if properly understood to mean that the church is both centrifugal and centripetal, will challenge and enrich both the traditional and the emerging churches.

My book, in revisiting John's image of the church in John 20, will seek both to vindicate and to nuance the missional or "mission-shaped" church (UK) concept. It will do so by indicating that the church that is deeply intimate with the triune missional God cannot fail to be intentionally and widely influential in all aspects of mission, the mission of fulfilling the cultural mandate that calls us to be fully human in all aspects of human life—marriage, family, vocation (Gen 1–2); the mission of loving our neighbors (Mt 22) through acts of compassion and justice seeking, because we love the God who created them and has in Christ reconciled the world to himself; and the mission to evangelize and make disciples of all nations (Mk 16; Mt 28).

What motivates this book is that the church's missional nature, as this was expounded principally by David Bosch and Lesslie Newbigin in the last century, is still not nearly well enough known by evangelical churches of the traditional kind, and that some of its nuances have been missed also by some emerging church proponents. If the former were to discover the theological roots of the missional story, they would discover with delight that the essence of the triune God they profess to worship is missional, and indeed, that his mission is the essence and primary hermeneutic of the biblical story. They could then re-envision their churches as communities of deep communion with that missional

triune God of the gospel, and communities who therefore can participate in his mission to the world. This will bring needed change to
many of these churches that are more indiscriminately enculturated
within the culture of modernity than they may realize, on the one
hand, and who are unable to discerningly inculturate the gospel into
contemporary culture, on the other.

They would, to their surprise, realize also that the depth of church
life would in fact be enhanced by a proper understanding of the missional concept. Formation of the church community and of persons
within it by its deep practices would enhance the missional impact of
these persons. However, they would be awakened to the fact that even
in the deepest of church practices, the church acts for the world of humanity in its holy priesthood, and can never, therefore, forget mission.
As holy priests gathered, the church represents the world to God. Furthermore, as royal priests scattered, the church mediates the presence of
God into the world, spreading shalom and inviting people into reconciliation with God so that they may become Christian and fully human.
In this *wide* scattered work, the people of God are further deepened as
they encounter Christ in the stranger, the prisoner, the poor. So, depth
has width in mind, and width results in depth. This is the missional
church, and in this sense, I propose that *missional* is a better term than
deep for the church. The missional church is *both* deep *and* wide.

Vital to this concept is the grounding of the church's nature, or ecclesiology, in theology proper, and furthermore, within a specifically
and fully trinitarian theology proper—one that is from and to the
Father, and that is both christological or incarnational *and* pneumatic.
Irenaeus's analogy of the revelation of the Father by his "two hands" the
Son and the Spirit provides an important set of criteria for evaluating
just how the church needs to be missional. My concern with calling a
church *deep*, therefore, is that the emphasis returns to ecclesiology or
ecclesiological practices. Whereas the term *missional* runs the risk of
creating all kinds of misconceptions until explained, its core derivation
is the God of the gospel, the self-revelation of God in Christ by the
Spirit. That major creedal understanding, then, in proper order, leads
to ecclesiological practices that are both deep and wide.

The concept of the deep church is an important corrective also for some emerging churches that have lost all connectedness with the church catholic and historic. Belcher's treatment of this is compelling. The foundation of these deep concepts is again the triune missional nature of God. For example, it is the incarnational nature of the historic church modeled on the incarnation of its Head, Christ, that necessitates that the church of today see its connectedness creedally and liturgically with the church of yesterday. Furthermore, the seeming neglect of the pneumatic in some forms of the emergent and missional emergent churches finds a corrective in a nuanced understanding of the missional which, because it is trinitarian, is pneumatic as well as incarnational. Emphasis on engagement with culture requires an openness to the work of the Spirit for discernment. Pursuit of solidarity and social justice, often justified within an incarnational rubric, will without the energizing of the Spirit lead to a de-emphasis on evangelism, and a false equating of political liberation with the kingdom of God.

Our treatment of the missional church in this Johannine context will interact also with the Anabaptist approach to church life championed by John Howard Yoder, Stanley Hauerwas, William Willimon and other authors. These authors emphasize the exilic nature of the church and urge a model of church in which the integrity of church life and the formation of persons in community is of paramount importance. Faithfulness in the life of discipleship is key within this approach. The church is characterized by depth of community. *Deep church* as a descriptor can thus subsume this approach.

While I would be the first to applaud this communal depth, and the need for formation, I hope to offer a counterbalance in the missional approach, to what I perceive again to be an overemphasis on depth that neglects the width. If the church is an image of the Trinity, it should not be merely *communio* (communion), but *communio* in *ekstasis* (outpouring)—the communion of the Trinity flowed out in the creating of a universe in love, by an act of his will, and the reconciliation of a fallen creation. Similarly, the church does not circle the wagons to become merely a church faithful to its identity, filled with well-formed Christian persons in communion. Yes, its existence as a loving community will in itself be missional. However, this approach seems to suggest ever so slightly an ethos of isolationism. The church that is true to its mission to participate with the triune God in his mission to the world, by being the image of the Trinity in the world, will have a profound sense of engagement with the world of people and the public square and culture and culture-making and creation care. It will meet for deep practices but always with an awareness that it is a sign of the kingdom of God, a harbinger of a redeemed new humanity. There will be a distinction made between the Christian and the non-Christian, but there will be an openness to the seeker that invites her to belong before she may believe, precisely because the church must take the desire of God that all should believe seriously, precisely because the intended scope of the justification accomplished by Christ in his vicarious humanity, death and resurrection was humanity—all of it.

In sum, for those who stress the sentness aspect of the missional approach to an extent that any concept of a gathered church with a deep inner life is neglected, or who promote the idea that meetings with seekers at Starbucks constitutes the church, I wish to offer the corrective that to be truly missional in participation with the missional God means acknowledging that there is a bringing dimension to the nature and mission of God, and that therefore there ought to be a concomitant bringing (centripetal as well as centrifugal) or gathering dimension to the life of the church.

What I offer here is a theology of the church that is, in a nutshell, *participational*, that its missional identity is an organic consequence of union in and participation with the missional God, who is bidirectional in His missional nature. He *both sends and brings*. The church in union with God will therefore be a bidirectional, a sending and a bringing church. It will gather to press into that union. It will therefore as gathered be a missional presence in the world and a priesthood representing humanity to God. Its outgoing mission as the scattered church is also a participation in the ongoing mission on earth that Christ began and then entrusted his people to finish (Jn 20:21; Acts 1:1). Its task is not to do mission but to join God in what he by the Spirit is already doing. It must be deep and it will be wide in its character as the missional church participating in the life and love of its Head. Its deep and wide missional identity is the only hope for the re-evangelization of the West.

I seek here, then, to justify an eccesiology that is missional, and to push back just a little on the *deep church* approach, even though I suspect that when all is said and done, the sentiments I offer will find large resonance with that approach.

In sum, in this book, I seek to offer hope for the re-evangelization of the West in the twenty-first century by promoting the concept that mission is participation of the church and its members in the missional God. It will describe the missional church as the church that participates in the love and life of the triune God, as a continuance of the mission of the Son from the Father, by the Spirit. A theological exposition of the pronouncement by the risen Jesus of the "Greatest Commission" in John 20:19-23, it will be a call for churches to break through their walls by rediscovering their missional identity in the missional God, creating awareness that when they do so in a fully trinitarian way, the following traits may be found to coinhere, rather than collide: missional width *and* spiritual depth, openness to the world *and* integrity of the church, cultural relevance *and* confessional rootedness in the grand narrative of the Christian tradition and historic orthodoxy, openness to the surprising new works of the Spirit *and* a catholicity that reflects the depth of a liturgical and sacramental tradition.

Acknowledgments

■ ■ ■

I WISH TO THANK THE FOLLOWING PEOPLE without whom this book would never have been written. It was barely begun when my wife, Sharon, was diagnosed with ovarian cancer. She passed away 21 months later, on September 23, 2008. Its writing was therefore put on hold until after she passed away, and much of it was crafted in a season of deep grief during which the exercise of writing provided some structure and escape from profound sense of loss. How much Sharon shaped my life in our twenty-seven years of happy and deeply interdependent marriage, and therefore whatever is enriching in this book, is impossible to estimate. I am unable to express the fullness of my gratitude for her gracious spirit and all the sacrifices she made in enabling my pastoral and academic pursuits. I express gratitude also to my children Martyn and Heather for their love and support and sacrifices made in the years I pastored churches in the missional pursuit, and during my studies, all of which prepared me for what is written in this book. The book has been finished in the last year in the course of the development of a relationship with my new wife Tammy, who lost her husband, Carlos, to cancer five weeks before Sharon died. We were married in November 2011. The "resurrection" experience of newfound love, an expanded family life with Keila, Brandon and Celia, and the great personal inspiration of Tammy, have contributed significantly in the finishing stages of the process. That I have embraced the mission of the triune God is in significant measure the result of the influence upon me of my

Scottish parents, Willie and Betty Hastings, who have served with distinction as missionaries in Africa for over sixty years.

I wish also to thank my students in the course "Empowering the Church for Re-evangelization of the West," which I have taught at Regent College for the past six years. I have learned a great deal from them. I owe a debt also to Darrell Johnson and Charles Ringma, who taught this course before me and left for me a legacy and rubric on which I have sought to build. I am grateful also for the granting by Regent of a gracious leave of absence and sabbatical time for writing. I wish to thank my teaching assistants, Lydia Cruttwell, Rebecca Pousette and Ricky St-Pierre, for their assistance with the bibliography and proofreading. I am grateful also to Robert Hand for his editorial assistance in an earlier draft. The people of the churches I have served in Westminster Bible Chapel, Westview Bible Church and Peace Portal Alliance Church have also made a great contribution to my development as a missional pastor. I am indebted to all my fellow elders and pastors in the latter church, with special mention of the late Len Hordyk, Scott Dickie, Jon Imbeau, Phil Vanderveen, Jim Postlewaite and Mike Richardson, who especially journeyed with me in missional thinking.

On the theological front, I owe a great debt to two particular scholars: J. I. Packer, my master's thesis supervisor, whose foundational influence has helped me craft a book which I hope may be described as "Knowing the Missional God," and Alan Torrance, my theology Ph.D. thesis supervisor, who helped impart to me the fresh understanding of the glory and mission of the specifically *triune* God of grace that grounds and pervades this book. I am very grateful also to IVP for giving me the opportunity to publish and specifically to Gary Deddo for his influence and editorial guidance.

1

The Greatest Commission

■ ■ ■

On the evening of that first day of the week, when the disciples
were together, with the doors locked for fear of the Jewish leaders,
Jesus came and stood among them and said, "Peace be with you!"
After he said this, he showed them his hands and side. The
disciples were overjoyed when they saw the Lord.

Again Jesus said, "Peace be with you!
As the Father has sent me, I am sending you." And with
that he breathed on them and said, "Receive the Holy Spirit.
If you forgive the sins of anyone, their sins are forgiven;
if you do not forgive them, they are not forgiven."

JOHN 20:19-23

Strictly speaking one ought to say that the Church is
always in a state of crisis and that its greatest shortcoming
is that it is only occasionally aware of it.

DAVID J. BOSCH, *Transforming Mission*

MUCH INK HAS BEEN SPILLED on the crisis state of the church in the
West in recent decades. While I do not wish to minimize the reality that
most churches in this area are not growing and that many professing
Christians have opted out of church, the intent of this book is to suggest

that no matter how dark things may seem, the church will never be in a worse state than that described in John 20:19, pre-Jesus, and that if the dynamics that are present post-Jesus in John 20:20-23 are rediscovered in the church today, it can be all that this little community became.

Such audacious optimism rests not in any idealistic foundationalism but in the roots of the church's being. It rests in the historical and organic continuity between that small group of disciples and the church today, and above all it rests on the triune God of grace who still inhabits that church despite its beleaguered state, and is at work in the world through it to bring to completion the new creation Christ has inaugurated.

The "before" picture of this group of disciples, this microcosm of the church, is of a motley crew of notable failures. They had ministered effectively alongside Jesus for three years and their level of competence toward the end of that season had led some of them to think they might even sit in close proximity to Jesus in his coming kingdom. However, then came the trial and the cross. They failed miserably, to a man. Even postresurrection, they were in a pretty sorry state, so far unconvinced for the most part by the sight of an empty tomb, and the claims of Mary Magdalene that she had seen him.[1] Sad though their chauvinism or jealousy may have been, this only magnifies the amazing grace of Christ who appeared to them on Easter Sunday evening despite all.

We can feel some sympathy given that they were undoubtedly numb with grief, a grief riddled with regrets. It is true that John attributes their isolation to fear. But it was a fear no doubt intertwined with sporadic numbness alongside the turbulent waves of grief and remorse. Most importantly, the total situation of the first disciples as John describes it—in a room behind locked doors for fear of the Jewish leaders of that day—is, I believe, a metaphor for their powerless state. Chrysologus notes that the "extent of their terror and the disquiet caused by such an atrocity had simultaneously locked the house and the hearts of the disciples."[2] This infant microcosm of the church hadn't a prayer

---

[1]*Homilies on the Gospel of John* 86.2, *Nicene and Post-Nicene Fathers* 1, 14:326; *Patrologiae cursus completus. Series Graeca* 59:471-72, cited in Joel C. Elowsky, *John 11–21*, Ancient Christian Commentary on Scripture IVb (Downers Grove, Ill.: InterVarsity Press, 2007), p. 355.

[2]Sermon 84.2, *Fathers of the Church* 110:49-50, cited in Elowsky, *John 11–21*, p. 356.

where world evangelism is concerned. They would have been voted the group of human beings "most unlikely to start a new world religion." They certainly could offer little by way of shalom, simply because they were experiencing none.

The "after" picture, however, is another story altogether! The difference is made by Jesus' presence in their midst. There was shock at first. The sudden presence of Jesus in their midst might have been a little hard to process! Each may have thought at first that he was seeing the kinds of apparitions grieving people see. But soon they realized they were *all* seeing him. This was real. By the time this occasion was over and the disciples had calmed down, they really might have begun to believe that mission was possible. The picture John paints here of that little shell-shocked gathering, with the risen Jesus standing in the center, imparting his shalom and then inspiring them with the greatest of all the commissions—mission as participation in God's mission—is evocative of what the church can be in every era of its existence as it once again makes the risen Christ the center.

After the day of Pentecost when they actually received what Jesus symbolically conferred on them here, the Holy Spirit, they would in fact accomplish the impossible—the evangelization of a significant portion of their then-known world. The shalom imparted by the risen Christ to his kingdom community was shared with a broken and alienated world. People were drawn into that gathered community of shalom, and the catalytic impact of that scattered community in turn ultimately brought shalom to the ancient and medieval world in all kinds of ways—the liberation of women, the humanization of children, hospitals, education, art, architecture and science.

This little community that began with the eleven apostles here and then 120 disciples prior to Pentecost, grew to 5,000 by Acts 4. Rodney Stark has estimated that the church then grew from around 1,000 in A.D. 40 to 25,000 by A.D. 100 to between 5 and 7.5 million by the start of the fourth century.[3] I don't wish by quoting these figures to convey any hint of a numbers obsession when it comes to mission, and I am

---

[3]Rodney Stark, *The Rise of Christianity: A Sociologist Reconsiders History* (Princeton, N.J.: Princeton University Press, 1996), p. 6.

certainly not wishing to suggest either that the Christianization of em-
pires is the goal of Christian mission. The call of the church in any age
is faithfulness to shalom sharing, the living and proclaiming of the
gospel in its fullness. The results are God's concern, not ours. The
church has historically actually done better in terms of faithfulness to
its identity and calling when it is a persecuted minority, just as it is depicted here in John 20, rather than when it is the ruling political entity
with a cultural hegemony.

That said, the missional call to which Christians are to be faithful
must include faith-filled engagement and shalom sharing with society
at every level. This will be done with awareness however, that the telos
in this "already but not yet" phase of the kingdom is not the political
reign of a Christian government. Christ's kingdom on earth is a sub-
versive one, and it is characterized by its smallness, making its dispro-
portionate influence so remarkable in this age and its massive nature, in
its fully realized form, so surprising. The parables Jesus told about the
mustard seed which surprisingly produces a large tree, and about the
yeast that surprisingly influences the large amount of flour to form a
large loaf, would not have meaning if the kingdom in this present age
was obviously and spectacularly large. The sense of triumph I am encouraging is not triumphalism, but it is triumph nevertheless. It is a call
to faithfulness, but it is an unapologetic call to raise our faith and expectancy in light of the dynamics still present to the church.

OUTLINES OF JOHN 20:19-23 AND OF THIS BOOK

This book will be a theological exposition of the factors that transformed the community of the early disciples, or the early church, as it
is proleptically depicted here in John 20:19-23.[4] The exposition is
grounded upon an assumption that John is doing much more than
merely describing a resurrection appearance of Jesus in this passage, all

---

[4]Whether this account is indeed proleptic or realized, with respect to the actual reception of the
Spirit, will be discussed later. On the one hand, there is evidence of the reception of the Spirit
in the joy the disciples experienced, and yet their profound failure to convince Thomas later in
this chapter argues against a realized view. This is, indeed, the reanimation of humanity and
these first followers become *nepeš hayāh*—living souls again as in the creation narrative, but I
suspect this is symbolic here in John and awaits fulfillment in Acts 2.

important though this appearance was.[5] He is giving us his picture of the early church, and in doing so offering hope for its mission. It is true that John does not in his Gospel ever reference the church. But this is his way. He does not reference the institution of the Lord's Supper either, yet many commentators see in his account of the feeding of the five thousand and Jesus' elucidation of the symbolism of that event the most profound eucharistic teaching of the New Testament.[6] Similarly, as John gives us his version of the Great Commission, he does so in a word picture, a word picture of the church in union with the risen Christ by the Spirit's inbreathing, as the missionary of God. John also presents this picture of the church in a new creation context, with the last or *eschatos* Adam present in its center as its defining reality.[7] He describes the breath of the last Adam (a man who is also God, cf. Gen 2:7), being breathed into the last Adam's race, the new humanity in Christ, the church, and anticipates all those who would be brought into its communion by means of its missional nature and action: "as the Father has sent me, I am sending you." John's is a commission with cosmic consequences, with covenant and creation together.

If there was hope for that motley crew of eleven disciples in John 20, there is hope for the church in the West despite its indiscriminate enculturation on the one hand and its cultural isolation on the other—if the realities that transformed that early infant church are permitted to transform churches and Christians today. This will lead me to encourage the church to rediscover the dynamics and reengage the practices of the early church and yet to reimagine these in a manner appropriate to our times, thus not succumbing to any romantic idealism of that church.

Certain realities began to transform this community of disciples in

---

[5]Rudolf Schnackenburg says, "It is the appearance which is of decisive importance for the Easter faith, for the life and future of the church" (Rudolf Schnackenburg, *The Gospel According to St. John*, trans. David Smith and G. A. Kon [New York: Crossroad, 1982], 3:321).

[6]Indeed one could argue that since the motif of the Passover is so prominent in John, the whole Gospel has a eucharistic context.

[7]This term *"eschatos* Adam" reflects the view that the first creation and Adam were in fact eschatological. Christ, as Irenaeus thought of him, for example, was the recapitulation of Adam, the true human in whom all humans find their intended purpose (retrospectively for the Old Testament) as relational vice regents in caring for and stewarding creation.

John 20. The emphasis is on the word *began*. They did not actually receive the Spirit until Pentecost, and even after that the fullness of all these trinitarian realities became part of them gradually. These realities can be structured around Jesus' repetition of the words *peace to you*.

Unlike Calvin, who thinks Jesus was just offering the customary "hello" here, I am in agreement with the idea that, at minimum, Jesus is calming their stated fears,[8] but more likely still that he is conferring shalom in its full redemptive and cosmic sense upon them. Jesus does use the customary Hebrew words when friends greet each other in Jerusalem: *Shalom ʿaleikhem!* However, in the context of this Gospel, it is certain that they heard much more, certainly when they reflected back on the occasion. They may have heard in Jesus' words here an echo of *peace* words spoken to them in his passion ministry in John 14:27: "Peace I leave with you; my peace I give to you," adding words that fit so well with this John 20 context where fear is the emotion explicitly spoken of: "Do not let your hearts be troubled and do not be afraid." What they heard reached far beyond a mundane "hello." As F. F. Bruce comments, "on this occasion it bore its literal meaning to the fullest extent."[9] The deepest and widest meaning of *peace* is intended. In light of the fuller teaching of the New Testament, it was a peace freshly accomplished between God and humanity by the cross, that is, a peace born of the reconciling work of Christ who made "peace through his blood, shed on the cross" (Col 1:20). It was a peace not only of a forensic kind (Rom 5:1), however, but one very much to be experienced in their hearts. Their emotional state changes from fear to joy (v. 20) in consequence of his impartational invocation. Appreciated as this was, however, they would as Jews know that shalom had yet a fuller meaning still, more than even a deep individual existential experience. It was social and cosmic in its scope, a state of well-being in the whole creation. The apostolic understanding of this peace impartation of Jesus would grow into the realization that its scope extended to "the world" of people (2 Cor 5:18) and indeed the whole fallen cosmos, as Colossians 1:19-20 indicates: "God was pleased to have all his fullness dwell

---

[8]Schnackenburg, *Gospel According to St. John*, 3:323.
[9]F. F. Bruce, *The Gospels and Epistles of John* (Grand Rapids: Eerdmans, 1983), p. 391.

in him, and through him to reconcile to himself all things, whether things on earth or things in heaven."

In fact, the twofold repetition of this blessing from Jesus was intended to indicate that they were not merely to receive this peace.[10] The second impartation, followed immediately by the commission ("as the Father has sent me"), indicates that they were, as the church, to dispense shalom to the world as the eschatological harbinger of the kingdom of God. Gregory the Great seems to support this idea by linking it with their soon to be given authority to forgive sins. Thus he says, "You see how they not only acquire peace of mind concerning themselves but even receive the power of releasing others from their bonds."[11] Maximus the Confessor (580-662) in the Orthodox tradition actually brings the greeting of peace together with the breathing of the Spirit upon them: "Through his greeting of peace he breathes on them and bestows tranquility as well as sharing in the Holy Spirit."[12] He also infers a connection between the receiving of the Spirit and the bestowal of peace through the mission the Spirit would empower. Schnackenburg confirms this connection, confirming that as an inner gift the peace the Spirit gives "is also to manifest itself outwardly. . . . The peace which the risen Lord brings the disciples from God is to go with them as they are sent out and to testify to the world what true peace is (cf. similarly, concerning the idea of oneness)."[13]

We can, therefore nuance Christ's peace benediction. There were *two* transforming realities that *imparted* shalom to them to make them a community of shalom—his risen presence and his presence as the

---

[10]Schnackenburg informs us that "It becomes an Easter greeting in a special sense, as the repetition in v. 21 suggests" (Schnackenburg, *Gospel According to St. John*, 3:323). He adds that between the two pronunciations of peace, there was a "narrative pause which leaves room for the joy of the encounter."

[11]*Cistercian Studies* 123:204, cited in Elowsky, *John 11–21*, p. 364. The connection between this peace and the reception of the Spirit is affirmed by other Patristic commentator, Cyril of Alexandria for example. *Commentary on the Gospel of John* 12.I. LF 48:668-69, cited in Elowsky, *John 11–21*, p. 357.

[12]*Maximus the Confessor: Selected Writings* 157, cited in Elowsky, *John 11–21*, p. 357.

[13]Schnackenburg, *Gospel According to St. John*, 3:323-24. Ramsey Michaels suggests that the three announcements of peace to the disciples on the consecutive two Sundays described in verses 19-29 suggest that "John puts these two appearances of Jesus together as one encounter of the Eleven" (J. Ramsey Michaels, *John*, New International Biblical Commentary, ed. Ward Gasque [Peabody, Mass.: Hendrickson, 1989], pp. 343-44).

once-crucified Savior. Then there were *three* further realities that would enable them to dispense that shalom to others as a sent community. That is, they could as a community of the once crucified, now risen Christ, both experience and express shalom. The shalom in their midst would make the community attractive (if not attractional!) and missional. But they would as those sent in participation with the Son by the Spirit, and in the Spirit's power, impart peace in being missional and in doing mission. As a community therefore, their missional message of the peace of forgiveness could be compatible with who they were as missional people, characterized by shalom, sharing it out of their own overflow of it. Another way to say this is that both the character and content of mission is the shalom of the gospel.

The structure of this passage may thus be presented in the following way:

> *The church discovering shalom through*
> 1. the presence and influence of the risen Jesus (v. 19)
> 2. the redemptive nature of the once-crucified One (v. 20)
>
> *The church disseminating shalom through*
> 3. the trinitarian and participatory nature of the commission (v. 21)
> 4. the impartation of the Spirit (v. 22)
> 5. the privileged task of pronouncing forgiveness (v. 23)

This structure will serve to form the skeleton of the book. I offer five perspectives that break the fear and despair around mission and bring shalom to sent people and those they are sent to. Chapters two and three will highlight the challenges facing the contemporary church. Then after chapter four, which provides some needed background on the doctrine of the Trinity and its general relevance to mission, there are three pairs of chapters on the first three themes (chaps. 5-10) with the first of each pair addressing the nature of the church community as a consequence of Jesus' death and risen presence and the Trinity, with the second in each pair addressing implications for the mission of the church.

Chapter eleven discusses how the presence of the Spirit has implications for the community's nature and mission, and similarly chapter twelve explains how the community's nature and mission is a consequence of its privilege in pronouncing reconciliation. Thus the structure of the book is as follows:

The church discovering shalom

- Chapter 5: the church *community*: in light of the presence of the risen Christ

- Chapter 6: the church's *mission*: implications of participation in Christ's resurrection

- Chapter 7: the church *community*: in light of the presence of the crucified Christ

- Chapter 8: the church's *mission*: implications of participation in the crucified Christ

The church disseminating shalom

- Chapter 9: the church *community*: in light of the nature of God as Trinity

- Chapter 10: the church's *mission*: implications of participation through Christ in the mission of the triune God

- Chapter 11: the impact of the Spirit on the church *community* and its *mission*

- Chapter 12: the influence of the church's nature as a *community* of reconciliation on its *mission*

I wish, then, to expound this commission given by Jesus in John 20, as the "Greatest Commission," because it is the deepest and the widest. It is wide in that it connects theologically with the fullness of God's mission in terms of creation and redemption. The presence of Jesus as the risen One imparting shalom to his people and through them to the world evokes the notion of the new creation and the reconciliation of all things. It is the commission above all, however, because it connects the mission of the church deep into the eternal purpose of the Godhead. The sentness of the church is connected to the sentness of the Son by the Father, a sending planned in eternity past within the covenanting counsels of God. Mission is expressed as flowing from within the very life of the Trinity.

MATTERS OF INTERPRETATION

Given that I am basing this whole book on a particular metaphorical interpretation of John 20:19-23, a few words on hermeneutics are necessary. First, I am consciously employing the interpretive method of the Patristic and medieval or "precritical exegetical" tradition. Although there were excesses in this tradition, it is preferred to the idea that there is only one meaning to a text and it is that uncovered by discovering the author's intent through historical-critical method. This latter idea is thoroughly modern and in the timely words of David Steinmetz, the "modern theory of a single meaning, with all its demonstrable virtues is false." It is not that the determination of the author's intent and the literal meaning are not important, but to limit meaning to this is to deny the Spirit-derived nature of the Bible, and indeed to deny the use Scripture makes internally of itself.[14]

Second, I offer justification for my metaphorical take on John 20:19-23 in light of the particular metaphorical richness with which the author of the Fourth Gospel writes. The conviction that there is in the Johannine mind a significance well beyond historical description here is strengthened by the promise-fulfillment motif of this passage.[15] I suggest it is a sign of the church community about to be birthed, a community defined by Christ's permanent presence through the Spirit's indwelling.[16]

A proleptic event. I assert that the impartation of the Spirit is enacted by Jesus in John 20:22 in a symbolic form, a prolepsis of what would actually be fulfilled in Acts 2. First, John is explicit about the

---

[14]David C. Steinmetz, "The Superiority of Pre-critical Exegesis," *Theology Today* 36 (1980): 27-38.

[15]See for example, Michaels, *John*, pp. 344-55, who illustrates the fulfillment of John 14:18 ("I will come to you"), pp. 23, 28, in John 20:19 ("Jesus came and stood among them"); 14:27 ("Peace I leave with you"); 16:33 in 20:19, 21 ("Peace be with you"); and so on.

[16]Michaels comments on the echo of the phrase "On that day," in John 14:20 here in v. 19a: "of that . . . day" (Jn 20:19) as indication of promise fulfillment (Michaels, *John*, p. 349).

timing of the giving of the Spirit when, upon Jesus' promise of the Spirit's giving, he comments that "Up to that time the Spirit had not been given, since Jesus had not yet been glorified" (Jn 7:39). Second, throughout the period between the resurrection and Pentecost, these disciples showed all the signs of disciples not yet filled with the Spirit, including the season described after the ascension when they were explicitly waiting for the Spirit![17]

Not all will agree with this, some preferring the idea that the Spirit was indeed imparted here. Calvin seems to offer a *via media* in this regard by suggesting that the Spirit was here only given in small measure as a harbinger of what was to come at Pentecost.[18] However, he confirms the superfluous nature of Pentecost if the Spirit was granted here, and indeed the seeming contradiction between this event in John and the clear command of Jesus for them to "wait quietly" for the Spirit in Luke 24:49 and Acts 1:5-8. He reaches the conclusion that "This breathing should therefore be referred and extended especially to that magnificent sending of the Spirit which He had so often promised."[19]

This event has weighty significance as John's depiction of the infant church. In this vein Cyprian, in speaking about the fact that it was the one Christ in their midst who made that infant church one, seems to hint at the idea that this moment has the gravitas of the church's origin.[20] Schnackenburg provides evidence of this also when he draws attention to the fact that it is not the functions of the Spirit which Jesus spoke of earlier in John that come into view here, such as reminding and teaching the disciples, conviction of the world and so on. Rather, he says, "The perspective is a different one; in our passage, only the fact

---

[17]Some Johannine scholars prefer to speak of this event as the Johannine equivalent of Pentecost (e.g., Michaels, *John*, p. 349). This seems misguided. The ministry of the Spirit to the disciples is evident throughout the Gospel records. It was a ministry "with" rather than "in" them as Jn 14:17 indicates.

[18]John Calvin, *John 11–21 and 1 John*, Calvin's New Testament Commentaries, trans. T. H. L. Parker, ed. David W. Torrance and Thomas F. Torrance (Grand Rapids: Eerdmans, 1959), p. 205.

[19]Ibid.

[20]Cyprian, *The Unity of the Church* 4, Ante-Nicene Fathers 5:422, cited in Elowsky, *John 11–21*, p. 362.

of the receiving of the Spirit which *is the foundation of the life of the church*, is mentioned."[21] In sum, the foundational idea that John is presenting a picture of the church and its mission in this passage finds support in the tradition.

A new creation context. The new creation context in John 20 is also an important factor in our interpretation of this passage as having critical significance. This has profound relevance to the creational and holistic dimensions of Christian mission. This context is inferred first by the fact that it occurs, as Tom Wright has indicated, on the "evening of the new creation's first day."[22] Wright draws an interesting parallel between the initial creation of God and what Christ had accomplished by his death and resurrection. With reference to the "first day of the week" (Jn 20:19), he states, "Jesus had accomplished the defeat of death, and has begun the work of new creation."[23] Wright suggests that the theme of new creation runs deep in this passage. On the day of humanity's creation, Adam and Eve "heard the sound of him at the time of the evening breeze." "Now," notes Wright, "on the evening of the new creation's first day, a different wind sweeps through the room," and noting the sameness of the words for wind, breath and Spirit in both Hebrew and Greek, he concludes, "This wind is the healing breath of God's spirit, come to undo the long effects of primal rebellion." Wright suggests a further echo in this passage of the creation account, relating to the parallel between this Johannine passage and Genesis 2:7,[24] the moment when Yahweh breathed into human nostrils the breath of life. "Now, in the new creation," Wright continues, "the restoring life of God is breathed out through Jesus, making new people of the disciples, and, through them, offering this new life to the world."[25] Ramsey Michaels adds the perspective that a comparison of the first and last Adams is implicit in this breathing act. Whereas the first Adam is the recipient of the breath of God in Genesis 2, the last Adam actually is

---

[21]Schnackenburg, *Gospel According to St. John*, 3:322, 326, emphasis added.

[22]N. T. Wright, *John for Everyone, Part 2* (London: SPCK, 2002), p. 149.

[23]Ibid.

[24]There may also be in this passage an echo of the double peace benediction on Ps 122.

[25]Wright, *John for Everyone*, p. 150. That the Spirit's impartation by the breath of Jesus seems to echo Gen 2:7 is confirmed also by Bruce, *Gospels and Epistles of John*, p. 391.

the breather himself, breathing the Spirit into those who were becoming the new humanity in him.[26]

Setting the stage. The assumption that John has the church in mind within a creational context in this passage sets the stage for the exposition of the missional church from this passage. It justifies the notion that the cultural mandate as given to the first Adam forms a crucial component of Christian mission under the last Adam, who recapitulates all that the first was unable to fulfill. The telos of Christian mission is thus human beings becoming humans fully alive. However, this equally asserts the ecclesial nature of the new humanity. God's mission was to be carried out by the church—the church as a signal of the new humanity, the church as the sign and servant of the kingdom of God, for the re-creation of the cosmos.

DEFIANT OPTIMISM

The point of this defiantly optimistic treatment of the church is to rekindle hope and fresh imagination in the face of various forms of discouragement and retreat I discern today even in the missional conversation. A few examples will suffice to make the initial point: emphasis on the church as exilic and of Christians as "resident aliens" without qualification by other metaphors such as "embassy" and "royal priesthood"; emphases on intentional community that lack awareness of the missional nature of the inner practices of the community as well as the need for engagement in culture; emphasis on social justice at the expense of evangelism or vice versa; the lacuna and suspicion of revival and the pneumatic in missional church life. This study is sympathetic with the cry of the missional church movement and exponents of the pilgrim concept. It is also deeply sympathetic toward the need for the church to be incarnational and holistic in its mission. There is, however, a danger that overemphasis on the incarnational can lead to a neglect of the work of the Spirit, yet without the unrealistic optimism that sometimes characterizes some overly pneumatic wings of the church, which seem to pronounce the reign of God triumphalistically without en-

---

[26]Paul may be referring to this event when he makes this comparison explicit in 1 Cor 15:45—
"So it is written: 'The first Adam became a living being'; the last Adam, a life-giving spirit."

gagement in the brokenness of the world, or who delight in ecstasy without concern for the lost.

I hope through an exposition of the trinitarian commission of John 20:19-23 to offer a via media or, better, a *fully* trinitarian account of mission that is both patriological, incarnational *and* pneumatic, which gives full cognition of the need for the church to be the church (deep church) of pilgrim exiles, vigilant toward cultural compromises (enculturation) in ecclesial life, *and* to be a royal priesthood fully engaged (wide church) in all aspects of the world (inculturation), and the creation that God is redeeming. As such, if indeed the church is true to the dynamics of the missional Trinity, I hope to show that the church will be both centrifugal and centripetal.

My own approach here builds on the work of authors like Darrell Guder, Alan Hirsch and especially Andrew Walker and Luke Bretherton. It reflects at a deeper level the influence of David Bosch, Lesslie Newbigin, Orlando Costas, as well as the renaissance of trinitarian theology in recent decades as a result of the work of Karl Barth, Jürgen Moltmann, Thomas Torrance and James Torrance, Colin Gunton, John Zizioulas and others who have advanced this conversation and who have served to place the mission of the church under the rubric of theology proper. My own particular emphasis arising from the fact that the church's mission is a consequence of its union with the triune God and his mission is to stress that the missional church is both deep and wide. It is to stress that mission is participation of the church and its members, in Christ, by the Spirit. The missional church will be as much concerned with the depth of its liturgical and sacramental and catechetical and catholic life as it is with the width of its influence in evangelistic, holistic, socially conscious, culturally and creationally engaged ways. It will be as intensive in its ecclesial life as it is extensive in its world engaging influence—precisely because it is the story of the coinherent incarnational and pneumatic missions of God!

The working out of this coinherence of the works of the divine persons in the church will ensure that its mission is reimagined as commitment: to being ecclesial in incarnational, located, imperfect churches of Christ, *and* as such, to be by the Spirit's empowering, the sign, servant and messenger of the kingdom of God; to being intentionally catholic in spirit *and* yet committed to the particularities with which one's own tradition has been gifted; to the practice of *both* social justice *and* evangelism; to articulating and practicing theologies of healing *and* suffering; to creation care now *and* anticipation of a new creation then; to solidarity with the poor, the disenfranchised, the marginalized, the uneducated *and* to working toward their holistic transformation; to the pursuit of work as a good gift from God, under the cultural mandate recapitulated in the last Adam, with the practice of sabbath and jubilee principles, *and* the moral transformation of the worker by the Spirit such that even in a fallen world, the telos of work becomes the glory of God, the good of the community, as well as individual fulfillment.

This proleptic picture of the early church given to us by that most creative of all the apostles, John, was given to remind the church of what it can be with and in Christ by the Spirit on the one hand, and what it can relapse into on the other, when it forgets its God and co-coons into a cozy and fearful community behind walls. Without the presence of Christ its entrapment is portrayed with crystal clarity. The utter impossibility of fulfilling its mission is clear: apart from the presence of the once-crucified and now-risen Jesus, apart from the power of trinitarian participation, apart from life in the Spirit. But, positively stated, this word picture was given as an image of what emerges when untrained, dispirited men and women, feeling desperately inadequate, begin to live as a community in the shalom of the triune God, and share it out with humanity and creation.

THE STATE OF THE WESTERN CHURCH

Many churches in the West in the twenty-first century need that picture. The church is beginning to look a lot like a fear-filled, re-treated, "walls-up," not-very-influential community. It is entrapped in various ways by forces at work outside of its walls and by capitulation to its cultural milieu to what it has become inside those walls. A thriving church that influenced Western culture and spawned mission movements that touched the far corners of the world is now under siege. Now the Two-Thirds World has 70 percent of the world's Christians, and missional activity is no longer primarily from the West to the rest of the world but from and to six continents. Mission now, therefore, is the movement of those with faith to those seeking faith. These churches have outstripped the Western overseas missionary effort with their own growing global missionary activities, including mission to the West.

Assailed by forces outside—first the "certainties" of reason and science and the relativization and privatization of faith that modernity brought, and then the radical doubt of postmodernity—and then nullified by its own insipid life through enculturation, Christian witness is at a low ebb. The church's mission to reevangelize the now highly secularized West seems to be in jeopardy. "Here," asserted Newbigin, "without possibility of question, is the most challenging missionary frontier of our time." More disturbing yet is the reality that the Third World is rapidly shrinking and that modernity, of all cultures, the "most resistant to the Gospel" is everywhere "driving religion into smaller and smaller enclaves."[27]

The technocratic triumphalism of the so-called church growth era did not deliver much growth. Charismatic renewal in its various forms from the 1960s to the 1990s brought deeply divided traditions together and seemed to offer hope of greater catholicity as well as life, and even mission, as Alpha emanated from this renewal. It has proved, however, to be an eschatological taste of things to come, rather than a permanently incarnate, ecclesiological reality.[28] Inevitably postrenewal feelings were depressive.

This book is an attempt to restore faith in the church as the church rediscovers its missional identity as the community of the triune God and the sign and servant of the kingdom of God—and to inculcate renewed commitment to the church along the directions of its *bipolar* missional nature. It is to be freely admitted the renaissance of the notion that the church is "missional" may have its accompanying imbalances and be prone to extremes, in response to cultural pressures. The question may well be asked, is the term *missional church* in fact nothing

---

[27]Lesslie Newbigin, *Missionalia* 17, no. 3 (1989): 213.
[28]Andrew Walker, "Recovering Deep Church: Theological and Spiritual Renewal," in Walker and Bretherton, *Remembering Our Future*, p. 8.

more than the latest evangelical fad, one that will soon give way to another? Already there are alternative terms afoot in the literature to correct the imbalances that the term *missional* seems inevitably to evoke, terms like *total church*, *deep church* and so on. Both the "total" and "deep" descriptors are not offered by their proponents as alternatives to the missional church, it seems to me, but rather as attempts to rectify different misconceptions that arise from the adjective *missional*. What I wish to argue is that the concept of the missional church is not a fad but is theologically foundational for the church, and more appropriate as an appellation than "deep" or "total." Despite its semantic ambivalence, I deem it important to persist with the term *missional* for the simple reason that the majority of Western churches still need awakening to this core identity, with the caveat that the missional church as this concept is derived from the biblical account and the theological tradition of the church (specifically as envisioned by the Johannine metaphorical description of it in John 20), is both deep and total![29]

I am somewhat invested in *not* actually coining a new adjective for the church, and in definitely not spawning a new denomination or even a new movement, especially one which distances itself proudly from the church catholic! One of the key points of this endeavor is to show that all churches, whether traditional or contemporary, intentionally litur-

---

[29]David Bosch's reference to Luke's church as bipolar in its orientation (*Transforming Mission* [Maryknoll, N.Y.: Orbis, 1991], pp. 119-20) will be discussed later. This idea of bipolarity is in keeping also with Paul Steven's conception of the church as existing at simultaneously as *diaspora* and *ecclesia*. See R. Paul Stevens and Phil Collins, *The Equipping Pastor: A Systems Approach to Congregational Leadership* (Washington, D.C.: Alban Institute, 1993), pp. 126-27. It accords also with Guder's creative notion of the missional community as centered and bounded sets by which organizations gain identity. A bounded set forms mechanisms for structure and appropriate control and serves to demarcate a group and define its identity. Centered sets, by contrast, do not differentiate members and nonmembers at the boundary of the community but rather are functions which facilitate a common journey toward a set of values and commitments. Both of these sets are needed to both foster true discipleship and engage those on the periphery. Such a conception provides a hospitable mode of being for a missional church in which there is a continuum from centered to bounded set by which those in a community can journey to becoming disciples of Christ through various points at which they can continue with integrity only when they are intentionally bound by a common language, story and set of practices particular to the Christian way. See Darrell Guder, ed., *Missional Church: A Vision for the Sending of the Church in North America* (Grand Rapids: Eerdmans, 1998), pp. 205-9. I am indebted to Michael Chase for drawing attention in a term paper to this consonant deep-wide aspect of the missional church as expounded by Guder.

gical or inadvertently liturgical, church plants or church parents, whether of Orthodox, Roman Catholic or Protestant traditions, and every stripe and brand of church within the latter, is called to *be* the church where the risen Christ lives by the Spirit, and if so, they *will* be missional *like* he is, and *as* he is (as a sent one of the Father by the Spirit). But this will look very different in each of these churches. Missional churches are likely to be multicolored, not monochrome, in their methodology. They need to study to *be* the church and themselves!

This is not a book about methodology. Rather than a book to build models on, this one offers "models of permission"[30]—that is, that will encourage churches to have particular identities that flow from the vast array of particular cultural identities of the communities of the world, and yet which have a common identity in the life and love of the one God and Father of our Lord Jesus Christ, in the one Spirit and in confession of the essentials of trinitarian faith.

A note of caution is warranted about the hubris that can characterize those who "get it" with respect to the missional church paradigm. As Avery Dulles warns, churches that proudly say "They've got it!" or even worse, "we've got it!" easily lose the stance of humility before Christ to whom the church belongs.[31]

---

[30]This phrase is borrowed from a recent book by Derek Tidball, *Ministry by the Book: New Testament Patterns for Pastoral Leadership* (Downers Grove, Ill.: IVP Academic, 2009).
[31]Avery Dulles, *Models of the Church*, 2nd ed. (Garden City, N.Y.: Image Books, 1987), p. 15.

2

Breaking Free Through
Discerning Inculturation

■ ■ ■

Embracing what God does for you is the best thing you can do
for him. Don't become so well-adjusted to your culture that you fit
into it without even thinking. Instead, fix your attention on God. You'll be
changed from the inside out. . . . Unlike the culture around you, always
dragging you down to its level of immaturity, God brings the best
out of you, develops well-formed maturity in you.

ROMANS 12:1-2 *The Message*

I didn't take on their way of life. I kept my bearings in Christ—but
I entered their world and tried to experience things from their point
of view. I've become just about every sort of servant there is
in my attempts to lead those I meet into a God-saved life.

1 CORINTHIANS 9:20-21 *The Message*

RETURNING TO THE BESIEGED STATE of many Christian churches in
the West, many of which are like that community of disciples before
Jesus stood among them, I turn now to the two primary ways they have
been rendered ineffective: on the one hand, *cultural disconnection*, or the
failure to engage in appropriate *inculturation*, and on the other, *indis-*
criminate enculturation.

INCULTURATION WITHOUT ENCULTURATION

I use the term *enculturation*, which has sociological roots, to describe the process whereby an existent, prevailing culture influences an individual or community (e.g., the church) to imbibe its accepted norms and values so the individual or community is pressured to find acceptance within the society of that culture. *Inculturation* however, is a missiological term which refers to ways to adapt the communication of the gospel for a specific culture being evangelized. The term inculturation is exemplified prototypically in the evangelistic (pre-evangelistic?) sermon Paul preached at the Areopagus in Acts 17, which is very different to that by Peter in Acts 2 to Jews who knew Scripture. In Athens Paul interacts with two strands of Greek philosophy and even quotes two Greek poets in his presentation of the gospel. The term can also be used somewhat interchangeably with being incarnational, that is, entering in to a culture for missional purposes, as Jesus did when he came into a Jewish world characterized by poverty and by particular cultural characteristics that included the type of food he ate, the clothes he wore, the language he spoke and the accent he spoke it with. My contention is that the challenge the Western church faces is that it is often enculturated in ways that it ought not to be, and that it is not inculturating the gospel in ways it ought to be.

Culture is a complex of traits and ideas that characterize a community. It is the product of two influences, the creation of humankind in the image of God on the one hand, and the fall of humankind and its proneness to demonic corruption and counterfeit on the other. Cultural disconnection is the phenomenon that I am using to describe Christians and churches when they fail to relate the gospel relevantly because they do not adequately affirm and adapt to the positive aspects of human culture, and fail to distinguish between what is mere culture and what is the kerygmatic core of the gospel. This area of entrapment of the church and the challenge it brings to mission will be considered first. Positively stated, there is a valid inculturation which the church needs to undergo in every era and every distinctive community.

However, much care is needed in light of the second area of potential entrapment for the church with respect to culture, that of *indiscriminate enculturation.* This has to do with the possible inappropriate response to the dark side of culture. Instead of speaking and acting prophetically against such elements of culture, the church can easily become inappropriately enculturated and swamped with the waters of insidious influences incompatible with the gospel. This has been aptly described by Darrell Guder, who states that North American "churches have become so accommodated to the American way of life that they are now domesticated, and it is no longer obvious what justifies their existence as particular communities."[1] In the third chapter we will look at forces at work in Western culture that are resistant to and incompatible with the gospel which the church can inadvertently take on board. As we expose the entrapments related to the positive and negative aspects of culture, I will offer positive solutions that arise from considering culture in light of the triune God and discover ways the church can break free of entrapment and be missional precisely around culture.

CULTURAL DISCONNECTION OF WESTERN CHURCHES AND BREAKING FREE

In every culture there are positive elements, elements of beauty, such as distinctive dress styles and musical genres, ways of relating in community, the multitudes of dialects and accents, the varied sports and leisure forms, and so on. These are to be admired, enjoyed and preserved because they reflect the fact that humanity was created in the image of God (the *imago Dei*). There are also customs, trends and ideas which the Spirit of God positively shapes in preparation for the reception of the gospel. There are even areas of brokenness that the Spirit uses to create hunger for God and the gospel. Cultural disconnection in church environments is the failure of churches to connect relevantly with people in areas of positive culture that define being human, to both preserve host cultures and even be culture makers. The profound marginalization of the church from society in the West is not just a consequence of the secularization of the culture, though that is a significant factor. It is due to the failure of church people to engage re-

---

[1]Darrell Guder, ed., *Missional Church: A Vision for the Sending of the Church in North America* (Grand Rapids: Eerdmans, 1998), p. 78.

demptively in all areas of human culture, sharing in the mission God has given them as humans in Christ, by their presence and the perspectives they are able to share intelligently. Second, it is due to the failure of the whole people of God to appropriate a theology spacious enough for all of life, for the "other six days" and not just their Sunday worship experiences. It is due, third, to the failure of churches to gather in ways that contextualize the gospel without compromising its core or the essence of the church as the community of the triune God. It is, fourth, a consequence of failing to discern the "openness" to the gospel that the Spirit creates as he is at work in the midst of every culture and community. Espousing a positive view of what God is accomplishing in history causes the Christian to ask, How is the Spirit at work in my culture and in my community to create openness to the gospel? We will look at each of these four areas in turn.

Discerning God's good creation and culture. The relationship of the church to culture has sometimes been expressed in the exilic or pilgrim language of the apostle Peter. While he does use the metaphor for the church of "pilgrims and exiles" (1 Pet 2:11), the question is just how far Peter's metaphor of the church as "pilgrims in exile" is to be carried. It expresses the distinctiveness of the people of God, their separation from the world of ideas and ideologies contrary to the gospel, and indeed their rejection by that world. Is it, however, a justification for withdrawal of the church from all aspects of human culture? It does reflect the fact that the world as it is now is not the final destiny of the people of God. But is it a rationale for the all-too-prevalent tendency for the church to circle the wagons and form its own exclusive subculture behind impenetrable walls? While the character of Christians does need to be formed through ecclesial practices in churches as alternative communities that are profoundly distinctive, does this mean that a profound disconnect is necessary between church and the rest of humanity, a humanity which Christ assumed, of whom Christ became a neighbor and for which he died?

The same Peter will refer to the people of God as a "royal priesthood." This metaphor implies a kingly mediation of the creational-redemptional purposes of God on earth by the church as the new humanity of the last Adam. Through Christ's humanity, the real humanity which the first Adam's only prefigured, culture is to be engaged and redeemed, and new forms of culture made that reflect the beauty of God. The words of Robert Farrar Capon relate well:

> It is through that Sacred Humanity—and through the mighty working whereby he is able to subdue all things to Himself—that He will, at the last day, change these corruptible bodies of ours, make them like His own glorious Body and, through them, draw all things into the last City of their being. The world will be lifted, as it was always meant to be lifted, by the priestly love of man. What Christ has done is take our broken priesthood into His and make it strong again. We can, you see, take it with us. It will be precisely because we loved Jerusalem enough to bear it in our bones that its textures will ascend when we rise; it will be because our eyes have relished the earth that the color of its countries will compel our hearts forever. The bread and the pastry, the cheeses, the wine, and the songs go into the Supper of the Lamb because we do: It is our love that brings the City home.[2]

Do the church's ways of relating with the world differ when its circumstances differ—when it is a beleaguered minority or when it has cultural dominance? Or is it rather that in every era the church must be exilic in the sense that it is called to be the holy people of God (discerning, lest it be enculturated) yet also engaged in a royal-priestly way (discerning how to inculturate in order to be missional to the world for whom Christ has died)?

This is an important discussion in the contemporary missional conversation, and it relates to the salvation-history events of creation, fall, redemption *of creation* and consummation *of creation*, and where we find ourselves on that trajectory. The church is never intended to exercise a cultural hegemony. It is, however, called to be salt and light in its culture and country. Crucial to a biblical theology of culture and the praxis of engagement in culture is a theology of the relationship between God the Creator and Redeemer of the creation, including the culture made by humans in his image, and those created and

---

[2]Robert Farrar Capon, *The Supper of the Lamb: A Culinary Reflection* (New York: Smithmark, 1969), p. 190.

fallen humans. This will involve us in a discussion of the theology of participation.

The Christian metanarrative of "creation, fall, redemption and consummation" actually stems from the work of Abraham Kuyper as particularly expressed in his *Lectures on Calvinism* in 1898.[3] In fact, we owe in large part to Kuyper (and the Kuyperian school of thought) the now-popular notion of "worldview," which refers to the fundamental and global perspective with which one or one's community sees the world, or the beliefs and "stories" about the world and reality that are so basic as to be not so much rationally proven as presupposed. Kuyper presented the idea that Calvinism is more than a set of doctrinal propositions; it is an all-encompassing Christian worldview grounded in the sovereignty of God, and expressed in the trajectory "creation, fall, redemption." Kuyper's view of the mission of the church was holistic and one of engagement in the human endeavor, not withdrawal. The sovereignty of God over all realms of creation, the prominence of the cultural mandate given to humanity in Genesis and fulfilled in Christ, and the salvation-historical markers of creation-fall-redemption all contributed to Kuyper's world-affirming theology. Equipped with this worldview the people of God could profitably engage in all areas of culture toward the redemption of humanity and creation in this era of history.

A Kuyperian influence may also be traced in the worldview and theology of philosopher-theologian Nicholas Wolterstorff, whose pilgrimage took him away from intellectual foundationalism into a more holistic way of knowing and educating beyond just the mind to involvement of the whole person in the pursuit of justice and shalom.[4] James Smith similarly builds on Kuyper but advances the category of "worldview" (ensconced as it is within a Cartesian anthropology)

---

[3]Abraham Kuyper, *Lectures on Calvinism*, Stone Lectures of 1898 (1931; reprint, New York: Cosimo, 2007).

[4]Nicholas Wolterstorff, *Educating for Shalom: Essays on Christian Higher Education*, ed. C. W. Joldersma and C. C. Stronks (Grand Rapids: Eerdmans, 2004). For a discussion of foundationalism see William Carl Placher, *Unapologetic Theology: A Christian Voice in a Pluralistic Conversation* (Louisville: Westminster John Knox, 1989), and John E. Thiel, *Non-foundationalism* (Minneapolis: Fortress, 1994).

beyond the merely cognitive, in light of the fact that humans are "desiring beings" or "persons-as-lovers," not cognitive "thinking things."[5] The influence of Kuyper is also evident in *The Transforming Vision: Shaping a Christian World View* by Brian J. Walsh and J. Richard Middleton who, in turn, had a profound influence on the work of N. T. Wright as indicated by the dedication of *The New Testament and the People of God* to Walsh.[6] Wright's work and his influence on Christian mission has drawn attention rightly to the "story" dimension of the Christian worldview by seeking to point out the continuity between the story of God's redemptive dealings with Israel and the Christ story. Christ in fact recapitulates the story of Israel. He fulfills the mission of God in all the ways that Israel failed. But in turn, just as Christ is for Israel, so also the people of Christ, in union with him, are *for* the world.

Various other authors have continued to favor this narrative approach over the foundationalist theology that has characterized much Christian theology since the Enlightenment, with its high emphasis on reason and its narrow propositionalism. The approach of Kevin Vanhoozer has been to offer the category of "drama" as preferable to that of "story," in light of the idea that this category implicitly incorporates the mission of God and his people within it.[7] Michael Goheen and Craig Bartholomew (influenced greatly by Newbigin) have also attempted to integrate the Reformed signposts of "creation, fall and redemption" with Wright's narrative of Jesus' life as "for Israel, and hence for the world."[8] Interestingly, the tenets of the Lausanne Covenant Issue Groups documents[9] reflect the influence of Kuyper and Wright toward the participation of Christians within God's story or drama for the redemption of the world, in a world-affirming manner.

---

[5]James K. A. Smith, *Introducing Radical Orthodoxy: Mapping a Post-Secular Theology* (Grand Rapids: Baker Academic, 2004).

[6]Brian J. Walsh and J. Richard Middleton, *The Transforming Vision: Shaping a Christian World View* (Downers Grove, Ill.: InterVarsity Press, 1984). N. T. Wright, *The New Testament and the People of God* (Philadelphia: Fortress Press, 1992).

[7]Kevin Vanhoozer, *The Drama of Doctrine: A Canonical-Linguistic Approach to Christian Theology* (Louisville: Westminster John Knox, 2005).

[8]Michael W. Goheen and Craig G. Bartholomew, *Living at the Crossroads: An Introduction to Christian Worldview* (Grand Rapids: Baker Academic, 2009).

[9]www.lausanne.org/2004-forum/documents.html.

This viewpoint, has much in common with the primary sentiments of the contemporary Roman Catholic tradition as represented by the papal encyclical *Caritas in Veritate*, the latter being grounded not so much in the worldview or "story" category but "rather on an emphasis on a "common humanity," which unites the church with the world.[10] In this way the Church's mission is for the whole world in a certain partnership with the rest of the world, for they share a common goal and a common good. This emphasis on "common humanity" is derived from a broader theological outlook that is participatory."[11] Both traditions emphasize the holistic nature of mission and the call of the church toward engagement in culture and human life, locally and globally, albeit from a different foundation. The theologies of participation in particular are different. The Catholic version draws heavily on two ideas: (1) the Thomist concept of the analogy of being (*analogia entis*), by which the being of created things is analogous rather than of the same order (as in Duns Scotus's univocity of being), and (2) the neo-Platonic concept of material participation (reflected in the Greek term *methexis*) of all things in God.

The Protestant tendency has been to suggest that "participation" (Gk, *koinōnia*) should be used only to refer to the union of persons, divine persons within the Trinity, and Christ and the church,[12] and rather than using material participation to undergird providence and

---

[10]"Caritas in Veritate," *Vatican*, 2009, www.vatican.va/holy_father/benedict_xvi/encyclicals/documents/hf_ben-xvi_enc_20090629_caritas-in-veritate_en.html.

[11]Alex Abecina in a document prepared for Disciple the Nations Alliance, Appendix: The Latest Theological Development of Biblical Worldview and Wholistic Ministry/Mission. I am indebted to Alex for his helpful outline of some of these trends in Christian mission, though the Barth-Bosch perspectives are mine.

[12]Karl Barth was of the opinion that the way Paul uses *koinōnia* "factored personal relationship into what was formerly a philosophical and cosmological conceptual tool" (*Church Dogmatics* IV/3, ed. G. W. Bromiley and T. F. Torrance, 2nd ed. (Edinburgh: T & T Clark, 1975), p. 535. As Alan Torrance indicates, "participation derived closely from New Testament references to *koinōnia*, 'commit us to an irreducibly relational conceptuality denoting a radically interpersonal overlapping or interpenetration of being, where this is conceived in such a way that personal hypostases are fully realized in this and not in any way subsumed by it' " (Alan Torrance, *Persons in Communion* [Edinburgh: T & T Clark, 1996], p. 256). Similarly, Julie Canlis argues that even Calvin portrays a doctrine of participation consonant with the transcendence of God, and along with Irenaeus, "refashioned Platonic participation on the anvil of their perception of the trinitarian relations" (Julie Canlis, *Calvin's Ladder: A Spiritual Theology of Ascent and Ascension* [Grand Rapids: Eerdmans, 2010], p. 8).

the ongoing influence of God upon creation and all humans, Protestant theologians like Bonhoeffer and Barth have preferred to speak rather of the relations of the personal God to creation and all humans as a relation founded in grace, mediated through the incarnate Christ, rather than mere being, that is, by means of an analogy of relations, not an analogy of being. Regardless of what view of participation one adopts, a theology of engagement in culture and the cooperation of the church with non-Christians who also seek the good without necessarily being aware of theological motivations is important to full-orbed Christian mission.

With regard to the status or condition of humans who are not Christians, Calvin (on Canlis's account at least) and the neo-Calvinists (e.g., Kuyper and Dooyeweerd) have affirmed a strong theology of creation and the *imago Dei* as extant despite the Fall and a non-*methexis* participation by which God's providence operates in all aspects of the pursuit of human knowledge and government. The work of the Spirit is invoked in particular. Barth's Christological recasting of the theology of election and emphasis on Christ as *the* image of God and the man for all humanity brings the added incentive for mission in the broadest sense, including engagement in the public square, on the basis of the fact that all humans are "designated Christians."

Irrespective of the differences by which the Catholic, Orthodox and Protestant traditions arrive at this, all three great traditions affirm that God is at work redemptively in cultures. The distancing of the evangelical movement from these great traditions, especially under fundamentalist influence, has led to entrapment in this area. Rediscovering that God is at work in the world of culture and that the telos of his work is the renewal of creation breaks Christians free for missional engagement in culture. It also enables them to see that their work can be participation in his work in the world.

Discovering a theology for all of life. Sometimes churches and their member Christians live with a poor creational theology. They forget the full implications of the reality that God created humanity in his image and that in Christ that image has been recapitulated for humanity and shared with his people. They therefore fail to embrace elements of human culture that are good and wholesome, in fact that are aesthetically beautiful reflections of the image of the triune God. These churches are prone to isolationist traits, in that their members disengage from the world of people and fail to support the pursuits of the creational, cultural mandate that was given to all humanity. Many Christians in many churches, be they traditional or emergent, are frustrated by not having a theology of the things they spend most of their lives doing: work and play. This hampers their general sense of joy and shalom in life and therefore their effectiveness in mission, not only because that lack of shalom shows in their relationships with non-Christians but also because it pressures them to press for unnatural opportunities for evangelism which are usually counterproductive. Even the popular notion of the move from "success to significance" in some evangelical literature for second-career people is tainted with the false assumption that ordinary work in first careers lacks significance. A sense of depression thus pervades the vocational lives of so many Christians.

Liberation from this entrapment comes when we see that the triune God calls us to evangelistic mission in, and only in, the wider context of his first mission given in Genesis 1–2. These two commissions (the cultural mandate and the Great Commission, along with the Great Commandment) are integrated in a Christological and trinitarian manner. Christ is the fulfillment of the creation/cultural mandate first. When we come into Christ as believers, we can begin therefore to fulfill the creation mandate more effectively. We have been brought into the redemptive reconciliation of God in Christ in order to work out the shalom of the kingdom here on earth. We are called first to be subcreators with God. Being a Christian makes me all the more concerned to assume my role as a vice regent of God's rule on earth with renewed vigor and redemptive grace. Therefore, I can pursue my vocational and artistic and environmental and political involvements with a sense of peace that I am fulfilling God's mission for creation, and that peace will be a missional influence on those I rub shoulders with as I go about these pursuits, creating opportunity for sharing the good news in natural and relational ways.

The imparting of a theology and mission for all of life and specifically work, leisure and communal engagement will be a common theme in the preaching of a missional church and in expressions of the vision of our church for mission to the world. It is important to commission not just pastors but those of every vocation. All fulfill their mission as God's vice regents in Christ on earth by doing their work to the best of their ability to the glory of God.

Relativizing and forming/reforming church culture. The church, any church, is itself a subculture. Within weeks of starting a new church it becomes a subculture. It has sometimes been said that churches need to distinguish between bad tradition (the dead faith of the living) and good tradition (the living faith of the dead, time-tested liturgy). Bad tradition relates to cherished forms of the church that once fulfilled their functions well but now no longer do and have become idolized. Churches can be idol factories. Forms or subcultural norms must ever be under scrutiny with respect to how they fulfill the functions of the church.

When a church loses its sense of connectedness to humanity and its missional telos, it can easily lose touch with the fact that the customs of its subculture are alienating to the world it has been designed to reach. The church is not, in my opinion, intended to be seeker-driven. The gatherings of the church, though intended for the church to be the church (Acts 2:42-47), are however to show missional awareness. If a passage like 1 Corinthians 14 is anything to go by, we should be sensitive toward seekers in the church's practices so that the essence of the gospel is not obfuscated. It is imperative that there is intentionality concerning the church's functions such that the church's inevitable subculture deeply forms the character of its people, as missional people. However, the specific *forms* by which this liturgy of Word and sacrament and community is fulfilled should be sensitive to the shifts in culture and the seekers who come.

How can the deep practices of the church deeply form disciples of Jesus and avoid obscurantism? It should be pointed out that the practices of the church which form its disciples as persons-in-relation or, to use the phrase suggested by James Smith, "persons-as-lovers," have a profound missional goal.[13] Reflecting Augustinian thought, Smith suggests that the telos of the church and its persons-as-lovers is love. The vital connection between the church and the world is that the love is directed toward humanity and the coming of the kingdom of God and the reconciliation of all things.[14] These culture-forming practices within the church can extend into culture forming in the world. In a manner somewhat reflective of Charles Van Engen's extrapolation of the four Nicene marks of the church into "mission verbals,"[15] Smith states that the telos of the ecclesial practices of the church, which he describes as the "deepest" liturgies, are specific characteristics of the kingdom such as hospitality, reconciliation, economics and so on. In other words, the deep practices of the gathered church become the wide (my words) "practices beyond Sunday" (Smith's words) of the scattered church. This expanding of the language of liturgy beyond Sunday services has as its purpose, as Smith's reviewer Brent Aldrich states, "to suggest an ordering of the world in which everything is charged with the immanence of the kingdom."[16]

Crucial to avoiding the idolatry of bad tradition and its hindrance to mission is the idea that the church does, as missional, have two dimensions. Lesslie Newbigin made a distinction between the church's missionary dimension (welcoming outsiders, equipping believers to serve) and the church's missionary intention (direct engagement in the world through evangelism and the pursuit of justice, etc.).[17] In a similar vein, Paul Stevens writes that "the church is a rhythm of gathering (*ekklēsia*)

---

[13]James K. A. Smith, *Desiring the Kingdom: Worship, Worldview, and Cultural Formation*, Cultural Liturgies 1 (Grand Rapids: Baker Academic, 2009).

[14]Smith's approach resonates with the deep church perspectives of Andrew Walker and Luke Bretherton (*Remembering Our Future* [Colorado Springs: Paternoster, 2007]), as well as the general approach that has arisen in the work of Stanley Hauerwas and William Willimon by way of the influence of Alasdair McIntyre and John Howard Yoder. Others who have been influenced by the McIntyre virtue ethic have opted for the new monastic communities (Jonathan Wilson, Jonathan Wilson-Hartgrove, Shane Claiborne) approach.

[15]Charles Van Engen, *God's Missionary People: Rethinking the Purpose of the Local Church* (Grand Rapids: Baker, 1991).

[16]Brent Aldrich, review of *Desiring the Kingdom* by James K. A. Smith, *Englewood Review of Books*, October 2, 2009, http://erb.kingdomnow.org/featured-desiring-the-kingdom-by-james-k-a-smith-vol-2-39. Similarities with Wendell Berry are noted.

[17]Lesslie Newbigin, *One Body, One Gospel, One World* (London: International Missionary Council, 1958), pp. 21, 43.

and dispersion (*diaspora*)," which involves movements referred to as the "come" structures and the "go" structures of the church.[18] This interwoveness of these two dimensions was perhaps more evident in New Testament churches than has been realized. The social features of the time, and specifically the fact that voluntary associations were a prevalent feature of Greco-Roman society, influenced the nature of the church significantly.[19] These associations gathered around philosophical schools, synagogues or households. The reality that the *ekklēsia* in those times engaged in a network of other voluntary associations offers a model for a church as much more engaged with the world of people and the *polis* than is popularly believed. Certainly, an interweaving of the coming and going dimensions of the missional church will keep the subcultural mores of inner church life under scrutiny and in perspective.

Some churches, perhaps most in the West, are so focused on their gathered life that there is little intentionality in equipping God's people for the dispersed life of the church. As Phil Collins and R. Paul Stevens say, "Most churches are havens of refuge rather than dynamic centers for transformation in society."[20] Such ecclesial introversion or self-centeredness is as Hendrik Kraemer says, "a betrayal of its nature and calling."[21] Similarly, Michael Frost and Alan Hirsch aver that the church today is overly engaged in attractional strategies that are effectively forms of extracting people out of the world instead of calling and then equipping people to follow Jesus in the world.[22] Then, reflecting the thought of David Bosch, they say that the New Testament vision of

---

[18]R. Paul Stevens, *The Other Six Days: Vocation, Work and Ministry in Biblical Perspective* (Grand Rapids: Eerdmans, 1999), p. 211.

[19]See, for example, Richard S. Ascough, "Translocal Relationships Among Voluntary Associations and Early Christianity," *Journal of Early Christian Studies* 5, no. 2 (1997): 223-41; Philip A. Harland, *Associations, Synagogues, and Congregations: Claiming a Place in Ancient Mediterranean Society* (Minneapolis: Fortress Press, 2003); James S. Jeffers, *The Greco-Roman World of the New Testament Era: Exploring the Background of Early Christianity* (Downers Grove, Ill: InterVarsity Press, 1999); John S. Kloppenborg and Stephen G. Wilson, eds. *Voluntary Associations in the Graeco-Roman World* (London: Routledge, 1996).

[20]Phil Collins and R. Paul Stevens, *The Equipping Pastor* (Washington, D.C.: Alban Institute, 1993), p. 126.

[21]Hendrik Kraemer, *A Theology of the Laity* (Vancouver: Regent College Publishing, 2005), p. 130.

[22]Michael Frost and Alan Hirsch, *The Shaping of Things to Come: Innovation and Mission for the 21 Century Church* (Peabody, Mass.: Hendrickson, 2003), p. 39.

the church implies a sending impulse, a sort of centrifugal force (moving or tending to move away from a center) movement rather than a centripetal (moving or tending to move towards a center).[23] Perhaps it is better to say that the church is intended to be centripetal as it is centrifugal. Some churches have emphasized the scattered dimensions to the detriment of the inner life of the church with God and the rich "one another" dimensions. The missional God is the sending and the gathering God, and the missional church will thus also be both a sent/sending and a gathering community. Clayton Schmit's book title *Sent and Gathered: A Worship Manual for the Missional Church* aptly reflects both aspects of the missional church.[24]

Awareness of the going and coming nature of the church will overcome blindness to the need for contextualization for a postmodern world of the language and music of the church's gatherings, as well as its degree of formality. Surely the incarnation of the Son of God into a Jewish world with all the culture and customs he engaged in is all the legitimization we need for contextualization of the gospel and the gospel-community in our day. *Semper reformanda.*

Discerning where the Spirit is at work in every culture. There is ample evidence that the Spirit is at work in all cultures and communities. In Matthew 9:37-38 ("He said to his disciples, 'The harvest is plentiful but the workers are few. Ask the Lord of the harvest, therefore, to send out workers into his harvest field.'"), Jesus startlingly infers that to pray for workers is legitimate, but that prayer for a harvest seems not to be necessary. This has to do with the missions of the Son, sent by the Father, and of the Spirit, sent by the Father (and, or through the Son). As a product of his own mission, Jesus spoke in John 12 of "much fruit" or "many seeds." The mission of the Spirit would ensure the drawing of

---

[23]Karl Barth speaks also of the intended centrifugal nature of the mission of the Old Testament people of God. This he does in his exegetical work on the uniquely universal orientation of Isaiah's call narrative in chap. 6 ("the whole earth is full of his glory"), where he states that the "overtly centrifugal motion is a *novum* in the calling of Isaiah" and affirms that Israel's election had a "centrifugal orientation towards the universal concerns of Israel's God." See Mark S. Gignilliat, *Karl Barth and the Fifth Gospel: Barth's Theological Exegesis of Isaiah* (Aldershot, U.K.: Ashgate, 2009), p. 71. On centripetal see Bosch, *Transforming Mission*, p. 388.

[24]Clayton J. Schmit, *Sent and Gathered: A Worship Manual for the Missional Church* (Grand Rapids: Baker Academic, 2009).

people to God and the application of that atoning work to people, to form "God's field," as Paul speaks of it (1 Cor 2:4, 10; 3:6, 9). Optimism about the presence of a harvest is grounded in what God has done in his Son and what he is doing by his Spirit. Our prayers are to be focused on the raising up of humans to participate with him as his "co-workers" (1 Cor 3:9). Disciples then, as now, need to be willing to become the answer to their own prayers.

The way the Spirit works to prepare the "harvest" has both an individual dimension as well as a larger dimension, either the direct shaping of culture or the turning of adverse influences in culture to create windows of light to draw people to himself. Within particular cultural trends, ideas, brokenness and events, the wind of the Spirit blows to bring about harvest.

The way the church views contemporary culture, influenced as it is by modernity and postmodernity, requires both vigilance toward insidious aspects and realistic optimism that in even this culture, God creates windows for the gospel and opportunities for the church to influence culture. Even within modernity, for example, good aspects may be affirmed, such as progress in science and the liberation of regimes from religious or ideological repression. As Graham Ward has noted, "a good dose of secularism would break the repressive holds certain state-ratified religions have over people."[25] The following is a brief discussion of modernity and postmodernity with an eye toward windows for the gospel.

Discussion of modernity and postmodernity is a complex matter.[26] Taking an appropriately critical stance toward modernity does not mean that we wish to promote anti-intellectualism or that we want to go back to a premodern age. The goal of the critique of culture is to affirm the good, the true and the beautiful, to critique that which is fallen, to denounce values opposed to the gospel and to exert prophetic and redemptive influences toward an alternative vision of

---

[25]Graham Ward, *True Religion*, Blackwell Manifestos (Oxford: Blackwell, 2003), pp. 1-2.

[26]Helpful discussions of the similarities and distinctions between modernity and postmodernity, including both the challenges to and compatibilities with the gospel are found in Jens Zimmermann, *Recovering Theological Hermeneutics: An Incarnational-Trinitarian Theory of Interpretation* (Grand Rapids: Baker Academic, 2011) and Craig Gay, *The Way of the (Modern) World: Or, Why It's Tempting to Live As If God Doesn't Exist* (Grand Rapids: Eerdmans, 1998).

modernity or postmodernity, as the case may be.

One of the key prophetic roles of the missional church, however, is to poke holes in cherished intellectual assumptions that undergird secular culture. The Spirit may be at work to unsettle people and draw them to repentance of their culture's idolatries. One myth of modernity is that there is a secular arena in which reason is free from the influence of religious bias. This has been a barrier to Christian engagement. True postmodernity has demonstrated that reason is never unprejudiced, and Radical Orthodoxy (RO) has shown convincingly that there is specifically no neutral secular sphere. As Jamie Smith suggests, "RO's project is aimed at unveiling the religious status of this modern vision, thus alerting us to the ways in which these core values or doctrines of modern life are, in the end, competitors of the Gospel of Christ." Secularism is an alternative confession. It does not merely form values by borrowing capital from its original Christian roots, but it is "actually constituted in its secularity by 'heresy' in relation to orthodox Christianity, or else a rejection of Christianity that is more 'neo-pagan' than simply anti-religious. Secular theory, then, is supported not by a neutral universal rationality (as it claims) but by simply another mythos, an alternative confession."[27] Smith's exhortation that Christians can engage in the public square of ideas on the basis that all engagement by everyone is faith-based, given the fideistic nature of reason, is timely. It is a prime example of how God is at work in culture to create openness to the gospel.

Postmodernity is notoriously difficult to define. One opinion is that postmodernity is in fact a misnomer, and that the characteristics of this era are in fact merely modernity taken to the extreme. The era is, for those of this persuasion, more appropriately termed hyper-modernity.[28] Smith comments for example that

> what is taken to be postmodern relativism is usually allied to a very modern skepticism, coupled with the Enlightenment emphasis on the

---

[27]Smith, *Introducing Radical Orthodoxy*, p. 127.

[28]Thomas Oden and Craig Gay, for example. Adherents of radical orthodoxy (Milbank, Ward) also tend to see postmodernity in this light, in a way that according to James Smith (*Introducing Radical Orthodoxy*, p. 139 n. 33) parallels Jürgen Habermas's critique of Derrida and Foucault in *The Philosophical Discourse of Modernity* (Cambridge, Mass.: MIT Press, 1987).

autonomy of the self, which is intended to secure the right for the individual to do whatever he or she wants. The pervasiveness of rights language and identity politics is a hyper-modern phenomenon, not a mark of postmodernity.[29]

Many of the so-called novel trends of postmodernity have much in common with Romanticism of the eighteenth century. Crucially, as Graham Ward has noted, the fundamental continuity lies within the commonness of the immanent ontology and the anthropology they share, and that within the common framework of autonomous secularity.[30] There is universal acknowledgment that the foundationalist paradigms of modernity have collapsed as a consequence of the insights of postmodernity, but that "the dogma of the autonomy of theoretical thought" persists.[31]

There is a great deal to be said for this opinion. Its relevance lies in the fact that modernity is still very much publicly viable, its core being the conclusions of the Enlightenment. The Enlightenment has as its heart the notion of "'prejudice against prejudice'—where the most dangerous prejudice is the religious."[32] As Smith concludes therefore, "political (and academic) rhetoric indicates that modernity is a thriving project."[33] Evidences that this has pervaded the church abound, but most notably in theologies of both a liberal and conservative kind, which are apologetic projects of correlation with secular thought, employing supposedly autonomous reason. Fundamentalism in particular is "but a mirror of modernism" in its engagement also on the assumption of neutral, objective reason.[34]

Having said all this, it is acknowledged that true postmodernity is in fact present alongside hypermodernity. Newbigin, in *The Gospel in a Pluralist Society* (1997), was much influenced in poking holes in the En-

---

[29]Smith, *Introducing Radical Orthodoxy*, p. 32 n. 5.

[30]Graham Ward, cited in Smith, *Introducing Radical Orthodoxy*, p. 139. In this vein, radical orthodoxy finds little new in supposedly postmodern theology or postmodern philosophy of religion (Derrida, Caputo).

[31]Smith, *Introducing Radical Orthodoxy*, p. 139.

[32]"Prejudice against prejudice" is a phrase coined by Hans-George Gadamer, *Truth and Method*, trans. Joel Weinsheimer and Donald G. Marshall, rev. ed. (New York: Continuum, 1989), p. 276.

[33]Smith, *Introducing Radical Orthodoxy*, p. 32.

[34]Ibid., p. 37.

lightenment and modernism by Michael Polanyi (*Personal Knowledge*) and Alasdair MacIntyre (*After Virtue*), who exposed the fallacies of a rationalistic worldview, scientism, the reliability of pure reason, suggesting that total objectivity is a myth, even for scientists.[35] The idea of the infallibility and supremacy of reason of the autonomous human mind, and of a pristine secular space untarnished by religious faith which so dominated many Western countries, has in fact by means of postmodernity (Lyotard) been shown to be a myth. Postmodernity's contribution to the contemporary postfoundationalist milieu does at minimum create some windows for the gospel and "unapologetically confessional theory and practice" of the Christian church. The realistic revelationism in Karl Barth's commitment to Anselm's epistemological conviction that theology is faith seeking understanding provides a window arising from a consonance between postmodernity and Christian theology done in this way.

As Tom Smail notes, "In our own day, the deconstructing skepticism that Feuerbach applied to religion has in much post-modern thinking been extended to all claims to know the truth about any reality that is objective to us."[36] Postmodernity has therefore exposed the gods of modernity as unreliable, and this can only be good for Christian mission. Hans Küng has stated that

> Atheism too lives by an indemonstrable faith; whether it is faith in human nature (Feuerbach), or faith in the future socialist society (Marx) or faith in rational science (Freud). The question then can be asked of any form of atheism whether it is not itself an understandable projection of man (Feuerbach), a consolation serving vested interests (Marx) or an infantile illusion (Freud).[37]

As Smail asserts, postmodernity has seen through this, but offers no alternative hope:

---

[35]Sometimes the distinction is made between "modernism," the era since the Enlightenment characterized by the idea of progress through rationality and hierarchy in public and artistic life, and "modernity," the era within modernism in which modernism was worked out into the fabric of life in the West. Thus both modernity and postmodernity come within the era of modernism.

[36]Tom Smail, *Like Father, Like Son: The Trinity Imaged in Our Humanity* (Grand Rapids: Eerdmans, 2005), p. 24.

[37]Hans Küng, *Why I Am Still a Christian* (Nashville: Abingdon, 1987), pp. 229-30.

The beginning of the twenty-first century does not have much faith or
hope left in human goodness, political utopianism, or psychiatric salvation and, indeed, in its more sophisticated post-modern expressions,
has little faith that there is any possibility of knowing any universally
binding truth about objective reality. When a society offers no common
vision of a reality beyond itself and no responsibility to values that are
given to it rather than created by it, that society fragments and disinte-
grates; the evidence multiplies that this is exactly what is happening to
our own society in our own day. [38]

In response to this the church, rather than despairing, can offer its
humble and honest "faith-seeking-understanding" apologetic grounded in
humble, admittedly circular, revelational trinitarian hermeneutics. One of
Karl Barth's central theological axioms, as Smail points out, was that
when we are talking of God, it is the actuality that determines the possibility and not the other way around. We do not limit our openness to what
God has done by prior notions of our own about what he could do; rather,
our basis for recognizing what he can do is what he has already done. The
incarnational revelation of God in Christ objectively, a historic narrative,
is the actuality to which we in faith point, trusting that the Spirit subjec-
tively will bring people into the awareness of the actuality of relationship
with God. This approach will have greater resonance with postmodernity.

The religious right, which has pursued the Constantinian project by
seeking to "colonize the public and political spheres by Christian morality (or the morality supposedly disclosed by 'natural law')," has, as
Smith has shown, in fact revealed itself to be a theological response to
modernity on the basis of modernity. [39] All such Constantinian projects
are accommodationist in that they are "attempts to accommodate and
synthesize the gospel with the interests of the nation-state." [40] Smith
advocates here for the approach taken by Hauerwas and Willimon in
Resident Aliens, who in contrast to approaches involving the revival of
natural law[41] suggest that the church is an alternative society: "The

---

[38]Smail, *Like Father, Like Son*, pp. 25-26.
[39]Smith, *Introducing Radical Orthodoxy*, p. 32.
[40]Ibid., p. 32 n. 3.
[41]The case of J. Budziszewski, *What We Can't Not Know* (Dallas: Spence, 2003) is cited by Smith
   in *Introducing Radical Orthodoxy*, p. 32 n. 3.

church, as those called out by God, embodies a social alternative that the world cannot on its own terms know."[42] This is a valid notion as long as it does not exclude the scattered *ekklēsia* and therefore the "salt and light" influence of the church on society, with the purpose of redeeming culture rather than isolating from it.

A further aspect of postmodernity that finds consonance with the values of the gospel relates to affectivity. Postmodernity has subverted the notion that we can only know things by means of the cognitive faculty. Graham Ward comments that new models of personhood in postmodernity give "renewed dignity to the affective side of human nature," which points to a knowledge "more profound and prior to rationality."[43] Drawing on the work of François Lyotard and Helene Cixous, Ward has explored "deeply affective experiences of the sublime" by looking at relationships between aesthetic and religious experiences. The importance of aesthetics and affective responses has caused proponents of radical orthodoxy to emphasize the importance of liturgy in the life of the church. The radical orthodoxy conclusion that "outside the liturgy there is no visible meaning, such that only a doxological account can underwrite the arts"[44] points to the arts as a significant window for the penetration of the gospel in the postmodern era.

Christopher Wright has also written encouragingly on the resonances of the Christian faith and mission with postmodernity, as well as on the limits of these resonances. He acknowledges that recognition that all Christian theologies are contextual, including the "standard" Western one, has coincided with the impact of postmodernity on hermeneutics and its welcoming of locality and plurality.[45] He also acknowledges that unlike postmodernism, which eschews the idea of any metanarrative, Christianity is a nonoppressive metanarrative, that there is objective truth for all in revelation of the gospel, and that there is

---

[42]Stanley Hauerwas and William Willimon, *Resident Aliens: Life in the Christian Colony* (Nashville: Abingdon, 1989), pp. 17-18.

[43]Graham Ward, *Theology and Contemporary Critical Theory: Creating Transcendent Worship Today* (New York: St. Martin's Press, 1999), pp. 121-23.

[44]Smith, *Introducing Radical Orthodoxy*, 78.

[45]Contextualization involves inculturation, which emphasizes the insertion of theology into culture and evokes connotations of the incarnation.

a "universal story" that "gives a place in the sun to all the little stories."[46] Since Christian mission has thrived in multiple cultural contexts, Wright affirms that contextualization "is rather the very stuff of missional engagement and missiological reflection." He concludes that "we may be challenged by swimming in the postmodern pool, but we need not feel out of our depth there."[47]

While culture must be critiqued and postmodernity in particular in its most radical forms for its deconstructionism, I fear that many evangelical Christians spend too much time exposing the subtle ploys of the evil one in the world of ideas and far too little time being present to that world and its broken people. It seems that most ordinary people in Western society would be unable to articulate a coherent postmodern way of thinking and being, but may best be described as holding fragmented belief systems. The need for churches to embrace people into communities in which they are formed by the Christian story is crucial. In reaction to the negative trends in culture, however, even sophisticated theologians can overreact and encourage an isolationism that runs counter to the church's nature as the new humanity. For example, while one can agree with the Aristotelian-MacIntryian notion of the church as a *polis*, it is a polis unlike any other. The word *polis* conveys a discrete entity, a well-defined community. The church is not a community circumscribed by a solid line but by a dotted line.

I believe we can feel positive about mission in this era insofar as we can see evidence of windows that the Spirit has created within postmodernity for receptivity to the gospel. There is a new openness to spirituality. There is a hunger for intimacy born of much domestic brokenness, and particularly the absence of fathers, as a result of the

---

[46]Christopher Wright, *The Mission of God: Unlocking the Bible's Grand Narrative* (Downers Grove, Ill.: InterVarsity Press, 2006), p. 47. Here Wright also references Richard Bauckham's exploration of "the constant oscillation between the particular and the universal, and its implications for a missiological hermeneutic, with special attention to its relevance to postmodernity," in *Bible and Mission: Christian Mission in a Postmodern World* (Grand Rapids: Baker Academic, 2003)." The idea of the Christian metanarrative absorbing all human stories into the one grand narrative may be traced to the work of postliberal theologian George Lindbeck, *The Nature of Doctrine: Religion and Theology in a Postliberal Age* (Louisville: Westminster John Knox, 1984).

[47]Wright, *Mission of God*, pp. 45-46.

drivenness for success and its symbols. There is an emotional authenticity about this generation that is very much consonant with gospel
values, and a refreshing change from the emotional pharisaism one
often finds in the church. There is a distrust of metanarratives, which
are considered to be oppressive, and yet the nature of Christianity, if
understood rightly, is not oppressive. Furthermore, the concern for the
poor that characterizes many postmoderns, inspired by popular artists,
creates opportunities for many to sense the appeal of Jesus who became
poor, lived among the poor and proclaimed a gospel for the poor.

Even as the church seeks to come to terms with postmodernity, the
world moves on, and it appears that the pendulum is swinging back.
There is talk of a shift that may mean the advent of an era dubbed as
"post-postmodernity." This may be a reaction to the sense of the moral
morass of subjectivity in which people are not able to make moral sense
of their lives. The Spirit will no doubt be at work in all of this. Whereas
the extreme cynicism of postmodernity rejects the Christian story out-
right, the post-postmodern may have ears more open to hear it.

Of course, care is required here. John Milbank is appropriately nuanced when he states that there is an "inevitable, if wary, affinity, which
must exist between Christianity and postmodernism."[48] Equally carefully, Smith states that "This affinity is neither an identification of the
two nor an accommodation of one to the other but rather the discernment of an opportunity afforded by the contemporary situation."
He states that the chink in modernity's armor is an opportunity for the
"church to be alerted to its complicity with modernity."[49] This highlights a further challenge for the contemporary church. Its failure to
inculturate is related to the fact that it is blind to its own indiscriminate
enculturations. We now consider this entrapment of the church.

---

[48]John Milbank, *Being Reconciled: Ontology and Pardon*, Radical Orthodoxy Series (London:
  Routledge, 2003), p. 196.
[49]Smith, *Introducing Radical Orthodoxy*, p. 141.

3

Breaking Free of the Entrapment of Indiscriminate Enculturation

. . .

"There exists in every church something that sooner or later
works against the very purpose for which it came into existence."
So we must strive very hard, by the grace of God to keep the church
focused on the mission that Christ originally gave to it.

WILL VAUS, *Mere Theology* (quoted material
by C. S. Lewis, *Letters to Malcolm*)

TO SAY THAT THE DISCIPLES in John 20:19-23 were temporarily disconnected from their culture is an understatement: "doors locked for fear of the Jewish leaders" says it all. However, what kept them entrapped was not just a disconnection from people based in fear; it was the grip of deeply embedded Jewish cultural thought patterns and expectations. The news Jesus had given them that he would die and rise again had never been fully computed in their minds, filled as they were with Jewish, political expectations of a Messiah. Peter's classic refutation of news of a suffering Messiah in Matthew 16, and Jesus' strong rebuke—Peter's darkest hour right after his brightest—provides some evidence of this. They didn't get the cross before it happened, and they didn't get it when it happened. The reason they were locked up had a lot to do with their lifelong enculturation in that kind of thinking. Who could blame them? The radical reshaping of values regarding power and prestige and possessions that Jesus had modeled in his life and kingdom teaching ran counter to their enculturation as normal Jewish, normal human, people.

Who could blame them also for the slowness in grasping that Jesus was risen? Resurrection was not something rational thought could handle very easily, even if they had seen Jesus raise others. At least one sector of the religious establishment of their day, the Sadducees, were pre-Enlightenment rationalists who denied the possibility of resurrection on antisupernaturalist grounds. That could have been in disciple minds, if only at the back of it. Much enculturation entrapped and prevented them from becoming the missional church Jesus had called them to be.

In similar fashion the church in the West finds itself severely enculturated in a mosaic of modern and postmodern influences, and not only in the positive dynamics of culture. This chapter is a survey of possible ways that churches and Christians experience entrapment concerning *indiscriminate enculturation*—even in the ways they react to this enculturation with movements that are themselves characterized by subtle enculturations. Drawing on what happens to liberate the early community that John pictures in John 20, I will outline how the church can break free of this to become the "sent" community that it is. In fact, the task of the church is not merely to wage war against prevailing culture but to offer a new, alternative culture, that of the church, which as a community and as its component persons become culture shapers in society.[1]

The enculturation of the church signals that there is more than the influence of the *imago Dei* on human culture. Every human being and every culture is a conglomerate of dignity arising from the *imago* and the distorting, corrupting influence of sin as a consequence of the Fall. In every culture there is evidence of an independence of God and ideologies in opposition to God. This is what is meant by the "world" in many New Testament passages. Idolatry is at the core of the aspects of culture that the church is called to separate itself from. These are often very subtle because they are often distortions of good things.

---

[1]In this vein see the work of Andy Crouch, *Culture Making: Recovering Our Creative Calling* (Downers Grove, Ill.: InterVarsity Press, 2009).

I will highlight the dangers of the church being indiscriminately enculturated (influenced in formative ways by values and ideas contrary to the gospel—some might prefer *acculturation*). There is a need for Christians and the church to contextualize without compromising the core of the gospel. Jesus himself, as God the Son, entered by his incarnation into a specific human context and communicated the nature of God and the gospel in ways that were culturally relevant without ever compromising his holiness and without capitulating to sinful cultural trends. By contrast the blindness of many modern and postmodern Christians to their own enculturation in gospel-violating ways compounds the challenge of contextualizing the gospel.

Indiscriminate enculturation is a result of ignoring the consequences of the Fall for human culture. There is a danger which lurks for those (especially in emergent or missional churches) who right-mindedly determine to recontextualize the gospel. The danger for those who seek to adapt the ways that the gospel community lives and worships with cultural relevance is that they may inadvertently capitulate to trends in culture that are fallen elements, or elements that are the consequence of the influence of demonic forces. There are elements in every ethnic and generational culture that are a product of the distortion of the image of God in humanity (1 Jn 2:15-17). There are ideological forces at work that are satanically originated and manipulated (1 Jn 5:19).

I will highlight some of the elements present in contemporary culture in the West and how the church may be entrapped by capitulation. In light of the Westernization of Two-Thirds World cultures and Christians, some of these entrapments may be relevant there also. We cannot naively enter this discussion. Just how difficult it can be to discern the good and the bad in culture, and just how nuanced the theological underpinnings of this issue can be is best illustrated by the famous feud between two theologians from similar theological stables, Karl Barth and Emil Brunner. Barth perceived Brunner to be capitulating to the negative influences of Nazism in their contemporary German culture by suggesting that fallen human beings retained a "point of contact" for receiving revelation. As Trevor Hart has insightfully commented, the differences could have been clarified by making a distinction between

formal and material capacity, and even Barth would have admitted that
fallen humans have at least the formal capacity to receive revelation.
That is, they, like Lazarus's body, have the capacity to receive the capacity to live.[2]

INDISCRIMINATE ENCULTURATION
OF THE WESTERN CHURCHES

Numerous elements of Western culture make it resistant to Christianity, and the church has imbibed them to some degree or another.
Some elements are more evident in the culture of modernity and some
more in postmodernity, though there is overlap.

In the late twentieth century Bishop Lesslie Newbigin returned to
England after years of serving as a missionary in India. He proposed
that the culture of modernity in societies in the United Kingdom and
other Western nations was pagan, and that because its paganism had
been born out of the rejection of Christianity, it was far more resistant
to the gospel than the pre-Christian paganism that crosscultural missions traditionally encountered. "We are in a radically new situation
and cannot dream either of a Constantinian authority or of a pre-Con-
stantinian innocence," he said.[3] Newbigin encouraged churches in the
West and their leaders to engage in the same kind of contextualization
that crosscultural missionaries do. What are the specific values of modernity and postmodernity that are resistant to the gospel, and how has
postmodernity made a difference if any?

Under the rubric of *modernity* I would suggest that the belief systems
or values which have been most gospel resistant and have infiltrated the
Christian mind and the church are:

- faith in autonomous perfectibility, and human progress

- consumerism

- secularism[4]

---

[2]Trevor Hart, "A Capacity for Ambiguity: The Barth-Brunner Debate Revisited," *Tyndale Bulletin* 44, no. 2 (1993): 290-91.
[3]Lesslie Newbigin, *The Gospel in a Pluralist Society* (London: SPCK, 1989), p. 224.
[4]See in this regard Leander Keck, *The Church Confident: Christianity Can Repent but It Must Not
Whimper* (Nashville: Abingdon, 1993). After exposing the secularizing tendencies of the con-

- the dichotomization of reason as verifiable and faith as unverifiable, leading to the privatization of values and faith, and religious pluralism

- the dichotomization of the natural and the "supernatural" (if acknowledged) such that God is exiled to the supernatural realm, and such that creation becomes "nature," in which God appears only as an intruder[5]

- dualism not only of the physical and the spiritual, but of the intellectual and the emotional

- materialism and entitlement to guaranteed security

- control

- individualism, as a consequence of the primacy of reason of the autonomous mind

- technocracy

- ethnocentrism

Many of these persist into the postmodern era. However, the values that more clearly characterize *postmodernity* and which have been indiscriminately imbibed by the church are:

- facile perspectivalism, which is a way of insulating all truth claims from critical evaluation; it also places talk about God into the background at the expense of talk about "my context, culture, gender, language, biology, auto-biography"

- undue cynicism about truth, which manifests itself sometimes in a "don't confuse me with the facts" arrogance

- hedonism, the pursuit of pleasure as a means to hide existential despair, expressed in the party lifestyle and sometimes involving binge drinking and drugs

---

temporary church, in the spirit of this book, Keck argues with conviction that the church has grounds to be confident about its proper nature and mission and urges a theocentric and doxological approach to church life.

[5]See in this regard William Carl Placher, *The Domestication of Transcendence* (Louisville: Westminster John Knox, 1996).

- technocracy

- antihistoricism: postmoderns tend to champion imagination as the premier faculty over against memory and thus over formation by the tradition[6]

- spiritualities of a demonic and New Age variety

- moral confusion and laxity

Much has been written about most of these values and trends, and one can find detailed commentaries on them in, for example, works like that of Wilbert R. Shenk and Darrell Guder et al.[7] I will comment mostly on how especially the most insidious aspects of modernity and postmodern culture have been indiscriminately absorbed by the Christian population. I will also highlight how some of these negative values have influenced those who have seen the indiscriminate enculturation of the traditional church and formed reactionary movements, which are themselves indiscriminately encultured. I will then offer hope for the unshackling of the church.

Here then are some comments on the *indiscriminate enculturation* of the Western church.

- *Consumerism.* Consumerism manifests itself in the church in the manner in which people come to church with expectations of getting, as opposed to giving to God their worship and to the people of God their ministry. Even the language we use, "going to church" or "doing church" as opposed to "being the church," reflects this. Consumerism makes it difficult for Christians to move beyond being demanding spectators to become participants. But then to get them to see that the church does not exist for them only but for the world, for the poor, for the needy and the broken, is even more challenging. Consumerism keeps us from mission. Behind locked doors.

---

[6]See in this regard George P. Schner, "Metaphors for Theology," in *Theology After Liberalism: A Reader*, ed. George P. Schner and John Webster (Oxford: Oxford University Press, 2000).
[7]Wilbert R. Shenk, "The Culture of Modernity as a Missionary Challenge," in *Church Between Gospel and Culture: The Emerging Mission in North America*, ed. George R. Hunsberger and Craig van Gelder (Grand Rapids: Eerdmans, 1996); Darrell Guder, ed., *Missional Church: A Vision for the Sending of the Church in North America* (Grand Rapids: Eerdmans, 1998).

- *Materialism.* The prosperity of the Western church poses a real challenge for Christian discipleship as Jesus expressed it. The pervasiveness of the idol of material advancement and guaranteed security makes the worship and service of the kingdom with an undivided heart extremely difficult.

- *Dualism.* Old Greek Platonic thinking still pervades Western culture with its assumptions about the evil of matter, including the human body, and the goodness of the immaterial or spiritual. Such dualism still influences the church of modernity, causing its mission often to be limited to the saving of souls to the neglect of the redemption of the whole person. As a result, evangelism is disconnected from concern for the poor, missions overseas is limited to church planting rather than expression of compassion for the whole person, and the pursuit of social justice for persons is somehow disconnected from their coming to know justification by faith. The incarnation of Jesus spelled the end of all such dualism, and his kingdom ministry to whole persons confirmed that.

  There are other dualisms that hinder mission. There is in our culture a prevailing openness to "spirituality." Such awareness does create a window for the gospel. Spirituality in our culture, however, takes many forms. They are predominantly dualistic and often demonic. There can be a tendency for Christian spirituality to become disconnected from earthy, incarnational reality.

  There is a dualism within postmodern thought that affects the church also. There is a sense that somehow what the Christian person does with their body does not matter much, and that giving way to its desire for sex outside of marriage is not an issue of concern. The incarnation and resurrection of Christ in a human body spells the end of such dualistic thinking.

- *Ethnocentrism.* To say that the disciples of Jesus depicted in John 20:19-23 had to overcome ethnocentrism is a gross understatement. God had to literally move heaven and earth to get the hardheaded Jewish disciples to preach to the Gentiles, let alone recognize them as equals in the church. Ethnocentrism still exists in the church.

Many white, predominantly Anglo-Saxon churches continue to worship in ways that are dominated by that culture. Furthermore, the "zeal" for missions overseas is often not coupled with a concern for the people of many nations in the proverbial backyard. Ethnic churches, which form for good reasons, often remain ethnically monolithic in ways that contradict the gospel. The risen Christ calls us to make disciples of all nations and to work with him by the Spirit toward the formation of an international community. Until we break down these barriers in Jesus, we are hindered in our mission. Locked behind doors.

- *Control.* Control is the particular challenge of modernity. This is demonstrated, for example, by an obsession with strategic planning.[8] In discussing the subtle impact culture has had on the church in the modern world, David Wells expresses that the church is "blinded" by the way modernity is "restructuring Christian ministry."[9] Or as Os Guinness has commented, the church's mimicking of the modern world in its control of its ends through rational means has meant that "more and more of what was formerly left to God . . . is now classified, calculated, and controlled by systematic application of reason and technique."[10] Church leaders are pressured to "take control," to be CEOs and technicians. Regrettably, this pursuit of control stands in contrast to the true essence of the church: a community that is gathered together through the Holy Spirit in the life of Christ and sent by the Holy Spirit to represent the kingdom of God. As Guinness notes, "One way this 'control' has infiltrated the church is within the ideas of the church growth movement with its technique oriented cause-effect reductionism. . . . The human agency within the church growth movement, as Van Gelder sees it, is also 'at the heart of the ethos of modernity.' "[11] As Jacques Ellul, well-known

---

[8]See, for example, Janice G. Stein, *The Cult of Efficiency*, rev. ed. (Toronto: House of Anansi, 2002).

[9]David F. Wells, *No Place for Truth: Whatever Happened to Evangelical Theology?* (Grand Rapids: Eerdmans, 1993), p. 79.

[10]Os Guinness, *Dining with the Devil: The Megachurch Movement Flirts with Modernity* (Grand Rapids: Baker, 1993), p. 58.

[11]Ibid. Guinness clarifies he is referring to the contemporary church growth *movement*, both the

critic of technique, states: "It is not [the Christian's] primary task to think out plans, programmes, methods of action and of achievement. When Christians do this (and there is an epidemic of this behaviour at the present time in the Church) it is simply an imitation of the world, and is doomed to defeat."[12] The kingdom of God is about God's reign, not human control. This control will keep the church from missional effectiveness. Behind locked doors.

• *Individualism.* In his list of Enlightenment precepts that have domesticated the church and its mission, David Bosch highlights that "everyone was an *emancipated autonomous individual*" and that specifically Protestantism has been afflicted with "rampant individualism" to such an extent that "church became peripheral, since each individual not only had the right but also the ability to know God's revealed will" and "could make their own decisions about what they believed."[13] Such trends violate the communal nature of persons and the notion of church community. Furthermore, individualism prevents the church community from being open to the world. God's primary agent for mission, the church, not its individuals, is thus entrapped. The postmodern hunger for community creates a Spirit-inspired opportunity for the church, but there can be resistance to this. The fundamental *in curvatus in se* orientation (curved in on ourselves) of the human condition (termed such by Augustine), can, by the power of the gospel of the God who is *for us*, transform his community to be *ex curvatus ex se*, turned toward the other.

Newbigin, in *The Gospel in a Pluralist Society*, exposed the Enlightenment Descartian view of the human self as autonomous—and with it, the individualism and successism that is part of the cultural captivity of the church. Newbigin famously said that Jesus does

---

"classical" church growth movement, initiated by Donald McGavran, and the "popular" church growth movement, as exemplified by the writings of George Barna, Rick Warren and Bill Hybels. These are linked by the similar commitments to techniques and strategies for the growth of the church. For instance, the classical church growth proponents seek to use the "new ground" from the fields of management, marketing, psychology and communications to help churches grow.

[12]Jacques Ellul, *The Presence of the Kingdom*, trans. Olive Wyon (New York: Seabury, 1967), p. 80.
[13]David Bosch, *Transforming Mission* (Maryknoll, N.Y.: Orbis, 1991), p. 273.

call his people to be "fishers of people" but that he did so by "forming a community."[14] Newbigin indicated also that the epistles are devoid of references to exhortation on evangelism and mission, and states that these are not the responsibility of the individual believer but rather a consequence of the power of the Spirit transforming the church. This of course needs to be understood within the assumption that the whole people of God in every vocation is the scattered church. The trinitarian nature of the Greatest Commission given in our John 20 passage will do more than anything to break the church free of its individualistic tendencies. Apart from this we will be ineffective. Locked behind doors.

- *Undue cynicism.* Cynicism about the possibility of knowing any truth, which manifests itself sometimes in a "don't confuse me with the facts" arrogance, may be present in postmodern culture. Unparalleled saturation with media has reduced concentration spans, leading to cultural decline in education standards, observable now in many postsecondary educational institutions. The disdain for the teaching of confessional truth in the church and the pressure also for sermons to be short and soundbite-ish is a result of these influences, sometimes negating the power of the Spirit in preaching.

- *Hedonism.* Hedonism also characterizes this generation. This may be a consequence of disillusionment with the successism of modern parents' generation, the availability of money made available by affluent parents, despair about the future of a world threatened by global warming and terrorism, depression and anxiety arising from the breakup of marriages in an unparalleled way. A concern is that Christian people can be so caught up in this culture of hedonism that their capacity for engaging in the spiritual disciplines can be adversely affected. Sadly, values and ethics come to be influenced more by the media and movie culture than by the gospel.

- *Technocracy.* Technocracy is another cultural reality that can impede the church in its mission, by which I mean the un-

---

[14]Newbigin, *Gospel in a Pluralist Society*, p. 227.

redeemed use of technology. It so easily becomes a surrogate God, a "broken cistern."

- *Antihistoricism.* Another feature of postmodernity, antihistoricism runs counter to the gospel. This is understandable in the sense that changes in trends and technology happen so fast in this time that all that precedes ten years ago can seem irrelevant. This aversion to history has tended to show up in emergent ecclesiology and its tendency to negate all that has gone before. The continuity of the church with Christ since its inception, however, and a belief in the providence of God over history suggests that we should value and listen to the past.

In summary, Lowell Noble, American sociologist, in *From Oppression to Jubilee Justice*, labels three primary evils of the First World—idols of individualism, ethnocentrism and materialism—and calls on the church to replace these with the values of the kingdom of God.[15] Similarly, Scott Hafemann says, "The secret to building a successful church is now thought to be getting to know the new trinity of technology, psychology and marketing, not the Trinity of the Bible."[16] When the North American trinity is replaced by the biblical Trinity we shall have missional churches. But how do we get there? Before unfolding the way into that, I want first to speak of some cultural entrapments of the movements that have reacted against the traditional church. Underlying each is a form of discouragement or despair concerning the church, which arises by neglect of one aspect or another of God's continuing work in the church as it is depicted in this John 20 picture.

DESPAIR LEADING TO ISOLATION

The evidence abounds that many in North America have opted not to "do church" at all. George Barna's twenty million "Revolutionaries" apparently live "a first-century lifestyle based on faith, goodness, love,

---

[15]Lowell Noble, *From Oppression to Jubilee Justice* (Los Angeles: Urban Verses, 2007), p. 6.
[16]Scott J. Hafemann, *The God of Promise and the Life of Faith: Understanding the Heart of the Bible* (Wheaton, Ill.: Crossway Books, 2001), p. 20.

generosity, kindness, and simplicity," and "zealously pursue an intimate relationship with God," apparently without the help of a local church. In fact, even Barna suggests that we should be excited because this new movement "entails drawing people away from reliance upon a local church into a deeper connection with and reliance upon God."[17] I cannot imagine a notion more contradictory to the communal nature of humans created in the image of the communal God, and more in violation of the biblical notion that without the church there is no salvation. This represents the hegemony of Western individualism at its worst. It is a notion incongruent with the reality that the Spirit of God brings every Christian into union with Christ and with his people, so that each is organically connected to the *historical church*, "the continuous embodiment of God's covenant with humanity stretching across the centuries of Jewish and Christian tradition"; the *geographical church*, "the present manifestation of God's work in Christ across all the continents and among all the traditions, including those with whom we gather in our bit of history and geography through the *local church*"; the *heavenly church*, all "those who have gone before us in the faith and who wait in the nearer presence of Christ for the coming of the kingdom's fullness"; and the *eschatological church*, "the community of the redeemed that includes not only the saints on earth and in heaven but also those whom the Spirit will draw into the people of God through the ongoing messianic mission of Christ."[18]

It furthermore takes away much hope for the spiritual transformation of human persons from self-centered to other-centered beings that is enabled by the hard work of fellowship with other believers. It also negates the transformation of the communal worship in the presence of Christ among his people such that his "worshiping self" is formed in us, and even more specifically the transformation of the self as it undergoes the eucharistic *habitus*.[19] The words of Christopher

[17]George Barna, quoted in "No Church, No Problem," a review by Kevin Miller, *ChristianityTodayLibrary*, January 1, 2006, www.ctlibrary.com/ct/2006/january/13.69.html.

[18]Christopher Cocksworth, "Holding Together: Catholic Evangelical Worship in the Spirit," in *Remembering Our Future: Explorations in Deep Church*, ed. Andrew Walker and Luke Bretherton (Colorado Springs: Paternoster, 2007), pp. 139-40.

[19]David Ford, *Self and Salvation* (Cambridge: Cambridge University Press, 1999), chap. 4. This concept will be developed further in chap. 4.

Cocksworth are apropos: "This is the catholic breadth of the Spirit's work in our worship: to connect us with all those to whom Christ is connected, to bring us into fellowship with, as Luther liked to say, 'Christ and all his saints.'"[20]

This anticipates a further trend—those who establish new forms they believe to be less enculturated can often have their own enculturations and neglect the unity and catholicity of the church.

DESPAIR WITHIN EVEN THE RADICAL EMERGENT

Doubt about the capacity of the institutional or inherited forms of church to incorporate many who have come to believe in Christ or are at least attracted to him has driven the agenda of emerging churches. Some pessimism is justified in light of the seeker and newcomer unfriendliness and inappropriate otherworldliness of many churches. One feature therefore of some emerging churches has been seeking to form churches in what are termed "church-world hybrid spaces." This may even mean that getting together with other Christians to worship God at dedicated times and places of gathering goes by the board. This merely repeats the problem that there is no such thing as believing without belonging. Furthermore, as Bretherton states, "Many of these non-church places are antithetical to the faithful practice of Christianity: for example, to be in a café is not to be in a neutral space but to be in a site of consumer capitalism." While admitting that the church itself is "a deeply contested place of consumption and cultural production and a site of negotiated power relationships and the interplay of a variety of identities," that is, that the churches themselves are hybrid places "in and of the world as well as sites of divine presence," he nevertheless affirms that the difference between participation in a local church and having coffee with a friend at Starbucks lies in "how a particular community is oriented both to its past (the tradition it has received from those who have gone before) and to the actions of Christ

---

[20]Walker and Bretherton, *Remembering Our Future*, pp. 139-40. The quote from Luther is from "The Blessed Sacrament of the Holy and True Body and Blood of Christ, and the Brotherhoods" 18, in *Martin Luther's Basic Theological Writings*, ed. Timothy F. Lull (Minneapolis: Fortress, 1989), p. 254.

and the Spirit in a particular context and place."[21]

Many in the emergent or even mission-shaped church movements have reacted to any form of traditional churches by consigning them to historical extinction much like the dinosaurs. For example, the approach of Alan J. Roxburgh in *The Missionary Congregation, Leadership and Liminality* is to reinvent the church in light of postmodern reality, a process with three "rites of passage": separation (the church is already marginalized by society), liminality (the negation of everything that has been considered normative and the possibility of transformation) and reaggregation (the church is once again compatible with society).[22] There is much to be said for this kind of reform. However, too extreme an attitude to church in the past surely betrays a lack of faith in God's providence in church history. This attitude has motivated proponents of new and emergent forms of church to assume that nothing much has been good about church until now. A tendency to ignore the depths of communion with the historic church pervades these movements grounded in the belief that the "root must be cut" rather than preserved. The words of Andrew Walker are timely:

> Deep church is not merely overdue: it is an ecclesiological and missiological imperative. Mission-shaped churches and emergent churches for all their resourcefulness, vigour and imaginative drive, will not succeed unless they heed the lessons from their charismatic precursors in the renewal and drop anchors in the deep waters of the church that goes all the way down to the hidden reservoirs of the life-giving Spirit that, like the water Jesus gives, gushes up like a spring to eternal life (John 4:14).[23]

The hidden reservoirs this author is referring to are discovered in the regular ministry of Word and sacrament, the practice of spiritual disciplines, and a devotion to sound doctrine as expressed in the orthodox confessions of the catholic faith. He contends that emergent churches, which are an offshoot of charismatic/Pentecostal churches,

---

[21]Luke Bretherton, "Beyond the Emerging Church," in *Remembering Our Future*, ed. Walker and Bretherton, pp. 42-43.

[22]Alan J. Roxburgh, *The Missionary Congregation, Leadership and Liminality* (Harrisburg, Penn.: Trinity Press International, 1997).

[23]Andrew Walker, "Recovering Deep Church: Theological and Spiritual Renewal," in *Remembering Our Future*, ed. Walker and Bretherton, p. 20.

for the most part, will fail to experience long-term renewal unless they maintain this depth. What is more, the proliferation of these churches will further violate the unity and catholicity of the church of the one risen Christ, unless they have roots into the depths of the historic church.

Luke Bretherton has commented that emergent churches have inherited the anti-institutionalism that characterized the Pentecostal and charismatic movements, as well as their view of the kingdom of God in opposition to the church or denomination. Bretherton asserts that "Theologically, the opposition between the kingdom of God and the church establishes a false dichotomy and tends to legitimise a Docetic ecclesiology: that is, that 'true' or authentic Christianity is exempted from ordinary and mundane patterns of human association." He goes on to say that to "emphasize the person of Jesus and the kingdom of God as somehow *necessarily* in opposition to the history of the church is to fall into a kind of Jesusology: an attempt to escape history as if Christians can simply copy the primitive church or ask what would Jesus do and ignore two thousand years of church history."[24]

Part of the discouragement in some emergent church thought also lies behind the legitimate disavowal of the "attractional" or "extractional" approach. The preferred "incarnational" approach carries with it some dangers, however: discouragement about the importance of the gathered church, and doubt that the gatherings of the church in the presence of Christ and by power of the Spirit can attract people. The idea now prevalent that church is two or three people who just happen to meet in Starbucks, or two or three people blogging or facebooking in a disembodied way, for that matter, is not only poor theological anthropology and worse ecclesiology, it is an isolationist defeatism.

I would be the first to agree that we are not trying to put "the Humpty-dumpty of Christendom back together again" or trying to revert back into the "centuries of ecclesiastical triumphalism."[25] It

---

[24]Luke Bretherton, in *Remembering Our Future*, ed. Walker and Bretherton, p. 37.
[25]Douglas John Hall, "Metamorphosis: From Christendom to Diaspora," in *Confident Witness—Changing World: Rediscovering the Gospel in North America*, ed. Craig Van Gelder (Grand Rapids: Eerdmans, 1999), p. 70.

would be foolish to minimize the failures of many mainline and traditional evangelical churches. I therefore have a great deal of sympathy for the emergent church movement. Church should always be emerging as it is always reforming. However, dangers exist of idolizing new forms and above all losing the focus of what church is as that has been experienced for twenty centuries. The community of the unmanageable transcendence as well as the terrifying and yet insatiably satisfying immanence of God. The community of the triune God. This is our hope for reevangelizing the West.

The Despair Undergirding Radical Orthodoxy

Another form of despair that has arisen in the wake of and in protest against modernity is a theological one. It underlies radical orthodoxy. While there is much to commend this movement, as James Smith has indicated, at critical points it falls short of a Christocentric and trinitarian approach in seeking for Christian theology to be present to the postsecular era (in fact to demonstrate that the *saeculum*, or reason without religious prejudice, does not exist). One of the twenty-four theses of radical orthodoxy states the following:

> One can only speak of God indirectly, so theology is always speaking of something else: culture, society, history, language, art, nature. Therefore theology is more mediatory than neo-orthodoxy allowed; it is not just one more positive discourse. To deny mediation is paradoxically too modern, too liberal.[26]

Crucial to this mediation to achieve a theology of culture, for radical orthodoxy, has been the notion of participation funded by neo-Platonic influence, especially that of Iamblichus. It is participation of the *methexis* variety, rather than personal participation of the persons of the Godhead with creation or culture. The warranted pessimism of the radical orthodox concerning contemporary theology and its absence from the public square relates to much of it being ensconced in modernity. They contend also that it suffers from the legacy of Duns Scotus's univocity

---

[26]Thesis 4, John Milbank in "Radical Orthodoxy: Twenty-Four Theses," in L. P. Hemming, ed., *Radical Orthodoxy?: A Catholic Enquiry* (Aldershot, U.K.: Ashgate, 2000), pp. 33-45.

prior to the Reformation, which gave to God and creation a common category of "being" and thus granted a freedom that allowed space for the secular, a realm where pure reason could reign apart from any influence of prejudice (including faith). Included in radical orthodoxy's critique is the theology of Karl Barth, for it seems that for radical orthodoxy only participation understood in a neo-Platonic way can overcome the myth of secularity.

Detailed rebuttal of these aspects of radical orthodox theology is beyond our scope here. I agree with Julie Canlis that "the Christian insistence on a mediator is undermined by a Plotinian ascending typology that suggests progressive, unmediated participation in divinity."[27] It seems far better to insist on mediation by Christ such that Christ is necessary and sufficient to a theology of participation. Joseph Mangina corrects radical orthodoxy's misconception of Barth as a "correlationist" who offered a secular theology, asserting that Barth's incarnational and resurrectional theology was world affirming.[28] His basis for engagement was by affirmation of the *analogia relationis* or *fidei*, that is, the idea that nature is always graced not as a static given but in a dynamic way, always being given, in and through Christ. This parallels yet transcends Henri de Lubac's reappropriation of the *analogia entis* of scholastic Thomism. Lubac's conclusion is that

> nature is always graced. As a dependent creation, nature is gift and therefore cannot be autonomous; correlatively, reason always participates in grace, so any dualistic opposition of faith and reason is a product of modernity. The natural and supernatural are not to be understood as two different levels or realities but rather varying intensities of grace.[29]

Barth would have insisted that any kind of mediation between God

---

[27]Julie Canlis, *Calvin's Ladder* (Grand Rapids: Eerdmans, 2010), p. 30. Canlis cites J. Eichler to the effect that *koinōnia* is *methexis* participation redeemed (*metechō* is used as a synonym for *koinōnia*). J. Eichler, "Fellowship, Have, Share, Participate," in *New International Dictionary of New Testament Theology*, ed. Colin Brown (Grand Rapids: Zondervan, 1975), p. 639.
[28]Joseph L. Mangina, "Mediating Theologies: Karl Barth Between Radical and Neo-Orthodoxy," *Scottish Journal of Theology* 56, no. 4 (2003): 427-43.
[29]Smith, *Introducing Radical Orthodoxy*, p. 44, reflecting here the work of John Milbank and Catherine Pickstock, *Truth in Aquinas*, Radical Orthodox Series (London: Routledge, 2001), p. 21.

and human reason that relates to essence rather than as mediated by Christ is suspect.[30] Calvin and Irenaeus before him were at pains to transform all participation into *koinōnia* of the Christological and personal kind.[31]

One crucial reason why Barth's approach is more hopeful with respect to offering a missional public theology is that his "point of departure in the *Church Dogmatics* is the *presence of the resurrected Jesus, the bearer of God's new creation.*"[32] The gracedness of creation and all humanity is a consequence of its relation with the Christ who is both the mediator of creation and the one who has entered it that he might by his resurrection reconcile, renew and reaffirm it. The church, as a *koinōnia* between the person of that risen Christ and his church, is the beginning of the new creation, the mediation of peace to the world and to creation as it engages the public square. "The overall effect," of this Christo-centric resurrectional vision, Mangina concludes, "is more like a Russian Orthodox Easter Vigil, where joy and wonder, ecstasy and solemnity stand strangely mingled. If there is crisis here, it is the crisis created by grace itself—news we falsely imagine too good to be true."[33]

Barth's is thus a more optimistic yet still realistic (theologically, as well as psychologically!) way of achieving the valid aims of radical orthodoxy with respect to a theology of culture and the Christian presence in the public square. It reflects our John 20 passage in a striking way. A measure of optimism always results from placing Jesus back into the center. This is the elixir that is Karl Barth's theology, which is I believe necessary for evangelicals to appropriate if they wish to be truly evangelical. Mangina's commentary here evokes the picture of Jesus standing in the midst of his newly birthed church in John 20, saying twice over "peace be with you." This is the ontology of peace that drives radical orthodoxy, and it is my conviction that this is achieved by means of an unconfused Christocentric vision, both with respect to the mediating church and to its role in culture and the new creation.

---

[30]Karl Barth, *Church Dogmatics* IV/3, ed. G. W. Bromiley and T. F. Torrance, 2nd ed. (Edinburgh: T & T Clark, 1975), p. 535.

[31]Canlis, *Calvin's Ladder*, passim.

[32]Mangina, "Mediating theologies," p. 436, emphasis added.

[33]Ibid.

HOPE IN THE CHRISTOCENTRIC, TRINITARIAN CHURCH

Having outlined the enculturation of the church and the resulting forms of despair, we now turn to John 20 and what it suggests by way of inspiration for the church that rediscovers Christ at the center of its existence and mission as participation in the triune God's mission. We offer the church hope for carrying out its mission in the twenty-first century by moving beyond technique and even ecclesiology into the theology proper—the triune God.[34] The church is in union with God, in the Son, as his body, and in communion with the Father and the Son by the Spirit, and by its very nature then a missional church.

Some may consider the "missional church" the latest fad to hit the fad-prone evangelical church. It is no fad, however. Missionality is grounded in the ancient doctrine and reality of the Trinity. The church that lives into this will be a conceptually and confessionally deep church, both wide and deep. This construal has made a resurgence through people like David Bosch (1929-1992) and Lesslie Newbigin (1909-1998) over the last twenty-five years. But the foundation is much older; it is at the heart of this the Greatest Commission of Jesus—his trinitarian commission: "'As the Father has sent me, so I am sending you.' Then he took a deep breath and breathed into them. 'Receive the Holy Spirit,' he said." This moves the mission of the church back from ecclesiology into theology proper. It is a recognition that what ails the contemporary church is forgetting the essential theology that determines its ecclesiology: the theology of the *missio Dei*, or better, *missio trinitatis*. It gets us back to the basic understanding that the church is a sent community because it is the community of the sending triune God. Jürgen Moltmann put it well: "It is not the church that has a mission of salvation to fulfill in their world; it is a mission of the Son and Spirit through the Father that includes the church."[35]

It is not only the identity of God as Trinity and missional in John 20 that makes it the Greatest Commission. The consequence of un-

---

[34]"Mission [is] understood as being derived from the very nature of God. It [is] thus put in the context of the doctrine of the Trinity, not of ecclesiology or soteriology" (Bosch, *Transforming Mission*, p. 390).

[35]Jürgen Moltmann, cited in Bosch, *Transforming Mission*, p. 390.

derstanding that the triune God himself is on mission is that we understand our place in mission in an encouraging way. In fact, of all the commissions the gospel writers give, this one makes it most clear that the motif for mission involvement is not so much command as encouragement. It is a consequence of our union with the triune God in Christ (theosis) by the Spirit. It is something that arises from our *participation* in God's mission, participation of the *koinōnia*, persons-in-communion kind. In other words, we are given encouragement to engage in mission as a consequence of who we are in Christ, not by a command from outside ourselves. The indicatives precede the imperatives, and usually the commands are actually hortatory, not imperatives. And that I find encouraging.

Why? Because by participation *our* being and doing as sent people will be ensconced and directed and empowered in *his* being as the missionary God, in the sent Son by the sent and sending Spirit. Our being and our practices as the missional church gathered in union with him, and our being as the sent people of God engaged with him in his mission will enable us to *be* Christ to the world and to *do and teach* as he did (Acts 1:1).

The missional church concept has to do not with programs or evangelistic pep talks or ramping up missions programs. It is an identity in God's identity. Mission should not be understood as one of many activities the church does but rather as something that constitutes its very essence. As Guder comments, "The church's essence is missional, for the calling and sending action of God forms its identity."[36] The church is missional because it is the continuation of Christ's mission as sent by God to the world. As Jesus instructed his disciples after his resurrection, "As the Father has sent me, I am sending you" (Jn 20:21).[37] It is this

---

[36]Guder, *Missional Church*, p. 82.

[37]It should be noted that the other major commissions are also set in the indicative rather than the imperative and that they are also participatory, if less emphatically so. Acts 1:8 is a promise that the disciples would be his witnesses, rather than a command, and that by the empowering of the Spirit. Even Matthew's edition of what is popularly called the Great Commission is not, as some translations have it, a command to "go" so much as it is a statement about what they are to do *as they go*." The point is not so much to deny that we are under command but to suggest that the gestalt of the command is that of the gospel, and that the power for the fulfilling of the command is through our trinitarian participation in it.

phrase in context which I want to unpack to form the core message of this book. This will, I hope, move us from despair to encouragement concerning the church today. Surely if the community of disciples in John 20 could be transformed, so can the churches in the West.

These eleven people who turned the first-century world upside down were not naturally blessed with great intellect or even much intestinal fortitude. The irony in John 20 is that the people behind locked doors are *apostles*, that is, sent ones! Mary Magdalene had not only shown up these cowardly male apostles with regard to courage, but she had in fact demonstrated for them what it means to be an apostle. Mary is first at the tomb, receives the first appearance and is the first declarer of the good news of the resurrection. She, ironically, is the "apostle to the apostles" in that she is sent to tell them the good news. What's more, the challenges for these weak apostles of bringing the gospel to a stubbornly religious Jewish culture and then an intellectually challenging dualistic Greek and then a polytheistic Roman culture would be no picnic. Whatever happened in that encounter with the risen Jesus in that room and what transpired from it is profoundly relevant for us.

Before turning to consider in detail the dynamics at work to transform these apostles, which John's picture of the missional church reveals, it is needful to provide some background on the doctrine of the Trinity, which forms the core of this passage and therefore these dynamics.

4

Greatest Co-Mission

The Missional Trinity

■ ■ ■

As the Father has sent me, I am sending you.

JOHN 20:21

Our social programme, said the Russian thinker Feodorov,
is the dogma of the Trinity. Orthodoxy believes most passionately
that the doctrine of the Holy Trinity is not a piece of "high theology"
reserved for the professional scholar, but something that has
a living, practical importance for every Christian.

TIMOTHY WARE, *The Orthodox Church*

IN THIS CHAPTER, I WANT TO PROVIDE an introduction to the doctrine of the Trinity as necessary background for embarking on the theological exposition of the five factors that form a deep and wide missional church. Over the course of the late twentieth century, missiologists drew on the insights of the renaissance of trinitarian theology and made the term *missio Dei* the foundational term of mission and the missional church. Whether they always did this appropriately with a robust and fully Christian doctrine of the Trinity, we will consider later. Irrespective, it is fair to say that participation in the life of the triune God as revealed in Christ is the greatest key to releasing the church from its besieged and defeated position. This dynamic of participation in the mission of the Trinity seems to be the only way to account for how the eleven disciples behind these locked doors could have transformed the known world.

The church can only interpret the gospel for the modern-postmodern world if it reflects the story and deeper reality behind it of the triune God who in Christ and by the Spirit is open for human relations. The strategy for mission is not demonstration (of a rational, verbal kind) but "narration—or more specifically, *out*-narration," the presentation of the Christian story in embodied practice as a better story.[1] Smith's conviction about this, in addition to his Reformed belief that the serious hamartiological effect of the Fall suppresses the witness of creation to human universal reason, is based on his view that the valid postmodern critique of the autonomy of reason "spells the end of apologetics."[2] The church *is* this apologetic when the dynamics of the triune life and love of God continue in and through it, and when the sentness of Jesus by the Father is perpetuated in the sentness of the church, by the Spirit. As the Spirit is at work in the gathered life of the church, enabling it to reflect the triune story of the gospel and as the Spirit is at work in the scattered lives of the whole people of God through their stories the Spirit will remove the barriers to perception that make apologetic appeals to mythical "pure and universal reason" fruitless and draw people into the ongoing triune story.

The greatest wonder of the Christian gospel is that the Trinity is open for human relations! It was rendered open by the sending of the incarnate Son, and humans enter that openness by the work of the Spirit and are birthed into the church. And now, this is the crucial point that gives hope for mission, *mission is God's mission first*, and we participate by grace in who he is and what he is doing. Therefore, to the extent that the Western church rediscovers its identity by inhabiting the story of the Trinity; to the extent that it lives in communion with

---

[1] James K. A. Smith, *Introducing Radical Orthodoxy* (Grand Rapids: Baker Academic, 2004), p. 181. Here Smith reflects John Milbank.
[2] Smith, *Introducing Radical Orthodoxy*, p. 180.

the triune God; to the extent that it has an openness for human relations reflective of God's openness; to the extent that it works in participation with what he is doing; to the extent that it works incarnationally, modeled on and in union with Christ; to the extent that it lives
in communion with the indwelling, transforming, empowering Spirit;
to the extent that it reflects the oneness of the Trinity in catholicity and
unity; and to the extent that it reflects the diverse, irreducible identities
or character of the three persons in a coinherent way, there is hope for
the Western church, and indeed the whole church of God.

The phrase that evokes our consideration of the Trinity is John
20:21, "As the Father has sent me, I am sending you," the Greatest
Commission because it is a "co-mission," the "supreme passing on" of
Jesus' "sentness" and therefore, authority.[3] The tense of the verb used
for Jesus' sending in John 20:21 (perfect, *apestalken*) is one that communicates the idea that "his sending by the Father still continues."[4] The
Father's sending is to continue in the disciples' sending "for the earthly
continuation of his work." Jesus' statement is thus not merely motivation by example—you are sent because I am sent. There is an actual
correspondence between his sending from the Father and their sending
from Christ. Each assumes a union. Just as Christ is sent as the Son in
union with the Father, so now they were sent ones because of their
union with Christ, by the Spirit he was about to breathe into them. The
Spirit would mediate the presence of Christ in them so that they would
be his body, his hands and feet on earth. This is the miracle of theosis,
the union of Christ with his church. Note that this is a communal or
specifically ecclesial reality, though it also related to each individual
person in the community. The "fellowship of the disciples is to make
him present in the world" and each was to continue Christ's ministry of
reconciliation (2 Cor 5:11-21).

In light of all that John conveys in his Gospel about the being and
actions of the triune God, I feel justified in investing the phrase "As the
Father has sent Me, I am sending you" with this fuller Johannine back-

---

[3]Rudolf Schnackenburg, *The Gospel According to St. John*, trans. David Smith and G. A. Kon
(New York: Crossroad, 1982), 3:324.
[4]Ibid.

ground and content. In chapters nine and ten I will say much more on the implications of recovering the relevance of the Trinity for the church's missional identity and life. In this chapter the theme of the Trinity will be the primary focus with a view to demonstrating its relevance for mission. The tougher questions about the legitimacy of the nature of God as missional or missionary will be postponed until chapter nine.

WHAT DOES IT MEAN TO BE TRINITARIAN?

I am suggesting that the John 20 commission has a timely message for the contemporary church precisely because it is trinitarian. But what does it mean to be trinitarian? And could such a difficult doctrine have any relevance for Christian mission and evangelism in these modern and postmodern times? Surely the mysterious three-in-one doctrine should be hidden in missional enterprise, some might say. The trend of avoidance is not new as suggested in Lesslie Newbigin's recounting that "At the Chapter House of the ruins of the Fountains Abbey in Yorkshire there is engraved a text which says 'Here the monks gathered every Sunday to hear a sermon from the Abbot, except on Trinity Sunday, owing to the difficulty of the subject.'"[5]

Actually, a concern about numerical oneness and threeness betrays a rationalistic, modern epistemology rather than that of encountering revealed mystery in faith, then seeking understanding. It is also a red herring, for as Paul Fiddes has well stated, "the doctrine of the Trinity is not an exercise in mathematics."[6] He notes that Christian apologists, for example, in response to the charge that $1 + 1 + 1 = 3$, not 1, have countered that $1 \times 1 \times 1 = 1$. But God, as Fiddes responds, is not and cannot be the result of addition or multiplication! He reminds us that Barth has correctly emphasized the reality that the oneness of God is not to be confused with the "singularity" that is connected with numerical unity. Unlike numerical oneness, the "revealed unity does not

---

[5]Lesslie Newbigin, "The Trinity as Public Truth," in *The Trinity in a Pluralistic Age*, ed. Kevin Vanhoozer (Grand Rapids: Eerdmans, 1997), p. 2.
[6]Paul Fiddes, *Participating in God: A Pastoral Doctrine of the Trinity* (Louisville: Westminster John Knox, 2000), p. 5.

exclude but includes a distinction."[7] In other words, what oneness in the Trinity means is as that is revealed in the self-revelation of God, not by mathematics. God is Father, Son and Holy Spirit, three persons sharing the one divine nature, in a oneness of communion God has revealed himself as the one God in three persons. The relational God, who is the personal God. The God who is open for human relations in Christ. The God who draws humans into his life through his people by the Spirit. This is central to mission, not peripheral. To be missional is to be trinitarian, and to be trinitarian is to be missional.

Isn't every Christian trinitarian? Well yes and, sadly, no. All Christians, believers in the deity of Christ (and the Holy Spirit), must by confession, be trinitarian. However, being trinitarian is not just to believe confessionally in the Trinity. The nature of the Trinity as persons-in-relation is not a subsidiary doctrine or even an attribute of God among others. It is who God is, and it is the very center of Christian theology and therefore of mission. Reminiscent of Barth, Lesslie Newbigin helped in his writings to place the Trinity back in the center of Christian mission and dialogue in the marketplace and with other faiths. In expressing his debt to another in this regard, Newbigin states that

> [Charles Norris] Cochrane showed me how the trinitarian doctrine provided a new paradigm for thought, which made possible the healing of dualisms that classical thought had been unable to overcome—the dualism between the sensible and the intelligible in the world of thought, and between virtue and fortune in the realm of action. The doctrine of the Trinity, in other words, was not a problem, but the solution to a problem that classical thought could not solve.[8]

This is an encouraging incentive to inspire our perusal of this subject.

THE TRINITY AND THE POWER OF RELATIONALITY

To be trinitarian means first to understand the fundamental loving relationality of God and the power of that relationality. It is the power of

---

[7]Karl Barth, *Church Dogmatics* I/1, ed. G. W. Bromiley and T. F. Torrance (Edinburgh: T & T Clark, 1975), pp. 354-55.
[8]Newbigin, "The Trinity as Public Truth," p. 2.

love. No reality could be more relevant to Christian mission. Jonathan
Edwards believed he could prove the necessity of the triune nature of
God if he were eternal and if he were love. In his apologetic works in
defense of the Trinity, Edwards was concerned that the church's prevailing approach was to adhere to this doctrine for pragmatic reasons.
The most common defenses were on the basis of the utility of the economic Trinity. The doctrine of the deity of Christ was needed to validate the atonement, and the doctrine of the Spirit's coequality was required to explain sanctification. Edwards, however, felt that the
doctrine should be defended because it was an integral part of understanding the nature of God.[9] Thus, for Edwards "God is love" means
that he has "a disposition to abundant self-communication." I suspect
that C. S. Lewis has Edwards's writing in mind when he speaks about
a similar "proof" of the Trinity:

> All sorts of people are fond of repeating the Christian statement that
> "God is love." But they seem not to notice that the words "God is love"
> have no real meaning unless God contains at least two persons. Love is
> something that one person has for another person. If God was a single
> person, then before the world was made, he was not love. [Christians]
> believe that the living, dynamic activity of love has been going on in
> God forever and has created everything else.[10]

Lewis goes on to say that whenever love exists between two persons,
in addition to the two persons of the lover and the beloved, there is a
third reality. This is the spirit of love that unites them. In human relationships this is a real relational bond, whereas in the divine being, the
eternal, infinite spirit of love that unites the Father and the Son is "such
a live concrete thing that this union itself is also a Person"— the Holy
Spirit. God is thus, if he is love, "God in three Persons, blessed Trinity."
This is a Western way of looking at the Trinity.

This a priori philosophical approach runs contrary to the revelatory
or historically empirical approach to theology, and to the discovery of

---

[9]The reasoning that Edwards employed in determining the logical necessity of the ontological
Trinity is found in his early work *Miscellany* 94, the later *Miscellany* 308, *The Mind* ("Excel-
lency") and in his posthumously published *An Essay on the Trinity* and *End of Creation*.
[10]C. S. Lewis, *Mere Christianity* (New York: HarperCollins, 2001), pp. 151-52.

the doctrine of the Trinity in the church fathers and its resurgence in Karl Barth. Though it may have secondary value, the proper grounding of Christian theology is the revelation God has given us of himself in Christ, by the Spirit, as received by faith. In fact, the doctrine of the Trinity was formulated by the church in response to the church's historical experience, its experience of the gospel, its experience of a man who was God, its experience of the Spirit, who they came to understand as being God also. As Fiddes states, "When the early Church Fathers developed the doctrine of the Trinity, they were not painting by numbers; they were finding concepts to express an experience."[11] Methodology aside, however, both the revelatory and rational schools of thought were convinced that "God is love" and "God is Trinity" are inseparable. The Trinity has powerful relevance now and in every age, because it represents the profound relationality of God within himself and therefore as expressed in his creation and sustaining and reconciling of the universe and humanity.

How profoundly unrelational (toward anyone but themselves) these poor early disciples were in this locked room in John 20! The contrast with the burgeoning, open-hearted communities and the role the apostles played in them, described in the book of Acts, is quite marked. As these New Testament communities developed, they did so with a profound openness to the world. The boundaries between church and world were real and yet fluid as suggested by the passage in Acts 5:13-14: "No one else dared join them, even though they were highly regarded by the people. Nevertheless, more and more men and women believed in the Lord and were added to their number." As the Archbishop of Canterbury Rowan Williams writes, "We have frequently lost a sense of the church as sign of the Spirit rather than its domicile. The church signifies (means, points to) the humanity that could be."[12] Another case in point is the church community in Corinth, in which Paul's expectations seem evident that there will be seeking people in the gatherings of the church (1 Cor 14:24-25). But it is much more than just

---

[11]Fiddes, *Participating in God*, p. 5.
[12]Rowan Williams, "Word and Spirit," in *On Christian Theology: Challenges in Contemporary Theology* (Oxford: Blackwell, 2000), p. 124.

having an openness to unbelieving people in our gatherings. It is a way of seeing the world. Just as the triune God has become one with humanity in Christ by his incarnation, the church is to recognize that having become one with Christ by the Spirit, it too is incarnational, in union with all humanity and the means by which the Spirit is drawing all to find their place in the new humanity in Christ. The church is the sign and servant of the kingdom to come.

There is a profound correspondence between the fundamental relationality of the Trinity's inner life (*in se* or *ad intra*), and the expression of that relationality in the economy of creation and redemption (the Trinity *ex se*). If who God is, as revealed in salvation history, is not who he really is in himself, we are, as Barth said, back on our quest looking for God. If the church is an icon of the Trinity, then similarly it will be characterized by a profoundly deep relationality in its inner life, but this relationality will have an orientation toward the world. The nature of the missional church of the missional God will be bidirectional. It will be deep and wide in its relationality. *Mission* is an appropriate term for what the church is as gathered and what it does as scattered, and its gathering will always have sentness in mind, and its scattering will always have bringing in mind. It is for this reason that John F. Hoffmeyer has suggested that "the rhythmic movement of gathering in and being sent out is certainly embedded in our liturgy . . . our gathering as church is a sending and our sending is a gathering."[13] The rhythm of gathering and sending in the church is a complex one, he suggests, given two factors: (1) the center of our gatherings, the "crucified and risen Christ . . . is a very odd center" in that he is, in solidarity with the marginalized "on the outside" (an emphasis similar to that of Orlando Costas);[14] (2) the nature of the Lord's Supper as eaten with openness to the world in "anticipation of the eschatological banquet."[15] This awareness leads us to "enact that openness" when we leave our worship gatherings to engage in mission, feeding the poor, advocating for just

---

[13]John F. Hoffmeyer, "The Missional Trinity," *Dialogue: A Journal of Theology* 40, no. 2 (2001): 110.

[14]Ibid. See notably Orlando Costas, *Christ Outside the Gate: Mission Beyond Christendom* (Maryknoll, N.Y.: Orbis, 1983).

[15]Hoffmeyer, "Missional Trinity," p. 110.

legislation on behalf of the hungry, in ways that invite others to the next celebration of the Eucharist and anticipate the great banquet.[16] Crucially, Hoffmeyer concludes, "To neglect our missional sending as church is not just to be weak on mission while possibly still being strong on word and sacrament. To neglect our missional sending is to *betray the inherent dynamic of word and sacrament.*"[17]

These disciples hunkered down in this upper room had struggled with exclusive tendencies. Some of them had expressed the desire for privileged places in the kingdom because they had been chosen by Christ. A tendency toward exclusivism has plagued the church often down the centuries, as it characterized the people of Israel in Old Testament times. There is something about human nature that loves to protect privilege for itself. The social club phenomenon creeps into churches. There is a clique in leadership that relates to longevity and sometimes who has given what to the church. There have been movements birthed with great openness to the whole people of God which in a few years have degenerated into exclusivity that has scarred many adherents and marred the gospel of the triune God who is for all humanity. As we shall note later, election was always for missional responsibility to bring others in. This has not yet dawned on the Eleven. It may not yet have dawned on many of us present-day Christians either.

Relevance to postmodernity. The relationality of God is a point at which there is some convergence between postmodern thought and the gospel. Part of that convergence lies in disillusionment of postmoderns with the success ethos of modernism and its replacement instead with the prime value of friendships. Climbing the corporate ladder and having a career involving travel has become less important for postmoderns than maintaining friendships and experiencing all there is in life. This relational trend is an obvious window for the relationality of the gospel. But another more fundamental piece of this convergence is the place within Christianity for story or narrative. Postmodernism has expressed incredulity toward the notion of metanarratives, which are

---

[16]Ibid.
[17]Ibid., emphasis added.

oppressive by drawing in and homogenizing individual narratives. Historically, the oppressive metanarratives have included Greek imperialism, Roman imperialism, medieval Christendom, Islam and post-Enlightenment rationality and progress.

But what if Christianity can offer a metanarrative that is not oppressive, and, significantly, one that is relational yet not collectivist, personal yet not atomistic, one that can absorb all the personal stories into one grand story without obliterating the identity of each story in doing so? Moreover, what if the significance of the particular narratives could be elucidated meaningfully by a universal narrative that was not only nonoppressive but in fact made sense of the whole of reality?

The nature of God's relationality (one in which persons and communion are eternally equiprimal) leads to just such a metanarrative, one that makes sense of each human's story within the human community in Christ, within the metanarrative of the gospel. God's revelation of who he is in himself is expressed as a grand narrative with eternal sweep from his covenanting counsels in eternity past to the future kingdom in which God's purposes for the whole of creation will have been fulfilled, as expressed in the overarching narrative of the Scriptures. Richard Bauckham confirms that though it does not have a storyline like a novel but a sprawling collection of narratives, it nevertheless as a whole tells a story. It is a canonical missional narrative which is "in its overall direction a metanarrative, a narrative about the whole of reality that elucidates the meaning of the whole of reality."[18] Bauckham suggests that such a hermeneutic "connects with the character of people's experience." "Stories," he continues, "come naturally to people." Citing Wicker, he notes that "the human world . . . is story shaped," and concludes that "if the Bible offers a metanarrative, a story of all stories, then we should all be able to place our own stories within that grand narrative and find our own perception and experience of the world transformed by that connexion."[19] Thus all human persons retain their identity: "the goal is not an abstract universal but the gathering of all particulars into the one kingdom of the one God." That one God is revealed in a narrative

---

[18]Richard Bauckham, *Bible and Mission* (Grand Rapids: Baker Academic, 2003), pp. 11-12.
[19]Ibid., p. 12.

manner as the God of the One and the Many, as Father, Son and Spirit, profoundly one in relationality and essence and profoundly three in irreducible identity as persons-in-relation. Thus in expressing the temporal movement of the metanarrative, Bauckham notes, "Mission is the movement that takes place between Jesus' own sending by his Father and the future coming of Jesus in the kingdom of his Father."[20]

The relational and personal nature of human beings made in the image of the Trinity also ensures that the call for human response is nonoppressive. The ontic relatedness of all human persons *to God* is not affected by the Fall (Acts 17:25-28), though the relationship is. The restoration of that relationship in Christ by the gospel restores the life of human persons so that they become humans fully alive. They retain their identity even as they become one with Christ in salvation and even after they are brought into likeness to God at the consummation. Union with God will not obliterate personhood, nor the stories of that personhood. For those who refuse to enter in, this is their choice, rather than the desire of God or his justifying design and its accomplishment in Christ. God loves even them too much to force them to be his followers.

Carl Raschke has written extensively on the consonance of relationality within postmodernity and the fundamentally relational God of Christianity. His somewhat categoric claim that "relational Christianity is postmodern Christianity" arises from his belief that the metamorphosis of the world by the power of God, despite the power of modernity in the West, is what the "postmodern moment" really is, and not merely the ideas of a French company of faddish philosophers and religious thinkers.[21] Raschke attributes this power to the *"power of relationship,"* "the power of establishing, sustaining, and purposefully pursuing relationships."[22] Raschke coined the term *GloboChrist* to show how this relational power of God is "manifesting itself amid the growing anxieties over what is happening under the impact of the force

---

[20]Ibid., p. 14.
[21]Carl Raschke, *GloboChrist: The Great Commission Takes a Postmodern Turn* (Grand Rapids: Baker Academic, 2008), p. 20.
[22]Ibid., p. 19.

we call globalization and the political, cultural, and religious upheavals that arise in its wake." "Christ," he assures us, "is showing his power not just among the nations but also for the nations."

Raschke is quick to demonstrate that the relational power of God for us (Latin, *pro nobis*) is a natural consequence of who God is in himself (*in se*), and this leads him into discussion of the Nicene Creed and a comparison of the Eastern and Western traditions of trinitarian thought. He states that Eastern Orthodoxy has stressed the relational character of God, "or at least the relationality that is existential and incarnational rather than strictly intellectual and conceptual." Quoting Bishop Kallistos, Raschke states that all trinitarian talk "implies a movement of mutual love."[23] The inner movement within the Godhead spills over through the *missio Dei*, the incarnational movement of the Son, in its historical and eschatological movement through his people, by the Spirit. And it is evidence of this in postmodern globalization that Raschke draws attention to.

Relevance to the exclusivism-inclusivism debate. The nature of the relationality of the triune God has profound consequences for the destiny of creation and humanity. God created, not because he was lonely but rather the richness of his intratrinitarian love flowed over in a joyful *ekstasis* of that love. It was an act of his will, and not an extension of his being. Given this origin of creation, including the pinnacle of that creation, humanity made in his image, we are not surprised that he pronounced it good. His love for humanity continued despite the Fall. Psalm 145:9 celebrates the fact that "the LORD is good to all; he has compassion on all he has made." The realization of that love toward creation is fulfilled in Christ who as the true head of creation has redeemed it and will one day reign over a fully reconciled universe with all humans who are in this new humanity. The Son of God entered humanity by the incarnation and in so doing a new ontic reality occurred. Deity and humanity were brought together in the hypostatic union. All that Jesus was and all he did in his life was vicarious for the new humanity, which is the true humanity. "Christ Jesus, himself human, . . .

---

[23]Kallistos Ware, *The Orthodox Way* (Crestwood, N.Y.: St. Vladimir's Seminary Press, 1995), p. 33.

gave himself as a ransom for all people." So, by way of the desire of God for humanity, we are assured by Paul that God "wants all people to be saved" (1 Tim 2:5-6). However, it is clear that God, who loves in freedom, will not permit humans to love him except in freedom either. By the Spirit he woos people to himself without coercion.

What does the relationality of God have to say to the exclusivist (or restrictivist), inclusivist, pluralist debate in soteriology?[24] There is a brand of "trinitarian theology" advocated by folks like Marjorie Suchocki, William Reiser, S.J., and Mark Heim, which, on the basis of what is deemed to be the generic relationality of the Godhead (emphasis is placed on the relationality of God apart from the revelation of Christ), promotes the idea that there is a diversity of ways through which humans may come to God. This is inclusivism of an unorthodox kind. Orthodox, biblical Christianity has to do with the God and Father of our Lord Jesus Christ, and the revealed unique Son and of salvation through Christ alone, by the one Holy Spirit. Evangelical Christians who take biblical and personal revelation seriously may differ as to whether restrictivism or orthodox inclusivism is the most orthodox position. Detailed discussion of these views is beyond our scope here. Suffice it to say that in light of the relationality of the real God precisely as revealed in Christ, who became one with humanity and who acted and now acts for humanity, we are charged with directing *all* humanity toward that Christ. The universal provision of salvation for all vindicates God's relationality. The command of God for humans to believe vindicates his relationality also, for he will not coerce the relational persons he has created. This demands of Chris-

---

[24]The conviction that it is only by the person and work of Jesus Christ that people may be saved is shared by both *exclusivists* or *restrictivists*, who believe that people can only be saved as a result of hearing the gospel and responding to it by faith (and there are three subsets of this position) and *orthodox inclusivists*, who believe that all who are ultimately saved are saved because of the salvific work of Christ for humanity, but that they may come through another religion, or on the basis of whatever light has been granted. The *three types of restrictivists* are (1) those who believe people must hear and respond to the gospel while alive to be saved, (2) those who believe that all humans hear the gospel in the moment of their death and are given an opportunity by the Spirit to respond then if they have not heard it before, and (3) those who believe that those who do not hear the gospel in this life will be given a chance in the life to come, perhaps, but not necessarily, in purgatory. For more on this see John Stackhouse's blog, http://stackblog.wordpress.com/2007/07/08/terminology-time-what-is-an-inclusivist.

tians in mission with people of other religions a relational and respectful orientation in dialogue.

What God will do with those who have never heard of Christ is a speculative matter at best. It is interesting to observe how Jonathan Edwards, venerated by many evangelicals of Reformed persuasion, wrestled with this issue. He is unfortunately often best known for his sermons on hell, when he should be best known for his development of a wonderfully aesthetic trinitarian theology,[25] one which included the possibility of the salvation of the heathen who had a disposition (an active and real tendency which has ontic reality even when it is not exercised) toward faith without ever hearing the gospel, and on the basis of elemental theological truths (the *prisca theologia*) which they could access.[26] These tendencies in Edwards bear no resemblance to Barth's doctrine of justification as a reality for creation and all humankind. Edwards's reasoning comes from general revelation, which Barth disparaged. Barth's understanding of a universal justification (which did not necessarily infer that all will be saved) came from a different source altogether. However, both had leanings toward grace for the heathen, Barth in a more Christologically obvious way than Edwards. The matter of how to account for the tension between the idea of an expression of the wrath of God in hell, in a fully reconciled universe is a vexing one which Edwards does not address.

THE TRINITY AND THE DIGNITY OF PERSONHOOD

To understand God as Trinity entails the concept of relationality or communion. Critically, however, it equally entails the concept of *persons*, though by definition, *persons-in-relation*. Because personhood and relationality are equiprimal (each is present eternally) in God,

---

[25]See Amy Plantinga Pauw, *The Supreme Harmony of All: The Trinitarian Theology of Jonathan Edwards* (Grand Rapids: Eerdmans, 2002); and Gerald R. McDermott, "Jonathan Edwards and the Salvation of Non-Christians," *Pro Ecclesia* 9, no.2 (2000): 208-27.

[26]*Prisca theologia* is ancient theology, a tradition in apologetic theology postulating that vestiges of true religion (monotheism, the Trinity, *creation ex nihilo*) were taught by the Greeks and other non-Christian traditions, and that all human beings were originally given this knowledge by Jews or by tradition going back to Noah's sons or antediluvians. Edwards made more of general revelation than Calvin. See McDermott, "Jonathan Edwards and the Salvation of Non-Christians," p. 211.

divine persons (hypostases) must be understood in a perichoretic fashion such that each is defined by and mutually internal to the other. The distinctiveness and dignity and power of personhood-in-relation in God serves to define human persons in a corresponding way, an analogy justified by way of Christ as the divine-human person. This understanding of human personhood has profound implications for mission. Before indicating some of these, I will first offer some justification for the assertions that personhood is a primal reality of the triune God, and then that human personhood is analogous to it.

Personhood in the Trinity. The great advance made by the Cappadocians (Gregory Nyssa, Gregory Nazianzus, Basil of Caesarea) was that *hypostasis* was elevated to supremacy as the ultimate ontological category in philosophy, as opposed to substance. This was, as Metropolitan John Zizioulas describes it, the "great innovation in philosophical thought, brought about by Cappadocian trinitarian theology," which, in turn "carries with it decisively a new way of conceiving human existence."[27] Thus the divine essence or nature could be shared by the three persons. This is the social or communion model of the Trinity, which, based on what we know of the Father and the Son in the economic revelation of the Trinity, is surely more consonant with Barth's previously stated methodology.

Whereas Augustine and the Western tradition defined "threeness" within the "oneness" of the "one mind" analogy, the Cappadocians were able to equate the "threeness" and the "oneness," such that the persons are persons in communion.[28] Gregory of Nazianzus, with the other Cappadocians, indicated that the *cause* or *aition* of divine existence is the Father, which, because he is a person, makes the Trinity, therefore, "a matter of ontological freedom."[29] The Cappadocians were able to account for the unity or oneness of God by suggesting that the *ousia* (substance) or *physis* (nature) in God should be taken as a general

---

[27]John D. Zizioulas, *Being As Communion: Studies in Personhood and the Church* (Crestwood, N.Y.: St. Vladimir's Seminary Press, 1985), p. 49.

[28]The equiprimal nature of the threeness and the oneness is reflected in Gregory Nazianzen's *Oration 40*, "On Holy Baptism," xli, www.ccel.org/ccel/schaff/npnf207.iii.xxiii.html.

[29]Zizioulas, *Being As Communion*, p. 51.

category that is applied to more than one person.[30] Commenting on this, T. R. Martland stresses that *ousia* is that which is common and *hypostasis* is that which is particular. *Hypostasis* is the "external, concrete, encountered deity" while "*ousia* is the single philosophical unit, disclosed . . . by internal analysis."[31]

The Cappadocians were even willing to run the risk of appearing to represent tritheism in order to secure the concept of the hypostatic uniqueness of persons. This they did, not because of the safety of a "one mind" psychological analogy as in Augustine or Edwards or the current Pope Benedict XVI, but because they knew that their use of the term *persons* was by definition that of "persons in communion." The Cappadocians were able to draw the important distinction between human persons as created on the one hand, in which case nature precedes the person, and the person as an "individual," that is, an entity independent ontically from other human beings, and uncreated divine persons, on the other hand, in which case the three persons of the Trinity, because God has no beginning, "do not share a pre-existing or a logically prior to them divine nature but coincide with it" (that is, they are equiprimal). "Multiplicity in God," therefore, "does not involve a division of His nature, as happens with man."[32]

However, there is still an analogy between divine and human persons as made in the image of God, and this is best defended with reference to Christ, the image of the invisible God.

Justification of the analogy between divine and human persons. Barth was squeamish about even using the English term *persons* for the Trinity because he perceived that it was too much endowed with the human idea of "individual." He therefore used the term *Seinsweise* or "modes of being," which sounds modalistic and yet was not intended as such.[33] Ironically,

---

[30]The manner in which the finally accepted terms *ousia* and *hypostases* were understood is well expressed by Basil of Cappadocia, "Letter 236," cited in T. R. Martland, "A Study Of Cappadocian and Augustinian Methodology," *Anglican Theological Review* 47 (1965): 254.

[31]Ibid.

[32]Zizioulas, *Being As Communion*, p. 48.

[33]This paralleled the Cappadocian use of the term *"mode of existence"* as that which communicates what is uniquely implied in the names of the persons of the Trinity, and that which communicates their peculiar characteristics as hypostases. It seems better to redeem the term "per-

given this and the concern of Barth for upholding God's transcendence, Barth actually provided a Christological way for pointing to the analogy between divine and human "persons" in a way that affects the gospel and mission significantly. Barth believed that if we wanted insight into the relational nature of God, we would see it in the humanity of Jesus, and, critically for this discussion, that human personhood of Jesus was then determinative of the destiny of human persons.[34] This was expressed as the analogy of relations, or *analogia relationis*.

First, Barth's assessment of Christ noted that he was the man for God and the man for others, his fellow humanity. Jesus in his deity is from and for God, and in his humanity he is from and to his fellow man.[35] Barth follows the Chalcedonian formula carefully in his Christological anthropology in that Jesus being for God and for his fellow man correspond to his divine and human natures: the "I" of Jesus is determined by the "Thou" of God the Father, but also the "Thou" of his fellow humanity.[36] Critical to defining human personhood is that Jesus as the prototypical human was first and foremost the man for others. As Barth states, "What interests him and does so exclusively, is man, other men as such, who need him and are referred to him for help and deliverance."[37] But Jesus is not presented to us merely as an example. He is ontically related to humanity. He became truly human to become one with us and to act for us. Thus his personhood, determined as it is by his relations within the Godhead is also related to ours as we are his fellow humanity. This fundamentally defines what real personhood is and the direction of human sanctifi-

---

son" for the triune hypostases and to qualify it as carrying the meaning of "person-in-relation." See Alan J. Torrance, *Persons in Communion: An Essay on Trinitarian Description and Human Participation with Special Reference to Volume One of Karl Barth's "Church Dogmatics"* (Edinburgh: T & T Clark, 1996), p. 245.

[34]Karl Barth, *Church Dogmatics* III/2, ed. G. W. Bromiley and T. F. Torrance (Edinburgh: T & T Clark, 1975), p. 248.

[35]As Daniel Price, *Karl Barth's Anthropology in Light of Modern Thought* (Grand Rapids: Eerdmans, 2002), points out, Barth used two terms for "human," *der Mensch*, and then sometimes a more inclusive term *der Kosmos*, which refers to man together with his historical setting, such that humanity is redeemed not abstractly, but as human in the cosmos. See Barth, *Church Dogmatics* III/2, p. 216.

[36]Ibid.

[37]Ibid., p. 208.

cation. It is not individualistic, though the identity of each human person is unique, as was that of Jesus. Rather personhood as defined by Jesus is defined in relation to the other, just as in the Trinity. Human persons have as their origin and destiny to be in relation with the other (God) and the other human. This is the goal of missioners and their mission.

However, in worship we also recognize that we are in union with Christ and therefore called constantly to be for humanity as he is the man for humanity. This will shape our understanding of what it means to develop as a person, and it will profoundly affect our closest relationships. Gary Deddo has written extensively of the application of Barth's ontology of relations for family life, for example.[38] This is the crucible in which human persons are meant to be shaped to be for the other (God and human). However, in addition to our "near" neighbors, Barth's conception of humanity in relation to Jesus calls us to consider our relatedness and mission to all of humanity. Our connectedness to all challenges our concern for global poverty and exposes our culpability in it.

Second, this nexus of the relations of Christ as the Son of God within the Trinity and his relations with all humanity for Barth expresses the appropriate analogy between God and humanity by the technical term, the *analogy of relations* (*analogia relationis*). As Barth states, it "follows that the person who corresponds to, and reflects, the being of God bears the stamp of God's own dynamic character. Each human person then is destined to be in relation: to be I and Thou. I implies Thou, and Thou refers back to I. I and Thou are not coincidental or incidental but essentially proper to the concept of 'man.'"[39] The *analogia relationis* is a critical concept in Barth's anthropology and a major contribution to human thought. This was the notion that when speaking of human persons we must speak of relations, not merely of being. Barth preferred this over the Thomistic *analogia entis* (analogy of being), foundational to much Catholic theology.

---

[38]Gary W. Deddo, *Barth's Theology of Relations, Trinitarian, Christological, and Human: Towards an Ethic of the Family* (New York: Peter Lang, 1999); "The Grammar of Barth's Theology of Personal Relations," *Scottish Journal of Theology* 47 (1994): 183-222.

[39]Barth, *Church Dogmatics* III/2, p. 248.

The work of Barth has demonstrated in a profound way the relationship between the divine personhood within the Trinity and human personhood, without confusion as to the essence of divinity and humanity. It is an analogy of relations, not essence, and it is a relationality from beginning to end that flows from the grace of God. It also defines personhood in a way that reflects the person of Jesus and the nature of God as love, and thus in a way that both evokes inspiration for mission and defines its goal.

Implications for mission. The truly Christian concept of a human *person* is not that of an autonomous individual, and especially that of the Western Cartesian notion of the self. Rather its meaning should be governed by an understanding of trinitarian persons. The nature of human and divine persons is not identical, but the notion of a human as person-in-community, in formation toward an "other" orientation, is determined by that of Christ and divine persons. The distinction is that whereas divine persons are mutually *internal* to one another, as understood from biblical passages like John 14 and the terms *perichoresis* or *coinherence*, humans can only know mutual interdependence and imperfect intimacy at best. The trajectory, eschatologically speaking, is an other-orientation toward God and all humans.

What then does it mean for human persons to encounter the gospel and be transformed by it? Does it mean that they are simply "souls" now granted an insurance policy for an eternal heaven and longing for disembodiment? Or does it mean rather that having been brought into union with the one person who epitomizes true personhood and humanity, and having been brought into communion with the triune God, they can, yes, be assured of justification and eternal life in Christ, but much more to the core of Christian soteriology, recover in the fullest way the dignity of human personhood, a personhood that as with the Trinity is defined by community with the other (God), characterized by love of God and neighbor and creation. This is the recovery of the "human being fully alive," which reflects the glory of God.[40]

---

[40]This is a quote from Irenaeus which is more fully "The glory of God is man fully alive, and the life of man is the vision of God. If the revelation of God through creation already brings life to all living beings on the earth, how much more will the manifestation of the Father by the

The implications of this for mission are massive, leading to a dissolving of the tension between evangelism and the so-called Social Gospel. Trinitarian missioners will be concerned with both proclamation of the saving message of Christ and the development of persons to their fullest human potential by means of education and health care, and with the transformation of communities so that converts might discover the dignity of work, healthy community and creation care. More will be said of this later.

THE TRINITY AND COINHERENCE

By "trinitarian" I mean fully mutual relationality *with* the irreducible identity of personhood. This requires a definition of persons who are mutually internal to one another in both being and act, by perichoresis. Medieval theologians referred to the coinherence of the persons by two Latin terms. The perichoresis of the *being* of the persons was termed *circuminsessio* (literally, their seatedness in one another). The perichoresis of *actions* in the economic Trinity was referred to as *circumincessio*. The latter depends on the former. The profound coinherence in the work of Christ and the work of the Spirit is evident even in John 20, where the sentness of the Son is conferred to the apostles by the indwelling of the Spirit. This reflects both the trinitarian doctrine of appropriations (that to each person there has been given certain distinct roles) *and* the doctrine of the indivisibility of the works of the divine persons—*opera extra sunt indivisa* (that each person is coinherently at work on the appropriated work of the other).

The coinherence of the persons in relation is critical to fully trinitarian mission. That due weight is given to the person and work of each of the divine persons is very evident in our Johannine text: the Father has sent, the Son was sent and has now died and risen, and the Spirit is being given and will soon be received by humans to baptize them into the body of Christ, to transform them and to empower them for their sending. However, it is equally important to acknowledge the coinherence of each

---

Word bring life to those who see God" (*Adversus Haereses* 4.20.7). Care must be taken with this quote in that what it means is that human life is for him the glory of God, provided that the human remains in communion with the Creator.

in the other for the removal of dualisms and the avoidance of extremes sometimes present in the Christian church and in mission. This will be developed in further chapters.

By way of illustration, Paul Stevens has stated that he sees the importance of coinherence of the work of the persons of the Trinity for every member ministry of the whole people of God, or the *laos* (people). He says,

> The Father creates, providentially sustains, and forms a covenantal framework for all existence. The Son incarnates, mediates, transfigures and redeems. The Spirit empowers and fills with God's own presence. But each shares in the others—coinheres, interpenetrates, cooperates—so that it is theologically inappropriate to stereotype the ministry of any one.[41]

The people of God tend to emphasize more the Father, the Son or the Spirit, but God is one for the sake of himself and also for his people. A trinitarian mission seeks the unity of the church. "God is more than the sum of the three. God is not God apart from the way the Father, Son and Holy Spirit give and receive from each other what they essentially are."[42] This is a critical analogy for the missional church, which if it really is a reflection of the missional God will value the equipping of the whole people of God for ministry, which makes the church healthy, and for mission in their worlds, thus usually making the church a growing one.

THE IMMANENT AND THE ECONOMIC TRINITIES
(Two Trinities or One?)

We come now to the relationship between who God is in his own being (*in se*), that is the immanent Trinity, and who he is as revealed in his works (*pro nobis*, for us), or the economic Trinity. The coinherence of the works of the divine persons in the economic Trinity (God as he has been revealed by his actions in creation and redemption, that is God *ex*

---

[41]R. Paul Stevens, *The Other Six Days* (Grand Rapids: Eerdmans, 1999), p. 57.
[42]Ibid., p. 58.

se) is a necessary consequence of who he is in himself in the immanent Trinity. Two issues related to this topic are relevant to mission.

First, the distinction *and* the correspondence between who God is *in se* and who he is as revealed is a key assumption of trinitarian theology and therefore the gospel. If there is not a correspondence between what we know of God as he has revealed himself in the economy of redemption and what he really is, we are in difficulty and revelation will have proved to be unreliable, and the Christian gospel will be no more than a groping in the dark. Mission does not exist. As Barth famously said, if the revealed God does not reflect the real God, "the real God would remain behind revelation and we would be back on our quest."[43]

Second, we gain our understanding of the immanent Trinity from the revelation of God in Christ by the Spirit in the economy. If this indeed is the case, then the place of the Trinity in how we think about the gospel and mission should be central, not peripheral.

On the first point, the language used of the Son and the Father in many sections of John's Gospel connotes that in the economy, they are distinct in personhood ("the Father is greater than I" [Jn 14:28], understood with respect to economic role) and role (it is the Son who is the Word born into humanity and who dies on the cross, and not the Father) and yet that each was always in the Other ("I am in the Father, and . . . the Father is in me" [Jn 14:10]; "Anyone who has seen me has seen the Father" [Jn 14:9]; cf. Jn 5:19). Thus we must assume that this is reflective of who the Father and the Son are *in se*. If not, the gospel is not the arrival but the beginning of an impossible quest. Barth's chief contribution was to reassert that God's being *ad extra* corresponds to his being *ad intra*. God does not become in the economy what is alien to his essence.

We can then say that the functions of the persons in the economy of creation and redemption are reflective of the relations within the immanent Trinity. Edmund Hill expresses the relationship between the missions and the processions of God in this manner: "The sendings of

---

[43]Barth, *Church Dogmatics* I/1, pp. 350-51. Thus Barth states "if the *tropos apokalupseos* is really a different one from the *tropos huparxeos* and if the *huparxis* is the real being of God, then this means that God in his revelation is not really God" (ibid., p. 353).

the Son and the Holy Spirit reveal their eternal processions from the Father (and the Holy Spirit's procession as well), and thus reveal the inner trinitarian mystery of God."[44] This does not remove all mystery from the Godhead, but it prevents us from casting a veil over what has been unveiled!

Some theologians, Catherine LaCugna, for example, have said that the revelation of God in Jesus, by the Spirit, is identical with who God is and thereby have coalesced the immanent and economic Trinities.[45] While the revelation of God in Jesus Christ, if reliable, must truly reveal God truly and is sufficient to bring about human knowledge of God and salvation, it need not tell us all there is to know about God within Godself, which still remains shrouded with some elements of mystery. This is evident from texts written after the incarnation event, such as 1 Timothy 6:16: "who alone is immortal and who lives in unapproachable light, whom no one has seen or can see. To him be honor and might forever. Amen." Nevertheless, our primary focus will be on what is revealed as sufficient for Christian life and mission. Jason Vickers has some wise counsel in this regard:

> The trinitarian Theologian can, with Chrysostom, encourage initiates to remain focused on that birth that we have seen and heard and not to become overly distracted by what we have not seen or heard, namely the manner of eternal generation of the Son from the Father, the manner of the Spirit's procession, and so on.[46]

Related to the second point, Barth spawned the recovery of the Trinity's centrality for Christian theology, after theologians like Schleiermacher had all but dispatched it into obscurity, when he affirmed that the noetic logic of trinitarian theology moves from the differentiated love of Father, Son and Holy Spirit in the economy of salvation (the economic Trinity) to the ultimate ground of their threefold love in

---

[44]Edmund Hill, *The Mystery of the Trinity* (London: Geoffrey Chapman, 1985), p. 89.
[45]Catherine Mowry LaCugna, *God for Us: The Trinity and Christian Life* (San Francisco: HarperSanFrancisco, 1991).
[46]Jason E. Vickers, *Invocation and Assent: The Making and Remaking of Trinitarian Theology* (Grand Rapids: Eerdmans, 2008), p. 196.

the depths of the divine being (the immanent Trinity).[47] In rescuing the Trinity from Schleiermacher's dusty basement, Barth set the doctrine in the prolegomena of his dogmatics and then made it the architectonic of his theology. One of the most perceptive interpreters of Barth, Eberhard Jüngel (1933-), observes "The *Church Dogmatics* is the ingenious and diligent attempt to think the proposition 'God corresponds to himself' through to the end."[48] Far from being a theological afterthought, the doctrine of the Trinity has both a positive and critical function in Christian theology and the gospel according to Barth.

In affirming who God is in himself as revealed by his external works, Barth was reacting to a tendency in some theologians, especially of the Scholastic (both Catholic and Reformed) tradition, to speculate on the nature of the Godhead in an a priori philosophical manner. This tradition has often drawn from Augustine, who most famously used the concept of God as the great *Nous,* or eternal mind (Father as Memory, Son as Understanding, Spirit as Will/Love),[49] a psycho-philosophical analogy drawn from Neo-Platonism, which is fundamentally impersonal and unsatisfactory, and a distancing of the God who is for us from who he is in himself.[50] The development of the doctrine of the Trinity, as Lesslie Newbigin expressed it,

> was not the result of any kind of theological speculation within the tradition of classical thought. It was the result of a new fact (in the original sense of the word *factum,* something done). God had done those things that are the content of the good news that the Church is commissioned

---

[47]The term *noetic* when used as here in a Barthian manner must include knowledge that is participational and relational, and inclusive of the whole person, not merely the intellect.

[48]Eberhard Jüngel, *The Doctrine of the Trinity: God's Being Is in Becoming,* trans. Horton Harris (Edinburgh: Scottish Academic Press, 1976), p. 7.

[49]Augustine writes "we find in memory, understanding, and will a triad of certainties with regard to the nature of the mind. They present a single, substantial reality, in differing relations to itself" (Augustine, *Later Works,* trans. John Burnaby [Philadelphia: Westminster, 1960], p. 72).

[50]This view of Augustine's Trinity has been challenged, especially by Brad Green, "The Protomodern Augustine? Colin Gunton and the Failure of Augustine," *International Journal of Systematic Theology* 9, no. 3 (2007): 335. Those less critical of Augustine (Green, Danaher, Ratzinger) suggest that the Cappadocian ontology was already a given for him and that his analogies were an attempt to illustrate a truth already revealed and believed. These analogies were offered with reverent, speculative reticence as windows into what the beatific vision of the triune God might be like.

to tell, the gospel. This fact required a complete rethinking of the meaning of the word "God."[51]

Thus, the doctrine of the Trinity was formulated by the church in response to the church's experience of the persons of the Godhead in real history and, critically, as encountered in worship.

What is sufficient for Christian mission, and indeed crucial to it, is the awareness that the Trinity as revealed in the sending of the Son and the giving of the Spirit is the essence of the gospel, and indeed that the extent to which the church lives in the experience of the Trinity, it will accomplish its mission. If the church articulated the doctrine of the Trinity because of its worshipful response to the incarnational revelation of the Son and the work of the Spirit, then it will reveal that triune God and his gospel by remaining true to its nature as a community worshiping the triune God. It does not need to sacrifice its worship depth to become missionally wide. It becomes missionally wide by being deeply engaged in the worship of the triune sending God.

Jason Vickers wrote about another person who maintained this emphasis on the revealed Trinity as encountered in worship and lived out in mission in the time period where Reformed Scholasticism and Enlightenment theology had all but relegated it to a doctrinal curiosity—Charles Wesley. William Jones's 1767 treatise *The Catholic Doctrine of the Trinity, Proved by Above an Hundred Short and Clear Arguments, Expressed in Terms of the Holy Scripture* formed the inspiration and pattern for Charles Wesley's 1767 *Hymns on the Trinity*, of which his brother John wrote, "If anything is wanting, it is the application, lest it should appear to be a mere speculative doctrine, which has no influence on our hearts and lives; but this is abundantly supplied by my brother's Hymns."[52]

Vickers writes that he "may have done more to preserve the Trinity than he could have by writing the technical kinds of treatises on the Trinity that were so common in his day." "Indeed," Vickers continues,

---

[51]Newbigin, "The Trinity as Public Truth," pp. 2-3.
[52]John Wesley on the Trinity, in a letter to Mary Bishop, April 17, 1776.

"Charles Wesley's contribution to modern theology may lie precisely in that he reminds us that theology's true home is in worship and prayer, its true task the work of praise and thanksgiving to God."[53] In other words, *Wesley moved the Trinity back from assent to invocation!* He thereby helped toward a recovery of emphasis on the Trinity as the proper personal name of God, grounded in the economy of God's revelation and reconciliation and redemption, as the grammar and means of assisting the church

> in its proper task, namely, informing people through evangelism and catechesis about the saving activities of God in the coming of Christ and the coming of the Holy Spirit, as well as helping to facilitate the human encounter with the triune God in worship, prayer, and praise through the hard work of initiation and Christian formation.

Vickers adds, "Instead of conceiving of the Trinity as a network of propositions to be 'explained,' such a move will help clergy think of the Trinity as divine persons to be *introduced*."[54]

Commenting on the fact that coming to know God personally is more like developing a capacity for art or music than it is like learning the alphabet, Vickers states that

> teaching people how to pray is of the *very essence of trinitarian theology.* . . . The *trinitarian theologian* as the midwife of the Holy Spirit will assist Christians to encounter Jesus Christ in baptism and the Eucharist, in joining with Christ in obedience and surrender to God the Father. The end of trinitarian theology as such will not be to explain God but to worship God, to give thanks and praise to God, to surrender one's will and one's life to God in obedience, and ultimately to become like God.[55]

In other words, trinitarian ecclesial and personal mission is the goal of trinitarian ecclesial doxology, and the goal of trinitarian ecclesial doxology is ecclesial and personal mission. The church deeply immersed in the life of the Trinity will inevitably be missional.

---

[53]Vickers, *Invocation and Assent*, p. 189.

[54]Ibid., p. 193. He adds, "To be a trinitarian theologian in this setting is not to set one's mind to the tough task of solving the problem of the principle of individuation. On the contrary, to be a trinitarian theologian is to be a midwife of the Holy Spirit, actively participating in the birthing of new Christians in and through baptism" (ibid., p. 195).

[55]Ibid., p. 195, emphasis added.

THE TRINITY AND CREATION

To be trinitarian is also to see the self-revelation of God as Trinity to be the way of seeing all reality. For example, the healing of a dualistic view of the universe lies in the revelation that God has become incarnate in the Son. The ancient Greek view of the universe derived from Plato and expressed fully in Gnosticism entailed the notion that matter and all things physical were bad, and that only what is spiritual and intellectual was good. The soul was trapped within a body from which it needed to escape to be free. The revelation of the Trinity through the incarnation of the Son who became fully human in a real physical body reaffirmed what God had said about his creation in Genesis 1: "it is good." The resurrection of Jesus in a real, physical, though spiritually oriented body confirmed that message, anticipating that the future of humanity is not perpetual disembodiment but the immaterial spirit/ soul and body together in a new creation.

Dualism was dealt a fatal blow in Jesus, and yet regrettably it has persisted especially in the thinking of Western Christians. The legacy of Greek philosophy persists in Western education and thought, and the Enlightenment perpetuated that dichotomization. This has profoundly affected mission in evangelical history, with its tendency to pursue evangelism outside of the context of care for whole persons and outside of the pursuit of social justice of communities and nations. In general, it seems to me that evangelicals have in some ways tended to prize the "spiritual" over the incarnational dynamics of life, to the neglect of the following: a proper integration of science and theology, and the arts and theology; work as the fulfillment of God's cultural mandate or mission in Genesis 1–2; concern for the poor; the education, health care and engagement in society of converts in overseas missions; the historic manifestation of Christ on earth in his church as evidenced by a low concern with catholicity and liturgy; the routine of normal church life and "order" when refreshing renewal movements of the Spirit break out. Of course it is possible for Christians and churches to fail to be trinitarian in an opposite direction, in that they can become so mundane and earthbound that they neglect the work of the Spirit, who brings heavenly, kingdom perspective and spiritual power to the mundane.

Our preoccupation in the West with the material and the visible, and our sense of entitlement with respect to health, wealth and happiness, betrays a shallow spirituality.

These are simply examples of how Christians may be trinitarian in creed yet not in experience. To be trinitarian, in a nutshell, is to say that the climax of God's revelation of himself is in Son and by Spirit. We do well to make this our hermeneutic for understanding all reality, including the nature of the created universe, who we are as humans made in his image, and the nature of his mission, specifically to whole persons in whole communities, in whole nations and to all creation.

Our first task in the business of getting the gospel and mission right, in other words, is getting the God of the gospel right. Reevangelizing the West first means reevangelizing Western Christians with the good news of who God really is in order that we might reflect who he really is, and not projections of our psyches. He is first and foremost the triune God of love, the God who loves in freedom, the God who is *for* humanity and whose whole intent in his loving act of creation was to draw fallen human beings into relationship with himself in Christ. God's act of creation itself was a loving act of his will. God did not create because he was lonely. He did so out of the richness of his triune love, and he did so knowing what would befall it, and knowing that his Son would need to become human in order to redeem and reconcile it, indeed recapitulate it. In that sense, it is right to say that even the act of creation by God was kenotic.

It is also important to note that the creation was not an extension of God's being, for then creation would be God. A trinitarian distinction made by Athanasius centuries ago is necessary to distinguish between God and creation. The Father has *generated* the Son from his own being for all eternity, but at a finite point, the triune God *created* the universe. Thus the Son is God, but the creation is not. The relation between God and creation, or the universe, is not pantheistic or monist. Yet God loves his creation and pronounced it good, and has by the sending of his Son into creation reconciled all things in heaven and on earth to himself. It seems clear by comparison of John 1:1-14 and Colossians 1:15-20 with Genesis 1 that the Son was the primary agent within the

Trinity in the actual act of creation, and that he was, by a precreation covenant of God, destined to be its reconciler and the head of the new humanity he would redeem to reign over it with him, the last or *eschatos* Adam. The creation or cultural mandate for the relational rule and stewardship of creation, given to the first Adam, is thus the first "mission" given to all humans in Christ. Our relationship with Christ holds together this command of God and those of the Great Commandment and Great Commission.

THE TRINITY AND ELECTION

It would be naive to pretend that mention of God's decrees and purpose for the creation and humanity do not raise some hard questions. The doctrine of election has been difficult for Christians to understand down through the centuries. Sometimes it has facetiously been called "the doctrine of the lucky ones," referring to the seeming capriciousness of a God who appears to elect some but not others, and in not electing some apparently damns them for all eternity before they were even born. Some theologians have thus coined the term *double predestination*, meaning that God has predestined some to heaven and some to hell.

Despite its difficulties, Paul, who was no intellectual slouch, is completely unapologetic and nondefensive about this doctrine. He considered it a doctrine to be delighted in, not avoided, not something to feel vaguely guilty about. That was perhaps because, in the spirit of biblical revelation about election, he saw it as a responsibility as much as it was a privilege.

There are Reformed, Wesleyan and Arminian camps on this issue. I wish to offer an alternative to these, but before doing so I would point out that all traditions can affirm the universal love of God for humanity and his desire that all should be saved (with the exception of the extreme hyper-Calvinists). Even within the Reformed camp there has been a conviction that election is an incentive for evangelism and not a discouragement. After all, no one knows who the elect will be and so one can preach with the assurance that the Father will by the Spirit be drawing those people to himself. If this were not the case, preaching would be pointless. It should not be forgotten that the father of modern missions is William Carey, who came from precisely this Calvinist background, even if he did have to battle his more extreme mentors to do so.[56] But is there a way in which election might in fact be deemed to be the best news of the gospel, and not an embarrassing doctrine to hide in the proverbial theological cupboard, along with the Trinity? Karl Barth thought so.

Barth refreshingly turned much of traditional Western theology on its head by recasting many of its doctrines in a Christological, trinitarian way. Barth's whole movement is away from man as the subject to God and Christ as the subject of theology. This does not negate humanity or human experience of salvation, even though when grappling with Barth's theology of election and justification, sanctification, reality and experience, we do sometimes feel like we have indeed taken "an excursion into a dogmatic Wonderland in which familiar values and assumptions are turned on their head."[57]

What does it look like to recast election Christologically in a trinitarian manner? First, it means to see election as referring first to Christ. Barth suggested that the true subject of election in the precreation covenant of God was not human individuals but rather *Christ*, and thus *all humanity with whom Christ has become one by the incarnation*. In that trinitarian covenant, God elected to be *for* humanity, in Christ. When Paul speaks of "the God and Father of our Lord Jesus Christ" (Eph 1:3), he is speaking of the God of covenant.[58] He goes on to say, "*he chose us in him*" (v. 4). The juxtaposition of the three pronouns in this sentence is noteworthy. This is evidence that God put us and Christ together in his mind in precreation eternity when he formed his purpose concerning creation. The subject of God's election is primarily Christ himself and only secondarily, by derivation, those in Christ: "For he chose us in him before the creation of the world to be holy and blameless

---

[56]John Ryland is reported to have exclaimed, "Young man, sit down; when God is pleased to convert the heathen world, He will do it without your help or mine," though his son has disputed this.

[57]Trevor Hart, *Regarding Karl Barth: Essays Toward a Reading of His Theology* (Carlisle, U.K.: Paternoster, 1999), p. 58.

[58]This covenant language infers a new covenant in which Christ and his new humanity are now the new Israel, the covenant community.

in his sight" (Eph 1:4). Covenant thus involves the election of the triune
God to be our God: "I will be their God." The covenant made within
the Godhead to be for humanity specifically involved the election of
the Son to become human. The Son was chosen to become incarnate
and thereby to represent humanity as the last Adam, the real Adam of
which the first Adam only prefigured. In taking on our full humanity
by the incarnation, humanity was healed and taken into the Godhead,
relationally: "they shall be my people." What Christ did by way of his
life and death was done vicariously for humanity as an ontic entity.
Christ justified humanity, indeed creation by means of his vicarious
humanity, death, resurrection and ascension. Thus, all humanity is, in
Christ, elect, ontically speaking.[59] Only those who noetically participate in Christ through faith enter in to awareness that they are ontically elect and receive salvation and eternal life, but in Barth's way of
thinking, no one goes to hell because they are nonelect. In fact they do
so refusing to accept God's verdict of them that they are justified.[60]

In fact, for Barth, *election is indeed the best news of the gospel* because it
tells us that God is for humanity in Christ, and missioners can announce that *all* are included in its scope. Barth even took the Calvinist
doctrine of double predestination and turned it on its head in Christ.
What he averred was that Christ was the elect and predestined one,
and that on the cross Christ also endured the rejection of the nonelect.
Barth is supralapsarian in a unique manner here.[61] Election in Barth is

---

[59]Barth in fact saw humanity in Christ as the only true humanity. In this sense he reflected the
anthropology of Irenaeus. The form of humanity that is concrete and has real historical existence and is the eschatological goal of humanity is the humanity of Christ.

[60]Ontically speaking the "real" reality of the election and justification of humanity has been
established by God in Christ. The noetic act is not to be construed as an additional and equal
aspect of "union," as if this were our contribution to the union that makes it actual and real.
There is an asymmetry of the ontic over the noetic. The noetic aspect is our participating in
the reality cognitively and affectively and conatively by the gift of the Holy Spirit. Furthermore, the "ontic" in Barth is not just static being but an "onto-relational" reality established in
and by Christ. Barth and T. F. Torrance, when referring to ontological reality actually intend
a meaning other than that in standard Western philosophy, that of *onto-relational* (Torrance's
term), by which they intend to say that the ontological is inherently and essentially relational.
The relations are constitutive of the being. See T. F. Torrance, *The Christian Doctrine of God*
(Edinburgh: T & T Clark, 2001), pp. 123-24; *The Mediation of Christ*, rev. ed. (Colorado
Springs: Helmers & Howard, 1992); and Paul D. Molnar, *Thomas F. Torrance: Theologian of the
Trinity* (Aldershot, U.K.: Ashgate, 2009), pp. 59-63.

[61]Barth gleaned his views on election from the *Scots Confession* of 1560 and also from Pierre

pushed back into the triune God and Christ, specifically, and it is not a reaction to the Fall.

Second, it means to see election as communal rather than individual. Election is always spoken of as communal in the New Testament. For example, near the beginning of Paul's great trinitarian symphony of praise in Ephesians 1, he writes "He chose *us* in him before the creation of the world to be holy and blameless in his sight" (emphasis added). In our Western way of thinking we stress the importance of the individual, and therefore we tend to interpret that matter of election as an individual matter—who's in and who's not. Rather its object is the community of humanity that has been forever conjoined with Christ by his incarnation. Those who believe enter awareness that they are, like Israel of old, the elect covenantal community of God, in the One who is the new Israel, Jesus.

Third, it means to see election as a responsibility to be borne, not an exclusive privilege to be hoarded. Those who become aware through conversion that they are elect then treat election not so much as a privilege for a few but as a responsibility. They are to be humble and holy bearers of that election to the many, who are also within its purview. Barth builds a robust theology of mission first in the election of God to be for humanity as demonstrated in the cross-resurrection event of reconciliation. Then he speaks of the church as God's human partner, in union with Christ, taking part in God's mission because God has taken the congregation as his partner in service. Most important, election was a narrowing with expansion in kind; that is, it was for mission. In this vein Lesslie Newbigin speaks of election, "the doctrine that permeates and controls the whole Bible," as that which resolves the scandal of particularity in mission. He sees the doctrine of election as resolving the tension between the universality and the particularity of God's concerns. Newbigin's point is that God's intent to bless was always universal, but that this was not accomplished "by means of a universal revelation to all humanity." Rather, "there is . . . a process of selection: a few are chosen to be the bearers of the purpose; they are chosen, not

---

Maury at the International Congress of Calvinist Theology of Geneva in 1936 (see *Church Dogmatics* II/1, pp. 154-55).

for themselves, but the sake of all." Thus, "the one (or the few) is chosen for the sake of the many; the particular is chosen for the sake of the universal."[62] This, says Newbigin, was in keeping with how election is always presented in the Scriptures, that is, that it is a narrowing with a view to expansion.

The ultimate narrowing with a view to expansion was of course in Christ himself. It is in Abraham's seed that all nations of the world are blessed. It is in Christ that all humanity has been chosen, as Barth would say. The church as the elect community, participating with Christ noetically, is simply mirroring the role of Christ. Its role is to draw all people to the Christ who has been lifted up and is now present in the church. Therefore, to fail to be engaged with our near and distant neighbor is to misunderstand the nature of election and the missional nature of Israel in the Old Testament and now the church.

THE TRINITY AND THE CHURCH
Unity with Diversity

Karl Barth's contribution to a missional understanding of the church is inestimable. His grounding of mission in theology proper and the Trinity first, rather than ecclesiology, was not the only move made by Barth that encouraged missional thinking. His grounding of the church in the being and the eternal election of the triune God to be for humanity is, to be sure, inseparable from the divine commissioning of the church for mission to the world. However, his *ecclesiology* in turn, as shaped by incarnational and trinitarian thinking and his doctrine of reconciliation, further emphasized the core identity and orientation of the church and the Christian as missional.

With respect to the former, Barth expresses his view of the church in *Church Dogmatics* IV/3 as the "people of God in 'world-occurrence'" on the basis of and in correspondence with his view of the church as the "fellowship of the Spirit" and the "body of Jesus Christ." Mission in Barth's ecclesiology so understood is spoken of as vocation. This is extrapolated for the individual Christian as the church scattered. As

---

[62]Lesslie Newbigin, *The Open Secret*, rev. ed. (Grand Rapids: Eerdmans,1995), p. 34.

Kimlyn Bender states, "In Barth's understanding, the vocation of the church is complemented by the vocation of the individual Christian: both the community and the Christian are commissioned and sent to bear witness to God's reconciliation of the world in Jesus Christ (*CD* IV/3.2, 681-3)."[63] All three concepts of the church as fellowship of the Spirit, body of Christ and people of God in world occurrence are expressed analogously to the incarnation of Christ (unity and differentiation, asymmetry [deity over humanity] and correspondence) and, in the case of the first two, logically ordered such that the church is second. But in the third case, with respect to mission, the church is assigned priority concerning witness. This in turn permits a reciprocal but asymmetric relation between the church and the world.[64] This leads Barth to express a theology of history in which ecclesial history takes precedence in world history. As creation is grounded in covenant in Barth, so general history is the basis and context for the particular history of Jesus Christ and, as his own history includes with it his community's history, so the history of the world exists so that the particular history of Christ and his church exists. This is a reason for further hope with respect to the mission of the church in this and every age, no matter how things may appear on the surface. For Barth the relationship between the church and the world is asymmetric. Just as the divinity of Christ prevails over the humanity in Barth's Cyrillic view of the hypostatic union, so he insists that in the reciprocal relation between the church and the world, the church will prevail in its influence for the mission of God, despite its evident weaknesses and contrary to appearances:

> In theory and above all, in practice, we have to confess that church history does actually have priority over all other history, that with all its

---

[63]Kimlyn J. Bender, *Karl Barth's Christological Ecclesiology*, Barth Study Series (Burlington, Vt.: Ashgate, 2005), pp. 225-26.

[64]The relation between the church and the world suggested by this conception is expressed well by Gordon Preece: "Put christologically rather than eschatologically, the center of human action and vocation is witnessing to reconciliation in Christ at the center of God's triune action, and invoking social transformation through God's coming kingdom (*CD IV/3*, 481-680)" (Gordon Preece, "Barth's Theology of Work and Vocation for a Postmodern World," in *Karl Barth, a Future for Postmodern Theology?* ed. G. Thompson and Christiaan Mostert [Hindmarsh: Australia Theological Forum, 2000], p. 153).

insignificance and folly and confusion in history generally, it is still the church and decisive history to which all the rest is as it were, only the background or accompaniment.[65]

The church's identity as missional is further accentuated by Barth's ensconcing of the church in the great work of the divine reconciliation of the world to God. His massive exposition of this doctrine is beyond our scope here, but suffice it to say that the third of its three movements, *vocation* (justification and sanctification being the first two) is crucially defined as the mission of the church and the Christian. Barth's understanding of vocation (German *Berufung*) was not that of the particular callings of individual Christians but, as Flett indicates, it was intended to convey "that calling, active participation in service to Jesus Christ's prophetic office is the nature of Christian existence." Similarly, the term *service* (*Dienst*) was intended by Barth to convey "the missionary nature of the Christian community."[66] As Barth himself stated, "Remember: every Christian is a missionary, a recruiting officer for new witnesses! That she is this constitutes the knowledge and orientation without which our communities cannot be missionary communities, and, in point of fact, cannot be truly Christian communities at all."[67]

One of the further crucial relevancies of the Trinity for the church as elect is the necessity for it to demonstrate its unity in Christ, within its great diversity. It is striking that the one and the only great missional strategy revealed in the high priestly prayer of Jesus in John 17, which in the context follows the "as you sent me into the world, I have sent them" passage that parallels John 20:21, the burning desire of our great high priest in his prayer is the unity of the church. Notice how Jesus makes trinitarian relations the ground for the unity of the church and therefore for its effectiveness in mission. Verse 20 marks the beginning of the third section of the prayer where he expresses his concern for mission: "those who will believe in me through their message" (Jn

---

[65]Barth, *Church Dogmatics* III/3, p. 207.
[66]John G. Flett, *The Witness of God: The Trinity, Missio Dei, Karl Barth and the Nature of Christian Community* (Grand Rapids: Eerdmans, 2010), p. xi.
[67]Barth, *Church Dogmatics* III/4, p. 505.

17:20). He has prayed first concerning his own mission to the cross (vv. 1-5) and then for those who are already in the elect community (vv. 6-19). Now his prayer is that the message of the elect ones, the disciples, will bear fruit "that the world might believe" (Jn 17:21). This is the narrowing of election for the bearing of mission to all. But notice how this is to happen: "I have given them the glory that you gave me, that *they may be one as we are one—I in them and you in me*—so that they may be brought to complete unity. *Then the world will know* that you sent me and have loved them even as you have loved me" (Jn 17:22-23, emphasis added).

It is the oneness of the Father and the Son, and then the church's relational oneness with God by its union with the Son as a consequence of sharing the glory of intradivine relations with us through him. That is the reason the unity and catholicity of the church are so important for mission. The unity of the church represents the unity of the Godhead! The experienced unity of the church Jesus is praying for (it must be more than organic or ontic unity, which was a given) is critical if we are accurately to represent who God is, as the God whose oneness includes differentiation. And it is critical if we are to represent the intended oneness of the human race in Christ. The church is to be a sign of the kingdom to come in this sense.

New methodologies and technologies, seeking cultural relevance, challenging the institutionalism of the corporate church, calling the church to feed the poor—all these have their rightful place, but they pale in insignificance when placed alongside the prayer of Jesus, which I assume he is probably still praying as our great high priest, given that we seem to need it more than ever. The most powerful dynamic in mission remains the church in unity. This needs to temper reform movements within the church—emerging churches and church plants must do all they can to remain within the catholicity of the church. Jesus calls the church to missional effectiveness by working at unity.

Controversy surrounds the matter of how Protestant or evangelical churches of free church heritage, as opposed to the Roman Catholic and Eastern Orthodox Churches, can practice unity and catholicity necessary for missional life. Surely their schismatic origin precludes that, some might say, cynically adding that *catholic free* is an oxymoron. A key issue in this discussion relates to the difference between diversity and division. Miroslav Volf has written perceptively on the manner in which different views of the Trinity affect the views of unity and catholicity held by the three great traditions of Christian faith, and offered the view that the social Trinity of the Athanasian variety (the correct one in his opinion) supports the free church view that the local church has autonomy. He thus suggests that catholicity can indeed be pursued within this tradition, as reflected in a catholic attitude and hospitality (including admission to the Eucharist) toward all Christians, collaboration in missional ways and by celebrating diversity within the basic unity of the historic orthodox faith, recognizing that ultimate organized unity will be experienced only in the fullness of the *eschaton*.[68]

In concluding this chapter introducing the triune God of mission, it is appropriate therefore to say that the greatest secret to fulfilling God's mission for a church is for it to be experientially participating in the triune God. This involves its deep commitment to know this God, like theologians such as Edwards and Barth and von Balthasar, to demonstrate an intoxication with God and his triune glory as the source and end of Christian mission. In his book *The Sacrament of the Present Moment*, Jean-Pierre De Caussade wrote, "Let us set off at once and lose and intoxicate ourselves in the very heart of God."[69] It is the church intoxicated with God, actively participating in the life of God, the church in worship, that is the missional church. The church of Acts 2 was just such a church. The evangelism was effected through the church at worship. The three thousand converts were attracted first by the disciples' "declaring the wonders of God" (Acts 2:11) in their own tongues. The church was accused of being drunk. When the church is accused of being drunk with worship, intoxicated with God, it is most missional.

Why does this trinitarian understanding of God matter in general?

---

[68]Miroslav Volf, *After Our Likeness: The Church as the Image of the Trinity* (Grand Rapids: Eerdmans, 1998).

[69]Jean-Pierre De Caussade, *The Sacrament of the Present Moment* (San Francisco: HarperSanFrancisco, 1981), p. 35.

It matters profoundly in the matter of mission that we represent who God really is. He is not a generalized unitarian mysterious God we cannot know. He is the God and Father of our Lord Jesus Christ, made known through Jesus historically and by the Spirit experientially. And he draws his redeemed people into participation in his life and love to continue his mission on earth.

PART ONE

Discovering Shalom

■ ■ ■

On the evening of that first day of the week,
when the disciples were together, with the doors
locked for fear of the Jewish leaders, Jesus came and stood
among them and said, "Peace be with you!" After he said this,
he showed them his hands and side. The disciples were
overjoyed when they saw the Lord.

JOHN 20:19-20

5

Communities of
Christ's Risen Presence

. . .

On the evening of that first day of the week,
when the disciples were together, with the doors locked for
fear of the Jewish leaders, Jesus came and stood among them
[εἰς τὸ μέσον] *and said, "Peace be with you!"*

JOHN 20:19, emphasis added

Ivan Illich was asked what he thought was the most
radical way to change society; was it through violent revolution
or gradual reform? He gave a careful answer. Neither. Rather,
he suggested that if one wanted to change society, then
one must tell an alternative story.

ROWLAND CROUCHER, review of Alan Hirsch's
The Forgotten Ways

THIS IS A VIVID NARRATIVE. Into the midst of a community of disciples wondering what their future might be now that their Jesus is dead comes that very Jesus, now risen. But how he comes is what is so remarkable. The doors were locked! He came through them anyway. How did he do that? Jesus was still human, and that is an important reality for human salvation and the renewal of all creation. However, now his humanity is of a different order, no longer orientated toward mere earthly existence. His new humanity is oriented toward a new creation in which heaven and earth are in perfect union. Jesus now is in a body that is prototypical of the resurrection bodies Paul speaks of in 1 Corinthians 15:42-44: "So will it be with the resurrection of the dead. The body that is sown is perishable, it is raised imperishable; it is sown in dishonor, it is raised in glory; it is sown in weakness, it is raised in power; it is sown a natural body, it is raised a spiritual body." The meaning of "spiritual body" is "spirit-oriented body," a body able to transcend normal earthy limitations. But beyond the metaphysics of his human body, which is more our concern in chapter six, lies an important ecclesial reality suggested by his presence among the disciples.

Church as Christocentric Community

Jesus came and stood among them.

John 20:19

As communities of the presence of the risen Christ, churches should be *intentionally Christocentric communities*.

Calvin is surprisingly complimentary toward these disciples, for without ignoring their fear, he suggests that the fact that they were actually together as a group denotes faith and some courage:

> It is a sign of faith, or at least of a godly attitude, that they had all assembled. . . . [A]lthough they act less courageously than they should have done, they do not give way to their weakness. They certainly seek concealment to escape danger, but they pluck up enough courage to remain together; otherwise they would have been scattered and none would have dared to look at another.[1]

They seemed to know that they were still a community. However, without Jesus at the center they were not all they could or were intended to be.

---

[1]John Calvin, *John 11–21 and 1 John*, Calvin's New Testament Commentaries, trans. T. H. L. Parker, ed. David W. Torrance and Thomas F. Torrance (Grand Rapids: Eerdmans, 1959), pp. 201-2.

This vivid word picture depicting the incarnate, once-dead, now-risen Son standing among the community of his disciples evokes the very essence of the church. The "before" picture of dejected, disillusioned and fearful disciples behind locked doors conveys a "nonchurch," which both then and now arises when the risen Head as its source and center is absent. When "Jesus came and stood among them" everything changed. The "after" picture is what the church really is and how it becomes a community able to break free of walls and doors to fulfill the mission of God that Jesus began. Jesus had said, according to Matthew's account, that "where two or three come together in my name, there am I with them [ἐν μέσῳ αὐτῶν]" (Mt 18:20). This is depicted in John's picture here: "when the disciples were together, with the doors locked for fear of the Jewish leaders, Jesus came and stood among them [εἰς τὸ μέσον]." This is at ground level what defines church.[2] This validates my contention that John has in mind here a little picture of the infant church. I am well aware that Acts 2 is presumed as the day of the inception of the church. However, it seems that John has in mind here a prefiguring of that moment. The proleptic nature of the conferral of the Spirit by Jesus in this event seems suggestive of this notion.

It is of course unlikely the "two or three" in this instance had gathered "in his name." Christ came in sheer magnanimous grace. In this case, Jesus had to burst in on them through closed doors, not open doors! To say mission was not yet possible for this church at this point is an understatement. Their door wasn't open for Jesus, let alone anybody else! Before a community of disciples will ever break out of rooms with closed doors, or at least open the doors for others to come in, it must first have an open door for Jesus. Once he came and spoke, they were church. And then they could begin to hear his Greatest Commission: "As the Father has sent me, so I am sending you."

In sheer grace, again, when the risen Christ comes to them he does not do so with condemnation. He comes instead with outstretched arms and words of shalom upon his lips. How precious was the real presence of Jesus for those disciples—the same yet different Jesus. There was a

---

[2]Miroslav Volf makes this point convincingly in his defense of free church ecclesiology in *After Our Likeness* (Grand Rapids: Eerdmans, 1998).

continuity of identity. He was still fully divine and fully human, yet there was a discontinuity with respect to the nature of the humanity. This picture is a strong encouragement for Christians in churches that have lost their way missionally because they have lost their center in Christ. Instead of discussing the glories of the risen Christ, they now squabble over carpet colors and who's in charge of what and how much money should be given to whom. John's description of a local church in Revelation 2 depicts the frightening possibility that the risen Jesus does sometimes remove candlesticks when churches forget their first love and the reality that they are all about him (Rev 2:4). This is happening at a frightening speed in the Western world, and especially Europe, where church buildings now form pizzerias and pubs and domestic dwellings. A community of professed Christians who have failed to treasure Jesus as the source and center and mission of their gatherings is apparently better off not existing than existing for its own sake.

Yet that same passage in Revelation conveys hope, in that it contains an invitation for the church to repent and make things right. For those churches who come to be aware that they have displaced their risen Head from the center, there is hope if there is repentance. In another of the seven churches, the lukewarm church in Laodicea, Jesus stands at the door knocking. He does not easily shut down a lamp stand. He longs to be invited back to the center of the affections and worship of his people. In John 20:19, Jesus did not knock. He just came in because his disciples then did not know any better. So, there is hope for any church that repents of its enculturations and self-orientation and invites Christ to return. This will make them Christ-oriented and inevitably mission-oriented. Perhaps the place for many churches to begin, led by their leaders, is with services of public repentance and prayers of invocation of the living Christ to assume his rightful place again.

Many things can occupy the center at his expense. Without spiritual vigilance, bands and music and technologies designated to facilitate worship, the style of the worship or the charism of the leader or the eloquence of the preacher becomes the focus. This is true whether the ethos of our services is modern or postmodern, whether our churches are traditional or emergent. The frequent absence of that which was designed by Christ to keep his memory central in the church is most symptomatic of the church's eccentricity. I refer to the Lord's Supper—which seems to define the purpose of the gathering of the church (Acts 2:42, 46; 20:7; 1 Cor 11:20). Yet rigidly held ways of observing this can also become idolatrous. Preaching genres and exponents can become an idol too. The Word preached in a eucharistic context and within frequent liturgical affirmation by the church of the historic trinitarian creeds retains its importance but does not as easily assume a place of idolatry and become a source for Christian consumerism. What above all else will keep Jesus central is awareness that worship is not what we do anyway, but a grace-filled participation in the liturgical leadership of our risen great high priest (Heb 8:2, *leitourgos*). This latter point is suggested in this instance of the disciples' gathering in John 20, because as we have noted, they weren't capable of worship until he came. They were overjoyed once they saw him, and we can assume that they worshiped. A week later on a similar occasion, Thomas made this explicit. But Jesus took the initiative. After he came he led them in worship and added his perfume to their joyful praises as they ascended to the Father.

This record in John's Gospel of the appearing of Jesus in the center of his people to define them as his and therefore as missional is history as reliable as history can be, but it is not mere history. The risen Jesus of history is the risen Christ of contemporary Christian experience. He is alive today and his presence as the risen One still constitutes and then transforms the people of God from fearful captives behind locked doors to faith-filled missioners. But we must keep him at the center.

CHURCH AS CELEBRATORY COMMUNITY

The disciples were overjoyed when they saw the Lord.

John 20:20

As communities of the presence of the risen Christ,
churches should be *communities of celebration*.

The evident joy that emanated from this group once Jesus had returned to its center indicates that church worship should have a celebratory tone. Why? The One in the center who gives it its existence and life has been dead and is now risen! This does not mean superficial happy-clappy services that are inauthentic, or the absence of space for lament and contemplative meditation on the sufferings of Christ and of the world. I will express the need for the centrality of the cross in worship in chapter seven. Nevertheless, he was the risen Christ among his people, and that set the tone of that gathering. They now knew what they had not known before, that the cross was not the end of the story. This tension of celebration with depth is how Luke actually describes the tone of the worship in the infant church of Acts 2:46-47—"They broke bread in their homes and ate together with glad and sincere hearts, praising God." In all of our worship, even when we keep the cross central there must be a pervasive sense that this was not the end of the story. That hope is a reality because of Jesus' resurrection from the dead. People need to leave a service or community group with a sense of authentic hope. God knows how much despair there is in their lives.

The presence of Jesus as risen One here really does evoke an image of his reign and thus its joy. "All authority in heaven and on earth" (Mt 28:18) has been granted to him. This is good news! This little band of apostles with the risen Jesus in their midst depicts the kingdom of God with the good news that the reign of God is at hand! The mission of the church, then, is to continue Jesus' mission to represent the reign of God.[3] As its representative the church is not identical with the kingdom of God but is its community, its servant and its "sign" or "foretaste" of its final culmination of the kingdom of God. It must therefore be a community of joy![4] This joy was indicative of their beginning to experience the shalom Jesus' words had imparted.

CHURCH AS A COMMUNITY OF SHALOM

Jesus came and stood among them and said, "Peace be with you!"

John 20:19

---

[3]Darrell Guder, ed., *Missional Church* (Grand Rapids: Eerdmans, 1998), p. 100.
[4]Ibid.

As communities of the presence of the risen Christ, churches should be *communities that experience and express shalom.*

What is shalom? Is it a state of mind? It may include that, to be sure. We are told that these disciples were experiencing the "un-shalom" of fear, and I suspect that anger was not far away either, given the blocking of their hopes of exalted positions in the messianic kingdom they envisioned and their disillusionment with the claims of Jesus. Fear and anger are secondary emotions. Underneath them lies vulnerability of some kind. Insecurities. Grieving, for example, has an anger component because the loss of a person who has kept us grounded or who has enabled us to pursue our careers threatens our stability and our achievement. Often underlying anger is our vulnerability to failure, fear of failure. The insatiable desire for achievement is often fueled by the need for somebody's approval, and it has another side—anger at those we set up as the people we need to impress or please. Fear of failure keeps us feeding the beast. That is, the idol of what it is I fear.

It is only in the place of abject failure that peace actually comes to the disciples. What we dread, they experienced. They had failed. Miserably. Failed their best friend in his hour of deepest need. All the big, brave claims that Peter made, for example, have now proved hollow. He has denied his Lord and has with all the others forsaken him and fled. But actually it could be no other way. If they had contributed in any way to helping Jesus on the cross, they would have been taking credit for it and using it as a "one-up on the others" ploy. A means to say, "you see, I *will* sit at the right hand of Jesus in his kingdom." A means to point to achievement. The peace or shalom comes when achievement can no longer be the source. They would achieve a lot after this, but it would be as those participating in the shalom of participation with God. It would not be as those driven by need for recognition or human approval, but as those already in that peace of being the beloved of God.

However, shalom is much more than an interior subjective state. It is that state of harmony and goodness that is intended by God in his ultimate creation, as reconciled in Christ. Shalom or shalomic harmony is about being—and being as properly related, being-in-relation. It is creation and humanity in its proper relatedness to God. And that begins with the new humanity already reconciled, and disseminates from there. Thus shalom involves a whole-creation, all-of-humanity orientation. Henri de Lubac, a Catholic writer, has demonstrated the meaning of shalom profoundly in his close associating of the ecclesial and the social justice missions of the church. In *Catholicism: Christ and the Common Destiny of Man* he has shown the innate missionary trajectory of the church toward the totality of human needs in a way that flows out of the sacramental nature of the church, and the telos of shalom.

CHURCH AS A MISSIONAL, OPEN COMMUNITY
A Community of Hospitality

> Again Jesus said, "Peace be with you! As the Father has sent me,
> I am sending you." And with that he breathed on them
> and said, "Receive the Holy Spirit. If you forgive
> the sins of anyone, their sins are forgiven."
> JOHN 20:21-23

As communities of the presence of the risen Christ, *the church as one with Christ (not individuals) is God's primary missionary.*

This picture of the risen Christ identified fully with his failing, feeble, fearful people evokes the notion of his union with the church, and that he issues the "Greatest Commission" in this context is significant. They would be initiating a community of forgiveness. What is anticipated proleptically here is the church, in union with Christ, as missionary, not first and foremost individuals. It is significant that the presence of Jesus, having freshly accomplished the work of reconciliation, not only defines the new humanity but connotes that its mission lies in being a community of reconciliation, but only as he was central and definitive of that community, indeed, in union with it.

Barth greatly emphasized the fact that mission is first Christ's prophetic office and only the church's derivatively. As Waldron Scott notes, "One must be careful not to overrate the relevance of missions. Revelation is exclusively Christ's. The church can never take the place of Christ's place in missions."[5] Scott supports this statement by citing Dieter Manecke, who wrote, "Barth does not consciously leave any voids in the Christ event which the church could or must fill."[6] This emphatic statement about the sufficiency of Christ's person and work should not, however, be interpreted in such a way as to negate the missional nature of the church or that the church fills up what is lacking in the sufferings of Christ in that it too suffers as it engages in mission. It serves, however, to emphasize that the church's mission is fulfilled *in participation with Christ*, and that its function as such is to point to Christ and what he has already done by way of reconciliation and revelation. "He is the true missionary," Scott adds, "The church merely accompanies him in mission, assisting as it can."[7] This fundamental Christ orientation of mission will therefore cause the church to preserve the centrality and supremacy of Christ in its life, recognizing that as the church lives out its union with Christ and offers reconciling hospitality its mission can be fulfilled.

Two conclusions arise for the church based on this understanding of the nature of the church as being one with the missional Christ. *The first* is to suggest that the church will be both attractive (not attractional or extractional, but attractive for organic and not programmatic reasons) *and* incarnational. For the people of God to be incarnational as Jesus was, living among humanity from the poor to the rich, is a clear calling of the church as a community, which will therefore be known in its larger community as being "for and with" that community, as Jesus was "for and with humanity" in his life on earth. But for the church *also* to be attractional in the right sense, a sense I am trying to capture by

---

[5]Waldron Scott, *Karl Barth's Theology of Mission* (Downers Grove, Ill.: InterVarsity Press, 1978), p. 12.
[6]Dieter Manecke, "Die Theologischen Voraussetzungen der Mission" in *Mission als Zeugendienst* (Wuppertal: Theologischer Verlag Rolf Brockhaus, 1972), p. 210, quoted in ibid. This quote was translated by Waldron Scott.
[7]Scott, *Karl Barth's Theology of Mission*, p. 12.

using a different word, *attractive*, is *a necessary conclusion of a fully Christologically determined ecclesiology/missiology, that is, if we are to reflect not just one side of incarnational Christology.* Christ not only came down to become human, he became one in order to form a new community of humanity in particular located places, in which he still dwells. Christ and his church are together, as Bonhoeffer famously said, the collective Christ. What tends to characterize those who emphasize the incarnational nature of Christology is the going out to be with people. This can lead to inadequate ecclesiologies. To be at Starbucks and wherever else folk meet in our culture is crucial. However, if we are to be truly missional, the same folks we encounter need to be brought into the gathered community, which, after all, if it really is the community in Christ, will be irresistibly attractive. As Gordon Smith has expressed it, community is "necessarily the mediator of religious experience."[8] The church that truly sees itself as the community of the presence of the risen Jesus and pursues the mediation of that presence with passionate intentionality will be irresistibly attractive. Stereotypes about church are overcome when people discover churches of resurrection celebration and the intimate presence of Jesus. If "they want Jesus but not the church," let's give them Jesus in the church. It's not that we have an option—we are in union with him.

The second conclusion of the nature of the church as one with the risen Christ is that it will be an open church. That is, it will never be an exclusive community that hoards the goods, as it were. This is indeed where the incarnational nature of the church does have profound relevance. The disposition of Jesus in becoming incarnate, both throughout his incarnate life and in this moment in John 20 as he constitutes the church (at least proleptically), is always toward the world of humanity. The church is the community chosen in order to invite others into it, in the spirit of a biblical view of election as this has been outlined in chapter four.[9]

---

[8]Gordon Smith, *Beginning Well: Christian Conversion and Authentic Transformation* (Downers Grove, Ill.: InterVarsity Press, 2001), p. 35.

[9]For further treatment of this understanding of election see also Lesslie Newbigin, *The Open Secret*, rev. ed. (Grand Rapids: Eerdmans,1995), pp. 64ff.

CHURCH AS ESSENTIAL COMMUNITY

When the disciples were together, . . . Jesus came and
stood among them. . . . "As the Father has sent me, I am sending you."
And with that he breathed on them and said, "Receive the Holy Spirit.
If you forgive the sins of anyone, their sins are forgiven;
if you do not forgive them, they are not forgiven."

JOHN 20:19, 22-23

As communities of the presence of the risen Christ
("where two or three are gathered, there I am in the midst"),
the *church* is essential and definitive of Christian salvation and life.

The metaphorical presentation of the infant church in John 20 fulfills
the definition given by Jesus of the church at its most basic: "Where
two or three come together in my name, there am I with them" (Mt
18:20). Here is the inaugural ecclesial community made by the presence
of Jesus in their presence, at the center. This communal picture communicates Christ's intentions for his people. These Eleven would not
be his apostles alone but as a community. Here we see the men called
to be fishers now in a community formed for that purpose in Christ, at
least symbolically.

Actually, John throughout his Gospel has a particular angle on community, more profound than that of any other apostle. It is grounded in
the notion of trinitarian union and *theosis*, the union of the Christian
with God. The snapshot of the infant ecclesial community John provides here must be seen to be undergirded by a profound set of theological realities he has recorded earlier in his Gospel. He has heard
Jesus say a number of things about the day when the Spirit comes, and
now when he records Jesus "breathing" on the community, we are
meant to read into this event all of that theology. These passages in the
passion ministry of Jesus in John 14–16 convey the crucial concept of
relational union that is, first, the very essence of the Trinity, second,
the union of the Son with humanity ontically by the incarnation, and,
third, a corresponding counterpart for every Christian—that by the

Spirit's indwelling each would be placed into relational union with Christ, and each would by the Spirit's indwelling enter into the bond of love between the Father and the Son (Jn 14:20, 23). And if all that were true, then unavoidably all persons in relational union with Christ and the Trinity were thus also to be in a union with each other, the community of the church, the bride of the Bridegroom and the body of the Head.[10] It is for this reason that John is so adamant and repetitive about his appeal for love, which he saw as the defining mark of the church and as its primary means for mission (e.g., Jn 13:34-35). The "as I have loved you" union in John becomes the basis also for the "as the Father has sent me, so send I you" passages.

As communities of the presence of the risen Christ, therefore, its constituent Christians will rediscover church as an identity and not just a responsibility to be juggled alongside other commitments. The identity of the disciples around Jesus in that community in John 20 was forever *to be* the church. The missional nature of the church derives from whole-life integration of the people of God in a community where they are loved and they love, and where the life and love of such a community is known (Jn 13:34-35). What this looks like is a lot different than attending a service once a week on a Sunday, or even doing that and a small group midweek. This means having enough engagement with the church community to be in formation together, to be aware of and responsive to one another's physical and financial needs, to be ministering with our *charismata* to one another, ministering Christ to each other and embracing his centrality in community. At the same time it means to be constantly engaged with the world of people and creation, and hospitable to the seeker and the stranger as a community. To recognize that their salvation is wrapped up in the church where Christ dwells.

All through the centuries converts to Christian faith have become conjoined to that apostolic community spawned by Jesus among the

---

[10]I have chosen to qualify the term *union* with "relational" to avoid any notions of monism or indeed Mormonism. The possibility of speaking of union or theosis (deification or divinization) without confusing the divine and the human is much more readily achievable within a persons-in-relation social Trinity. A Trinity grounded in a psychological analogy and philosophical idealism leads to all kinds of confusion, by contrast.

apostles. They are never Christians alone. They are a community. From the experience of their first faith inklings as mediated by the church on into their initiation into Christ in baptism and throughout their ecclesial practices in the journey into Christian maturity and missional life, and indeed into life beyond the grave, their way of being is communal or more specifically ecclesial.[11] That the prevailing view of saving faith and Christian life is so individualistic is a consequence, as I noted in chapter three of capitulation to the individualism of the West. My point here is to emphasize the essential communal nature of the Christian (human), the essentiality of the church for salvation and the primacy of the church over the individual as God's missionary. It is also to help overly idealistic and usually overly pneumatic, and inadequately incarnational, Christians to come to terms with the imperfection of people in the church and the inevitability of institutionalism.

Miroslav Volf has expressed the nature of local churches as communities in which faith is mediated, and as polycentric communities analogously to the social Trinity, in which all persons can express their priesthood through the charismata of the Spirit. In this context he states that "the essential sociality of salvation implies the essential institutionality of the church. The question is not whether the church is an institution, but rather what kind of institution it is."[12] Volf's thought on the life of the free churches in the West is crucial for the development of appropriate personal spirituality and mission that does not succumb to either Western individualism or gnostic naive anti-institutionalism. Structure is inevitable in any church, as it is in any living organism, with its organelles and cells and organs and limbs. Structures are either functional and liberating or they are dysfunctional and oppressive. In fact, at their best they bring security and safety along with life and power. Institutions are just part of incarnational life.

Of course institutions can be institution*al* and get in the way of the life and mission of the church, in which case they may need to be de-

---

[11]Volf in *After Our Likeness* provides a convincing Protestant version of the dictum "there is no salvation outside of the church."
[12]Volf, *After Our Likeness*, p. 234.

frosted. In fact, I suggest that one of the greatest seductions of North American churches in the last two decades of the twentieth century was the uncritical imbibing of the most dominant influence in Western society then, what Jacques Ellul called "Technique."[13] This was particularly manifested in the presuppositions and influence of the church growth movement. The idea was that, in the absence of spiritual power, there was a tendency to reduce its life to technique, that is, to assume that organization and methodology and marketing would make a church grow. With the right preacher and the right megachurch structures, church growth was guaranteed. With this also came an idolatry of the power of "vision."[14] That success itself became an idol was testimony to this all-absorbing baptism in technique in a way that the words of Bonheoffer address with conviction: "The figure of the Crucified invalidates all thought which takes success for its standard."[15] This applies even in preaching, and perhaps especially so, in an era when preaching is so often anemic, dumbed-down, feel-good, mood-swaying communication designed to keep the church "happy" and the offerings up.

Technique along with individualism in Western churches can also pervade how spiritual growth through spiritual practices can be viewed. Individual, often prescriptive, regimens of the spiritual disciplines or practices are offered, at the expense of ecclesial ones. Whereas the New Testament account is fraught with descriptions of what the church did together, it has precious little to say about individual disciplines. There are references to personal prayer and fasting, and Jesus does model silence and solitude and listening prayer. But formation is

---

[13]Ellul is most widely known in North America for his sociological writings and most notably *The Technological Society* (1954, ET 1964; *La Technique* is the original French title). The term *technique* is not original to Ellul, but his unique contribution lies in his insistence on the *dominance* of technique and its effects on all of life.

[14]Bonhoeffer did speak of the dangers of vision, but this clearly requires qualification, for Bonhoeffer was himself a "man of vision" (see Eberhard Bethge, *Dietrich Bonhoeffer: Man of Vision, Man of Courage* [New York: Harper & Row, 1970]). It is not that vision or being a visionary is wrong per se, but rather that vision can easily be driven by questionable motivation and subverted by presuppositions unworthy of the kingdom of God.

[15]Dietrich Bonhoeffer, *Ethics* (New York: Touchstone, 1955), p. 78. See also Patrick Franklin, "Bonhoeffer's Missional Ecclesiology," *McMaster Journal of Theology and Ministry* 9 (2007-2008), pp. 96-128, for an extensive discussion of this theme.

envisioned primarily through communal practices, especially the sacraments. Even personal practices, including solitude, have as their end community and mission.

CHURCH AS THE ONE CATHOLIC COMMUNITY

Jesus came and stood among them. . . . The disciples
were overjoyed when they saw the Lord. . . . Again Jesus said,
"Peace be with you! As the Father has sent me, I am sending you."
JOHN 20:19-21

As communities of the presence of the *one* risen Christ.

The pristine oneness of the church envisioned in John 20 in its proleptic form, gathered around its one Lord as it receives its commission, speaks eloquently to preserving the unity of the body of Christ as critical to its mission to reveal the one Christ as one with the Father (cf. Jn 17:21). That includes unity within churches and between churches, or catholicity. What of the vast proliferations of forms of the church within our Protestant heritage? Are we all to abandon these and join the magisterium? If, as Volf suggests, the free church understanding of catholicity as functional, invisible, eschatological and indeed missional is the superior concept to that of the more visible and incarnational Roman Catholic or Eastern Orthodox views of it, we will nevertheless find in these ancient traditions the creedal undergirding for taking catholicity and unity seriously, if we want to be missional.

Diversity of churches need not necessarily contradict catholicity, although an uncatholic attitude has often been at work in formation of new denominations. African theologian Lamin Sanneh has made a case that the diversity of churches and their lack of cultural uniformity can be evidence of the adaptability of the Christian faith within cultures, of its ability to be contextualized, grounded in the model of the incarnation, even of "the triumph of its translatability."[16] I take comfort

---

[16]Lamin Sanneh, *Whose Religion Is Christianity? The Gospel Beyond the West* (Grand Rapids: Eerdmans, 2003), p. 130.

that somehow, in the providence of God, all our splits according to denominational foibles can be somehow redeemed missionally, but that we will avoid further unnecessary splits (those not grounded in the essentials of the faith), and that in new ventures of church planting, emergent groups will do so in communion with their parent denominations where possible, and that all of the people of God will convey an openness, a catholicity of attitude toward all fellow believers and wings of the church, and that all will work together toward eschatological catholicity, of which the church gives a sign. Pneumatically charged denominations, maybe even especially in Africa, can tend to neglect the incarnational and ecclesial reality of the "one Head-one body" nature of the church, giving rise to further unnecessary divisions.

CHURCH AS COMMUNITY THAT IS BOTH LIVELY AND OLD

Jesus came and stood among them. . . .
The disciples were overjoyed when they saw the Lord.
JOHN 20:19-20

As communities of the living Christ, churches should be
*living and lively, valuing continuity with the good tradition of the past,
but always open to change necessary for contextualization.*

There is a profound lesson for the church to be gained from the appearance of Jesus in John 20 in a way that was brand new—and yet old. He was there in resurrection power with a changed body, but the essential point of this story is that of continuity of identity. It was the same Jesus with the same scars he had before he died. This is in part the reason he shows the disciples his hands and side, confirming it was really him and he was really human. Beyond the fact that this symbolism suggests that the cross and the resurrection should be held together in tension in worship, and beyond the demonstration here of the perpetual humanity of Christ which evokes thoughts of his high priesthood, a greatly neglected reality in the life and worship of the evangelical church, this is a metaphor for shaping the ethos of the church in all times.[17] Its worship needs to be living and lively, yet with continuity with redemption history and liturgy. There are many times in the Psalms where the writer appeals for the covenantal community of God to sing a "new song." However, these new songs celebrated the old creational and redemptive actions of the unchanging God.

Church communities should be very much alive as Christ is. There is a name for organisms that have no change—dead. But church communities must also reflect a continuity of identity in a similar manner to Christ. Thus the church will be both open to change and yet embracing of the continuity of the church throughout history. History should not be negated, nor should all tradition. There is good and bad tradition; the former has been called the living faith of the dead, as opposed to the latter which is the dead faith of the living.

Specifically, the gathered *worship* of the church must in every age be characterized by both change and continuity. Change that reflects the appropriate inculturation that is required to contextualize and communicate the gospel story in every age. Continuity that is derived in the faith once for all delivered to the apostles and developed by the doctors of the church until now. Continuity through community with the saints of the past that is reflected in the practices of the sacraments and in the liturgy that rehearses the major tenets of historic orthodoxy. As Luke Bretherton states, "taking church history seriously as an arena of God's activity in the world is part of what it means to live within the tension of continuity and change that is at the heart of Christian existence."[18] Evangelicals need to recover from the "theological amnesia"[19] that has been perpetuated since the considerable influence of evangelist Charles Finney in his orientation of church services toward the purpose of "producing of converts" and promoting "a pragmatic approach to worship," which "argues that, since worship forms

---

[17]The work of James Torrance is important in this regard. See also the recent publication by Robin Parry of *Worshipping Trinity: Coming Back to the Heart of Worship* (Carlisle, U.K.: Paternoster, 2005).

[18]Luke Bretherton, "Beyond the Emerging Church," in *Remembering Our Future*, ed. Andrew Walker and Luke Bretherton (Colorado Springs: Paternoster, 2007), p. 38.

[19]A term used by D. H. Williams in *Retrieving the Tradition and Renewing Evangelicalism: A Primer for Suspicious Protestants* (Grand Rapids: Eerdmans, 1999), pp. 9-10. This amnesia not only robs Christians of their past, it also diminishes their sense of identity in the here and now.

have changed over time, nothing biblical or historical is normative except that which works at the present."[20] Pragmatism thus flourished under revivalism. "Conversion was now the point of worship. The previous two-fold emphasis in Christian worship of 'word and meal,' was replaced with a block of songs before the sermon and then the issuing of the altar call."[21]

The road ahead for the church is to reflect the newness of resurrection with creativity that is applied to the oldness of the tradition. The road ahead does not involve a return to any era. In what era was the church perfect? Not even in the book of Acts! There is a need to recapture the faith of the church as it has been expressed for twenty centuries, however. Liturgy and catechesis and preaching together accomplish *paradosis*, that is the handing over of the faith of the apostles, in such a way that the people of God are formed and find the meaning of their stories within the much larger story of God's work in the world. Telling again and again, in creative yet continuous ways, the creation-redemption-new creation story of the gospel, and all the stories of those who have entered in to that story, will subvert the secular story that so influences our formation spiritually and morally. Applying creativity to the presentation of the creeds, confessions and liturgies to contextualize them will, in addition, form us well.[22]

I find a significant community of interest with the recent collection of essays called *Remembering Our Future: Explorations of Deep Church* regarding these sentiments.[23] Intended as a corrective for the "fad-driven, one-dimensional spirituality of the evangelical church" (back

---

[20]James F. White, *Documents of Christian Worship: Descriptive and Interpretive Sources* (Louisville: Westminster John Knox Press, 1992), p. 114. See more on this trend in evangelicalism in Robert Webber's *Worship Old and New* (Grand Rapids: Zondervan, 1994).

[21]Lance Odegard, "A Peculiar Identity: The Church as Alternative Community and Communal Witness," a term paper in the course "Empowering the Church For Re-evangelization of the Church," Regent College, April 17, 2009, p. 7.

[22]As Rodney Clapp has indicated, "Any culture lives and dies by the vitality of its rituals and symbols" (*A Peculiar People: The Church as Culture in a Post-Christian Society* [Downers Grove, Ill.: InterVarsity Press, 1996], p. 112).

[23]The editors are Andrew Walker, professor of theology and education at King's College, London, and an ecumenical canon of St. Paul's Cathedral, and Luke Bretherton, lecturer in theology and ministry, Convener of the Faith and Public Policy Forum and D.Min. program director at King's College London.

cover), it is an appeal for the emergent and even "missional" or "mission-shaped" church movements to balance their concern with relevance to emerging culture with a rootedness in the "grand narrative of the Christian tradition," the past twenty centuries of the work of the Spirit in the church.[24] The authors demonstrate astute awareness of dangers on both sides of this issue.

> The vision for a deep church is neither an attempt to simply restate or repristinate the Christian tradition, this is tantamount to ancestor worship; nor does it take its bearings from the emerging culture, to do this is simply to assimilate to the prevailing hegemony; rather, to be a deep church means to stand on the cusp or the breaking point of both the Christian tradition and the emerging culture, deeply rooted in the former while fully engaged in the latter.[25]

The dichotomization of institutionalism (the "grand narrative of Christian tradition") and the "work or freedom of the Spirit" (and therefore the emergent movement) is challenged strongly (as by Miroslav Volf in *After Our Likeness*). The institutional and the charismatic (or emergent, for that matter) are not in opposition to one another but rather coinhere, just as the work of the Son and that of the Spirit coinhere.[26] There are dangers to avoid on both sides of the issue. On the one hand, church communities that have "accessed the living memory of the common tradition but are not sharing in the *life* of the triune God are mere antiquarians rummaging around in the tradition like children looking for hidden treasures in a dusty attic."[27] On the other hand, however, "charismatics and religious enthusiasts should take heart: deep church does not mean abandoning spiritual experience and inspirational insight for the sake of intellectual clarity and doctrinal exactitude."[28] Tapping into good tradition is life-giving for the church, for as William Abraham states, reflecting Orthodox scholar Florovsky, "the great ecumenical councils of the first five centuries are

---

[24]Walker and Bretherton, *Remembering Our Future*, p. 12.
[25]Ibid., p. xviii.
[26]Ibid., p. 12.
[27]Ibid., p. 11.
[28]Ibid., p. 12.

charismatic events in the life of the church which are still operative today through the Holy Spirit."[29]

A specific application of this new-old approach to worship may be with regard to the arts, for example. How can the arts reflect resurrection newness in a way that still demonstrates continuity with the one Christ who is the same yesterday and today and forever? At a recent Transforming Culture Symposium conference in Austin, Texas, Jeremy Begbie spoke about how he sees the next fifty years of art in the future of the church. As described by Rosie Perera,

> Jeremy demonstrated "hopeful subversion," starting not with where we are now, but rather with a vision of God's future and working backward from there. . . . The Spirit recreates (the Resurrection was the first day of the New Creation). . . . The Spirit improvises (the new heaven & new earth is surprisingly, endlessly new). For many, God is dull because he seems so "ordered"—all word/*logos* and no spirit. Jeremy invited us to embrace "non-order" (as distinct from disorder), which is the realm of laughter and the Spirit.[30]

CHURCH AS A MISSIONAL COMMUNITY

As the Father has sent me, I am sending you.
JOHN 20:21

As communities in union with the living Christ, God's missionary, the church, will be *missional in its identity*.

Churches, because they are communities of the presence of the risen Christ (by the Spirit, postresurrection), the sent One who has now sent them, will be "missional" or "mission-shaped" churches. They will not be shallow, dumbed-down churches in order to be missional, because their very essence is their connectedness in intimacy with the risen missional Christ, who was sent that we might be sent in him. Churches are by identity missional because they are conjoined to the sent Christ and

---

[29]William Abraham, *The Logic of Renewal*, cited in ibid., p. 63.
[30]Rosie Perera, "Transforming Culture Symposium," *Space for God* (weblog), April 10, 2008, http://spaceforgod.blogspot.com/2008/04/transforming-culture-symposium.html.

because they are thereby grounded in the nature of the missional triune God. Charles Van Engen has helpfully shown that the Reformation definition of church as the community of the presence of Christ served to rescue the descriptors of the church in the ancient trinitarian Nicene Creed ("one, holy, catholic, apostolic church") from various semantic abuses of these terms with ecclesio-political ends. In asserting the presence of the risen Christ as definitive of the church, Charles Van Engen was able to redeem these terms by transforming them into missional verbals.[31]

First, the *unity* of the church translates in the term *unifying*. In John 20, Jesus unifies his disciples, drawing them together around his own person, after they had scattered during his hours of trial and crucifixion, and then commissions them. By the time Jesus' promise and symbolization in John 20 comes to fruition in the early chapters of Acts, they "all joined together constantly in prayer" (Acts 1:14), "all together in one place" (Acts 2:1). It is as one that they are birthed by the Spirit's descent on the day of Pentecost, and it is as one that the church in Acts fulfills its mission. Thus, the unity of the church is a unifying force in mission to humanity, for it is and it signals the new humanity in Christ. This, as Van Engen puts it, involves the church in the tasks of inviting, gathering and incorporating.

Second, the *holiness* of the church translates into the term *sanctifying*. Van Engen speaks of the church as Immanuel in the world. I see this as the *priestly* function of the church in that, first, the church (and its members) has access to the holy presence of God, by sheer grace, through the mediation of Christ. It is sanctified in that process. That is, through ecclesial life, church folks are meant to be transformed so that they live in right relationship with God and other humans. That is, they live out ethics which are truly *evangelical*, gospel-informed and motivated ethics grounded in being ("*is* before *ought*"). They live grace-filled lives in which there is growth, but no perfection this side of the *eschaton*. I suggest that the church is missional around holiness in some sense by the transformation of regenerate and always-converting lives,

---

[31]Charles Van Engen, *God's Missionary People* (Grand Rapids: Baker, 1991).

but mostly because it is a community of grace and forgiveness in which people are pursuing holiness, but with imperfect results, and only as they are in union with Christ. The last thing intended for the church is that it be a pharisaic community of pretense where only successful people can come. This anticipates a second dynamic of priesthood, which is that the priestly church community is one in which confession is made and forgiveness imparted, both for those in the community and those coming into it seeking reconciliation. The third aspect of priesthood is that priests undergoing transformation under the influence of God's practiced presence (granted by God yet verbalized by their fellow humans) then mediate the presence and forgiveness of God, with grace, into their world. The John 20 image of the church corresponds to this in that the commission imparts the words that made the church a community of the forgiven and the forgivers. Peter also pulls these concepts together in 1 Peter 2 when he speaks about the church relating to God in holiness (1 Pet 2:4-10) and to all humans with respect and integrity (1 Pet 2:11-17), with this purpose in mind: that "they may see your good deeds and glorify God on the day he visits us" (v. 12).

Third, the noun *catholicity* for the church transforms, according to Van Engen, into the term *reconciling*. The church as the immediate locus of the reconciling event in the world that Christ has reconciled at the cross (Col 1:20) is thus the church calling the world to reconciliation to God. It is the church calling alienated people into the shalom community. This is evident again in the John 20 vignette, where Jesus pronounces shalom to his church and then repeats it before commissioning it. In John 21 we gain an insight into what that meant practically for a disciple in dire need of reconciling. Jesus' gentle, yet probing, reconciliation and then reinstatement of Peter is a worthy model of what the church's ethos inside, and then its influence in the world, should be. The whole-humanity and whole-creation scope of the reconciliation work of Christ ("God was reconciling the world to himself in Christ" [2 Cor 5:19])—("all things, whether things on earth or things in heaven" [Col 1:20]) implies by way of our union with him and his mission that we as the church ought not only to be preaching personal reconciliation for all but also in the forefront of reconciliation in social justice, ethnic and national reconciliation, and issues of ecological and environmental management. Of course, in order to do this with any credibility, it needs to flow out of an ethos and attitude of catholicity within the church, as stressed earlier.

Finally, the *apostolic* adjective describing the church translates into the term *sending*. This refers to the fact that the church was, in terms of the human dimension, formed and founded by apostles, as is again evident in John 20:19-23, where those present were the apostles of Jesus. They gleaned their title "apostles" because they had been sent out by Jesus on two occasions in the Gospel records, and again now in John 20 by the risen Christ. However, that they were called "apostles" (sent ones) gave character to the church, both defining the content of the doctrine of the church as apostolic and also giving it an identity as dynamically a "sent" or missional community, leading every Christian to embrace a fundamental identity as a sent person. This intended democratizing of apostolicity was lost, as Darrell Guder has stated, when Christianity became Christendom: "apostolicity no longer described the action of the people of God in missional engagement. Instead it meant the succession in priestly authority."[32] In a similar vein, Paul Stevens has stressed the importance of the laity as the apostolic people of God, stating, "Together the *laos* of God is the creation of God's sending and the means of his further sending."[33] This should not negate the fact that apostleship is a continuing leadership gift designed to keep the church true to its missional identity and purpose. Beyond the clearly one-off foundational identity of the Twelve, others are mentioned in the New Testament as apostles (e.g., Acts 14:14, Barnabas; Romans 16:7, Andronicus and Junia). How the church incorporates this first-mentioned, character-setting gifting, and indeed all five giftings of Ephesians 4, should be a matter for thought in the church today.[34] I suspect that these people are among us and function either informally

---

[32]Guder, *Missional Church*, p. 192.

[33]Stevens, *Other Six Days*, p. 198.

[34]Peter Wagner has written on this topic in *New Apostolic Churches*, ed. C. Peter Wagner (Ventura, Calif.: Regal, 1998) and *Churchquake: The Explosive Dynamics of the New Apostolic Revolution* (Ventura, Calif.: Regal, 1999).

as visionaries on pastoral staffs or elders boards, or more formally yet not explicitly as bishops or missionaries or denominational leaders overseeing church-planting movements. They have a bird's-eye view of the kingdom work of God and strategize new missional ventures.

CHURCH AS A CATECHETICAL COMMUNITY

Jesus came and stood among them and *said*, "Peace be with you!"
After he *said this*, he showed them his hands and side.
The disciples were overjoyed when they saw the Lord. Again
Jesus said, "Peace be with you! As the Father . . ."
JOHN 20:19-21, emphasis added

As communities of the presence of the
risen Christ who *speaks* shalom to his church,
churches will be communities of the Word.

Just as the proleptic church in John 20 heard Christ speaking shalom comfort and then commissioning them, so for churches to be communities that experience and then express shalom, the pervasive preaching and teaching of the Word is necessary. This is because in a participational view of preaching and teaching, Christ preaches through his servants such that he, the living Word, is encountered in the exposition of the written Word. Is it going too far to suggest that the relation between Word and sacrament is suggested by the consecutive events John describes at this first meeting of the proleptic church: "After he said this, he showed them his hands and side" (Jn 20:20)? Jesus' scars suggest the visual sacrament, and his speaking is the verbal sacrament of preaching.

This notion of preaching is most often associated with Karl Barth and is in keeping with the New Testament concept of preaching, as reflected in Peter's words, "If you speak, you should do so as one who speaks the very words of God" (1 Pet 4:11), and those of Paul, "My message and my preaching were not with wise and persuasive words, but with a demonstration of the Spirit's power, so that your faith might not rest on human wisdom, but on God's power" (1 Cor 2:4-5). Enabled by the Spirit the preacher becomes a conduit of the very words of God. This was the essence of preaching for Barth; preaching was a primary revelation event, for in exegetically based, Spirit-enabled preaching, the "words of man become the words of God." Barth considered preaching at its best to be the living Word speaking in the written Word. It was even seen as sacramental. Thus even the form of Scripture needed to be respected when preaching. This viewpoint was built around Barth's theology of revelation, one which not all evangelicals may affirm but which led to an expository approach that many evangelicals with a "higher view" of Scripture ironically neglect. Barth preached beyond the obsession with relevance. The preacher who is true to the text as exegeted carefully would find him- or herself relevant, for it is the text itself that is relevant.

In a similar vein, John Webster, speaking concerning Bonhoeffer's conviction that "Christian proclamation becomes relevant through *Sachlichkeit*, that is, through being bound to Scripture"[35] and that "the 'matter' of the NT is Christ present in the word," concludes with, "Crucially, this means that the task of establishing relevance is not pre- or post-exegetical: on the contrary, exegesis itself performs this task, and does so because the textual word which is the concern of exegesis is Christ's address to church and world in the potency of the Spirit."[36]

This would enable people to discover meaning in their stories outside of themselves in the Christ story. Bonhoeffer believed strongly in the importance of attentiveness to the word of God, as Webster says, "precisely because the self is not grounded in its own disposing of itself in the world, but grounded in the Word of Christ." He adds, "Reading the Bible, as Bonhoeffer puts it in *Life Together*, is a matter of finding ourselves *extra nos* in the biblical history."[37]

Of course, it is not just preaching that facilitates encountering Christ in the Scriptures. One of the crucial needs, if evangelical churches are to be sustainable missional churches who truly "make disciples," is cat-

---

[35]"*Vergegenwärtigung neutestamentlicher Texte*," in *Gesammelte Schriften* (Munich: Kaiser, 1966), 3:307, cited in John Webster, *Holy Scripture: A Dogmatic Sketch*, Current Issues in Theology (Cambridge: Cambridge University Press, 2003), p. 82.

[36]Webster, *Holy Scripture*, p. 82.

[37]Ibid., p. 83.

echizing new converts for baptism and postbaptized converts who hear the shalom word of Christ through teachers or disciple makers. Andrew Walker expresses that "What a deep church most needs today . . . is for a theology of Christian basics . . . catechesis for all beginners in the Christian life whether they be infants or adults. . . . Catechesis should be the prolegomenon to a life-long educational process in and for a deep church."[38] He insists that catechetical content should be trinitarian and gospel-centered to be life-giving. This captures the essence of our concern. There are so many resources available for this endeavor that can build on the very helpful Alpha program, moving people into baptism and on into maturity.[39]

In sum, the recovery of the evangelical church and hope for reevangelization of the West is a function of recovering the risen Christ, once-crucified, as the center and influencer of its character. This involves a change-continuity tension, imagining fresh ways of being the church that are both culturally relevant and grounded in the word, that are catholic in their orientation rather than splintering and yet innovative in fresh contextualizations, that embrace the history of the church rather than assuming all has been bad until the era of this "enlightened" generation, and yet are always reforming. In light of the recovery of Christocentric missional church life, we can achieve *both* incarnational width through cultural relevance and engagement, *and* confessional, ecclesial and spiritual depth.

[38]Walker and Bretherton, *Remembering Our Future*, p. 14.

[39]See, for example, in the Anglican tradition, "Catechisms: More than Remembering," an article by Kevin Donlan which gives an excellent apologetic for catechesis and references a number of tools (www.globalsouthanglican.org/index.php/comments/catechisms_more_than_remembering_kevin_donlan), and in the Roman Catholic tradition, *The Post-Synodal Apostolic Exhortations of John Paul*, ed. J. Michael Miller (Huntington, Ind.: Our Sunday Visitor, 1998).

6

Mission of Incarnation and Resurrection

■ ■ ■

On the evening of that first day of the week,
when the disciples were together, with the doors locked for
fear of the Jewish leaders, Jesus came and stood among
them *and said, "Peace be with you!"*

JOHN 20:19, emphasis added

The Resurrection was the first day of the New Creation!

ROSIE PERERA, summarizing Jeremy Begbie

IF THE DISCIPLES IN THAT ROOM on resurrection day were in a mist concerning their past, there was now a fog over their future. Our passage describes that moment when Jesus in risen power "came forward out of the fog to meet" them![1] It is the impact of his resurrection on them and the mission of the church that we now will explore.

We now look at how the *mission* of the church takes its character from its relational union with him, exploring two primary questions: What does it mean to be missional in light of our union as the church

---

[1]N. T. Wright, *Surprised by Hope: Rethinking Heaven, the Resurrection, and the Mission of the Church* (New York: HarperOne, 2008), pp. xiii-xiv.

with (1) the *incarnate*-risen Christ and (2) the incarnate-*risen* Christ?

The first question is this: given that the resurrection of Jesus reasserts Jesus' incarnate state and reaffirms the goodness of the created order, how do we become missional in a way that is fully creational? Mission in light of the incarnation, or as "incarnation-al," actually implies the following concepts: (1) the justification of the gospel as holistic, with the convert's telos being an appropriate world-engaging way of being, including reappropriating the dignity of work as honorable; (2) solidarity of the Christian with all humanity in light of the fact that through the incarnation God became a neighbor to all humanity; (3) the legitimacy of contextualization involving engagement with culture, or inculturation without enculturation; and (4) commitment to an ecclesial way of being. This latter concept includes commitment to being the local church in a particular space and time, in communion with the expressions of that body through all time. Because this final point is expounded in other chapters, only the first three are unpacked in this chapter.

Second, I ask, How does the church engage missionally in a way that is properly incarnational *and* properly "resurrection-al." Jesus, who was incarnate, has died and is now risen as the beginning of the new creation, as the Last Adam representing a new humanity. I noted earlier that the theme of new creation runs deeply in this passage. If that is true, then how does the church's mission move beyond being creational to be new creational? Orlando Costas, perhaps one of the most incarnational of recent evangelical missiologists, indeed, an evangelical liberationist, noted that "incarnation without resurrection is only half a mission."[2] In other words, if mission is merely solidarity with humanity but does not impart the hope of the resurrection through personal, vocational and communal transformation encountered in the now and fully in the "not yet" of the kingdom, then it is only half a mission.

---

[2]Orlando Costas, cited in Samuel H. Moffett's review of Orlando Costas, *Christ Outside the Gate* (Maryknoll, N.Y.: Orbis, 1983), in *Theology Today* 43 (1984): 214, http://theologytoday.ptsem .edu/jul1984/v43-4-bookreview4.htm.

THE INCARNATION-RESURRECTION DYNAMIC REAFFIRMS GOD'S CREATION AND CONFIRMS THE CHURCH'S MISSION AS A CREATIONAL MISSION

That Christians today would need to be informed that mission is holistic would come as a surprise to their forebears. This would have been true of Calvin, for example, whose church donated its tithes to the city's poor, and of the eighteenth- and nineteenth-century forerunners of evangelicalism. To do evangelism without also caring for the poor and building hospitals and schools would have been inconceivable to them. It is telling that it was the influence of North American fundamentalism, in reaction to the liberal Social Gospel that this new idea of mission as "evangelism only" evolved. Thankfully a return to the whole gospel for the whole person in whole communities has occurred, though warnings like that of Orlando Costas still need to be heeded: "When people claim to be born of the Spirit and then icily continue to turn their backs on the outcast and disenfranchised, then it is time for us to ask whether they have been born of the Spirit of the crucified Christ or of the spirit of the antichrist."[3]

Justification of holism and world-engaging mission. When God created the world he said that it was "good." The fact that God the Son became human in a real created body, that he reconciled all things in heaven and earth in that body, and was raised and has ascended in that body reaffirms that created matter is good.[4] A Christian theology of mission therefore is inherently creational, world-affirming and holistic, and it moves us to engage the world to seek the whole personhood and full humanization of each person. It is concerned with evangelism *and* compassion *and* justice, and with both local and global contexts (the eschatological horizon of mission). The mission of the Christian church is to be undergirded by the telos of God for humanity, that is, what he intended when he created humans in the image of God and more particularly when he sent the last Adam to be its fulfillment and archetype.

---

[3]Orlando Costas, *Liberating News: A Theology of Contextual Evangelization* (Grand Rapids: Eerdmans, 1989), p. 82.

[4]This notion is expressed eloquently in Oliver O'Donovan, *Resurrection and the Moral Order*, 2nd ed. (Leicester, U.K.: Apollos, 1994).

To use Irenaeus's words, this incarnation-resurrection dynamic shapes mission to be a participation in God's work, which has as its goal the forming of human persons "fully alive," that is, in his image and likeness as recapitulated in Jesus.[5] The matter of mission is the redemption and restoration of humans to be persons-in-relation, fully alive, and not escape from their humanity.

Christian mission operates with awareness of the nature of the human being as made in the image of God (imago Dei) as recapitulated in Christ.

The anthropological theme of the image of God in Scripture is an important theme in mission, given that its fully Christological understanding defines the aim of mission. Humans, as they exist today, are the product of three influences: creation in the image of God; the Fall, which defaced and distorted the image; and the process of restoration of that image in Christ.

First, then, humanity was created in the image of God (Gen 1:26-27), and all humans since are likewise made in the same image. That image has been blurred and rendered eccentric (off-center) by the Fall. However, the Fall did not destroy or obliterate the image of God (Gen 9:6). Even Augustine, Calvin and others in the Reformed tradition who emphasize the debilitating effects of sin nevertheless concede that fallen human beings still reflect the image of God in their intellect, affections, community life and culture.[6] Karl Barth, for example, makes the clear and helpful distinction in section 45 of the *Dogmatics* that our humanity is something ontically good and that sin cannot alienate us from that declared goodness (Gen 1).

All humans, therefore, irrespective of religion, race, color or gender, as made in the image of God and as one with the true man (*verus homo*) Jesus, are to be accorded full human rights and treated with dignity and the privileges of nutrition, education, meaningful work and just legal

---

[5]"The glory of God is man fully alive, and the life of man is the vision of God. If the revelation of God through creation already brings life to all living beings on the earth, how much more will the manifestation of the Father by the Word bring life to those who see God" (Irenaeus, *Against Heresies* 4.20.7, ANF 1:469).

[6]It is for this reason that "total inability" is a preferred term to "total depravity," which sounds as though all humans are as bad as they possibly can be and are unable to reflect anything God at all.

recourse. This doctrine of human rights based in the creation of all humans in the image of God, as reaffirmed by the incarnation, has been at the center of Western civilization. Regrettably, secular advocacy of rights is expressed without awareness that the underpinnings are in fact "borrowed capital" from the Christian heritage of this civilization. It is indeed quite hard to imagine an ontological grounding for human rights other than that based in a common Creator who has made all humans equal. The church is called in its Christian mission to influence society to protect the rights of all human beings. These privileges help in part to define the telos of Christian mission. There is more than that involved, but certainly not less.

What then constitutes the difference between the Christian and the non-Christian? Clearly it is not the question of being human or having human rights. The difference relates to becoming *fully* human, as Christ defined that. One way to look at this is to say that all humans are in a condition of *relatedness* to God as creatures to the Creator-Reconciler (whether they are consciously aware of this or not), but not all are in conscious *relationship* with God. Furthermore, all humans, as a result of Christ's assumption of humanity as an ontic entity and his vicarious humanity and death on its behalf, are *ontically* or at least, by the design of God, the new humanity in Christ, the true image of God. However, only those who acknowledge Christ by faith are brought into noetic participation with the last Adam, become the church, and by the Spirit's restoration begin to be re-formed into the fullness of the image of God in Christ. The consummation of that process will be in the kingdom to come, where all in Christ will be glorified (Rom 8:30) and be "like him" (1 Jn 3:1-2) who is the "image of the invisible God" (Col 1:15). Mission must therefore be conducted in a manner that is respectful of the design and destiny of all humanity in Christ.

One obvious consequence of awareness that all humans are made in the image of God is that coercion and manipulative techniques for mission/evangelism will be avoided in that they ethically violate what Christians believe about the dignity of all humans. Mission as participation in what God is doing leads the Christian missioner to dialogue and persuade in the Spirit's power, but to avoid manipulative ways that violate others' personhood. Converts are mysteriously made willing to be made willing. They are resurrected spiritually by the work of regeneration, having "the formal capacity to receive the material capacity" for it. In all this, human instruments of mission are important, but they work only as God works, and God works in their work.

The difference being a Christian makes is not to have more or less human rights or more or less native intellectual ability than any other human. Rather the difference has to do with an aliveness to the God of creation-reconciliation and a sense of shalom arising from consciously functioning as God's vice regents in this world, in relationship with him. It is to receive the gift of spiritual responsiveness to God (regeneration) and a right relationship with God (justification) and to undergo lifelong transformation (sanctification) into the fullness of the image of God seen in Christ, completed in the consummation (glorification).

We have anticipated an important question: *What is the nature of the image of God (imago Dei)?* We now consider this question in three dynamics (creation, fall, restoration in Christ) seeking to answer the crucial missional question, how do fallen humans become human persons "fully alive"? This has a Christological orientation, not only in light of John 20 (the new creation dawns here!) but in light of the overall manner in which this issue is resolved in Christ.

Humans are formed by the image of God. Much ink has been spilled in the Christian tradition on what the image of God in humans actually means. There are three main clusters of interpretation, as derived from the Genesis text in the wider context of biblical revelation: these entail the ideas of *relationality* (the relational view), *reason* (the substantial or structural view) and *rule/reign*, which includes being coworkers with God in his ongoing reign over creation (the functional view).[7] The reason for this variety of opinion relates to the brevity of the Genesis reference and the paucity of references to the term elsewhere. Jeremy Kidwell has wisely commented that "appreciation for the polyvalence of

---

[7]Stanley Grenz offered a slightly different classification involving the structural view, the relational view and the dynamic view. See Stanley Grenz, *Theology for the Community of God* (Grand Rapids: Eerdmans, 2000), p. 169.

the doctrine allows for a composite meaning."[8] Even so, most theologians have opted for the elevation of one of these viewpoints as primary, even if polyvalence is evident.

1. Imago *as relationality of persons*. The first viewpoint is that the image has to do with relationality, specifically the notion of humans as "persons-in-relation." God as revealed in the Old Testament is profoundly covenantal and relational, and the triune being of Yahweh as revealed fully in the New Testament is confirmed to be essentially relational, so, inevitably, human beings made in his image are "in relatedness" to God and are therefore relational beings. The first man and woman were made "facing God," if you like, and they are immediately spoken of as facing each other in gendered relationship ("male and female created he them" is explicatory of the phrase *image of God*). At an ontological level this means that by the very act of being created by God, humans are related to God as creature to Creator and in relatedness to their fellow human.

Prior to the Fall this ontology corresponded with an actual relational intimacy between God and Adam and Eve, between each other and between themselves and creation. Furthermore, in that a stated purpose of the creation of humans is ruling on behalf of God in creation, the *imago Dei* seems to mean that humans were made with the capacity for relationship with God so that reigning over his creation is done in communion with him as his coworkers. This did necessitate the use of reason. Thus relationality takes precedence over and is foundational to the structural and functional aspects of the *imago*.

2. Imago *as reason*. Primarily, this structural view entails the human capacity for reason as self-reflection and self-love, following Augustine, who conceived the Trinity according to a psychological analogy in which the Son is the Father's self-reflection and vice versa, and the Spirit is the self-love or mutual love of the Father for the Son and vice versa. More broadly it relates to human intellect, emotions and volition, although even bodily features, such as uprightness, have a place in the tradition. A primary concern motivating the structural view has been

---

[8]Jeremy Kidwell, "Elucidating the Image of God: An Analysis of the *Imago Dei* in the Work of Colin E. Gunton and John Zizioulas," master's thesis, Regent College, 2009.

the distinguishing of humans from the rest of the animal creation.

If the relational dynamic is primary, what is the relationship between reason and the relationship of humans with God? Reason is not anywhere stated as a feature of the image of God in Scripture, yet it seems implicit that human intellectual, emotional and volitional capacities image these personal capacities in God and are necessary for relationship with him. The primacy of love over knowledge expressed in biblical passages (1 Cor 8:1; 13:1-2) and the fact that loving God with the mind is a subcategory of the Great Commandment to love God point both to the primacy of relationality and yet to the validation of reason as a component of the *imago*. A key issue within the structural view is how the capacity for reason is affected by the loss of relationship with God. There are a number of New Testament passages which suggest that the cognitive capacity for relationship with God has been removed by the Fall and that spiritual resurrection or regeneration is needed for their recovery (Eph 2:1-10; 1 Cor 2:14-16; 2 Cor 4:3-6). The distinction between relatedness and relationship is of value here, however. It is not the case that the IQ of Christians is any higher or lower than those of non-Christians. The structural view has value in that it helps to describe human capacities and indeed human rights (Gen 9:6 speaks, post-Fall, of the value of human life as a consequence of the creation of humans in the image of God) that have not been affected by the Fall. These are ontic and are a consequence of humanity's relatedness to God by creation and providence, whether humans are spiritually awakened or not.

3. Imago *as participative, caring rule.* The "ruling" (stewardship) aspect of the image of God is evident in the first reference to the *imago* in Genesis 1:26: "Then God said, 'Let us make human beings in our image, in our likeness, *so that* they may rule over the fish in the sea and the birds in the sky, over the livestock and all the wild animals, and over all the creatures that move along the ground" (emphasis added). However, the creation act that forms humans in relation to their Creator precedes and therefore qualifies the ruling function, as does the emphasis on the inherent relationality of humans as gendered (v. 27b). In communion with God and with each other, as male and female in un-

conflicted complementarity humans were commanded to manage creation as its stewards.

That this command of God, sometimes called the cultural mandate, included the creation orders of marriage and family and work (v. 28), is explicit here and again in Genesis 2: "The LORD God took the man and put him in the Garden of Eden to work it and take care of it" (v. 15). The nature of the ruling function of the human in the *imago* is thus qualified by submissive relationship with God, as defined by the cultural mandate, in a state of shalom. This is the first commission ever given to humanity, not the Great Commission of Matthew 28 or John 20, and not even the Great Commandment of Matthew 22. It is of great interest, however, that the notion of shalom is central in the commissioning of our Johannine context, perhaps indicative of the wide scope of the sending by Jesus. All this leads to another important principle of the mission of the church and the Christian:

> *Christian mission operates within the context of the cultural mandate of Genesis 1–2, and not in isolation from it.*

It is critical for the church to see evangelism within the wider context of the shalom experience and expression of the people of God, that is, within the creational/cultural mandate of Genesis 2 and the relationality of the Great Commandment. The helpful paradigm set by Rick Warren in *The Purpose-Driven Church*, which placed the Great Commission within the circle of the Great Commandment, requires a wider circle yet—that of the cultural mandate (see fig. 6.1). Mission most certainly includes evangelism, but its wider aim is the recovery of the humanness of humanity as this was anticipated in creation and recapitulated in Christ. Humanization is the goal of mission, not merely the saving of "souls."

The Great Commission facilitates the return of alienated humans into relationship with God, in turn enabling the cultural mandate to be carried out in relational participation with God. Figure 6.1 intentionally places the cultural mandate at the circumference because this is the goal of the Great Commission and the Great Commandment, that is, the goal of Christian mission. This goal is not only that people are reconciled to God as the church carries out the Great Commission. Reconciliation also brings the convert into the journey of loving God and neighbor, and fulfilling the mandate to exercise loving stewardship over creation through work and in all aspects of the human endeavor. The aim of mission thus is Christian humanism. Mission that focuses purely on evangelism is truncated and misses the trajectory of divine intention for humanity. The humanization entailed in mission is of

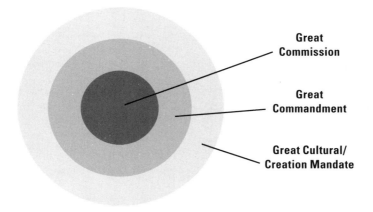

Figure 6.1. Christian mission in the context of the Great Commandment and the Cultural Mandate

course, not possible apart from the One human in whom humanity was recapitulated—Christ. It is this Christological theme that keeps creation and covenant together, and therefore demands that evangelism and rehumanization, through education, employment and justice, be kept together also.

There is another way to view figure 6.1 that has to do with the church's effectiveness in mission. If we move from the outer to the inner circles, we get the sense of the pathway by which most humans are brought to Christ. It usually begins with noticing Christians who truly live in the shalom which the outer circle represents. The sense of shalom demonstrated in the work and family lives of Christians is attractive. This resonates with the picture of the disciples in John 20 receiving shalom from Jesus on new creation morning. Living in the shalom of the second circle and expressing love to our neighbor is also usually crucial in the journey of unbelievers toward faith. Christians thus engage in loving friendships with their neighbors in work, homes and communities, hoping for their conversion but loving them unconditionally.

On being asked the difficult question, which of the three circles of mission comes first? there is no easy answer. Clearly all three would be in operation at once. The triquetra which imperfectly depicts the coinherent relations of the Trinity is an apt depiction of this (see fig. 6.2).[9]

The notion of mission is related to the concept of vocation. Klaus Bockmuehl conceived the wedding cake analogy for the three aspects of vocation that characterize the work of being human. First, as the bottom layer is what he termed *human vocation*. This involves the cultural mandate and within it the creation orders of marriage, family and

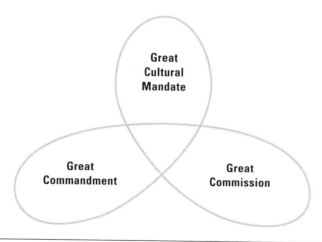

Figure 6.2. **The triquetra of missional commandments**

work. This is a mandate given by the Creator God for all humans. Mission must help restore the human being in all these critical areas that define him or her in the image of God, so that he or she may become the human being fully alive. This corresponds to the cultural

---

[9]I am indebted to Sandeep Jadhav for this insight.

mandate commandment in figure 6.2. The second layer of the vocational wedding cake is the *Christian vocation*, which may be summarized as the Great Commandment in its two inseparable facets, love of
God and love of neighbor, with a special concern for my neighbor in
need, or the poor and marginalized. This layer is, for obvious reasons,
associated with Christ. The unregenerate person cannot do this. These
commandments of course sum up the whole of Christian ethics. The
top layer of the cake represents *individual vocation*. This has to do with
the particular calling of the Christian concerning the nature of the
work they are called to and where they are called to fulfill this work.
This is associated with the person of the Holy Spirit, because it is as the
Spirit gifts and leads persons that they discover their individual vocation. This is a valid area of concern, but it can be overly emphasized
in an individualistic manner at the expense of the general moral will of
God and the creation commands. Irrespective of what a particular
calling may be, each Christian person will discover what it means to be

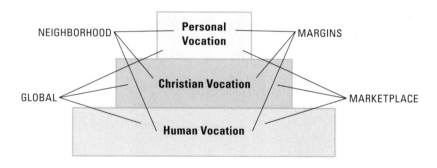

**Figure 6.3. The four loci of mission in the missional church and their
relation to vocation**

missional in the full-orbed sense of that term, whether he or she is a
pastor, layperson, janitor or CEO. This is diagrammed in figure 6.3.

When considering the mission of the church, all these concepts seem
to boil down to four aspects or quadrants that fill out the fullness of its
mission.[10] These must of course be deeply intertwined and are insepa-

---

[10]I am indebted to Wayne J. Kirkland of Wellington, New Zealand, who crystallized these
concepts for me in private conversation.

rable, but they can be distinguished as mission to the margins, the neighbor, the marketplace and the global. These are diagrammed in figure 6.4.

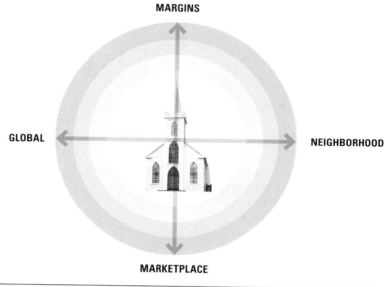

Figure 6.4. The four loci of mission in the missional church

A theology of work is inherent in the functional view of the *imago*. In Genesis 1 God himself worked for six days of creation and then, at the end of that day, passed the baton to his vice regent, humankind, to continue the work of creation and its management. Various forms of work emerge in the early chapters of Genesis, some to do with agriculture, primitive science and the arts (Gen 4:2, 17-22). Our call and our desire to work is a function of our createdness. Our work matters because it is done in partnership with God and because it fulfils his desire for the earth and its full development. God invented work. It is not a consequence of the Fall. The Fall brings a dose of reality to work, making it fraught with challenges like vocational ambivalence, frustration, boredom and management-union tensions. But the actual reality of work is a fulfillment of God's creation or cultural mandate. The New Testament makes some very specific statements about work and the workplace that are designed to restore God's intent for human work. Work will no doubt be our lot when humanity is glorified in Christ in the new creation.

In sum, relatedness to God is the dominant of the three aspects of the *imago* in that it precedes and qualifies the structural and functional aspects. It is in rediscovering relationship with God in Christ that we as humans will again fully image the triune God. All humans are related ontologically to God because he created all. All therefore have intellectual capacity and human rights, ethically speaking. But not all are in relationship with God through Jesus. It is as we live in union and communion with Christ, the true image of the invisible God, that we can fulfill God's creation mandate. Before discussing the nature of that mandate in more explicit ways, however, a second force at work in the forming (deforming) of human beings needs to be considered.

Humans are distorted by the Fall. Sin is the second influence that is at work in human persons, to cloud, twist and distort the image of God in them.

If we adopt the language of Irenaeus, we have by sin lost not the image of God but the likeness of God, the former relating to human capacities such as freedom and responsibility and the latter to moral character. Others prefer to see these terms as interchangeable and suggest that the image or likeness of God in humans has by sin become effaced, but not erased. Alternatively we can say that the spiritual capacity for relationship with God has been deadened by the Fall, but that the relatedness remains, as do the ontological capacities for reason and rule, although sin does affect the telos toward which these function. The presence of conflict where there was once shalom is another way of looking at the Fall. This is apparent in Genesis 3 with regard to the relationship between God and humans, to the relationship between the genders and to the area of work.

Whereas the Eastern tradition has tended to articulate the Fall in terms of the immaturity of the human race and its redemption as the movement toward maturity, the Western tradition, and particularly the Reformed wing of it, has articulated a much more serious, endemic and sin-oriented view of the Fall. The latter tradition expresses this as "total depravity," which in the tradition of Calvin is actually better expressed as "total inability" for relationship with God. It is not that in Calvin's theology humans are as bad as they possibly can be but that all are unable to respond to God relationally apart from the intervention of divine grace through the regenerating work of the Spirit. The ontological or structural aspects of the *imago* remain, albeit they are tarnished.

The question of the locus of the *imago* in the reasoning capacity, and specifically as that relates to discerning right and wrong, is a key issue in the Fall. The desire that enticed Adam and Eve was to "be like God, knowing good and evil" (Gen 3:5). It was the place of reason in ethical knowing, specifically reason outside of a faith relationship with God, that expressed the essence of sin. As Bonhoeffer so eloquently indicated, the pursuit of ethics, or being good and doing the good, outside of embeddedness and participation in the self-revealing God in Christ is futility.[11] Ethics can either be the very antithesis of the gospel or the very content of the gospel. Ethics that are not grounded in who God is as the triune, covenant-keeping God, and that are not evangelical, that is, enabled and shaped by the gospel, are an expression of self-righteousness and futility. It is this precise futility into which the Fall plunged humanity in its endless obsession with right and wrong. The missional church lives into personal and communal moral formation in union with Christ and seeks to influence communal and national justice as an outflow of this evangelical orientation toward ethics.

Mission must address the locus of the image of God in all of these areas: reconciliation for humans alienated from God and each other. It brings the essence of shalom into the areas where humanity is most conflicted—human to human relationships, as these are epitomized in the gender relationship, vocational struggles, all aspects of our embodied state and knowing in general and ethics in particular. This can only be accomplished in relationship with the triune God, in Christ the true *imago* and by the Spirit who fashions Christ in us as persons-in-relation and as ecclesial communities, who in *ekstasis* influence the world in all these arenas. So what is to be done for us to recover our

---

[11]Dietrich Bonhoeffer, *Works*, vol. 6, *Ethics*, trans. R. Krauss, C. C. West, and D. Scott, ed. Clifford Green (Minneapolis: Augsburg Fortress, 2005), pp. 47-55.

personhood-in-relation, our secure identity, our profound connect-edness to spouses and friends, our joy in work, our moral sense? The answer lies in the incarnation of the true *imago*, Jesus Christ.

Re-formed in Jesus: Jesus for us and we in Jesus, as the image of God. We should not imagine that God was taken by surprise by the failures of Adam and Eve, or that God did some serious handwringing when he discovered how his experiment had worked out. God's plan was from eternity to redeem a fallen world. Various passages (Acts 2:23; 4:28; Heb 5; Rev 13:8) indicate that Jesus was assigned within eternity past to enter humanity and become the last or *eschatos* Adam and redeem humanity by becoming one with that humanity so that humans might become one with him. This was always God's intent.

Irenaeus articulated the notion that the last Adam, Jesus, was in fact God's first intent for humanity. Jonathan Edwards much later ex-pressed the idea that what God reveals last he often intended first.[12] It was in the man Christ Jesus that humans would be what God intended them to be. What is stated by way of intention for the first Adam is recapitulated in the last Adam. Significantly, Christ is spoken of as the last Adam, not the "second Adam." The sense of "last" or *eschatos* conveys an ultimacy of purpose on God's part, for not only is it true that there are no more, he was the first intended anyway.

The human capacity to rule wisely is recovered in Christ and those in him. All humans can exercise care for creation and work to that end, but only those who have discovered life in Christ can do this fully alive in themselves and fully alive to God's present and eternal kingdom purposes. In the fullness of the eschaton the whole creation will be re-stored in shalom. If that is the aim of the kingdom of God, it is what the church is to pursue now, as the sign, foretaste and servant of the kingdom of God. People of the kingdom are to work consciously in participation with Christ the worker and as unto God. They are to work with an eye to how their work meets the needs of human com-munity and how their work affects creation. Industries that rape cre-ational resources will be the subject of kingdom scrutiny. The church

---

[12]Jonathan Edwards, *Dissertation I: Concerning the End for Which God Created the World*, vol. 8, *The Works of Jonathan Edwards* (New Haven, Conn.: Yale University Press, 1957-2003), pp. 405ff.

will be leading the environment charge, not lamely following it. Not because creation is God but because it was created by God as good and reaffirmed by the resurrection. Paul's stated intent is that all creation will one day be reconciled and renewed, not destroyed. This is the justification of the holism of mission in the incarnation of Christ. But the incarnation has a second consequence for mission, that of the solidarity of the Christian with all humanity.

Solidarity of the Christian with all humanity. If the *imago* is from its inception a relational reality, calling humans toward the telos of reflecting the Trinity as persons-in-relation, the incarnation reinforced this concept and provided the means toward the redemption and reconciliation of humans alienated from God and each other. Karl Barth's emphasis on the incarnation in theology found a particular emphasis with respect to mission in the "neighbor principle." By the incarnation God in his Son became a neighbor to all humanity. This reality provides an added incentive for Christians to love their neighbor globally and locally. Karl Barth did not go as far as Karl Rahner in suggesting that all human beings are "anonymous Christians," but in light of the solidarity of God with all humanity, he was comfortable with the term *designated Christians*. In commenting on what love of neighbor means, and in particular as that is determined by its relationship to the other half of the one Great Commandment (a "duality-in-unity"), Oliver O'Donovan brings together the responsibility of all Christians to include both evangelism and social justice in their missional lives:

> We must be wary, on the one hand, of evangelistic zeal that ignores all aspects of the neighbour's being, and on the other hand, give consideration to the possibility that repudiation of evangelism which is fashionable in some ecclesiastical circles may in fact reveal a refusal to take the neighbour's vocation seriously.[13]

But O'Donovan has a point to make beyond considering that all humans need to be evangelized in light of God's saving disposition toward them. The relationship of the love-neighbor command to the love-God command, especially in light of its weighty Christological

---

[13]O'Donovan, *Resurrection and the Moral Order*, p. 229.

reassertion, promotes the only true grounding for the doctrine of universal humans rights. Love of neighbor has no meaning were it not for God and love of him. The common origin of myself and my neighbor is in God by creation. The common end of myself and my neighbor, according to the gospel, is the high calling and destiny of fellowship with God. Were these assertions not true, love of neighbor would not have any ontological grounding. It would collapse into one of two possible corruptions: the tyrannizing of our fellow human or the enslavement of the self to the fellow human.[14]

Contextualization which involves engagement with culture or inculturation without enculturation. Another significant aspect of human existence that is addressed by the incarnation and the call to be incarnational is the communal dimension of culture. The presence of humans in community with one another produces culture. The etiology of human culture, formed by human persons together, unsurprisingly arises from the same sources—the image of God, on the one hand, and sin on the other. All cultures reflect both the beauty of God and the ugliness of sin. The relationship between culture and Christ is complex. H. Richard Niebuhr's classical yet controversial definition of five ways in which Christians have seen this relationship is well known. These may be summarized as the antagonist, accommodationist, synthesist, paradoxical and transformational views.[15] Each can be divided into

---

[14]Ibid., p. 230.

[15]H. Richard Niebuhr (1894-1962), in *Christ and Culture* (New York: Harper & Row, 1951) outlined these five types. He outlines five prevalent viewpoints:

1. "Christ against Culture": all culture is to be rejected as it is the product of the "world" and satanic control. This is the extreme of dissociation from culture.

2. "Christ of Culture": the extreme of uncritical accommodation of all culture.

3. "Christ above Culture": Christ is transcendent above culture, but as he himself acted within culture, he directs us to do likewise and to be subject to divinely instituted representatives. Culture is the product of human nature created in God's image, was pronounced as "very good" and even though fallen is still subject to God. Christians are simultaneously in and yet beyond the world, leading people to salvation in heaven yet encouraging all that is best in this world's culture. Strong emphasis on natural law and common grace to all humanity. This is the first of three attempts to synthesize Christ and culture. It stresses the good in culture over its fallenness.

4. "Christ and Culture in Paradox": Christ is Lord over one kingdom that has two realms, that of the world, which requires the moral law to curb sin, and that of the church, which has no need of moral law as guide consisting of free lords who are under grace not law. A complete synthesis of Christ and culture on earth, such as in Christendom, is not possible. Christians

subcategories. For example, the extent to which transformation of culture and society may occur even within the fifth view may vary considerably. In light of the incarnational-resurrection perspective offered here, I suggest that a category somewhere between the fourth and the fifth view, or one at the realistic end of the fifth view, may be somewhat congruent. John Howard Yoder expressed the complexity of the church's relationship in a well nuanced way:

> Some elements of culture the church categorically rejects (pornography, tyranny, cultic idolatry). Other dimensions of culture it accepts within clear limits (economic production, commerce, the graphic arts, paying taxes for peacetime civil government). To still other dimensions of culture Christian faith gives a new motivation and coherence (agriculture, family life, literacy, conflict resolution, empowerment). Still others it strips of their claims to possess autonomous truth and value, and uses them as vehicles of communication (philosophy, language, Old Testament ritual, music). Still other forms of culture are created by the Christian churches (hospitals, service of the poor, generalized education, egalitarianism, abolitionism, feminism).[16]

A return to Constantinianism, or the synthesis which undergirded Christendom, is not realistic or even necessarily desirable. A healthy dose of realism is needed, based on the fact that human culture crucified the Son of God. Yet it is the church's role to be a "salt and light" force within culture, preserving it from its fallenness and corruption, to do so primarily as the open, ecclesial community of the risen Christ

---

nevertheless are subject to both realms as they still sin in this life (*simul iustus et peccator*) and are therefore also obedient to temporal civil law. This is still a synthesis view also, but is more culturally conservative one that takes the fallenness of culture more seriously. It stresses the "not yet" as opposed to the "already" view of the kingdom. Preservation of society more than transformation.

5. "Christ Transforming Culture": Christ is capable of redeeming fallen culture as it is inherently good as created and capable of reform. He does so by grace through his church which offers an alternative culture and influences the world from the inside-out accordingly. Known as the "conversionist" view, it looks to the possibility of present renewal rather than with conservation of what has been given in creation or with preparing for what will be given in a final redemption. It stresses the "already" aspect of the kingdom of God. It looks toward participation now in the new creation.

[16]John Howard Yoder, "How H. Richard Niebuhr Reasoned: A Critique of Christ and Culture," in *Authentic Transformation: A New Vision of Christ and Culture*, ed. Glen H. Stassen, D. M. Yeager and John Howard Yoder (Nashville: Abingdon, 1996), p. 69.

offering a holy and harmonious culture, influencing from the inside out. It is the church's role also to speak evangelically into the public square on matters of justice and aesthetics whenever it has a place there, to participate in all shalom-bringing ventures with other humans doing so, to offer alternative forms of culture as was the case with the art and music which came in Medieval and Renaissance eras from within the church, to bear the cross when our attempts from the inside out at preservation and transformation are rejected, and in doing all this, to function as the incarnational-resurrection community of Christ, the sign, servant and messenger of the kingdom to come, which is already here and yet which universal resurrection will bring to completion.

What has just been described is an integral part of Christian mission in light of the cultural mandate, and it applies to churches in all cultures in all times. However, a view of culture as both a good product of the *imago Dei*, and fallenness, has repercussions for the Great Commission also, or how the gospel is affirmed and proclaimed in mission across cultures. In light of the incarnation, which led God the Son to live and work and reveal himself within the particularities of Jewish human culture, and in light of the fact that his apostles were able to communicate his resurrection and message across the Greco-Roman cultures, I am convinced that the gospel can be contextualized in all human cultures. The free act of God in the incarnation, by the cross, resurrection and the coming of the Spirit, has brought Christians into union with Christ such that they are now the continuation of his incarnational mission. This facilitates ongoing acts of contextualization as the gospel has been brought to nation after nation and people group after people group. This is evidence of the veracity of Christianity that it is culturally transferrable and that it can and should reinforce what is good and beautiful in cultures. We can pursue mission confidently in culturally appropriate ways, for as Andrew Walls affirms, the Christian church has "developed ever-growing pluriformity, taking root in culture after culture, while preserving the essential nonnegotiable and transcultural objective core of the gospel."[17] That such has not always been

---

[17]Andrew F. Walls, *The Missionary Movement in Christian History: Studies in the Transmission of Faith* (Maryknoll, N.Y.: Orbis, 1996). Christopher Wright, *The Mission of God* (Downers

the case is a commentary on the failure of missioners to be aware that their own brand of Christianity was culturally conditioned and that there was value and beauty in the host cultures they were sent to.

Indian Christian Sadhu Sundar Singh once spoke eloquently to this concern: "This is what I have been trying to say to missionaries from abroad. You have been offering the water of life to the people of India in a foreign cup, and we have been slow to receive it. If you will offer it in our own cup—in an indigenous form—then we are much more likely to accept it."[18] Sadly, much Protestant mission in the modern mission movement falls largely into what missiologist Paul Hiebert terms "the era of non-contextualization . . . roughly from 1800 to 1950."[19] The missiological paradigm that characterizes this period is encapsulated in "the doctrine of *tabula rasa*, i.e., the missionary doctrine that there is nothing in the non-Christian culture on which the Christian missionary can build and, therefore, every aspect of the traditional non-Christian culture had to be destroyed before Christianity could be built up." This unfortunate missiological paradigm is rooted ideologically in colonialism, with its belief in the superiority of Western culture and the firm enmeshment of Christianity in Western civilization. It was further enhanced by the cultural anthropology of its time; as Hiebert points out, "anthropologists until 1915 spoke of 'culture,' not of 'cultures.' They saw all cultures as different stages of development of the same thing; some were more advanced and others more primitive."[20] Small wonder that the missionaries did not make a concerted effort in contextualizing the gospel. Sadly many churches in our present culture resist contextualization for similar reasons.

Contextual theology seeks to interact and dialogue with cultural values, social change, social location, ethnic identity, and present and past conflicts. Contextualization is more than a tool for evangelism; it

---

Grove, Ill.: InterVarsity Press, 2006), p. 46 n. 20. The work of Martha Franks in this area is also highlighted by Wright.

[18]Sadhu Sundar Singh, cited in K. P. Yohannan, *Revolution in World Missions* (Carrollton, Tex.: Gospel for Asia, 2001), p. 144.

[19]Paul G. Hiebert, "Critical Contextualization," *International Bulletin of Missionary Research* 11, no. 3 (1987): 104.

[20]Ibid., 104-5.

goes far beyond the mere identification of cultural metaphors in the receptor culture which then may serve as bridges for communicating the gospel. Rather, contextualization is a matter of identifying the very worldview undergirding the culture and working to subvert this worldview by way of investing it with Christian content.[21] While the contextualization of the gospel is crucial for the task of evangelism, it is just as important for the health of the local church and for teaching. Hiebert makes the observation that noncontextualization ultimately leads to syncretism. Deeply ingrained cultural patterns do not simply die out with conversion but go underground and keep on impinging both on the life of the individual believer and the church.

With respect to the West in particular, what *are* the contextualizations required in a postmodern context?

- a humble posture of "faith seeking understanding," which has always been theology at its best

- presenting Christianity as a metanarrative, yet one that is not oppressive[22]

- a story of trinitarian love—presenting a gospel of the God who is in his being most fundamentally love

- a story of the Father heart of God

- a story of the incarnate Son of God—a God who has become one with humanity, who is not distant from our suffering and plight

- a story and a gospel of an incarnation and death that expressed solidarity with the poor

- a story of a servant, crucified Christ, who is truly represented by servant, crucified Christians in churches that serve their communities

- a story told in reliance on the Spirit, who through us and the Word

---

[21]This reflects the work of Dean Flemming in his fourfold assertion of contextualization as affirmation, relativization, confrontation and transformation (Dean Flemming, *Contextualization in the New Testament: Patterns for Theology and Mission* [Downers Grove, Ill: InterVarsity Press, 2005], p. 151).

[22]Not all may agree that Christianity is in fact a metanarrative, depending on how this term may be defined. See, for example, Merold Westphal, *Overcoming Onto-Theology: Toward a Postmodern Christian Faith* (New York: Fordham University Press, 2001).

pronounced brings regeneration, not by human coercion or argumentation but by his sovereign and gracious wooing

- a story told with fundamental respect for the human person being addressed in nonmanipulative fashion, and that seeks restoration of the full humanity of persons (not just salvation from sin's judgment) that emphasizes the primal filial (not just the forensic intentions of God)

- a story lived out in communal life that is attractive because it is fraught with the love of God and hospitality. Though this community is open for relations with all, it is loving enough to seek the transformation of all within it; its love like God's is unconditioned, but not unconditional.

Having considered the relevance of the incarnation of Jesus toward various aspects of humanity and human culture, and therefore toward mission, we now examine what difference the resurrection makes.

THE INCARNATION-RESURRECTION DYNAMIC AFFIRMS THAT CHRISTIAN MISSION IS A NEW CREATIONAL MISSION

The incarnation-resurrection dynamic (Jesus was as fully human raised from the dead to form a new humanity) affirms that Christian mission is a *new* creational mission. That is, it remains creational in its focus, but with a new creation in mind, one which transcends the old in beauty and wonder. The gospel will make us fully the new humanity.

The resurrection body of Christ, as revealed to the disciples in John 20, had a spiritual and heavenly orientation, with both a continuity with his preresurrection earthy body, reflected in his wounds and in the fact that they recognized him, and a discontinuity related to the new creation, as indicated by his miraculous entrance.[23] That his resurrection (and now ascended) body had capacities his kenotic body did not, is hinted at elsewhere in the postresurrection narratives. This new

---

[23]William Hendricksen records antisupernaturalist opinions on how Jesus entered (*NT Commentary: Exposition of the Gospel According to John* [Grand Rapids: Baker, 1954], p. 458). For most conservative scholars, there are two main opinions. He entered miraculously because his resurrection body had the capacity to pass through matter, having a spiritual orientation or even ubiquity, or that he passed through the door by miraculously unlocking it.

capacity is a consequence of the *communicatio idiomatum* (the exchange of the properties of divinity and humanity in the one Person, Jesus Christ, by the hypostatic union) on one account, or, more likely, just in the nature of a new order of creation. The immediate point for us is that the incarnate body of Jesus was still extant but now in a resurrected, "new creation" form. *That resurrected body signified the trajectory of the gospel for humanity*, which is resurrectional transformation beginning in the "now" through new birth and sanctification that affects all of life to be fully fulfilled through bodily resurrection when Christ returns in the kingdom to come, the new creation.

Two foundational texts and one crucial chapter form my thinking on this subject: Genesis 1:26-27 in total biblical context, Colossians 1:15 in context, and Hebrews 2. The latter two texts reveal that only Christ, the God-Man, truly fulfills the concept and reality of the image of God on earth, and that only in oneness with him can humanity become the fullness of that image. There are two aspects of that union. The first is ontological. The Son of God became one with humanity as an ontic entity by his incarnation. He has sisters and brothers because he entered their humanity. The intent of this was that he might be, and vicariously, for humanity. Thus, his life was lived vicariously for humanity, his death was the atonement for humanity, his resurrection results in the resurrection of humanity, and his ascension took humanity into the Godhead. He sits at the right hand of the Father as the man for humanity, the one who reigns invisibly over the earth through his church, which is the sign and servant of the kingdom that has already come, and who will yet reign visibly in his kingdom fully come. The rule over creation depicted in the *imago Dei* is thus entrusted to Christ and the new humanity in him. In this sense, Jesus is the man *for* us.

However, where the ontic union of humans with Christ is acknowledged, believing humans participate consciously with God through Christ. In this participatory relationship, Christ is not just *for* us but *in* us, one with Christ in a *relational* sense, not just a *relatedness* sense. Through faith, humans are brought into union with Christ and experience the spiritual regeneration that the bodily resurrection of Jesus pictures (Tit 3:5). Thus, humans not only enter into the reality that they are justified through the death and resurrection of Jesus (Rom 4:25), as a consequence of *his* union with humanity by the incarnation, but also they enter into life, resurrection life, as a result of *their* union with Christ.

I stress again, all humans have *relatedness* to God and have rights and dignity. This is the foundation of a Christian ethic for all humanity. However, those who come into *relationship* with God through Christ can become not just persons but human persons fully alive! This picture of Jesus in John 20 in a resurrection body is precisely that of a human person fully alive, and the picture of his disciples in communion with him, as those who have been told that his Father is now their Father, anticipates their journey to become human persons fully alive.

We will now discuss how the various aspects of *imago Dei* are restored through its recapitulation in Christ and in human persons in him, through their union and communion with him. In other words, what it means for Christians and their mission that Jesus enables us to become human persons fully alive. This involves first the recovery of a personhood toward that exemplified by Christ within the Trinity, and as the man for others. This entails both rediscovery of the security of personal identity and the relationality of human persons as persons-in-relation. Character formation and behavioral transformation will be a consequence of this reformation of persons in loving relation with God, with humans and creation, in such manner that the triune God is the ground and the power for ethics or "the good."[24] However, as ethics is beyond the scope of this book, little more will be said of this. Rather, attention will be given to what it means for such persons to be persons of gender, and persons in the human vocation of work.

Human persons fully alive as persons-in-relation in the image of God. The Christian gospel of the mission of God is the story not only of the forgiveness of sins but of human persons becoming sons and daughters of God, and therefore of the redemption and recovery of the fullness of our human life in union with the risen Christ and as modeled in the

---

[24]Dennis Hollinger's excellent introduction to Christian ethics outlines trinitarian ethics in favor of virtue ethics, or at least as a wider rubric than the latter, in his *Choosing the Good: Christian Ethics in a Complex World* (Grand Rapids: Baker Academic, 2002).

richness of his personhood. The Christian gospel is not first about morality but about union in the resurrection life of Christ that brings love, and with this morality! This change has as its aim recovery from individualism and into personhood-in-relation as imaged concretely in the person of the incarnate risen Christ, the true *imago* in this particular sense of the divine persons-in-relation.

The resurrected Christ is the *window* into what trinitarian personhood means. Human persons are a glorious reflection of what it means to be persons-in-relation, individuated but not individualistic, persons with irreducible and unique identity, yet formed in that identity by relatedness to others—God, their parents, their siblings, their friends and their spouses. Yet we do not merely seek to imitate Christ from a distance. We are united with him in resurrection, and our reformation occurs in the crucible of our communion with him as church and persons.

Incarnation with resurrection means, therefore, that as we discover God's redeeming transformation in our lives and mature as people, we discover healing for brokenness, our selfishness and self-absorption, and move out to become exocentric persons, living our lives to serve the other. Our orientation becomes Godward, worshipful, contemplative and sacrificial, and our orientation becomes the things in our world, both people, who he loves and calls us to serve in deed and word, and creation, which God loves, and has called us to steward.

Human persons-in-relation are given distinctiveness as persons and yet are influenced profoundly by their relatedness in at least three respects: (1) with respect to physicality (each has unique DNA), (2) with respect to personality, which is the product of both genes and social environment, and with that character, and (3) gender. The nature of the Fall was such as to make each of these a profound area of struggle. In our era of massive population explosion the prominence of media and its glorification of stars, as well as the migrancy of modern life and the extent of marital breakdown, significant depersonalization has resulted, with the consequence that many people struggle to find a secure sense of identity. A fundamental discontent with our bodies, their looks and their sizes, characterize us. Insecurity and lack of groundedness are profoundly felt in Western culture. Furthermore, although gender has since the Fall always been a war zone, in contemporary culture this seems to be more acute than ever, manifested in various forms. I will now develop the path to recovery in these areas as we examine what personhood is as revealed in Jesus and the *imago trinitatis*, by focusing in first on the legitimate security of identity that human persons can have, and then the profound manner in which relationality characterizes healthy humans. We will then move on to speak about gender, ethics and work. In each case Jesus fulfills the image of God as a human person fully alive but also can impart healing and wholeness in these areas to us. This will serve to define the breadth of Christian mission.

Human persons fully alive as persons-in-relation in the image of God with secure identity. We all need healing to become human persons fully alive because we are people of personhood who lose our identity in a depersonalizing world. A byproduct of family mobility through international migration as well as frequent inter- and intracity movement within nations, as well as frequent marital breakdown that in some part has been sacrificed on the altar of vocational success of various kinds, is that often we have a very fractured sense of home and who we really are. Even persons with a fairly good sense of identity struggle in a world where we attend large schools, work in large corporations and see doctors who barely know us, let alone our parents and grandparents, and who through no fault of their own see us for ten-minute appointments. One fears for the contemporary generation, many of whom are so formed by popular media; they barely have the capacity to differentiate what and how they think from how and what the prevailing culture thinks. Any sense of mission that excludes the matters of personal identity and belonging will be profoundly inadequate.

Contemporary culture has, to its detriment, neglected the creation orders God ordained for healthy human development and soul formation. More factors than just mobility go into a healthy sense of identity. Abuse within a family that never moves can be as damaging as a hundred moves made with parents who are supportive and nurturing. The end of all human journeys is the discovery of our home in God as he has made his home in us, and identity in light of who he is, and who he is for us. This does not negate all aspects of earthy cultural identity, but these are best appropriated and relativized when the deep roots of our longings for home are found in the incarnate, risen Christ, in the triune God of love. The fundamental irony of a secure sense of identity as humans comes only as we know Christ, and the triune God, and are known by him. John Calvin commented on this principle of "double knowledge" in the opening of his *Institutes*. We only know ourselves as we know God. Jesus in resurrection was vindicated and affirmed by the Father in his identity as Messiah—Son and Lord (Acts 2:36; Rom 1:4; Heb 1:5). In the risen Christ we discover a similar affirmation and security of identity, as the beloved of God (Eph 1:6).

Paul's great prayer in Ephesians 3 moves toward the goal of experientially grounding human persons in the infinite, multifaceted love and fullness of God, that is, their formation into human beings fully alive in the image of the triune God. The road to an internalized sense of the love of God that makes us whole persons with secure identity arises from relationship with the Father, whose orientation is to bless ("according to his glorious riches"), through the Spirit's strengthening and by making the risen Christ's home in human hearts. The recovery of self-worth, or a proper sense of self, is a product of realizing and internalizing the trinitarian work of each of the divine persons: that we are the unique creations of the Father, that the Son has died for and reconciled us and that by the Spirit we have been gifted with unique gifts and abilities, and are being formed and transformed by him. This enables a disseminating of the triune God's love to others as the very heart of mission. People need to know that God is *for* them! And it enables persons to serve rather than be served, for as Jesus illustrated in John 13, only he who has nothing to prove is free to serve. He had nothing to prove because he knew he had come from the Father and was returning to him. Every Christian hoping to be missional needs to press into their secure identity in the risen Christ. Too much damage is done in churches by pastors and people trying to shore up fractured identities and poor self-worth through people's approval and acclaim. Jesus comes in the fullness of this identity as the risen One in John 20, fresh from resurrection as the act by which his Father's approval had been shown. He will commission them in light of that approval and theirs in it.

Human persons fully alive as persons-in-relation with profound relationality. Every human needs healing with respect to relationships, for it is in being known that we know ourselves. Becoming human persons fully alive is as persons-*in-relation*. Humans not only have fractured identities but struggle with relationality because of our sin-induced inwardness and self-absorption, which is exacerbated by influence of the Western world's individualism since the Enlightenment. The recovery of an orientation toward the other is inspired by contemplation of the risen Christ who was a person-in-relation within the Godhead and was affirmed as such as a man by the resurrection. He was also, however, the man in union with humanity and demonstrated he was a man for others in his ministry. Now, as the risen man in John 20, he is still the man for his disciples, comforting and empowering them. By his Spirit imparted to them, his life would be shared in them. This would enable them not merely to look away to Christ to inspire their recovery as persons-in-relation but to actually be in relationship with him and the triune God. Contemplation and communion facilitate the recovery of relationality in human persons-in-relation.

The Ephesians 3 Pauline prayer reflects three realities concerning perfect relationality in God, which are to be contemplated and participated in to enable human emulation of it.

- *Perichoresis.* The first is coinherence (perichoresis, interanimation). The Father is prayed to, but what the Father is asked to do is fulfilled in what the Spirit and the Son are asked to do in this prayer. "I pray that out of his glorious riches he may strengthen you with power *through his Spirit* in your inner being, *so that Christ* may dwell in your hearts through faith" (Eph 3:16-17, emphasis added). The pray-er of this prayer is caught up in the communion between Father, Son and Spirit. The triune God is the paradigm that moves us toward relationality. The basic nature of human persons is intended to be correspondingly mutual and interpenetrative and communal. It is by participation in the life of the relational God, and by developing interdependent relationships with our fellow humans, that we can recover our relationality and become fully alive. This flies in the face of the atomistic and individualistic view of humans prevalent in Western culture and disloyalty in core relationships. When we learn to love God and be known deeply by God, we will begin to know and love ourselves properly. Furthermore, ironically, it is as we give ourselves away to our fellow humans that we will discover ourselves. The missing piece in much of our healing journey, which often tends to be inward looking, is to begin to be outward looking (*ex curvatus ex se*) and to serve others, to be sacrificial in our marriages and in our parenting.

- *Love.* The second manner in which relationality is recovered lies in the way the triune God loves, as revealed in this prayer, and the way he enables Christians to receive his love. Love is defined here in all its infinitude, flowing from the Trinity. But it cannot be experienced apart from prior work on God's part, which enables us for relationship with the Trinity and then all humans. He has not only given us his love: he has given us the capacity to receive it! "I pray that out of his glorious riches he may *strengthen you with power through his Spirit* in your inner being, *so that Christ* may dwell in your hearts through faith."

God's love has been expressed objectively in the historical event of the Son's coming. However, it is received by the Spirit's indwelling and strengthening to overcome stubborn resistance to love and increase human capacity to receive it. And then, because Christ indwells us by the Spirit, we become rooted and grounded in love! Although Paul mixes his metaphors here (botany and building), the idea is clear: groundedness and rootedness bring recovery of a true sense of identity in the affirmation and acceptance of his love. As trees and homes of love, persons-in-relation disseminate that love in mission.

This reformation in love toward becoming persons-in-relation seems to be a lifelong process; there are crisis moments to be sure. Interestingly, when Paul in Ephesians 3 speaks about Christ making his home in our hearts, he uses the aorist or point tense in Greek. This tense does not mean an unrepeatable event but communicates the idea of a discrete event, nevertheless. How are we to understand this, particularly given that Paul is addressing church people who have already received Christ in the initial sense, long ago? Handley Moule resolves this tension by stating that at whatever stage of the Christian life, we are all always in need of that fresh realization, a "new arrival and entrance" of the presence of Christ within us.[25] Moule notes: "Local images are always elastic in the spiritual sphere; and there is no contradiction thus in the thought of the permanent presence of One who is yet needed to arrive."[26] The disciples in John 20 experienced a wonderful arrival of his presence as the risen One that transformed them in a quantum manner which was, however, built on three years of his presence, often in more mundane circumstances. They were moved along the journey toward becoming resurrectional, persons-in-relation like their Master, with readiness to serve others even to the death.

A life of prayer articulating this Ephesians 3 prayer will facilitate this "again and again" experience of the love of God that transforms Christians into persons-in-relation like the risen Christ, to become missional people in actuality, pouring out God's love.

- *Community.* Third, relationality as revealed by the risen Christ cannot be recovered apart from human community, specifically ecclesial community. Resurrection persons-in-relation are just that, in loving community with other humans, especially others who have been brought into the same union with God. Paul says, "I pray that you, being rooted and established in love, may have power, *together with all the Lord's people*, to grasp how wide and long and high and deep is the love of Christ" (Eph 3:17-18, emphasis added). Paul is emphatic that we cannot experience the fullness of God's love apart from togetherness with the church. This speaks loudly to those who wish to do Christianity solo. It is as community that Christians receive the love of God and become persons-in-relation like Christ.

The essence of the mission we are entrusted with as the beloved

---

[25]Handley C.G. Moule, *Studies in Ephesians* (Grand Rapids: Kregel, 1977), p. 97.
[26]Ibid.

people of God reestablished in our identity as persons-in-communion, or persons-as-lovers, is to impart that love and recovered
identity to our fellow humans, that they too may discover themselves
to be God's beloved. We can do this only as church and as persons in
participation with Christ, by the Spirit, out of the love the Father is
pouring into our communities and lives. This requires that the
people of God develop gathered practices that enable them to live in
the love of God and scattered practices that bring them into contact
and relationship with lost and broken people.

***Human persons fully alive as persons-in-relation in the image of God
differentiated by gender.*** That Christ as fully incarnate and even risen
was gendered, as a person-in-relation, is true to what the image of God
entailed. The first theological statement about humans in the Bible
(Gen 1:26-27) established that the genders together in their complementarity are crucial to defining the image of God in humanity. The
sign of our cohumanity is, as Barth noted, first in human gender. Barth
interpreter Joseph Mangina says,

> Note that Barth is not speaking in the first instance of marriage, but
> about the distinction of male and female as such. Man and woman exist
> to help and serve each other; no person is sovereignly autonomous in the
> way that modern culture tends to celebrate; in their fundamental depen-
> dence on each other, human beings live out their vocation to be an
> image of the Trinity.[27]

Mangina sums up that in his discussion of gender, Barth "affirms
in modified form the existential picture of the human being as self-
transcending subject."[28] That Jesus lived as a single, gendered person in
holiness speaks to the fact that sexuality transcends sexual activity,
demonstrated that humans are self-transcending and that healthy sexuality is contemplative—it drives us to seek relationships with God and
other humans. Jesus' representativeness and accessibility for all humans
of both genders also relativizes the importance of gender. Thus humans

---

[27]Joseph Mangina, *Karl Barth: Theologian of Christian Witness* (Louisville: Westminster John
Knox Press, 2004), p. 96.
[28]Ibid., p. 97.

are persons first and gendered second. This is not to underplay the fact that gender and sexuality are the locus of the image of God in us. It is not surprising that it is often the place humans are most broken, and where much healing is needed to become persons-in-relation of gender. Mission cannot neglect this dimension of human life.

Resurrection life in Christ is needed to bring Christians into freedom to be sexual beings, delighting in sexuality as the gift of God, yet guiding its expression according to his commands in order that hope may be offered for freedom to our fellow humanity. The following are some of the areas of human brokenness with respect to sexuality and gender which require transformation.

1. Christians often fail to positively embrace themselves as sexual beings, human persons fully alive sexually! They do so because of a Platonic heritage in which the body is bad and only the spiritual is good. Sex was created by God and is therefore good. In fact, when God created humans on the sixth day of creation, he pronounced it "very good," and presumably that meant the sex organs too! Doubt that sexuality is good is removed in the incarnation and resurrection.

This owning and celebrating of sexuality extends both to the possession of sexuality (whether a person is single or married) and to the actual practice of sex between a man and a woman within the heterosexual covenant of marriage. Sex within marriage is to be enjoyed and celebrated as a unique sign of the image of God. The two becoming one flesh in the fullest sense of that term is a picture of the intimacy of the persons of the Godhead. But nonsexual relationships between singles and sexual relationships in marriage are equally important for imaging God. Stanley Grenz has written that in our nonsexual relationships as single people, we reflect the inclusiveness of God's love, whereas in marriage we mirror the exclusive nature of God's love, that is, his covenant faithfulness to his people, and we do so in a manner that reflects gender distinctiveness in oneness.[29]

Single people are not thereby penalized because they reflect one aspect of the love of God and not the other. John Stott, who was single all his

---

[29]Stanley J. Grenz, *Sexual Ethics: An Evangelical Perspective* (Louisville: Westminster John Knox, 1990), p. 252.

life, comments adroitly that "Sexual experience is not essential to human fulfillment. To be sure, it is a good gift of God. But it is not given to all, and it is not indispensable to humanness."[30] If marriage were required for sexual wholeness, Jesus would have been short-changed! The single person's sexuality is expressed in his or her capacity to love and be loved. Loving does not need to be genital to be intimate. In the context of deeply caring and emotionally fulfilling and healthy relationships, sexuality can be experienced without being expressed genitally and sexual energy thus dissipated. Marriage, in fact, does not in itself create sexual wholeness. Many married people are not sexually whole, and in fact sex in marriage can become a battleground precisely for this reason.

The need to receive the healing love of God is paramount for human persons to become fully alive, embracing their sexuality. Sexuality is evidence of the image of God in us, a God who is three persons who are exocentric, facing the other, interpenetrating and moving outward in creation and redemption. In knowing this God, in participating in his love, we become like him in that exocentric way. As Jim Houston says, "To know the Triune God is to act like him, in self-giving, in inter-dependence, and in boundless love."[31] Specifically this means being like Jesus!

2. But we also fail as people of gender who abuse the opposite sex by sexualizing them and making their gender their whole identity, treating them patronizingly at best and pornographically at worst. For this we need the recovery of the sense of the dignity of the other gender's personhood, as God has given that, to love whole persons, not just bodies, and above all to keep sex in perspective and seek to satisfy the wells of our thirst in God.

Although we don't attribute sexuality to the Godhead, we know that our sexuality mirrors something in him. So we take *both* gender equality *and* gender differentiation seriously, but are careful not to sexualize humans so that being male or female overshadows who individuals are as persons. Being persons-in-relation, as people of gender fully alive,

---

[30]John R. W. Stott, *Same-Sex Partnerships? A Christian Perspective* (Grand Rapids: Revell, 1998), p. 70.

[31]James Houston, cited in R. P. Stevens, "The Mystery of Male and Female: Biblical and Trinitarian Models," *Themelios* 17, no. 3 (1992): 20-24.

means that we treat people as people first and as people of gender second.

3. We fail as people of gender when we arrogantly assume we can flout the controls God has placed on the sex act. We are commanded to express sexuality in the sex act only within the covenant relationship of marriage, for very good reasons. Contemporary culture, and an enculturated Christian subculture, has chosen to ignore this to its own peril. It seems that sex is too powerful a force to be unleashed outside of covenant. We choose to ignore this and wreak the lifelong confusions and consequences of all premarital and extramarital sex. For this we need forgiveness from a loving Father and a return to the covenant faithfulness he models for us in his long love and inspires within us by his indwelling by the Spirit.

4. We fail as people of gender when we fail to show hospitality to persons who struggle with sin and brokenness in this area *and* when we fail to call them to repentance and healing. Jesus' interaction with the Samaritan woman at the well in John 4 illustrates the unconditioned and yet not unconditional hospitality of Jesus. On the one hand his offering of hospitality to this broken woman expressed unstinting grace and the offer of living water for her spiritual, affective thirst. In doing so he reflects what missional communities need to be doing. Our church communities are often nice little social clubs filled with people who are culturally and economically alike. We think we are offering hospitality, but we are, as missional theologian Alan Hirsch has expressed, often more about "huddle and cuddle" than we are about extending hospitality to strangers as Jesus did.[32] As Anthony Robinson says,

> The danger is that in our close-knit fellowship, our friendly church, there is no room for God, who comes to us as a stranger, the outsider. The danger is that our friendly churches have no room for the God who is, often as not, intrusive, disruptive, and not always "friendly"! Instead of aiming to be a friendly church, perhaps we ought to hope to be a church that practices hospitality.[33]

---

[32]Alan Hirsch, *The Forgotten Ways: Reactivating the Missional Church* (Grand Rapids: Brazos, 2007), p. 277.
[33]Anthony B. Robinson, *Transforming Congregational Culture* (Grand Rapids: Eerdmans, 2002), p. 108.

True hospitality is what grows out of missional communities who portray Jesus, and they welcome Christ in the stranger. Again, Robinson says, "When we extend hospitality to the stranger, we make no assumption that this person will have anything at all in common with us, much less that we will like one another. It could be someone unpleasant, even dangerous; we are still obligated to offer hospitality."[34]

However, quite clearly the hospitality of Jesus did not avoid the issue of sin and the call for transformation. His hospitality was unconditioned—in that there was not anything in the object of his hospitality that could or would have changed his love for the other—but it was not unconditional, in one sense. The invitation into Christ's community is an invitation to discipleship, which includes transformation, not settling for our moral and spiritual status quo, but the pursuit of holiness. Jesus loves us as we are, but he does not leave us as we are. We are invited into his house for healing and repentance and change.

5. We fail as people who use sexuality to try to satisfy core needs for God and crucial needs for close human relationships, and who therefore easily develop sexual addictions and distortions. We are all people of broken sexuality to some extent or another. For this we need forgiveness and then change. Change that comes from being in union with Jesus, from contemplating Jesus. We need to be filled with him who alone can satisfy our deepest needs for affection and affirmation, the Son of God, the lover of our souls.

The question is: Was there ever a human being like that? Person-in-relation, individuated and secure but not individualistic. Was there ever a human person fully alive, fully secure in his or her identity yet fully formed and given to the other; a human person committed to working with God in the completion of creation; a human person who was not guilty of egocentricity; a human person who overcame the influence of the Fall so that he or she was not turned in on his- or herself; a human person who had gender and respected the opposite gender to the full, who was sexually whole without having sex; a man or woman for others? Jesus was precisely that—the incarnate man for others who, on behalf

---

[34]Ibid.

of humanity, has as the risen One made it possible to be transformed in all areas of human existence.

How does this happen? It is a crisis and a process. The crisis is receiving him by faith, having received his offer of forgiveness. But that is only the beginning of a lifelong process of the formation or re-formation of our character as we allow him as the risen One to be formed in us.

Human persons fully alive as persons-in-relation in the image of God as steward rulers called to work. A profound consequence of the fact that Jesus' resurrection reaffirms creation is that this spells the end of all dualism, and specifically to the question of the Christian (indeed, the human person) and work! Many Christians do not have a theology for the thing they do most in their lives—work. Many Christians view work as something other than God's work. The term the *Lord's work* has been restricted to what pastors and missionaries do, and not to what we do as mechanics or lawyers or nurses. And because Christians have no theology for the other six days, they are often plagued with guilt. Because they still need to do the "Lord's work" outside of work time, they are busier than non-Christians, in fact so busy that their lives lack the shalom they profess to receive. Similarly, because many Christians think of workplace only as a well-stocked lake for fishing for souls, they find it hard to believe that just by doing a good job of work they are actually pleasing God, without ever opening their mouths about the gospel. The gospel is not about saving disembodied souls, it is about restoring whole persons to be persons in relation with God, neighbor and creation. This involves what we do at work and how we work.

Before many Christians who do have jobs can help toward the rehabilitation of the poor, they need to gain an understanding of the dignity of work as devotion to the God who himself worked and works. Work is a basic human right for persons created in the divine image. By Jesus' death and resurrection, each human person may become fully alive in that image, as it pertains to work. Those who have experienced the effects of resurrection will show this in their work, realizing that it not only fulfills the cultural mandate but is a contribution to the new creation. The missional church will show solidarity with those who do not, through no fault of their own, have work. It will reflect a realism concerning the challenges of work and unemployment in a fallen world. But it will also, because of Christ's resurrection and the new creation offer hope along with solidarity. The truly missional church will pursue evangelism in the context of neighborly compassion and justice seeking, grounded in the creation or cultural mandate, recognizing that Jesus' resurrection recapitulates the full dignity of every human being as creatures made in the image of God. This includes work.

A resurrectional-incarnational theology of work. I noted earlier that work originates in God and not the Fall. I also noted that the Fall adds complexity and difficulty to work. Resurrection is needed in this area of vocation. Personal transformation of the worker through evangelism and Christian growth includes how work is envisioned and pursued. In fact vocation as a term used for work must be qualified. The vocation of all Christians is to glorify God through worship and life lived in communion with God. Work becomes "vocation" when it is lived within that wider vocation. There is a need for evangelism and discipleship if there is to be resurrection and transformation of persons (reemploying the poor) and communities (which promote justice concerning work) in work, in a lasting way. The resurrection destiny in Christ of all humans as recapitulated in Christ prompts this. Going back to how our three circles relate to the three commissions (see fig. 6.1), when Christians live out shalom in the workplace (fulfilling the cultural mandate, outer circle), and when they demonstrate love for neighbor in the workplace (second circle), they are likely to have the opportunity to bring people to Christ (inner circle). But going in the opposite direction, as people respond to the gospel and become disciples (inner circle), they work out their Christianity in movement toward loving ethics (second circle), and on toward shalom in the workplace (third circle) and as that affects the creation. As Paul Stevens says, "Evangelism has as its goal the restoration of the whole person in relation to God, to neighbor and to the environment."[35]

John Stott has articulated (in his book *Involvement*) a fine trinitarian way of understanding our work when he states that work does

---

[35]R. Paul Stevens, *Liberating the Laity: Equipping All the Saints for Ministry* (Downers Grove, Ill.: InterVarsity Press, 1985), p. 94.

have a role to play in our personal sense of value and significance; second, that it is most meaningful when carried out for the community and in ways that benefit human community and the creation; and, third, that work has meaning above all when it is done with an orientation toward God and in participation with God by the Spirit. These find their texture for us in the person of Christ who revealed the Trinity. By his resurrection he brings a new creation in which all those in him by the Spirit participate. How does the fact that Christians are in Christ, the Worker, and that he is in us help? Let's profile Jesus from a trinitarian work theology perspective and find hope that because he is now alive in us, we too can work in ways that have eternal significance:

1. He certainly knew his personal calling, and by age twelve at that! When his mother lost him and she and Joseph found him hanging with the theological heavyweights, he said, "Didn't you know I had to be about my Father's business?" On another occasion he said, "My food is to do the will of him who sent me and to finish his work" (Jn 4:34). There is a sense of fulfillment that Jesus has as he goes about his work. He does so with the Father's clear approbation and pleasure.

2. Jesus worked in and for community. He was the man for others. He labored intensely and even when seeking rest, he ministered to the people who found him.

3. His orientation was always to the Father, and he worked always in perfect participation with the Father. John indicates a number of times in his Gospel that Jesus worked always in response to and in harmony with the Father. This is the image of God in its perfection, Jesus as man coworking with God in finishing creation.

A resurrectional-*incarnational theology of recovering work for the poor.* Incarnation without resurrection is only half a gospel. On the one hand there are many Christians who desire resurrection for the poor without being incarnational with the poor. Many are "with the poor" vicariously, at best, by giving to organizations that pay people to be with the poor. I have no doubt that it is not the special vocation of all Christians to be like Mother Teresa. Yet surely all are called in some way to be with the poor and marginalized. Others are at the opposite end of the scale. They are with the poor all the time and their sole sense of calling is to "be with" without any concern to be resurrectional with the poor, lifting them out of poverty by means of addressing social injustices, where that is relevant, or by helping toward providing the dignity of meaningful and just work. It is critical to not merely be with the poor but to be with the poor in order to remove the injustices that keep them poor, to be with the poor with a view to changing their circumstances in ways that are harbingers of the kingdom that will come, and to be with them to impart hope through a gospel of resurrection that will sustain them even when poverty remains in the now.

In this chapter, I have spoken of what it means to be in the process of becoming human persons fully alive as they live in Christ and he in them, knowing that he is already for us. We are in him regenerated, and by his resurrection justified (Rom 4:25), and so we pursue change to become persons-in-relation like him, persons of gender like him, persons made to work like him and with him by letting him be formed in us, by participation in his resurrection life. Yet there has been an underlying tone of realism that we live in "in-between" times, and that transformation is slow at best.

But what are the implications of the resurrection for the age to come? Our resurrection is not just spiritual. It is holistic, as was that of Jesus. Keeping together the resurrection with the incarnation will serve us well as we look briefly at the hope resurrection brings when the new creation fully comes.

Human persons fully alive as persons-in-relation fully transformed into the image of God by bodily resurrection. A *resurrection*-incarnation theology involves the future, holistic resurrection of all humans in Christ whose resurrection is its firstfruits and prototypes. The nature of Jesus' body as he encountered the disciples in John 20 tells us something about the resurrection state. He is identifiable as Jesus and he is touchable. Thus there is a clear sense of continuity between his pre- and postresurrection bodies. There are differences however. He can pass through locked doors and walls. Caesarius of Arles asks, "You ask me and *say*, If he entered through closed doors, where is the bulk of his body? And I reply, If he walked on the sea, where was the weight of his body?"[36] Postresurrection, the nature of the body has changed. Jerome concluded with respect to the resurrection body of Jesus in this passage, that the "substance of our resurrection bodies will certainly be the same as now, though of higher glory."[37] He no doubt did so on the basis of Pauline insights: "So will it be with the resurrection of the dead. The body that is sown is perishable, it is raised imperishable; it is sown in dishonor, it is raised in glory; it is sown in weakness, it is raised in power; it is sown a natural body, it is raised a spiritual body" (1 Cor 15:42-44).

Augustine asserts what he knows with certainty—that resurrection bodies "will be spiritual in the resurrection of the faithful and righteous" and that "there will be no corruption in them, and for this reason they will not then need this corruptible food that they now need. They will, nonetheless, be able to take and really consume such food, not out of need." "Otherwise" he reasons, "the Lord would not have taken food after his resurrection." However, as to the exact nature of these spiritual resurrection bodies, Augustine professes much less clarity: "But I do not know the character of a spiritual body, unknown as it is to us, can be either comprehended or taught. He manifested himself as both incorruptible and touchable to show us that his body after his resurrection was of the same nature as ours but of a different sort of glory."[38]

With this awareness of what we can and cannot know for sure, we may well ask two questions. First, how does God maintain the continuity of human personal identity when death brings dissolution of the substance of the body, so that when resurrection occurs, the continuity continues (as well as the discontinuity illustrated by the nature of Jesus' resurrection body and expressed concretely in Paul's words "a spiritual body," in contrast with a "physical/natural" body [1 Cor 15:35-50])? Given that even the DNA breaks down when a body decays or is burned, this is a real question. Or is it? Is it any more a question than

---

[36]Caesarius of Arles, Sermon 175.2, Fathers of the Church 47:434, cited in Joel C. Elowsky, *John 11–21*, Ancient Christian Commentaries IVb (Downers Grove, Ill.: InterVarsity Press, 2007), pp. 356-57.

[37]Jerome, *Against Jovinianus* 1.36, Nicene and Post-Nicene Fathers 2, 6:374, cited in Elowsky, *John 11–21*, p. 358.

[38]Augustine, Letter 95.7, cited in Elowsky, *John 11–21*, p. 356.

how Jesus was raised from the dead? John Polkinghorne suggests that the soul is the *information-bearing pattern* of the body. He has invoked the ancient concept spoken of by Aristotle and by Aquinas, who believed that the soul is the form (or pattern of the body), but with the very significant adaptation that he is speaking of a soul-body unity, not of a dualistic "soul in a body" entity. Polkinghorne's concept does not rule out but rather includes our genome or genetic code of the body, which is crucial to the body-soul unity that humans are. But Polkinghorne wants especially to insist that this must include our relationships, which play so significant a part in the character of personhood, as well as all the experiences which have shaped our identity.[39]

Thus the soul possesses no inherent immortality. When someone dies the information-bearing pattern of the soul-body unity dissolves along with the decaying process. However, Polkinghorne crucially adds, and this is an *however* of divine faithfulness, not of naturalistic expectation: "It seems to me to be a perfectly coherent hope to believe that the pattern that is me will be preserved by God at my death and *held in the divine memory* until God's great eschatological act of resurrection, when that pattern will be re-embodied in the 'matter' of the new creation." He then adds "a credible Christian hope centers on death and resurrection, and not on spiritual survival."[40] This naturally leads to a second tough question, where does the person "go" when he or she dies and the soul-body unity decays in the ground or as ashes?

While I wish to affirm the broad strokes of Polkinghorne's thesis, I also want to challenge the now popular notion that soul-body integrated unity must mean that there is no hope that departed loved ones are in some sense in heaven now. I agree absolutely with the sentiments of N. T. Wright when he emphasizes that resurrection on a new earth is our destiny when we die, and that "going to heaven" is not the ultimate, and that the intermediate state is less important and in fact a temporary state in the way to the resurrection state.[41] Wright

---

[39]John Polkinghorne, *Science and the Trinity: The Christian Encounter with Reality* (New Haven, Conn.: Yale University Press, 2004), p. 162.
[40]Ibid., p. 163, emphasis added.
[41]Wright, *Surprised by Hope.*

does not in fact negate the possibility that departed saints are with Christ in heaven. However, on the basis of the straightforward witness of Scripture (Phil 1:21-24; 2 Cor 5:1-10—where Paul recognizes that the disembodied nature of the intermediate state is anomalous for human existence), I wish to be a little more emphatic on that, despite the risk of appearing to harbor Platonic notions as best, and Gnostic ones at worst.

The principle thing about our future in the risen Christ, however, is not that we "go to heaven and be there forever." Rather it is for heaven to come down to earth (Rev 21) and for humans to be embodied in resurrection bodies. The trajectory of human history is creation as embodied beings, "animated bodies," then the Fall, then redemption and finally consummation in a new creation in which humans are embodied, not spirit beings or angels. The cultural mandate will be fulfilled in the humans in the last Adam. We will reign as cocreators with Christ in a renewed and reconciled creation. We will work in union with Christ on the new earth to which heaven will have come down. The bodies we have then will have continuity with who we are now, as well as significant discontinuity. They will be spatially limited, yet have a spiritual and heavenly orientation.

What characterizes us above all in this new earth is a metaphysical likeness to Christ's risen body and a moral likeness to him as a result of having seen the beatific vision (1 Jn 3:1-2). And we will reign with him as persons-in-relation, with the triune God, as members of the new humanity in the last Adam. And all will be glorious and for the glory of God.

7

Communities of Christ's Crucified Presence

Beautiful Scars

■ ■ ■

When He had said this, He showed them His hands and His side.
Then the disciples were glad when they saw the Lord.

JOHN 20:20 NKJV

THE SHALOM AND JOY WHICH this little community in John 20 experienced was a consequence not merely of Jesus' risen presence among them. Strangely, it had to do with the presence of Jesus who was *once dead* and now risen. The scarred hands and side he showed them did not merely calm them, because they identified him as the Jesus they knew.[1] They signaled a triumph achieved through suffering. Ugly scars

---

[1]Given his position on the humanity of Christ referenced earlier, it is surprising to find that Calvin rather dogmatically dismisses the idea that the wounds Jesus showed his disciples were permanent: "it would be ridiculous, for it is certain that the use of the wounds was temporary until the apostles were fully persuaded that He was risen from the dead" (John Calvin, *John 11–21 and 1 John*, Calvin's New Testament Commentaries, trans. T. H. L. Parker, ed. David W. Torrance and Thomas F. Torrance [Grand Rapids: Eerdmans, 1959], p. 203). While it may be granted that Jesus does not bear open wounds, might it not be reasonable that he bears the scars eternally, given that this seems to be part of the continuity between his former and his resurrection body? The depictions of the ascended Jesus given to us by John in Revelation seem to carry forward this eternal freshness of the Lamb once slain (Rev 5:6). Augustine also supported such a possibility: "I have always taken these as scars, not as actual wounds, and saw them as a result of his power, not of some necessity" (Letter 95.7, cited in Joel C. Elowsky, *John*

became beautiful to them. His presence among them in that form, however, also communicated the cruciform essence of the nature of the church and the kingdom.

The joy the disciples received was to become permanent. It was the fulfillment of what Jesus had promised them in his precross address: "I will see you again and you will rejoice, and no one will take away your joy" (Jn 16:22). Supernatural joy is in short supply and may account for our weakness in Christian mission in the West. I have, ironically, seen it more in poverty-stricken communities in Africa. The joy the disciples felt here would be tested. In fact, it would be enhanced by their own identification with him in suffering, but they didn't know that then. Gregory the Great draws out the sober conclusion that the correspondence between the sending of the Son and the sending of the Son's people is one of suffering also:

> The Father sent his Son, appointing him to become a human person for the redemption of the human race. He willed him to come into the world to suffer—and yet he loved his Son whom he sent to suffer. The Lord is sending his chosen apostles into the world, not to the world's joys but to suffer as he himself was sent. Therefore as the Son is loved by the Father and yet is sent to suffer, so also the disciples are loved by the Lord, who nevertheless sends them into the world to suffer.[2]

In this chapter I will address first why the crucified Christ paradoxically brings joy by exploring the beauty motif of the atonement. Second, we will explore what the presence of Christ with scarred hands and side as the source and center of the community means for the nature and practices of the community. We will look at how the worship of the church, its teaching and its communal life, should be influenced by the scarred Christ, and we will affirm that the church's missional nature is a consequence of its nature as a community of Christ-centered, cruciform worship. In particular, a church community that understands that the presence of Christ as crucified is definitive of its

---

11–21, Ancient Christian Commentaries IVb [Downers Grove, Ill.: InterVarsity Press, 2007], p. 356). His attribution of the presence of scars to Christ's power is assumedly due to the fact that they should have been wounds so soon after the crucifixion event.

[2]*Forty Gospel Homilies* 26, Cistercian Studies 123:201-2, cited in Elowsky, *John 11–21*, p. 360.

essence will see the Eucharist as definitive of its life and nature, and it will understand that being a eucharistic community and being missional are not in opposition.

Our immediate focus is what the inner life of the missional church should look like in light of the nature of the One standing in its center. His presence among them, bearing those scars, was a sign of what they would soon become—the church centered on a *once crucified*–now risen Christ. John is well known for his use of signs to convey rich meaning. We are meant to connect the dots with John's writing. These scars were a sign of something crucial about Jesus and anticipated how they were to keep him in their memory and how their liturgies were to reflect his community-defining presence. Somehow, seeing those permanently scarred hands in the risen Christ was an *aha!* moment. The lights came on as they understood all those predictions Jesus had made about his impending death, and it therefore evoked a whole lot more than mere recognition of who he was. This is the Johannine way! The nail-scarred hands and side were a symbol of a completed redemption. This would become the constitution of their church, the core of their message, and the costly pattern of their lives as his apostles. His presence as the scarred One among them appears to be an apt metaphor of the church constituted by that presence.

COMMUNITIES OF CHRIST'S CRUCIFIED PRESENCE
Joy Generated by Beautiful Scars

Crown Him the Lord of love! Behold His hands and side,
Rich wounds, yet visible above, in beauty glorified:
All hail, Redeemer, hail! For Thou hast died for me:
Thy praise shall never, never fail, throughout eternity.[3]

It may appear somewhat macabre that the scars in Jesus' hands and side should be so endearing to Christian disciples then and today. That

---

[3]This verse of the hymn "Crown Him with Many Crowns" is thought to have been written by Godfrey Thring (1823-1903), who added it to the verses originally written by Matthew Bridges (1800-1894).

these were somehow beautiful to them relates to the richness of what they signify: the beauty which the Christ of the cross embodied in himself,[4] and what he revealed of the beauty of the love and triune harmony of God who defines beauty and who assumes the world's sin so as to redeem it within his own being,[5] the beauty of the reconciliation that his crucifixion and sufferings had accomplished. It is my own experience that worship that flows from contemplation of creational beauty can reach lofty heights, but greater depth of worshipful thought and feeling emerges from contemplative meditation of the Christ of the cross as the center of creation. It is not until one's eyes are open to see the beauty of the cross that the created world evokes our worship of the one true God. The fact that the cross occurred and that it was planned in eternity past before the world's creation makes us aware that even the act of creation was for God a kenotic event. God, who in freedom created a universe that was granted some degree of freedom, was willing before its creation to bear the pain of what that freedom would invoke. This was the perspective of Duns Scotus (1265/66-1308), a Scot from Duns (Scottish borders) of the High Middle Ages, and whether we accept his concept of the univocity of being or not, we have to admire his affirmation of the freedom of creation and his insight into the premundane centrality of the cross for the reconciliation of creation.[6] This brought creation and redemption together profoundly. Worship at the cross is therefore the greatest spring from which mission flows, and its ultimate outcome, the reconciliation of all things.

Wherein lies this overwhelming beauty and motivating power arising from what in reality were fresh and bloody scars of an appallingly ugly, barbaric event, the gore of which, had we witnessed it, might

---

[4]Karl Barth is emphatic that the cross does not merely illustrate the love of God but embodies it in Christ: "The beauty of Jesus Christ is not just any beauty. It is the beauty of God . . . it is the beauty of what God is and does in him" (*Church Dogmatics* II/1, ed. G. W. Bromiley and T. F. Torrance [Edinburgh: T & T Clark, 1975], p. 665).

[5]For a helpful discussion of the atonement as the restoration of beauty in the theology of Anselm of Canterbury, see Steve Holmes, "The Upholding of Beauty: A Reading of Anselm's Cur Deus Homo," *Scottish Journal of Theology* 54, no. 2 (2001): 189-203.

[6]The alternative positions to univocity, that is, the analogy of being (Thomas) or the analogy of relations (Barth) involve the concept of the participation of nature in God, and this too involves some measure of freedom for nature.

have evoked horrified nausea? How can that which was a "stumbling block" to the Jews and utter "foolishness" to the Gentiles (1 Cor 1:23) be beautiful? These wounds are beautiful because:

1. They are the revelation of the nature of the beautiful triune God. The beauty of the cross is evident for its centrality in the very being of God. Scripture confirms that the cross was not an afterthought in God or conceived as some kind of a "plan B" when humankind fell into sin. In Acts 2:23 Peter speaks of the cross as in accordance with "God's deliberate plan and foreknowledge." Revelation 13:8 speaks of "the Lamb who was slain from the creation of the world." Brad Green has shown that a chief polemical feature of Augustine's *De Trinitate* is the central role that Christ's death plays in human knowledge of the Trinity (bks. 4, 13, in particular). Conceding that its principal theme is "the vision of the triune God which is future for the believer," Green nevertheless stresses that 'it is clear that the only way by which anyone will ever see God is through the cross."[7] The beauty of the cross is evoked in Jürgen Moltmann, especially in his *The Crucified God*, the central theme of which is the unveiling of God's answer to the human experience of suffering or Godforsakenness in his own suffering as experienced on the cross.[8] Though envisioned within a Rahnerian theology of the Trinity, which coalesces the immanent and economic trinities, and a consequent panentheistic blurring of God and creation/history, Moltmann correctly argues that trinitarian theology *must* emerge from our understanding of the cross.[9]

When the Lamb is worshiped in heaven, it is perpetually depicted as freshly slain (Rev 5:6). The wounds of Christ, it would seem, will be a source of wondering adoration throughout eternity, in the new creation,

---

[7]Brad Green, "The Protomodern Augustine? Colin Gunton and the Failure of Augustine," *International Journal of Systematic Theology* 9, no. 3 (2007): 339.

[8]Jürgen Moltmann, *The Crucified God: The Cross of Christ as the Foundation and Criticism of Christian Theology*, (Minneapolis: Fortress, 1993), p. 4.

[9]Ibid., pp. 240-41. With Alan Torrance, I am happier to have the question "Can God suffer?" answered by the revelation of God in the incarnation than by Scholastic philosophical assumptions, and yet not to make suffering endemic to the Godhead but something he decides in freedom to assume. See Alan Torrance, "Does God suffer? Incarnation and Impassibility," *Christ in Our Place: The Humanity of God in Christ for the Reconciliation of the World: Essays Presented to James Torrance*, ed. T. Hart and D. Thimmell (Exeter and Allison Park, Penn.: Paternoster, 1989), pp. 315-68.

and, no wonder, for they are the source of the reconciliation and re-newal of that creation. That at the heart of the reconciliation of all things is the Son of God slain is evidence enough that this is at the heart of God's intentions for the universe he created. If the cross arises from the very center of God's being and intentions for creation, it must somehow be beautiful.

The trinitarian nature of what transpired at the cross further evinces its beauty. While the atonement's substitutionary nature is a reality, the cross event is first and foremost a transaction within the Godhead be-tween the persons of the Godhead. It was devised from the Father (Jn 3:16; 1 Jn 5:8), who sent the Son, who was conceived as to his humanity by the Spirit (Mt 1:20). It was the offering of the Son to the Father by the Spirit. That it was the offering of the Son to the Father is conveyed by Paul: "Follow God's example, therefore, as dearly loved children and walk in the way of love, just as Christ loved us and gave himself up for us as a fragrant offering and sacrifice to God" (Eph 5:1-2). That the Spirit was involved in this is made apparent in Hebrews, which tells us that it was "through the eternal Spirit" that Christ offered himself without spot to God (Heb 9:14). The Son in humility depended upon the Spirit in every aspect of his life, and it was by the same Spirit that the beautiful life of Jesus that breathed devotion to the Father was of-fered to him on the cross. These scars on the hands and side of Jesus were beautiful because they were scars of a total devotion to the Father's will. They are scars of a sweet savor offering to the Father—they are signs of the beauty of a fragrant offering made to God for all of us.

Modern objections that the atonement depicts a sadistic God say more about the limited vision and anthropocentric orientation of culture than anything else. The trinitarian notion that the man of-fering this sacrifice is himself God goes unnoticed. Our propensity is to see the atonement in a unitarian manner as the offering of a human life to a monadic God, rather than the reconciliation of a fallen uni-verse within and among the persons of the triune Godhead in ways that remain veiled in mystery. Our finite understanding of what justice is and what its satisfaction entails all too readily presumes to instruct the God who defines justice and who in his premundane counsels opts sov-

ereignly for the cross as he opts sovereignly in freedom to grant his
creatures freedom.

The fact that in the eternal counsels of God he conceives of a creation which will not be complete without reconciliation from the alien-
ation and brokenness of sin seems to point to the conclusion that in his
estimation a reconciled universe is more beautiful than one which has
never fallen. This seems be the only logical conclusion from the passages of Scripture revealing that the eternal purposes of God include a
crucified Son. In the divine counsels he had always intended that the
Son would become a part of creation as a human being and then be
crucified to bring about the reconciliation of creation. This is in keeping
with Karl Barth's revised supralapsarianism, which entailed the election
of Christ within the Godhead to be the incarnate Redeemer of a fallen
humanity.[10] That is, it was an election by God to be *for* a humanity he
knew would fall. All humanity was to be elect because Christ was
elected to become human as the man for all humanity and the repro-
bation of the nonelect humanity was to be endured by him on the
cross.[11] This view of election as involving a trinitarian God, a man who
was both electing God and elect man, and the community of humanity
in that God-man makes the cross very much central to God's purposes.
Holding to infralapsarianism or Augustinian-Edwardsean supralapsarianism entails a high view of the cross, but Barth's Christological
supralapsarianism offers the highest of all views. It is the place where
God declares most vocally that he is for humanity, that he has reconciled it in Christ and that he has endured in his Son the rejection, the
hell of the nonelect.

---

[10]Edwards's position as supralapsarian has no more than a nominal similarity with that of Barth.
The form of supralapsarianism that Barth opts for is a fundamentally revised one. As Geoffrey
Bromiley notes, supralapsarianism "can fulfil this promise, however, only if it is reinterpreted
christologically along the lines that Barth has attempted. Barth might be described, then, as a
reconstructed supralapsarian" (G. W. Bromiley, *Introduction to the Theology of Karl Barth* [Ed-
inburgh: T & T Clark, 1979], p. 88). Bromiley is referring here to *Church Dogmatics* II/1, pp.
127-45.

[11]Barth actually transforms Calvin's (and Augustine's) version of predestination by grounding
election in Christ. Edward T. Oakes has commented that fortunately Balthasar's seminal work
on Barth summarized the 806 pages of II/2 in a manner that led Barth's thought to have a
profound influence on Catholic theology, including that of Pope Benedict. See Edward T.
Oakes "Predestination in America," *Nova et Vetera* 8, no. 3 (2010): 683-702.

Thus, *the fact that God freely bears the evil of the universe himself at the cross and overcomes it is beautiful.* God's power is not like that of human autocrats. It is power that conquers by love. It is power that wins the victory by becoming victim. He vanquishes sin and Satan by servanthood and sacrifice. This is true beauty. Without the cross the true beauty of God remains unrevealed in its fullness.

The cross is therefore at the center of the premundane purposes of the triune God. This is confirmed by the assuming of humanity into the Godhead in the incarnate Son, that is, the presence of a cross-scarred man seen in John 20, in the very being of the triune God, forever.

Though all are related in some way to this first point, there are a number of other reasons for attributing beauty to the scars of Jesus and finding joy in them as the disciples did.

1. They are the scars of a battle won, of a conqueror over sin, death, hell and Satan. In the human realm of war we tend to idolize the conqueror. Scars won in the pitch of battle only enhance the conqueror's image. However, with Jesus, his particular brand of battle scars indicate that he won by becoming the victim. This is the true *Christus Victor* motif of the atonement (Col 2:13-15; Heb 2:14-15).

2. They are the scars of a sacrifice for sin (sin offering category, Lev 4–6) made to a holy God on behalf of sinful humanity. These scars are a sign of justification achieved for humanity (Rom 3:24-26; 4:25).

3. They are scars that represent the full identification of God with the suffering of a sinful humanity and a broken creation (Heb 2; 7).

4. They are the fleshy scars of *the* human for all humans, and therefore the hope for all humans of all nations and the restoration of all creation (Col 1:15-20).

These scars forever etched in the embodied, postresurrection Jesus are beautiful because they are carried into the presence of God in heaven, where they are the symbol and guarantor of an eternal salvation for all in Christ and the harbinger of resurrection and the restoration of the whole creation when he returns and the sons and daughters of God are raised and revealed. They give hope of a different day when tragedies, hunger, poverty, death and tears will be no more.

COMMUNITIES OF CHRIST'S CRUCIFIED PRESENCE
Through Christocentric, Cruciform Worship,
Teaching and Community Life

The shalom of the church is always given as the redemptive presence of Christ is treasured, experienced and lived out in participation with him. Its attractiveness and capacity to share shalom with others is dependent on its cruciformity, that is, its likeness to the nail-scarred, risen Christ and the degree to which that Christ can be accessed by the world.

A cruciform church centered on the sacraments of baptism and Communion is the manner in which it reflects the beauty accomplished by the cross and is how the church perpetuates the vision of it suggested in John 20:19-23. This is accomplished by a much higher emphasis on baptism than is often present in our grandest evangelistic efforts as the church, which are often focused on the unseen spiritual dimension of conversion and not sufficiently focused on the physical concretization of the act in an incarnational way. This would immediately communicate the cruciform as well as communal nature of Christian life, recognizing that baptism of the Spirit in conversion and water baptism as its sign is an incorporative act, a baptism into the body of Christ (1 Cor 12:13). It would thus redress the issue of individualistic "Jesus and me" conversion, as it is popularly proclaimed. Furthermore, it would begin the convert's life in the right cruciform pattern and practices of continual mortification of self and sin, and continual vivification, a death and resurrection life lived toward the face of God and the face of our neighbor. It would thus help to address the challenging ethical state of the church, which often causes a credibility gap for mission.

When Karl Barth expressed his change of views on baptism in the preface to his final volume of the *Church Dogmatics*, he expressed that his desire was to put baptism "at the head of the Christian ethics with which the doctrine of reconciliation concludes."[12] His desire was that baptism, the Lord's Prayer and the Lord's Supper would fill out his

---

[12]Barth, *Church Dogmatics* IV/4, p. ix.

final work. With regard to baptism "at the head," in particular, his aim was that "The Christian life would thus be set forth in its most intimate form in a progression beginning with recollection of the divine gift that demands this answer thus posed for man as his task," and thus this "doctrine of baptism (as God's own work: baptism with the Holy Ghost, and also as man's liturgical work: baptism with water) was to be expounded as the foundation of the Christian life."[13] Developing the full picture of the Christian life as the baptized life is beyond our scope here. I merely draw attention to the need in some church traditions to raise the profile of the objective and subjective dimensions of baptism in ecclesial life and witness in order that cruciform pilgrims may be more frequently formed and that churches may fulfill their nature as cruciform and missional.

This is especially well accomplished if the Lord's Supper is restored to prominence. The "as . . . so" structure of John 20:21 is fairly common in John. As noted elsewhere, these statements found earlier in the Gospel can illumine the meaning of the "as . . . so" sentness in this commission. For example, pertinent to the cruciform theme in this chapter is the statement by Jesus in John 6 where, on one account at least, we find the deepest teaching in the New Testament on the Eucharist (compensating for the fact that John does not ever mention its institution like the other Evangelists): "Just *as* the living Father *sent* me and I live because of the Father, *so* the one who feeds on me will live because of me" (v. 57). This is preceded by the clarification that to feed on Jesus meant to feed on his flesh and blood (v. 54). The "as the . . . Father sent me" of verse 57 anticipates the same phrase in chapter 20. The order is instructive. The sentness of the disciples (Jn 20:21) is contingent on their feeding on Christ, that is, the possession of life sustained by feeding (Jn 6:57). Sentness is an outflow of life, and life is shown by and depends on feeding! At minimum what these Johannine sayings of Jesus mean is that those who feed spiritually on the benefits of Christ's death are those who possess spiritual life that spawns and sustains mission. If one can assume a eucharistic intention in John 6,

---

[13]Ibid.

this is accomplished especially through the feeding on Christ that is the Lord's Supper. Pauline assertions that the Lord's Supper is a participation in the body and blood of Christ (1 Cor 10:16-17) support the notion that the Eucharist is a feeding on Christ. It became a principle motif for the Eucharist within church history, in all traditions, even though the manner of this feeding is conceived differently. The way in which the Lord's Supper pervaded and defined early church life confirms the high place that feeding on Christ held for the church's life and mission. This is further confirmation that the missional church is the deep church—it is the church that has life sustained by frequent feeding on Jesus that comes through his real presence in the Eucharist, accompanied by the reading and teaching of the Word.

Christocentric, cruciform worship: A case for the centrality of the sacraments. Ironically, the greatest evidence of the cultural entrapment of the church today is the absence of the cross in its worship, teaching and community life. Who is this figure in the middle of this proleptic church community in John 20, who makes it what it is? It is a figure with eternally scarred hands and side! How can we use the term *worship* in the church today and not be referring to its central element, the Communion or Eucharist? Worship, as it is influenced by this image of Jesus standing in the community with scarred but risen body, will be eucharistic, keeping the polarities of celebration and contemplation, the paschal and the resurrection, together, and making it missional.

So what does a crucified Christ at the center mean for the church? It means that the church is a baptismal and eucharistic missional community. By means of the Eucharist the church is reminded of its source and center. The church, when it comes together, is meant to *remember* Jesus and *feed* on Jesus, and so be in *communion* with the triune God. John's metaphor of the church in John 20 has as its center not just a risen Jesus. It is a risen Jesus we can't see without remembering the cross, because his scars will always be there. If the church is to be what it really is, it needs to recover the centrality of the Lord's Supper. In one sense the Eucharist is the mother of all semiotics. It is the very essence of the gospel, which is the very essence of our mission! It conveys the image of Jesus standing with scars in his hands and side. It is the symbol of his presence as the scarred One in our midst, the sacrament that reminds us of his wounds. The church is only beautiful when the beautiful scars of Jesus are front and center. Remember what these disciples were without Jesus present? It is a picture of failure and fragility and fear. But with Jesus in their midst those same people become beautiful because he represents and leads them. They take on his beauty before the Father.

Holy Communion as the source and center of the missional church: Missional because of what it signifies. There is a significant strain of biblical scholarship that supports these sentiments that Communion defined the church and that its gatherings were synonymous with Communion. New Testament scholar I. Howard Marshall says, "The Lord's Supper should be celebrated frequently in the church, and there is good reason for doing so on each Lord's Day."[14] As Acts unfolds, the breaking of the bread or Communion comes to be not merely one of the marks of the church (Acts 2:42) but the primary descriptor of the gatherings of the church (Acts 20:7). The church cannot possibly be the missional church it is intended to be if this key aspect of its identity is missing.

The seminal description of church life in Acts (2:42-47) depicts its missional nature to be a consequence of devotion to *being* the church. Mission, not one of the marks of the church but the very nature of the church, was a consequence therefore of its deep life, characterized by Communion. When churches devote themselves to being *deep*, that is, to the teaching and learning of apostolic truth revealed in the Scriptures, to sharing their lives so as to be the *koinōnia* on earth that images the *koinōnia* of the Trinity in heaven, to the breaking of the bread or Communion, and to the prayers (definite article indicates public prayers), they will be *wide*, they will be missional: "they devoted themselves" to being the church and "the Lord" devoted himself to "adding to their number"!

---

[14]I. Howard Marshall, *Last Supper and Lord's Supper* (1980; reprint, Vancouver: Regent College Publishing, 2006). The relegation of the Lord's Supper to a monthly or even annual event in some Protestant denominations is not in keeping with a key Reformation impulse. The Reformers without exception, in reaction to the annual practice of the Eucharist in Medieval Catholicism, increased the frequency. Calvin, for example, wished for weekly communion but did not get his way in Geneva. See John Calvin, *Institutes of the Christian Religion*, ed. John T. McNeill, trans. Ford L. Battles (Philadelphia: Westminster, 1960), 4.17.44, 46.

It is useful to note that the two sacraments were prominent also in this missional church—the initiating sacrament of baptism in Acts 2:41, the constitutive sacrament of the "breaking of the bread" in verse 42. The latter is revisited in verse 46, where there is evidence that it was practiced as a eucharistic meal, shared in an environment of close communion and where feeding people was practicable. It would have been impractical in temple gatherings to feed over three thousand folk. But pertinent to our point here, there is no reason to believe that the breaking of the bread was any less frequently observed than the teaching or the prayers, and, in fact, when the church is more fully developed as described in Acts 20:7 ("On the first day of the week we came together to break bread. Paul spoke to the people and, because he intended to leave the next day, kept on talking until midnight") and again in 1 Corinthians 11:18, 20 ("when you come together as a church, . . . [W]hen you come together, it is not the Lord's Supper you eat") it apparently became the descriptor that trumps all the others, the gathering's primary purpose, even though in the former case Paul preaches for a long time! The view that the Eucharist defines the church and its mission has been present for centuries in the Eastern Orthodox Church.[15] Even if we may not be convinced of this viewpoint, we can hopefully acknowledge that Communion is at least central to and inseparable from the life of the church and therefore its mission.

Despite this emphasis on the Eucharist as "feeding on Christ," I venture to say that this description is subservient to that of "communion." Nor is it merely remembrance, though clearly that is accomplished by the repeated act and by meditation that should characterize both our preparation for communion and the service surrounding it (Western evangelicalism with its prominently Zwinglian memorialist view has tended to limit Communion to this, and this has been encouraged by the rationalism of modernity—despite this, minimal space is provided for meditation in observing the Eucharist in most traditions. In the ethos of rush and the noisiness of current society, the Lord's Supper is more like a snack). Nor is its best description "Eu-

---

[15]See Alexander Schmemann, *For the Life of the World: Sacraments and Orthodoxy* (Crestwood, N.Y.: St Vladimir's Seminary Press, 1988).

charist," though this word reflects the appropriate human response involved and says something about our speech in the act of Communion. Rather its most essential definition is to do with being, not doing. We take Christ afresh into our being spiritually. In so doing we enter afresh into communion with the triune God: in and through Christ, by the Spirit, to the Father. We go forth from the act freshly renewed in the communion of being that facilitates our participation in his mission, taking the bread and feeding it to the world, seeking to draw others into that communion. In the act of Communion as the gathered church, we act representatively, and so, again and again, participate in his mission to the world. In its gatherings centered on Communion, the church is itself a semiotic missional expression of Christ given for the life of the world. It should be a table of gospel invitation to all. It is after all an occasion for the church to "*proclaim* the Lord's death" (1 Cor 11:26). The Passover and the covenantal dimensions of the communion serve to reinforce the missional nature of Communion.

A perspective on the Lord's Supper that is frequently overlooked in the midst of philosophical discussions of its meaning is its historical rootedness in the Passover, in the context of which Jesus instituted it. Markus Barth draws attention to this. Grounding the church's history within Israel's history, he highlighted four aspects of Passover that have implications for the Christian Eucharist. Drawing attention only to the first here, which relates to memory, Barth recalls that the Passover is celebrated in memory of God's complete historic act of freeing the Israelites from Egyptian captivity. This redemptive-liberation motif provides further insight into the missional orientation of the Eucharist.[16]

The relationship between the Lord's Supper and the new covenant also serves to give it a profoundly missional orientation. Iain Provan speaks of the biblical covenants as critical markers in the continuing story of God's intentions for the world's redemption with the helpful image of an hour glass. Beginning with a covenant that includes all of creation, the scope then narrows to humans, then to the people Israel,

---

[16]Markus Barth, *Rediscovering the Lord's Supper: Communion with Israel, with Christ, and Among the Guests* (Atlanta: John Knox Press, 1988), p. 12.

then to one Israelite, before it begins widening again.[17] The new covenant points toward the widening scope of redemption to include all people and all creation. Knowing our place in that continuum as people of the new covenant that Christ initiated, and observing where we are in the longer story of redemption, helps orient ourselves. The Lord's Supper, which is a celebration of "the new covenant in his blood" prepares us to participate in a redemptive process of universal scope. Similarly, Craig Nessan has referred to the future kingdom orientation that participation in the Eucharist evokes, and of the use of imagination in encouraging us to envision that future, even "pretending" the kingdom as it ought to be, including in a missional sense, imagining that we are already that which we hope to be.[18]

Holy Communion as the source and center of the missional church: Missional because it is an open invitation. There is an obvious connection in John 20 between Jesus' scars and what he says concerning the disciples' ability to communicate forgiveness in verse 23. This last piece in Jesus' speech communicates the message that the church was to communicate—that it exists as a community of forgiveness. But that was only possible through what Jesus did here. The saving presence of Jesus in the midst of his people is what grants them the ability to communicate the offer of forgiveness. The giving and receiving of forgiveness should characterize the community of Christ, not pretense and Pharisaism. It has been the church's practice for centuries to offer confession before Communion, or to have within the liturgy of Communion prayers of confession and receiving absolution before taking the bread and wine. This practice is derived from 1 Corinthians 11:28: "Everyone ought to examine themselves before they eat of the bread and drink of the cup." This text has become in some traditions a basis for extreme soul examination and avoidance of Communion if the test is not passed. This is surprising given that this sentence simply says that there should examination and then eating. Underlying this Pauline text are sentiments

---

[17]Iain Provan, "The Pentateuch, II. Creation and Covenant," Old Testament Foundations lecture, Regent College, Vancouver, September 30, 2009.

[18]Craig L. Nessan, *Beyond Maintenance to Mission: A Theology of the Congregation* (Minneapolis: Fortress, 1999), p. 39.

of other texts that speak to confession in the New Testament (Jas 5:16; 1 Jn 1:9). That is, it seems fair to assume Paul means that examination leads to confession and receiving forgiveness and cleansing by God, as assured by the sister or brother or pastor or priest hearing the confession, and then Communion is received.

This is one reason why holy Communion is an open Communion, not a closed one. The Eucharist expresses the heart of the gospel and is by its nature an invitation for all to come and eat, if they have expressed confession and received assurance of forgiveness. The severe judgment expressed in 1 Corinthians 11 is not pronounced on seeking people who may in a church service take Communion without realizing its full significance. It is for Christians who know better, who are living aware of unconfessed sin and who still arrogantly take the elements. Judgment does fall on Christians of this nature in order to chasten, refine and restore them; if this does not have this effect, it can apparently lead to their untimely death. This is a sacred event. However, it is also a gospel event. I am not suggesting that unbelieving people be encouraged to take part in Communion apart from any expression of faith. I am saying that every time Communion is shared in the church, it should be done with an invitation for the seeking person to enter the confessional liturgy, to express faith in Christ, and to come and feed upon him for the first time. The exclusiveness that has characterized this feast in various traditions throughout church history is a scandal. It should be an invitational event, not a disbarring event. It should express hospitality, not exclusivity. It is, after all, for a community of sinners. Jesus frequently ate with tax gatherers and prostitutes, and he instituted this feast in the presence of his betrayer and his denier and the rest, who too abandoned him at the cross! I am not suggesting that serious lifestyle repentance in general and serious repentance on the occasion of taking Communion should not be practiced, but that not one single person is worthy to eat apart from Christ who is righteous for them. The church cannot be missional if it does not reflect that all who participate in Communion are sinners, and reflect an ethos of confession and forgiveness, not one of pharisaic superiority.

This notion and practice of an open Table is consonant with the nature of the church as a *koinōnia*, that is an open, missional community, which in turn is congruent and sacramental of the *koinōnia* of the Trinity, which has been opened to humanity through the incarnation, death, resurrection and ascension of the Son, who has taken humanity into the Godhead.

Holy Communion as the source and center of the missional church: Missional because of how it transforms the missional people of God. The importance of the Lord's Supper in making the church missional is also related to its profound formational influence on those who engage in its practice repeatedly. Mission is best accomplished through transformed persons and communities who reflect Christ in their character, ethics and compassion. This transformation is a consequence of what it means to take Communion.

1. Taking eucharistic bread and wine is an act of participation in Christ's body and blood (1 Cor 10:25-27). As the bread and wine reflect his participation in humanity for us, we in turn actually participate in his body and blood when we take these elements. This receiving has to do with our very being! Even if the bread and wine do not take on the nature of the body and blood of Christ *substantially*, what they become to us by the Spirit in epiclesis is *profoundly coinherent relationally with our beings while maintaining their own substantial integrity.* Thus, when we eat, this is spiritually nourishing for us, even apart from meditation on Jesus and thankfulness. But it is not only nourishing, it is profoundly hortatory. Anthony Thiselton says that this 1 Corinthians 10 passage,

> places at center stage (i) the commonality (with concern for the "other") and (ii) the exclusivity (in the framework of covenant loyalty) of a *cruciform lifestyle* which witnesses to *identification with Christ in the practical stance and lifestyle* of witnessing to the practical entailments of Christ's dying for "others" and being raised by God. Hence Paul sets up a dialectic between the sharing in shed **blood** or constituting **one loaf** (10:16, 17) and receiving a cup *of thanksgiving* or a **cup for which God be blessed** which together mark the **offering to God** not of the Lord's Supper as such but of the *life and lifestyle* which expresses its Christo-

morphic, Christocentric orientation in such a way that "you cannot take part in both the Lord's table and the table of demons" (10:21, NIV).[19]

2. When we take the eucharistic bread and wine, we are being formed again as the community of Christ. First Corinthians 10 speaks not only of believers' participation in Christ's historical, physical body (v. 16) but of a communal participation in his mystical body, the church (v. 17). By taking together we express that we have become one in Christ, as his mystical body the church. As by faith we share in the one eucharistic body (the bread), we participate in the benefits of his historical body, and the Spirit makes us one ecclesial body. This has profound warmth and profound challenge. This evokes the constant challenge for the preservation of the church's organic unity and pursuit of the mature unity Paul envisions in Ephesians 4, which is so crucial in the church's fulfillment of its mission as God's reconciling agent in the world.

The repeated practice of the Eucharist, in light of these Christological and ecclesial participational realities, is thus critical to the formation of the Christian self as an other-oriented person, in a manner that reflects the Trinity. This other-centered orientation, constitutive of a missional personality evokes David Ford's polemic for a contemplative understanding of spirituality such that the human self becomes a person facing God and other people. This, in a manner exemplified supremely in Christ, who Ford states "is a person who in facing God and other people embodies the other-orientated concept of self." A chapter in *Self and Salvation* speaks of the habit of engaging repeatedly in the Eucharist, what Ford calls the eucharistic *habitus*, as the manner in which the self is shaped gradually into an other-centered self.

Ford speaks of the Eucharist as a nonidentical repetition by which the Christian constantly recalls the blessing given at baptism.

> A eucharistic self is a baptized self in the routine of being blessed and blessing. Baptism is the archetypical Christian sign of personal identity, non-identically repeating Jesus' baptism, His death and resurrection,

---

[19]Anthony C. Thiselton, *The First Epistle to the Corinthians*, New International Greek Testament Commentary (Grand Rapids: Eerdmans, 2000), p. 751.

and the baptism of every other Christian. This is the initiating sacrament of blessing: being named and blessed in the name of the Father, Son and Holy Spirit. It signifies the reality and availability of the abundance it invites and initiates into a eucharistic practice in order to sustain a life of flourishing within the infinite love and joy of God.[20]

Ford goes on to speak of the transformation enabled by continuing this eucharistic *habitus:* "Repetition after repetition of hearing Scripture and its interpretation, of repentance, of intercession and petition, of the kiss of peace, of communion, of praising and thanking, all within a dramatic pattern that slowly becomes second nature: who can tell in advance what sort of self is being shaped year after year as these practices are interwoven thoughtfully with all the rest of life?"[21]

Yet, as Ford observes, the transformation of the self is actually not the principal issue. Becoming other-centered actually and ironically means not focusing on the self at all, even its transformation.[22] How does this happen? Ford suggests it is by practice, and yet thought and practice being inseparable, he suggests that a eucharistic *habitus* will be fostered by thought life that is dominated by orientation toward Jesus and other people. He summarizes the kind of self that is thus "accidentally" (my word) formed by habituation of the Eucharist in four ways that are very much in keeping with a trinitarian understanding of what humans are to become through salvation and for mission.

1. The self will be *blessed*. What the Eucharist does above all is to form the person as blessed and one who blesses others. This is in keeping with Calvin's appreciation of the Eucharist as a celebration of God's abundant goodness. Ford speaks of the Eucharist as the focal way by which the Christian copes with the abundance of God's blessing toward him or her. He speaks of

> the abundant meaning of a celebration which allows scope for dynamic relationship with God, other people and creation to be conceived in such rich terms: through taste and physicality; through drama and history; through being commanded, judged and forgiven; through mul-

---

[20]David Ford, *Self and Salvation* (Cambridge: Cambridge University Press, 1999), pp. 162-63.
[21]Ibid., p. 165.
[22]Ibid.

tifaceted responsiveness in word and action; through learning; through hospitality and a range of other exchanges; through individualization and incorporation.[23]

2. The self will be *placed*. Recognizing that selfhood involves particularity of place, Ford speaks of baptism and the Eucharist as a new placing of the self. He speaks of placing as being first of all, "under water" in baptism, and then "around the table." He speaks of baptism and the Eucharist as "ways of being placed before others, and they shape a *habitus* of facing. Above all they are oriented towards the face of Christ." He speaks of the Eucharist in light of the rich tradition of the "vision of God," that longing for an ultimate facing. He adds that the

> ultimate place is, therefore, "in the light of the knowledge of the glory of God in the face of Christ" (2 Cor 4:6); and the transformation of self happens in that facing of faith: "and we all with unveiled face beholding the glory of the Lord, are being changed into his likeness from one degree of glory into another; for this comes from the Lord who is the Spirit" (2 Cor 3:18).[24]

The transformation or beautifying of persons in this way into Christ's image is what makes a person missional as Christ is. It is a participation in both his being and acts.

3. The self will be *timed*. Whereas baptism "re-enacts the epoch-making event of Jesus Christ in its once for all character," the Eucharist continually places that event within time. In fact, habitually celebrating the Eucharist serves to form a self timed or regulated by it. Indeed, Ford suggests that by making the Eucharist the "timing event" that dominates our lives, it gives us guidance on the management of the rest of time.[25] This is the kind of shalom living related to the cultural mandate that draws others inexorably into its way.

4. The self will be *commanded*. In order that the theology of God's abundance should not lead to cheap grace, David Ford notes that if the posture of the eucharistic self is face-to-face with Christ, then it hears

---

[23]Ibid., pp. 162-63.
[24]Ibid.
[25]Ibid., p. 164.

the command of Christ. He speaks of this command first as the "Do this" command, which places the Eucharist's observance in an obedience and, therefore, an ethical context. Second, however, Ford speaks of the "new commandment," which figures prominently in the Johannine exposition of the Eucharist's institution.

The participant in the Eucharist is therefore under obedience, with the first, and perhaps greatest, testing ground being the arena of those around the table. The love commandment evokes the whole of ethical life as this is summarized by the love commandment and therefore mission. This involves death to the self. It involves resurrection in myriad ways of serving and loving Christ's people and our neighbor beyond. Integral to living out this ethical life is that it flows from the formation of the obedient self by the death and resurrection of Christ, a sphere into which baptism introduces the self, but a sphere which the Eucharist constantly reinforces.

The Eucharist is therefore missional, for as a practice that rehearses the crucial narrative of the Christian faith it forms people who are missional in character and in loving action toward the other. It is also missional in that it infuses *hope* within the human participant each time it is taken: hope of the kingdom to come, hope of societal justice and peace, hope of the comfort from sufferings encountered in the "now but not yet," hope of personal transformation when we will see Jesus in the fullness of his being, "face-to-face," hope of resurrection and immortality. And such hope infused is then disseminated in contact within the worlds of people for whom there often seems so little hope. It is disseminated into the *favelas* and townships and slums and communities and societies by the hope-filled presence and actions of kingdom people who live in anticipation of a new creation, working for it now. There is an eschatological dimension within the Lord's Supper suggested in the institutional words of Jesus in Matthew 26:29, "I tell you, I will not drink of this fruit of the vine from now on until that day when I drink it new with you in my Father's kingdom" and captured by the pregnant Pauline phrase, "you proclaim the Lord's death until he comes" (1 Cor 11:26).

We come now to what eucharistic priority and a cruciform ethos mean for the church's worship in general, as well as specifically for its preaching and the character of its community.

Christocentric, cruciform worship: A case for the great High Priest as worship leader. Though the Eucharist is central and determinative in the gathering, it is not the only thing in church worship. Recognizing that worship involves all of life, I will here nevertheless restrict my comments to the nature of corporate worship and how it should be affected by the centrality of the Eucharist and a cruciform ethos. The worship and thanksgiving of the church will take its cue from Eucharist. But what will that look like in a church? I will limit myself to two main perspectives. The first relates to what the Eucharist makes real by the Spirit—the presence of the One in the church's center, Christ who as *the* Priest, our great High Priest is the church's primary worship leader. The second is the priestliness of the many priests who take their character from the one Priest and worship in participation with him. If they come to remember, feed on and participate in the once-for-all sacrifice of the great High Priest, then they respond by bringing their own sacrifices of praise to God and ministry to the others in his mystical body. Both of these dimensions, if recovered and treasured and practiced by the church, would transform its character, making it a deep and wide missional church.

Worship, deemed by A. W. Tozer to be the "missing jewel" of the church in the mid-twentieth century, may by some be considered to be no longer missing.[26] In the later eras of the same century many churches moved away from preaching-dominated and Finneyesque evangelism-dominated church services, in which a few hymns and choruses were sung preliminary to the main preaching event. Instead came prolonged sessions of musical worship, influenced by the advent of renewal worship songs, which were more intimate than hymns and facilitated more contemporary styles of music and more emotionally and physically authentic expression. The presence of God could often be sensed in this practice. Many churches blended these songs with hymns. Services were no longer merely preaching sessions. The whole was considered worship,

---

[26]A. W. Tozer, *Worship, the Missing Jewel* (Camp Hill, Penn.: Christian Publications, 1992).

and significant time was given to singing as experiential worship, enabling the congregation to participate as priests, at least to some extent in this way to worship. This was, in my opinion, progress away from cerebrally dominant services. However, this has often led to the assumption that only singing constitutes worship. The absence of the Eucharist influence often remained. Furthermore, the missing jewel of the missing jewel remained missing: the realization of worship as led by the great High Priest, the church's liturgical leader. And with this the notion of worship as participation in God and specifically that of participation with Christ as our worship leader was also neglected.

Emphasis on objectivity in worship, not merely with respect to Christ as the object of worship but as worship leader among his people, initiating and presenting the saints' worship by the Spirit to the Father, is a rich concept rarely spoken of and even more rarely entered into. There has been a significant and welcome turn by many churches to ancient liturgy, the creeds and confessions of saints past and the reading of Scripture, and the Eucharist in many churches, blended with the experiential songs and hymns. This is a step forward in the deepening of the church. It will be a further step forward for that worship to gain the high priestly and trinitarian perspective.

Honoring the high priesthood of Christ our worship leader. Protestants who rightly eschew Pelagianism with respect to their soteriology have embraced Pelagianism in their practice of worship. Further, Protestants who by creed are trinitarian in fact express their worship in its subjective aspect in a unitarian manner. As James Torrance assessed it, there are, broadly speaking, two different views of worship in the church today. "The first view, probably the commonest and most widespread, is that worship is something which we do—mainly in church on Sunday." We may know that "we need God's grace to help us do it; we do it because Jesus taught us to do it and left us an example to show us how to do it. But worship is what WE do." This makes our human priesthood the only priesthood, "the only offering our offering, the only intercessions our intercessions." As Torrance confirms, it is "in practice unitarian. It has no doctrine of the Mediator or the Sole Priesthood of Christ. It is human centered, with no proper doctrine of the Holy Spirit, and is basically non-sacramental. It engenders weariness." It is, he asserts, "what our forebears have been called 'legal' worship, and not 'evangelical' worship. It is what the ancient church would call 'Arian' or 'Pelagian,' and not truly catholic."

By contrast, the second view is that worship is "the gift of participating through the Spirit in the incarnate Son's communion with the Father—of participating, in union with Christ, in what he has done for us once and for all in his life and death on the Cross, and in what he is continuing to do for us in the presence of the Father, and in his mission to the world."[27] The underlying assumption in Torrance's sentiments is of course the profound union between Christ and his church. Torrance's *totus Christus*, unlike the current pope's concept of it, is a full relational union in which human and the divine-human persons remain who they are. It is important when we come to worship that we not neglect the most important theological term of the New Testament, the prepositional phrase *in Christ*. Thus Torrance adds:

> This second view is Trinitarian and incarnational. It takes seriously New Testament teaching about the sole Priesthood and Headship of Christ, the once-and-for-all self-offering of Christ, life in union with Christ through the Spirit, with a vision of the church as the Body of Christ. It is fundamentally "sacramental"—but in a way which enshrines the Gospel of grace, that God in the gift of Christ and the gift of the Spirit, gives us what he demands—the worship of our hearts and lives. This is the heart of our theology of the eucharist.[28]

Torrance also includes mission in this concept of worship: "Our mission to the world and ministry to the needs of humanity, are they not the gift of participating in Christ's mission to the world and his ministry to human needs? Is this not the meaning of life in the Spirit?"[29] These sentences communicate how the worship and prayers of the church are in fact the mission of the church, before ever a hungry person is fed or an inquirer evangelized.

---

[27]James Torrance, *Worship, Community and the Triune God of Grace* (Carlisle, U.K.: Paternoster, 1996), pp. 36-37.
[28]Ibid., pp. 22-23.
[29]Ibid.

Honoring the many priests in the one Priest. Worship true to the image of Jesus standing in the community with scarred hands (Jn 20:19-23) is led by him, *the* Priest. This will bring freedom to the many priests who may imagine that if there is a worship leader up front doing his or her thing, along with the preacher who does his or her thing, then "my thing" is not very important, or, conversely, who may be plagued by a sense of the inadequacy of their feeble offerings of worship. Addressing the latter point, it will be heartening to both leaders in worship or congregational participants that even if they prepared diligently and even if they concentrated perfectly and didn't wander all over in their minds while singing or listening to the sermon, their worship would be imperfect. It is freeing to know that "to all our prayers and praises, He adds his sweet perfume" to make our feeble attempts at worship acceptable to the Father. This is not to say that we do not need to work at preparing for corporate worship or at concentration while in it, but we do even that in a spirit of dependence on the Spirit, not with fleshly fervor.

In at least some, if not all, of the church's gatherings, there needs to be movement beyond paying mere lip service to the priesthood of all believers. The New Testament, which speaks of every believer as holy and royal priests (1 Pet 2), not just the worship pastors and preachers or liturgical leaders, also speaks of various aspects of worship in terms of sacrifices or offerings. Hebrews 13:15 speaks of the sacrifice of praise, offerings of thanksgiving from our lips, of giving of our resources, and 1 Corinthians 14:26 pictures a highly participative ethos in gatherings where one "has a hymn, or a word of instruction, a revelation, a tongue or an interpretation." At the risk of saying the obvious, if every church member actually prepared before coming to offer offerings of thanksgiving, worship, songs, prayers, words of knowledge or wisdom, and of giving, and if there were space in our services for body expression, our gatherings would be transformed from the bus model (sleepy passengers led by the lone driver) or the orchestra model (a few performers up front and consumers in the rows of the audience) to the body model, and from relative passivity of the many to active participation of all.

I recognize that church is not just gatherings but a community doing life together and that there are opportunities outside of gatherings to serve. The priesthood of all believers involves service to God in participation with our great High Priest to others in the church (*holy* priesthood: "offering spiritual sacrifices to God through Jesus Christ" [1 Pet 2:5]). The church becomes an other-centered community in a way that extends beyond the members of the body to the world. This we may think of as *royal* priesthood (1 Pet 2:9, declaring his praises). As a charismatic other-oriented community of the Spirit, it is the sign of the kingdom of God. Priesthood is a concept inclusive of the mission of humans as designed by God to steward his creation. It includes participation with Christ, the full and true image of God, in creation care, in our work, in our family lives and in our leisure. This recaptures the widest circle of mission, expressed as the cultural mandate in Genesis 1–2. We are the many priests of creation, in the one Priest, giving creation a voice through our scientific discoveries, and protecting it from abuse through proper ecological and environmental management.[30] We are priests of creation also as we discover and enjoy its beauty and express that beauty through the arts.

However, there is a need within the church's gatherings for the expression of the priesthood of all believers. This can happen in smaller group gatherings, but this should not take away from the need for all priests to worship and pray and serve, albeit sometimes in silent prayer in the larger gatherings. The opportunities for all God's people to discover, develop and deploy their spiritual gifts in smaller settings seems at minimum, essential for the health of a deep and wide, missional church.

Christocentric, cruciform preaching: A case for preaching that is cruciform and sacramental. When Jesus stood among his people with nail-scarred body, his presence was all-important. Thus I have spoken of the Eucharist as the ongoing fulfillment of Jesus' spiritual presence to his people. However, Jesus also spoke words that day, words of comfort,

---

[30]This reflects an alternative rendering of Psalm 19:4. My colleague Loren Wilkinson has suggested that this rendering reflects well the creation mandate given to humans who give creation a voice by discovering and expressing how it is constituted and how it functions, and by protecting it from misuse.

imparting peace, and words of exhortation, encouraging them to disseminate peace in union with him, as sent by the Father. The church will analogously be a community in which the words of Jesus are heard just as in this early proleptic church. They will be words given context by the Eucharist. They will be words for the receiving of shalom. They will be words of exhortation, affirming mission, affirming that we are sent as he is sent because we are in him by the Spirit.

Preaching was touched upon in chapter five. The following are cruciform perspectives on preaching.

1. Preaching and the sacraments must mutually inform one another, and preaching, properly understood, is a sacrament.

2. Though it should cover all of Scripture and be expositional, preaching must in its content above all reflect the gospel imaged in the Eucharist.

3. Preaching is not reserved only for the public teacher but is the essence of what all God's people do as they articulate the shalom they have entered, and as they explain their nonverbal missional endeavors.

Christocentric, cruciform community: A case for community that is cruciform. *Community* is a buzzword in both the church and our world. It is, however, a rich word if it reflects biblical *koinōnia*. This term in context literally means a sharing *in* Christ and therefore a sharing in the love and life of the triune God, himself the divine *koinōnia*, which too is cross-centered, and then the sharing *out* of our lives and possessions with one another in a cruciform way. This is illustrated well in Acts 2:42-47, which includes *koinōnia* in the summary marks of the church in verse 42, juxtaposed with the "breaking of the bread." It is given color in its sharing out capacity in verses 44-45, where cruciform self-sacrifice is evident in the church's community life.

My particular interest, in this discussion of the presence of the once-crucified Savior in his community's center, is to point out that this is what defines the "sharing in" component of *koinōnia*. Much of what passes for *koinōnia* in contemporary church life seems to neglect the fact that the primary goal is not vulnerability or gut-sharing or even friendship, though all these are laudable. The goal is not even to advance each other's knowledge of the Scriptures, though that too is commendable. These are all secondary to helping one another know the crucified Christ more intimately. The ultimate goal of *koinōnia* is to discover common life in Christ, common union with Christ, common worshipful adoration of Christ, common soul-orientation toward Christ and our neighbor. For this reason when the gatherings that constituted *koinōnia* are further elaborated in Acts 2, a key element is that "they broke bread in their homes" (Acts 2:46). Its orientation was around the Eucharist, which was celebrated in these days in the context of a love meal.[31]

This may fly in the face of traditions in which the Eucharist is celebrated only with the whole church present or only when ordained persons are present, and there are dangers of making transgenerational assumptions from precedent without regard for historical context. I wish nevertheless to appeal to what seems a good pattern for the church here, from Acts 2:46. The Eucharist pervaded the fellowship of God's people. Just as the divine *koinōnia* was eternally cruciform, so the communities of the people of God in Christ were cruciform. As a result, the holistic nature of their *koinōnia* was demonstrated in their sacrificial and generous living. No one had any need because everyone shared generously. I wonder if more of this radical, costly fellowship would be evident in the Western church if its small groups or cell groups or pastorates were centered around the Eucharist. I wonder also if the willingness to sustain persecution when that came to the Jerusalem church was birthed in these cruciform gatherings.

Fear would be removed, as it was among the disciples when they saw that the death of their Master was not the end of the story. He was risen. But fear dissipated because that risen One bore scars that were profoundly sacramental. They understood that his atoning work on their behalf would mean that they need not fear death or the judgment of God. Fear about proclaiming this would go not only because the cross is a sweet fragrance to those who accept it but even when received as a stench and they faced persecution they were in good company—he would be with them, and they would be filling up

---

[31]See Joachim Jeremias, *The Eucharistic Words of Jesus*, trans. Norman Perrin (London: SCM Press, 1966), passim.

that which was lacking in his sufferings as the corporate Christ!

Furthermore, Christ's resurrection was a demonstration that redemption was complete. Seeing his scars as we gather to take Communion will help us as the Western church overcome our fearfulness. These scars remind us what it cost him and "makes our coward spirits brave." They remind us of a restored beauty, of what the cross accomplished for us and the world. They empower us to live in cruciform communities that are open and attractive to the world, and to live in our wider communities in ways that bring redemption and restore beauty to communities and people in them as we declare the good news alongside of living it. They remind us also to preach the depths of the cross to the people in our churches. Nothing will deepen their appreciation of their Savior and salvation more, and nothing will help them live more attractively as servant disciples and sent ones, and nothing will break their hearts more and enthuse them about expressing to a broken world God's identification with our suffering.

We and the people of our churches will be released in mission to the extent that we meditate upon, contemplate and feed on the Savior and the value of his saving, atoning, redeeming, propitiating, reconciling work, then live in the cross way of community life, and then declare its efficacy for all who believe.

8

Mission About the Cross, Mission Under the Cross

His Completed Redemption

■ ■ ■

After he said this, he showed them his hands and side.
The disciples were overjoyed when they saw the Lord.

JOHN 20:20

Christ's sufferings are for propitiation;
our sufferings are for propagation.

JOSEPH TSON[1]

How can this strange story of God made man,
of a crucified Savior, of resurrection and new creation become
credible for those whose entire mental training has conditioned them
to believe that the real world is the world which can be satisfactorily
explained and managed without the hypothesis of God? I know of
only one clue to the answering of that question, only one real
hermeneutic of the gospel: a congregation which believes it.

LESSLIE NEWBIGIN, "The Pastor's Opportunities"

---

[1]Tson was the pastor of the Second Baptist Church of Oradea, Romania, until 1981 when he was exiled by the government. Joseph Tson, cited in John Piper, *Desiring God: Meditations of a Christian Hedonist* (Portland, Ore.: Multnomah, 1986), chap. 10.

THE CONTRAST BETWEEN HOW MANY of Christ's disciples reacted negatively to his speech concerning his death in John 6 and how these disciples responded to the scarred Jesus in John 20 is remarkable. The John 6 "hard teaching" that Jesus gave about his flesh being "real food" and his blood "real drink" stumbled many. In John 20 his disciples begin to feed on his wounds with joy. That joy may have been tempered once they realized that in carrying out the mission in union with Jesus they too might be expected to bear scars.

Life and mission in union with Jesus' death, proclaiming his cross, seems to carry with it an inevitable consequence: those who do so will bear Jesus' scars (cf. "I bear on my body the marks of Jesus" [Gal 6:17]; "We always carry around in our body the death of Jesus" [2 Cor 4:10]). This seems to be the expected norm for New Testament Christians ("everyone who wants to live a godly life in Christ Jesus will be persecuted" [2 Tim 3:12]). But is this a uniform expectation in all periods of church history, even when it is not under siege? The church seems to have understood that it does not go looking for persecution. In post-Reformation eras of threatened persecution, for example, the church decided that the most ethical thing for Christians to do was (in this order) to engage, then emigrate if possible, then go underground if possible, and then to face martyrdom. In some periods of church history when Christianity was permitted within a state, its mission has moved forward unhindered, with unrestrained evangelism, ethical influence on governments and the establishing of educational institutions and charitable, holistic care through hospitals and so on. Yet as in the case of the post-Constantine era, all kinds of spiritual and ethical compromises seem to inflict the church when the waters are calm. This kind of malaise seems to characterize the church in Western countries today, even though most sociological and religious scholars agree that the days of post-Reformation Christendom are gone. Overt persecution is for the most part absent.

Is it possible that this is the case because a large majority of Christians do not reflect the values of Jesus and that our lifestyles simply do not challenge the world, perhaps because we are so indiscriminately enculturated? Some evangelical churches are in fact isolated globules of

Christendom, bereft of real Christianity, and unaware that the culture is now post-Christian simply because there is little interaction outside of their subculture that in any way challenges the larger culture. The reflections of Søren Kierkegaard on Danish Lutheranism, which had degenerated into a nominal state religion, might be just as true of these churches: "Christendom has abolished Christianity without really knowing it itself. As a result, if something must be done, one must attempt again to introduce Christianity into Christendom."[2] Charles Moore offers commentary on Kierkegaard's context:

> Three things, in particular, marred the church of his day: (1) Intellectualism—the "direct mental assent to a sum of doctrines"; (2) Formalism—"battalions upon battalions" of unbelieving believers; and (3) Pharisaism—a herd of hypocritical clergy that ignore the Christianity they were hired to preach. . . .
>
> Kierkegaard's contention was that despite sound doctrine, or the *what* of faith, "the lives people live demonstrate that there is really no Christianity—or very little." Genuine Christianity, according to Kierkegaard, is anything but doctrine. It is a way of being in the truth before God by following Jesus in self-denial, sacrifice, suffering, and by seeking a primitive relationship with God. . . . How, exactly, are we to *become* Christian, especially when "one is a Christian of a sort?"[3]

I am not entirely convinced that Christian life in our Western churches is that much different from how Kierkegaard describes the church of his day. Not many of our churches have grasped the cruciform nature of the church and its worship and ethos, and therefore not many Christians are living cruciform lives and proclaiming a cruciform gospel. This chapter may provide a gauge by which to assess this and be an evangelical catalyst for renewal of Christocentricity and cruciformity.

Two principle questions will be addressed. The first is, what is it that we preach when we preach the cross; that is, what has the cross accom-

---

[2]Søren Kierkegaard, *Practice in Christianity: Kierkegaard's Writings*, trans. Howard V. Hong and Edna H. Hong (Princeton, N.J.: Princeton University Press, 1991), 20:36.

[3]Charles E. Moore, ed., introduction to *Provocations: Spiritual Writings of Kierkegaard* (Rifton, N.Y.: Plough, 2011) From Introduction, pp. x-xi, www.plough.com/ebooks/pdfs/Provocations.pdf.

plished for God's mission to humanity and creation? The second is, what does it mean to do mission in union or participation with the crucified Christ as a church community, as a Christian? This will involve exposition of mission as mission *about* the cross, that is, I will seek to clarify the message that the church bears. Second, it will involve speaking of mission *under* the cross. That is, we will seek to understand what it means to be in participation with the crucified Christ and how the cross defines the missional way of life. This will entail elucidation of the relationship between the church as cruciform and the kingdom of which it is sign and servant, which will qualify how the church is to engage with society. We will also explore the implications of a scarred Christ for identification with the scarredness of the world. The way the cross serves to alleviate the objection of postmodernity to the oppressiveness of Christianity's metanarrative will be highlighted.

MISSION ABOUT THE CROSS

Proclamation of the message of the cross is as necessary today as it has been in every culture since Jesus' time. Postmodernity should not be any different. It remains God's appointed way for effecting the salvation of human beings, despite its apparent "foolishness" (1 Cor 1:23) in the two cultures Paul knew—Jewish and Greek—and our cultures, modernity and postmodernity, today. Paul professes with conviction, "For I resolved to know nothing while I was with you except Jesus Christ and him crucified" (1 Cor 2:2). He goes so far as to say, "Woe to me if I do not preach the gospel!" (1 Cor 9:16). When he speaks of the marks of the Lord Jesus in his body, he states, "May I never boast except in the cross of our Lord Jesus Christ, through which the world has been crucified to me, and I to the world," perhaps suggesting why he had such marks (Gal 6:14).

Preaching the cross is a critical piece of the *kērygma*, the core of our message. Paul highlights this in 1 Corinthians 15:3-4: "For what I received I passed on to you as of first importance: that Christ died for our sins according to the Scriptures, that he was buried, that he was raised on the third day according to the Scriptures." A lovely piece it is in every age. The privilege of offering the hope that Jesus' cross brings for human sin and ultimately for human suffering is inestimable. Here is the God who suffers *for* us and *with* us. Here is hope for a justified humanity and a reconciled universe.

One of the most remarkable missional passages of this gospel comes to mind. You may remember that some Greeks wanted to see Jesus in John 12. When they were brought to him, Jesus immediately launched into a description of his death. It didn't seem so seeker-friendly:

> Jesus replied, "The hour has come for the Son of Man to be glorified. Very truly I tell you, unless a kernel of wheat falls to the ground and dies, it remains only a single seed. But if it dies, it produces many seeds. Those who love their life will lose it, while those who hate their life in this world will keep it for eternal life. Whoever serves me must follow me; and where I am, my servant also will be. My Father will honor the one who serves me." (Jn 12:23-26)

First, they needed to understand that if they wanted to see Jesus as he really is, they must see him in light of his death, as a crucified Jesus, and, second, if they wanted to follow him, they needed to do the same, die as he did. They encountered Jesus as both the source of their pardon and the pattern of their lives.

Two issues rise to the top for consideration concerning preaching the cross of Christ in the missional church. The first has to do with the manner or style of the preaching, and the second, relating to the content of the preaching, has to do with the scope of the atonement the cross is declared to accomplish.

Perhaps most of us would agree that the cross must be preached in every culture. I want to assert that in every sermon ever preached, though it should be expository, must reflect and contain gospel, in the broadest sense—not a John 3:16 "simple gospel presentation" but the core of the Bible's message that God is for humanity in Christ! But the issue of controversy is how? How are we to preach the cross in this generation, in this culture or that? Both as the church scattered and as the church gathered, it seems entirely appropriate that we inculturate or contextualize the message as Paul does in Acts 17. Paul uses Athenian poetry and the truth in it to convey gospel. Much ink has been spilled on that passage elsewhere. I only say that preaching in the church and proclamation in personal witness must show awareness of thought patterns and cultural mores of the prevailing culture. That means awareness of the culture by being immersed in it, yet not being of it. In the gatherings of the church, using multimedia seems appropriate, though lines must be drawn between helpful use of media and that which ends up expressing the gospel in disembodied ways.

For example, what of the preacher's sermon being beamed into the gymnasium or other congregational sites? It is difficult to imagine that a disembodied or virtual sermon is consonant with the embodied notion of the church, and the immediacy of the encounter between the preacher and the community. I would not deny that God can use virtual preachers, but this seems to run counter to the idea of an organic body and even the essence of the gospel of an embodied crucified and risen and ascended Christ. What about dialogue or a chat between two folks up front in the church? Well again, no doubt God can and has used these methods, but it seems that the foolishness of preaching is just that—preaching: the anointed declaration of the gospel as the Word of God is expounded, accompanied by the power of the Spirit, humans speaking in such a manner that the words of man become the words of God (1 Pet 4:11).

Now to the matter of the *scope* of the atonement of the cross. The whole tenor of our discussion of the atonement, the beauty of the scars, in chapter seven, was such as to suggest that the life and death of Jesus were vicarious for humanity, *all* of humanity. This has sometimes been controversial in mission. Did Jesus really die for all humans, and if he did, why would they not all be saved? The classical arguments for and against particular atonement have run something like this: the atonement must either be limited in its scope or in its power. If it is unlimited in its power, all must be saved, so why bother proclaiming the good news. If it is unlimited in its scope, then its power is questionable, for all are not saved. The typical Reformed solution, notably that of John Murray, was to say that redemption has only been accomplished for those to whom it will be applied, that is, those who truly believe. Preachers of this persuasion are often careful for fear that they may not really be making a *bona fide* offering of salvation, lest they be offering eternal life to folks who were not the elect. They make sure they say that "all who believe will be saved."

I believe that this is a false premise. On the basis of the majority of clear texts in the New Testament, and above all, on the basis of the ontological significance of the incarnation of Christ as the man for all humanity, I believe that the life and death of Jesus was vicarious for all humanity. The issue of the atonement's power does not depend on whether folks accept the verdict of God upon them as a result of Jesus' death and resurrection for them. Their failure to believe and accept that verdict does not alter the verdict. If their entry into the epistemic and existential value of the justification that Jesus has effected does not have a volitional component, humans would not be free in any sense. Conversely, were God to force the human into faith it would no longer be faith.

If God really was in Christ reconciling the *world* to himself, as Paul tells us, then the world is really reconciled. Great freedom comes in proclamation, with the absence of concerns about a bona fide offer of salvation, when we announce reconciliation that is available to all in that all have in Christ participated in the cross event, and that all can enter into that reconciliation. It is the missional proclaimer's task to announce this *fait accompli* and call upon humans to repent. There is great freedom in proclamation in that the call to repentance is truly evangelical and not legal repentance; that is, proclamation that pronounces upon the sinner the reality that they are justified people in God's estimate and that they must merely acknowledge and accept God's verdict.

Missional preaching is fueled by the conviction that the atonement is a *fait accompli* for all since God has in Christ justified creation and all humanity representatively and yet that God will not push this "yes" verdict on anyone. This Barthian perspective on the One true human, Jesus, who has justified humanity and indeed creation, offers a perspective beyond the Calvinist and Arminian perspectives. I realize that there are different opinions on this matter, and that this is not the only way of seeing justification that is conducive to preaching the gospel. Obviously even those who hold a Reformed view of particular atonement are not precluded from Christian mission. William Carey, the father of modern Western missions, was a Particular Baptist (born 1761). Despite hyper-Calvinist influences in his denomination that worked against mission, Carey persevered, and in 1792 he published his groundbreaking missionary manifesto, *An Enquiry into the Obligations of Christians to Use Means for the Conversion of the Heathens*. The first part is a theological justification for missionary activity, arguing that the command of Jesus to make disciples of all the world (Mt 28:18-20) remains binding on Christians!

Carey was influenced by another proponent of particular atonement, Jonathan Edwards, whose *Account of the Life of the Late Rev. David Brainerd* influenced Carey positively toward mission. Actually, many in the Reformed tradition have influenced missionary movements despite this view of election and particular atonement. Particular election carries with it the notion of irresistible grace, which gives assurance that the Spirit will be at work in some to bring them to faith. It is in this manner that the Lord's encouraging words to Paul in Corinth are understood: "I am with you, and no one is going to attack and harm you, because I have many people in this city" (Acts 18:10).

Truly good news of justification for all. Acceptance of Barth's attractive alternative Christological viewpoint that all humanity and all creation has been justified in him, by his life and death and resurrection as the incarnate One, and that this is the *euangelion* to be proclaimed, does require an understanding of its underpinnings. A full treatment of this is beyond our scope here.[4] Suffice it to say that it is by means of God's eternal covenant to be for humanity and the concept of *homoousios* and incarnational theology that Barth links all humanity to Christ and by means of which an objective and real justification is actualized concretely for all humans. Thus, it is the primacy of the incarnate Christ in uniting creation and covenant, through his vicarious life and death, which paves the way for the Barthian doctrine of justi-

---

[4]For fuller treatments of Barth's work on this mainly in *Church Dogmatics* II/2, see Trevor Hart, *Regarding Karl Barth* (Carlisle, U.K.: Paternoster, 1999), pp. 62ff.; and Bruce L. McCormack, "*Justitia Aliena*: Karl Barth in Conversation with the Evangelical Doctrine of Imputed Righteousness," in *Justification in Perspective* (Grand Rapids: Baker, 2006), pp. 167ff.

fication.[5] Justification is not simply a declaration of righteousness with respect to the law, but is more fundamentally justification with respect to God's purpose for us as creatures and covenant partners. Barth maintains that the creation is declared "right" in Christ, in a manner reflecting its initial creation as "good," in that it was "able to be taken up by God in the incarnation and brought concretely to its telos in fulfilment of the covenant."[6] This divine assessment of creation anticipates an ontological aspect of justification which then determines that of the forensic, which is related to law, sin and justice. Barth's point is that justification, as ontological, means that we are not merely treated as if we were just, but that we actually *are* just in God's eyes. Through our relationship to this man, *incarnatus Deus* "his particular history is the pre-history and post-history of all our individual lives."[7] It should be noted, however, that universal justification of humanity did not, for Barth, necessarily imply universalism, the notion that all will be saved. "Whether man hears it, whether he accepts it and lives as one who is pardoned is another question."[8] For Barth, whether all will be saved from hell is an altogether different question than whether all are justified. Individuals can deny the reality that they are justified. They cannot undo this reality if they tried. They can continue to deny this reality and embrace hell in this state of denial of their true being.

Barth placed greater emphasis on justification *in Christ*, even more so than on justification *by faith*. When asked about the nature of the "self-demonstration" that is the essence of faith, Barth will respond that it is the self-revelation of Jesus Christ to the sinner, the incarnate Word of God, the "most concrete reality" in whom our justification is a completed reality before and apart from our acknowledgment of it. This is why faith is not a work that adds to justification to make it complete—justification is complete for us as an act of God in Christ—it cannot be augmented or set in motion by anything else. As Barth so eloquently expressed this, "What is the *sola fide* but a faint yet necessary

---

[5]Hart, *Regarding Karl Barth*, p. 51. Here Hart cites para. 61 in Karl Barth, *Church Dogmatics* III/1, ed. G. W. Bromiley and T. F. Torrance (Edinburgh: T & T Clark, 1975), pp. 369-70.
[6]Ibid.
[7]Ibid., p. 59. Quotation is from *Church Dogmatics* III/1, p. 27.
[8]Barth, *Church Dogmatics* IV/1, p. 568.

echo of the *sola Christus*? He alone is the One in whom man is justified and revealed to be justified. He alone has fulfilled the penitence in which the conversion of man to God is actually and definitively accomplished."[9]

For Barth justification is not a state but a history, that of the man Jesus in whom God has justified his creation by putting it to death and raising it up in a new form. Its location is in the history of the incarnate Son of God, Jesus Christ, as opposed to the histories of individual men and women. For Barth justification is therefore a history alien to our own but which we discover to be our own, and "which projects us into the crisis of eschatological transition, living out the Kingdom of God in the midst of the world, living by faith in that reality *which lies beyond our experience*, but which stands over against us as our reality nevertheless."[10] The depths of our being have been changed by the justification that God has brought about in Christ, Barth would say, but this reality is not locatable within our experience. God has brought it about by his electing grace, made concrete in Christ, irrespective of our experience of it. We are called away from our own experience and called into discovering ourselves "in Christ" and his situation. The nature of the journey is not, for Barth, toward *iustus* but rather the eschatological tension of *totus iustus simul totus peccator*. We live in the reality of being in Christ which is a "real being," one of total justification, and this is the ground on which we have hope of one day ceasing to be *totus peccator*. We are never more or less justified as we move along the journey.

Grace in Barth is God's self-giving, his standing in our place, his fulfilling of the obligations of the Torah for us. Thus *faith* is acknowledgment of a reality transition. Faith is a response to a reality, not merely a possibility. For Barth response in *repentance* to the reality of a justified creation and humanity is truly *evangelical* repentance; it is truly characterized by grace, a response to a reality already real before any human expression of repentance. *Assurance* of salvation for Barth is not gained by taking an inward journey to evaluate our religious affections, as in Edwards, for example. Rather he invites us to look away from

---

[9]Ibid., p. 632.
[10]Hart, *Regarding Karl Barth*, p. 62.

ourselves to the Christ who is for us.[11] In Christ we are righteous, new creatures, faithful covenant partners set free to live as such. This contemplative approach resonates with the disciples' joy in John 20 when they saw their risen Lord with nail-scarred hands!

This robustly Protestant theology of justification in Barth stands in opposition to the Augustinian justification theology reflected in the Catholic theologian Hans Küng, in which justification is the subjective side of salvation, the objective side being the redemption Christ has accomplished.[12] For Barth faith *is* the subjective aspect of justification. It stands also in contrast to a somewhat prevalent view within evangelicalism in which justification and sanctification become blurred by an introspective approach to assurance that makes sanctification the primary criterion for assurance of justification. This tendency has lived on from its roots in Jonathan Edwards. As in Calvin, for Barth union with Christ is the primal soteriological category, from which flow both justification and sanctification, these *duplex gratia* being distinct yet inseparable.

Barth's justification theology also stands distinct from the revisionist views of N. T. Wright, the "New Perspective." Though, like Barth, justification remains judicial in Wright, the latter distinguishes between subjective justification worked out in the believer's present life and objective justification, which is pronounced at a future apocalyptic event in which God vindicates himself and his people through the upholding of his covenant with Israel. This is a false dichotomy or dualism which Barth will not permit. Justification and sanctification in Barth "are two different aspects of the one saving event."[13] As McCormack points out, the dualistic way of thinking of justification as having been made possible by the cross and then made real by the subjective appropriation of it in the believer is a denial of the one work of

---

[11]Whereas the issue of human individual experience apart from our relation to Christ is anhypostatic abstraction, as Ingolf Dalferth notes, "our world of common experience is an *enhypostatic reality* which exists only insofar as it is incorporated into the concrete reality of God's saving self-realization in Christ" (Ingolf Dalferth, "Karl Barth's Eschatological Realism," in *Karl Barth: Centenary Essays*, ed. S. W. Sykes [Cambridge: Cambridge University Press, 1989], p. 29).

[12]Hart, *Regarding Karl Barth*, p. 68.

[13]Barth, *Church Dogmatics* IV/2, p. 503.

the one God through the one Christ through the one Spirit, in line with the trinitarian coinherence of act. For Barth,

> this way of thinking fails to understand that what Jesus Christ accomplished is not merely the possibility of reconciliation but the reality of it. Expressed even more concretely: justification is not first made effective when the Holy Spirit awakens faith in us; rather, the Spirit awakens faith in us so that we might live from and toward the reality of justification that is already effective for us before we come to know of it.[14]

As McCormack affirms, the Barthian view is firmly Protestant, in ways that may stretch evangelicals, even though it is more radically evangelical than standard evangelical views of justification.

What does it mean to preach this missional message? Ambiguities around proclaiming "Christ died for you" or "Christ died for the world" now disappear. All the New Testament texts that appear to clearly say that God loved the whole world and that Christ died and rose again for all need not be reinterpreted with subtleties like "all without distinction" as opposed to "all without exception." In 2 Corinthians 5, for example, Paul gives us the word of reconciliation we are to preach, quite categorically: "God was in Christ reconciling the world to Himself, not imputing their trespasses to them, and has committed to us the word of reconciliation" (2 Cor 5:19 NKJV). The truly good news, the *euangelion*, that God has justified all in Christ, is liberating to preach in that it moves away from the selection model of election and enables the proclaimer to proclaim the good news to *every* human being that God is for them and that he loves them. The primary point of considering the theology of justification as Barth developed it is the liberating power it brings to proclamation. The *how* question, in terms of the spirit of our proclamation, anticipates our next section, but let me say that it must be as one beggar telling another where to find bread.

MISSION UNDER THE CROSS

The pierced hands and feet not only convey an accomplished re-

---

[14]McCormack, *"Justitia Aliena,"* p. 179.

demption—they suggest the nature of the King and the kingdom. They reflect a Christ who is servant, giving his life for the world. They set a pattern for his disciples as to how they can expect to minister—as servants who give their lives for the world, who can expect to suffer in applying reconciliation and redemption to the world in mission. Christianity has, over the centuries, tragically been used to oppress people. The image in the Balkan Wars of a Serbian tank driver, with three fingers representing the Trinity of his Orthodox faith raised in triumph over his Muslim neighbors, is a striking example in recent history. True Christianity, if the image of Christ with nail-scarred hands is anything to go by, is a metanarrative that does not wield power and oppressiveness—it is revelation of a triune God in three persons who love each other with perfect mutuality and submission, and who creates and redeems human persons to love that way too. What's more, the heart of the Christian story is the story of God on a cross. The story continues with Christians on or under the cross—not trying to win approval or oppress people but offering service and sacrifice to bring liberation.

This latter perspective at first glance appears to be the downside of mission. The apostles would see in Jesus' scars not only an accomplished propitiation but also the cost of the propagation of mission in union with Christ. They would have recognized, at least in retrospect, that scars were what they too might incur in the fellowship of his sufferings, "filling up that which is lacking in the sufferings of Christ." It is not merely the pain incurred in propagation of the gospel that is involved here, however, and this may help to answer some of the questions about Christians in situations where persecution is not a reality. Being in union with Christ here on earth means entering in to the pain and suffering of the world as he did. Remaining aloof from this suffering is not an option for the Christian living in participation with Christ. As Andrew Walker poignantly expresses this:

> There can be no long-term renewal or sustained spiritual awakening of the Christian faith without sharing in the pain of the world. A *theologia gloriae* without a *theologia crucis*, Tom Smail has reminded us often

enough, is a cock-eyed gospel and, while it will always have popular appeal, it has no place in the soteriology of the deep church.[15]

But what does this way of life mean for a congregation and its identity as missional? The quotation at the head of this chapter from Lesslie Newbigin speaks of the only real hermeneutic of the gospel being "a congregation which believes it."[16] The following is a series of reflections that relate to the pattern of communal life of the "church that really believes it," that is, that really believes it is in mission with the crucified Christ. Alan Hirsch's concept of *Communitas* is an apt summary. This concept

> describes the dynamics of the Christian community inspired to overcome their instincts to "huddle and cuddle" and to instead form themselves around a common mission that calls them onto a dangerous journey to unknown places . . . where its members will experience disorientation and marginalization but also where they encounter God and one another in a new way. [17]

A pattern of communal life: From the church to the kingdom. As I have suggested, the cross is not just a message of pardon, it is a pattern of living, a way of being. Being in union with Christ and knowing him is resurrection power only as it is "participation with his sufferings" (Phil 3:10). The manner of the sending in John 20 takes its cue from the presence of scars in the hands of the Sender. This has relevance first of all to the relationship between the church and the kingdom of God. As Newbigin suggests, it bespeaks Jesus' intention "not to leave behind a disembodied teaching," but that rather "through his total consecration to the Father in his passion there should be created a community which would continue that which he came from the Father to be and to do—namely to embody and to announce the presence of the reign of God."

---

[15]Andrew Walker, "Recovering Deep Church," chap. 1 in *Remembering Our Future*, ed. Andrew Walker and Luke Bretherton (Colorado Springs: Paternoster, 2007), p. 21. Walker references Smail's chapters in Tom Smail, Andrew Walker and Nigel G. Wright, *Charismatic Renewal: The Search for a Theology* (London: SPCK, 1993), particularly "The Cross and the Spirit: Towards a Theology of Renewal," pp. 49-70.

[16]Lesslie Newbigin, "The Pastor's Opportunities: VI. Evangelism in the City," *Expository Times* 98 (1987): 356.56.

[17]Alan Hirsch, *The Forgotten Ways* (Grand Rapids: Brazos, 2007), p. 277.

These same marks symbolize the authenticating marks of the church, the body of Christ. That is, the church shares the passion of Jesus, and this shapes how it represents the reign of God. It is "not authorized," Newbigin notes, "to represent the reign of God, his justice and his peace, in any other way than that in which Jesus represented it, namely by being partners with him in challenging the powers of evil and bearing in its own life the cost of the challenge."[18]

The church represents to the world Jesus' name and face, and its being and proclamation and actions will be in the *way* of Jesus. This rebukes the dichotomizing of proclamation and deeds of compassion in the church's mission, for they are never separated in Jesus' mission. His people will fully enter the pain, the scars, of the world as he did. The giving of the Spirit to the church has also ensured that the church has the primal character of the kingdom because it is, as the body of Christ, made one with him by the Spirit's indwelling. When the church lives by the Spirit according to its kingdom nature, it will be open to the world, speaking words of hope but also challenging the ruling powers. This challenges the approach of preaching in isolation from societal concern. A church which exists only for itself, its members and its own enlargement is a contradiction of the gospel, because the church does not exist for itself "but as a sign and agent and foretaste of the kingdom of God." As such the church cannot give faithful witness to the kingdom of God if it is "indifferent to the situation of the hungry, the sick, the victims of human inhumanity." It will be, Newbigin suggests, a suffering church, for its challenge will not always be appreciated. It is "out of that conflict and suffering" that there will "arise the questioning which the world puts to the Church."[19]

As a community that embodies the kingdom values of a servant King, it will reflect triumph over principalities and powers, but not in triumphalistic ways. The scarred hands and feet are a reality check. The church's members will bear those scars when they invite people to leave their self-accomplishment to embrace the cross in repentance, relying only on Christ and his work for them. The church's members will

---

[18]Lesslie Newbigin, *The Gospel in a Pluralist Society* (London: SPCK, 1989), p. 134.
[19]Ibid., pp. 136-37.

also be expected to enter the scarred places of the world. Conflicts with the success motif of modernity will invite persecution. They will encounter social structures that discriminate against the poor, and they can expect persecution for confronting the principalities and powers. In other words, the nature of the church as a servant, cross-centered community reveals what the kingdom is, even if the kingdom is larger in scope than the church.

There is no set of prescribed programs for developing such a cruciform, kingdom mission. Its particular nature will be discovered in accordance with the location of a church and its community, in union with the crucified Christ and by communion with his Spirit, who is already at work in that church's community. The task of the church is to join God in his mission to its particular world.

In turn, the Christocentric and cruciform nature of the church will prevent use of the kingdom concept to "sacralize whatever is the contemporary program for justice and peace" such that "the message of the kingdom then becomes again a form of the law . . . a corpus of ethical demands," resulting in "hardening of conscience and mightily increasing the power of evil."[20]

A pattern of communal life: From the center to the periphery. The nail-scarred hands and side and the cross remind us that we serve a triune God who exercised a kenosis in creating and in his self-giving in the incarnation—and the cross. We serve a King who served and gave himself for all! And he was a King-Priest who, as Hebrews insists, died "outside the city gate":

> The high priest carries the blood of animals into the Most Holy Place as a sin offering, but the bodies are burned outside the camp. And so Jesus also suffered outside the city gate to make the people holy through his own blood. Let us, then, go to him outside the camp, bearing the disgrace he bore. For here we do not have an enduring city, but we are looking for the city that is to come. (Heb 13:11-14)

It is this image of where Christ died, outside the gate, that forms the

---

[20]Ibid., p. 134. This leads Newbigin to correct misuses of the "doctrine of the *missio Dei* . . . which bypass the Church and even bypass the name of Jesus" (ibid., p. 135).

missional thought of another important twentieth-century missiologist, Orlando Costas. In *Christ Outside the Gate: Mission Beyond Christendom*, he suggests that Jesus by his death outside the gate, the periphery, rather than at the religious center, set the pattern for missiological concerns. He suggests that mission done from the center to the periphery is not validated by the gospel and that true missiology is authenticated by identification with those who were banished "outside the gate." He exhorts us that the church must pattern itself after the incarnation of Christ, who emptied himself, was the suffering servant and who identified with the poor and the oppressed. We do not bear "the disgrace he bore" unless we are in solidarity and in community with the marginalized. Costas believes the church owes a debt to liberation theologians, and he is proud of their Latin American origins. As reviewer Samuel Moffett writes, "They have rightly challenged orthodoxy to recognize the authenticating demands of orthopraxis; 'faith without works is dead.' They have shaken theology out of passive thought into transforming, vitalizing action. They have prodded 'ethically impotent' ecclesiastical structures into a compassionate and responsible preference for the poor."[21] Costas was not uncritical of liberation theology, however, and its conflation of cultural identity and that of Jesus Christ. He insisted that "the true identity of Jesus Christ is not determined by our cultural identity," much less by Marxist ideology, but "by the New Testament," and specifically by the particularities of his death and resurrection. It was only by this insistence that the oppressed can "be sure that their Christ is not as much a distortion as the oppressors'" Christ, which they reject.[22] These critiques aside, however, Orlando Costas stridently called the church to be engaged in the liberation of the oppressed in ways that needed to be heard by the Christian church, which has often been passive and therefore complicit with oppressive regimes.

We can commit ourselves afresh to mission without fear as we reaffirm our gratitude for and confidence in the reconciling, redeeming

---

[21]Samuel Hugh Moffett, review of *Christ Outside the Gate: Mission Beyond Christendom* by Orlando E. Costas, *Theology Today*, http://theologytoday.ptsem.edu/jul1984/v43-4-book review4.htm.
[22]Ibid.

work of Jesus, confident to proclaim the gospel as the ground for personal salvation, but with incorporation of all—especially the marginalized—into the community of Christ where all are equal and have dignity. And we proclaim and affirm it in life as more than salvation of the soul—as reconciliation, redemption and transformation of the whole person, human beings fully alive, receiving health care, education, meaningful work, taking their place in society.

A pattern of communal life: Offering hospitality. This picture of Jesus standing with scarred hands conjures the notion of hospitality, and brings to mind the work of my colleague Hans Boersma. In his book *Violence, Hospitality and the Cross: Reappropriating the Atonement Tradition*, Boersma draws on the patristic tradition of seeing the cross as the place where the hands of God are stretched out to the world in hospitality.[23] Building on the words of Cyril of Jerusalem (A.D. 347) that "God stretched out his hands on the Cross, that he might embrace the ends of the world,"[24] Boersma states that "it is at the foot of the cross that we learn from God how hospitality is to function." He cites Reinhold Hütter, who wrote that the human practice of hospitality is "both a reflection and extension of God's own hospitality—God's sharing the love of the triune life with those who are dust."[25] In a way that might aptly summarize the word picture of John 20, Boersma adds, "At the very center of this hospitality stands both a death and a resurrection, the most fundamental enactment of truth from God's side and precisely therefore also the threshold of God's abundant hospitality."[26] Jesus standing in the center of his community with the signs of the cross upon him and uttering the words of mission to the world capture the essence of these sentiments.

This notion of hospitality may seem to have a meaning similar to that which arose within postmodern philosophy and specifically the "pure hospitality" work of Emmanuel Levinas and Jacques Derrida. These writers deconstructed the prevalent emphasis on metaphysics

---

[23]Hans Boersma, *Violence, Hospitality and the Cross: Reappropriating the Atonement Tradition* (Grand Rapids: Baker Academic, 2004).
[24]Cyril of Jerusalem, cited in ibid., p. 25.
[25]Boersma, *Violence, Hospitality and the Cross*, p. 25.
[26]Ibid.

(Being, *Dasein*) in modern philosophy and sought to ground philosophy in ethics rather than metaphysics, and specifically in the ethic of unconditional hospitality to the other.[27] This was a reaction to the oppression inherent in Enlightenment Western philosophy, which does violence to the other. Boersma summarizes this philosophical school in these terms: "The imposition of rational categories on the exterior world has undermined all that is different or other than one's self."[28] But Boersma goes on to point out that pure hospitality does not exist, especially not in a fallen world. He suggests that the concept of "good violence" (it must be endured by the conveyor of hospitality as part of responsibility for the other—a notion even Levinas accepted) is necessary within hospitality, and that this is true even in the cross event in order that hospitality might be extended to the world.

A Christian vision of hospitality has appropriate boundaries, as even the parable of the prodigal son (father) indicates in the son's expression of repentance and willingness to serve as a slave in the father's house. Miroslav Volf's *Exclusion and Embrace* is an exposition of the "phenomenology of embrace" built on the story of the prodigal son, demonstrating the limits as well as legitimacy of the hospitality metaphor.[29] Within the triune Godhead, each person offers and receives ultimate hospitality by perichoresis or coinherence. Yet there remains mysteriously an irreducible identity of each, such that the one God is still three persons. The coinherence or mutual internality does not violate the identity. On the more human level, Caroline Westerhoff has written extensively on the healthy boundaries that are required for abuse to be avoided in hospitality.[30]

Emphasizing the limited nature of hospitality, first in the God of the cross and second in his church, is necessary given that there are many churches or movements who have gone to the extreme with respect to hospitality, perhaps influenced by a postmodern philosophical

---

[27]Simon Critchley, *The Ethics of Deconstruction: Derrida and Levinas*, 2nd ed. (West Lafayette, Ind.: Purdue University Press, 1999).

[28]Boersma, *Violence, Hospitality and the Cross*, p. 28.

[29]Miroslav Volf, *Exclusion and Embrace: A Theological Exploration of Identity, Otherness and Reconciliation* (Nashville: Abingdon, 1996).

[30]Caroline Westerhoff, *Good Fences: The Boundaries of Hospitality* (Cambridge: Cowley, 1999).

construal. This is the notion of acceptance of all without concern for discipleship and transformation as necessary for those who profess to embrace the gospel, rendering any talk or action related to church discipline obsolete.

Having noted these legitimate boundaries, however, I want to stress that greater emphasis must be placed on the need for hospitality. The walls are so high that hospitality is impossible. The biblical vision of hospitality that welcomes the stranger is largely missing in many churches.[31] As Hans Boersma has written, permeable boundaries are needed for others to join the community of worship.[32] He adds that an evangelical hospitality is God offering his hospitality of forgiveness and reconciliation to everyone, and he contends that the church's gatherings have a public aspect involving the seeking out and extending of hospitality to people beyond church boundaries. Hospitality entails a welcoming of the other. The same philosopher mentioned earlier for the extremes of hospitality, Jacques Derrida, has nevertheless tellingly distinguished between two types of hospitality: hospitality by invitation and hospitality by visitation.[33] The first is the invitation of people we know or who are just like us, or who can serve some utilitarian purpose for us. By contrast, hospitality by visitation is risky because we are not in control. Risk is central to the idea of hospitality, as Derrida indicates. In this sense Derrida is consonant in his thought with the biblical idea of hospitality reflected in Hebrews 13:2, for example: "Do not forget to show hospitality to strangers, for by so doing some people have shown hospitality to angels without knowing it." The exact extent of the risk may be debated, but that churches should be riskily hospitable and should use their homes for risky hospitality is clearly the biblical way and the way of the triune God of the gospel.

A fundamental feature of all churches is that they ought to express the radical welcome of God to all, irrespective of class, race or sexual

---

[31]Patrick R. Keifert, *Welcoming the Stranger: A Public Theology of Worship and Evangelism* (Minneapolis: Augsburg Fortress, 1992), p. 80.

[32]Hans Boersma, "Liturgical Hospitality: Theological Reflections on Sharing in Grace," *Journal for Christian Theological Research* 8 (2003): 67-77.

[33]Jacques Derrida, cited in John D. Caputo, *What Would Jesus Deconstruct? The Good News of Postmodernism for the Church* (Grand Rapids: Baker Academic, 2007), p. 76.

orientation, irrespective of their initial moral condition.[34] They will, in so doing, be true to the Johannine vision of the church with Jesus standing at its center offering the welcome of his scarred hands outstretched. Most churches in the West need to get this right, and when they do, this next caveat will be needed. The welcome of Christ, that is, his invitation to follow him, is not unconditional. It is nail-scarred hands that he stretches out in welcome. This is an invitation to union with him in his death, which involves mortification of sin.

A pattern of communal life: Overcoming oppressiveness. Finally, when the church lives in the "way of being" of the cross as servants of humanity, and when this authenticates the proclamation of salvation by way of the cross, the objection of postmodernity to the oppressiveness of Christianity's metanarrative will be to some measure alleviated. Christians living under the cross present the gospel in the manner Jesus presented it—nonoppressively.

So, like Paul, we need to determine to preach and proclaim Christ and him crucified. And like Paul we will do so as those who have been crucified with Christ. Our lifestyles will be characterized by the putting to death of old sinful habits. Our demeanor will be as those under the cross. This will go some way to overcoming the postmodern fear of the oppressiveness of metanarratives. Not that we can remove the offense of the cross. And being willing to bear that is precisely what it means to be in union with the scarred Christ. But if we come under the cross at least the offense will be because of the cross itself, not our oppressiveness.

---

[34]This leaves no room for the Homogeneous Unit Principle of Donald McGavran and Peter Wagner. Eugene Peterson claims that "Scripture calls into question these 'domesticated accommodations' in light of the fact that Scripture stories do not court our favor but seek to subject us" (Eugene Peterson, *Working the Angles: The Shape of Pastoral Integrity* [Grand Rapids: Eerdmans, 1987], p. 132).

PART TWO

Disseminating Shalom

∎ ∎ ∎

Again Jesus said, *"Peace be with you!*
As the Father has sent me, I am sending you."
And with that he breathed on them and said,
"Receive the Holy Spirit. If you forgive the
sins of anyone, their sins are forgiven;
if you do not forgive them,
they are not forgiven."

JOHN 20:21-23, emphasis added

9

Communities of the Triune Missional God

Mission the Mother of Theology,
Theology the Mother of Mission

■ ■ ■

As the Father has sent me, so I am sending you.

JOHN 20:21 NLT

So then, no more boasting about human leaders!
All things are yours, whether Paul or Apollos or Cephas
or the world or life or death or the present or the future—all
are yours, and you are of Christ, and Christ is of God.

1 CORINTHIANS 3:21-23, emphasis added

The Bible is not the basis of missions;
missions is the basis of the Bible.

RALPH WINTER, U.S. Center for World Mission

HAVING LAID THE FOUNDATIONS for the trinitarian concept of the
missio Dei that undergirds the whole tenor and content of John 20:19-23
in chapter three, I feel it important to reinforce, clarify, defend and

nuance the trinitarian nature of the church's mission. It is a particular burden of this chapter to nuance the mission of the triune God toward humanity as bidirectional, not unipolar; the mission of the church is not merely sending but gathering.

First, then, some *reinforcement* of the heart of this passage: "As the Father has sent me, I am sending you." If we see only the challenge but not the core of what Jesus says here, we will miss his point altogether. Yes, we are called to be a missional community of sent ones, but this is because that is what we are. This commission is more an *is* than an *ought*. The ought is derived from the is. The church is missional, Christians are missional, because they are conjoined to the missional God and therefore enabled by him, the sending triune God. Peace to replace our fear, to get us out from behind locked doors, comes from the relational, participatory continuity between the Father and the Son and the Son and the Christian. This passage asserts that there is a relationship between Christ's sentness and ours. The meaning of "as the Father has sent me so am I sending you" in the larger Johannine context is certainly informed by the wider notion of a union in life and love. The correspondence of a sent nature is determined by a correspondence elsewhere inferred by Jesus in John between the relationship between the Father and the Son, and those "in the Son."

When Jesus spoke to his disciples of the Spirit's coming, he said, "On that day you will realize that I am in my Father, and you are in me, and I am in you" (Jn 14:20). The latter two unions make the logic of the *as . . . so* in John 20:21 inevitable. If we are in Christ (by his participation in humanity and our participation in him by faith) and Christ is in us (by the Spirit's indwelling), then his sentness is imparted to us. The *so* sending of the *you* has a relationship to the *as* sending of the Son by the Father. In sum, we are in Christ and Christ is in us by the Spirit. Therefore we do have a place in the *missio Dei* because we as church of Christ are participating in the mutual life (Jn 5:21, 25-26—the *as . . . so* of life), love (Jn 13:34; 14:21, 23; 15:9—the *as . . . so* of love), and *therefore* the mission (Jn 17:18; 20:21—the *as . . . so* of sentness) of the Father and the Son! Christopher Wright confirms this thinking: "All human mission . . . is seen as a participation in and extension of this divine sending."[1] Mission is a necessary consequence of our union with Christ. This is what gives hope for mission, because in that union with God we experience shalom and in that union with God we can spread shalom. Another way to say this is that if the character of Jesus is apostle ("the Apostle and High Priest of our confession" [Heb 3:1 NKJV]), then it will not be surprising if his people, who are one with him, have apostolic character, that is, they are sent ones. As Martin Hengel rightly claims, "the ultimate basis for the earliest Christian mission lies in the messianic sending of Jesus."[2]

Second, some *clarifying* is needed of this concept of participation in God, or theosis or relational union between God and human persons in Christ, by the Spirit, to emphasize that this does not entail any loss of distinction between divine and human persons, or the absolute distinctness of the relationship of the uniquely divine Son with the Father. The distinction as well as the correspondence in Jesus' trinitarian co-mission is actually suggested in the previous paragraph when Jesus tells Mary, "I am ascending to my Father and your Father, to my God and your God" (Jn 20:17). God is our Father, though not in the identical sense in which God is the Father of Jesus, the essential, eternal Son. The Son is sent in the economy of God's salvific purposes, which also mirrors the *in se* or essential or immanent nature of the relations between the Father and the Son (eternally generated), and so we are sent in not exactly the same sense. Yet we cannot shy away from the truth of the gospel, that by the incarnational union of Christ with us and by the indwelling of the Spirit, we have become relationally one with Christ and therefore we too are sent, not in isolation from Jesus but as those who continue his sentness as his mystical body. The incarnation also enabled a union between God and human "without confusion" of his humanity and deity. Humans stay human even as participants in the divine nature (2 Pet 1:4), just as there is no mixture of the hypostatic union of Christ's divine and human natures.

In light of its crucial importance for the discovery and disseminating

---

[1]Christopher Wright, *The Mission of God* (Downers Grove, Ill.: InterVarsity Pres, 2006), p. 63.
[2]Martin Hengel, "The Origins of the Christian Mission," in *Between Jesus and Paul: Studies in the Earliest History of Christianity* (London: SCM Press, 1983), pp. 61-63.

of shalom in our world, which is the essence of mission, the remainder of this chapter is dedicated to *defending and nuancing* the idea of mission as the mission of God himself in which we as the church participate, that is the *missio Dei*, specifically as a bipolar or bidirectional mission.

BIBLICAL EVIDENCE OF GOD AS MISSIONAL

The idea that God is missional and that his people inevitably participate in his mission is not merely a Johannine concept, though John is its primary exponent. It is the biblical story from Genesis to Revelation. Christopher Wright has demonstrated not only that mission must be seen as God's mission but that mission, as the mission of God, is a "fruitful hermeneutic framework within which to read the whole Bible."[3] His point is not just that Christian mission is grounded in Scripture. It is that mission is the paradigm by which Scripture should be interpreted. Wright's justification is that mission is the mission of God first: mission arises from the "one and only living God who wills to be known to the world through Israel and through Christ."[4] This implies that what might challenge mission as the determining hermeneutic for interpreting Scripture, that is, a Christological hermeneutic or even a doxological hermeneutic, is included in mission. In that mission is the mission of the triune God and inclusive of the centrality of Christ, and insomuch as it does arise within the being of God and emanates in the glory of God, it is broad enough to be that hermeneutic.

The interplay and mutual inclusiveness of mission and the triune God are expressed eloquently by Wright:

> So inasmuch as the Bible narrates the passion and action (and mission) of *this* God (specified as "the God revealed as YHWH in the Old Testament and incarnate in Jesus of Nazareth") for the liberation not only of humanity but of the whole creation, a missional hermeneutic of Scripture must have a liberationist dimension. Once again we are driven back to see how important it is to ground our theology of mission (and our practice of it) in the mission of God and in our worshiping response

---

[3]Wright, *Mission of God*, p. 26.
[4]Ibid., p. 27.

to all that God is and does. From that perspective, we are advocates for *God* before we are advocates for *others*.[5]

Space does not permit consideration of the full sweep of Scripture revelation concerning the grounding of mission in God and participation with him, which Wright has done admirably. I have chosen a few particular sections of the New Testament to demonstrate these concepts. For example, the notion of mission in union with God is central to continuity in the Luke-Acts story. When Luke begins Acts with the statement that his Gospel was about what Jesus *began* to do and to teach, the implication is that Acts is about what Jesus *continued* to do and to teach in and through his church, by his Spirit within it. Furthermore, Peter speaks of Christians as those who "participate in the divine nature" (2 Pet 1:4) in a context in which he urges the development of virtues flowing from this active participation, which has missional overtones: avoiding "being ineffective and unproductive in your knowledge of our Lord Jesus Christ" (2 Pet 1:8). And of course Paul's favored expression for the relationship between the church or Christian and Christ is "in Christ," the phrase that reflects the heart of the gospel.

In light of the primacy of this phrase in Pauline theology, Calvin famously spoke of union with Christ as the primary soteriological category, not justification or sanctification. These three concepts cannot be separated chronologically, but logically the priority is with the relational reality made possible by the participation of the Son in our humanity, and then our participation by the Spirit in Christ. The filial comes before the forensic. The twin graces are a consequence of our union with Christ. It is in him that we are justified and sanctified. These are a consequence of the Son of God becoming one with humanity, and so his righteousness has become ours. They become ours noetically when we are brought into the reality of our ontic union with Christ by the Spirit's regeneration and indwelling. It is as those brought into reconciliation reality in Christ that we become agents and ambassadors of reconciliation in the world: "All this is from God, who recon-

---

[5]Ibid., pp. 44-45.

ciled us to himself through Christ and gave us the ministry of reconciliation: that God was reconciling the world to himself in Christ, not counting people's sins against them. And he has committed to us the message of reconciliation. We are therefore Christ's ambassadors [embassy], as though God were making his appeal through us" (2 Cor 5:18-20). This passage is very important for both the trinitarian and theotic elements of the *missio Dei*. First, verse 19 makes it clear that God himself is in Christ, engaged in mission. This draws together the immanent being of God and his acts in the history of the saving economy. God *in se* was reconciling, was and is missional, and his reconciling presence in Christ in the economy is a manifestation of who he is. It is this reality that God has been and is at work in reconciling the world that provides the greatest incentive for mission. It gives hope to grieving, fearful, impotent and defeated disciples. But the second encouraging reality is that this God indwells us in Christ by the Spirit. That reconciling work continues today through his embassy on earth, the church. We participate in God's life and therefore in his missional work, as verse 20 indicates, "as though God were making his appeal through us." Participation does not mean that we are passive bystanders. He works and we work as he works.

Paul does not ever give what may be called a great commission. However, his assumption is that the church in union with Christ by the Spirit (Pauline equivalents to the three union phrases in Jn 14:20 may be found in Col 3:2; 2:9-10; Rom 8:9-10) will fulfill God's mission. This adjoining of union and mission is evident, for example, in Colossians 1:27: "To them [the people of God] God has chosen to make known among the Gentiles the glorious riches of this mystery, which is Christ in you, the hope of glory."

Admittedly the knot of Trinity, union and mission is most explicit in John, but hopefully I have demonstrated that Scripture is unified in its presentation of a missional God who works through his missional people to accomplish his reconciliation of the world. We return now to our Johannine text and to a theological exploration of the missional Trinity and therefore the missional church.

THEOLOGICAL CONSIDERATIONS
OF GOD AS MISSIONAL

The core of our passage expresses this connection between the Trinity, union and mission. Jesus' commission was "As the Father has sent me, I am sending you." There is a correlation between Christ's sentness by the Father, arising from trinitarian union, and our sentness by Christ, inferring mission in union with him, and therefore the Father. Thus, "mission by us" in Christ is a continuation of "mission by Christ" in the Father.

There are therefore two theological themes to be explored in our text:

1. "As the Father has sent me." Jesus' sentness is evidence of the great theme of the *missio Dei:* God is the sending God.

2. "So am I sending you." The sentness of Jesus is the paradigm for our sending because of our union with him: We are a sent community of people, the church.

The first theme will be our subject in this chapter, the second in chapter ten. The first phrase is a revelation of the Son's sentness, as the *ekstasis* (outward movement) of the triune communion. The sentness of Jesus is evidence of the great theme of the *missio Dei* that we will explore in some depth. This first theme, then, the sentness or mission of the Son, aptly anticipates Martin Kähler's now famous saying, "mission is the mother of theology," and the second theme, the corollary of this, theology (specifically that of participation) is the mother of mission.[6]

The claim that mission is the mother of theology is a bold epistemological statement. It is a recognition that the core of theology and the gospel is that God is the sending God, and that we can only know this because of God's two missions: the sending of the Son and the sending of the Spirit. That is, it was mission that led us to understand God as Trinity, and if Trinity is the distinctively Christian understanding of God, then mission, the missions of God that determine all mission, is the mother of theology. How do we understand the second phrase, that theology is the mother of mission? When we see God as the sending God, and when we see the church as his church,

---

[6]Martin Kähler, *Schriften zur Christologie und Mission* (Munich: Kaiser Verlag, 1971).

we come to see the church as fundamentally missional. We focus first on the missional God.

Claim: Mission is the mother of theology, mission is an attribute of God. Here I present the origin of mission in the sending actions of God (*ekstasis*), his incarnational and pneumatological missions and what this reveals about the sending God, and about a way of doing theology, a way of seeing the gospel. What ails the church with respect to its spirituality and ecclesiology is above all our poor theology proper. If the contemporary church truly grasped and lived by the truth that mission is the mother of theology and theology is the mother of mission, that is, if the church were intoxicated with the triune God, it would be transformed and a powerful transformer of culture. Many churches are beginning to come to terms with theology concerning the *missio Dei* and its implications for the church, given that the church is in union with the missional God. Missional theologians have refreshingly turned to the doctrine of God to guide their thinking concerning the church.

William A. Dyrness, for example, has pointed out that "theology consists primarily of reflection on mission. This is true on the most basic level: the most highly developed theological statements, those of the Apostle Paul, were forged in the context of the first expansion of the Church." This leads Dyrness to state that "mission lies at the core of theology . . . all that theologians call fundamental theology is mission theology."[7]

This is certainly true in an historical sense. The doctrine of the Trinity was a response to the missions of God—his mission in Jesus, the incarnate Son, and his mission expressed in giving the Holy Spirit. The doctrine of the Trinity was not arrived at through philosophical means, but rather was discovered empirically in the early church. The discovery by the apostles and then the church fathers that the person who had been in their midst is truly God and truly man, and then the recognition likewise that the Holy Spirit is God, led to the articulation of the doctrine of the Trinity in the Niceno-Constantinopolitan Creed, the foundational creed of the Christian faith.

---

[7]William Dyrness, *Let the Earth Rejoice! A Biblical Theology of Holistic Mission* (Eugene, Ore.: Wipf & Stock, 1998), p. 11.

The essence of who God is as Father, Son and Spirit has been revealed by the personal missions of God. It is for this reason that we say God is the missional God and also that we say that the *missio Dei* is only true because of the *missio trinitatis*. Paul Stevens, reflecting the sentiments of Colin Gunton, stated, "Mission is God's own going forth—truly an *ekstasis* of God. He is Sender, Sent and Sending (John 17:18; cf. 16:5-16; 20:21-2)."[8] But because all believers are in union with this God, because the church is an extension of who Christ is, this pushes ecclesiology back into the doctrine of God, making the conclusion that the church is missional inevitable. As Stan Grenz wrote:

> Christians declare that the touchstone of community is the eternal triune life and God's gracious inclusion of humans in Christ by the Spirit, constituting them as participants in the perichoretic trinitarian life. This theological-ecclesiological perspective leads Christians to view every social reality in accordance with its potential for being a contribution to, prolepsis of, or signpost on the way toward the participation in the divine life that God desires humans to enjoy.[9]

Thus I make the claim that (1) mission is God's defining attribute, in that his missions elucidate the triune being of God as love. It is from the missions of the Son and the Spirit in the economic Trinity that we come to know who God is in his immanent being. That God is *pro nobis* unveils who he is *in se*. The *missio Dei* is a term that expresses that God is a fundamentally missional God.[10]

And (2) I conclude that mission is a defining attribute of the church because it is the church of the missional God. Mission must be seen as the participation of the church and its persons, in the sending God. Interestingly, the term *mission* was until the sixteenth century used

---

[8]Stevens, *Other Six Days*, p. 194. This Sender, Sent and Sending paradigm reflects the same pattern as Barth's construal of the Trinity as Revealer, Revelation and Revealedness. See Colin Gunton, *The Promise of Trinitarian Theology* (Edinburgh: T & T Clark, 1991).

[9]Stanley J. Grenz, *Renewing the Center: Evangelical Theology in a Post-Theological Era* (Grand Rapids: Baker, 2000), p. 324.

[10]*Missio Dei* was supposedly coined by Karl Hartenstein when he had heard Barth teach on mission and the Trinity in 1928. The phrase originally meant the "sending of God," but at the Willingen World Mission Conference in 1952 it was modified to mean the activities of God in the world). See Wright, *Mission of God*, p. 133. We will revisit this claim later in light of research by John Flett.

only to refer to the sending (*missio*) of the Son and the Spirit, originating with Augustine and perpetuated by Aquinas.[11] The Jesuits first used the term *mission* for a mission project. It was and is very fitting, because the church's mission is an extension of God's mission. The church's mission is carried out in participation with the Son, empowered by Spirit.

Bringing these two strands of thought together, the *content* of proclamation in mission, the gospel, is also at its core about the Father sending his Son for the sake of all creation, as "drawing the world in the way of existence that is to be found in the Trinity."[12] As such, mission is not merely the proclamation of theological truth. The *way* of mission is to be a natural extension of the communal nature of the Trinity. This happens first through the church, which in union with Christ is the sign and messenger of that trinitarian life by its rich communal life.

But is all this simply wishful thinking on the part of the firebrand missional professors who wish to mobilize students into missional action with hyperbolic claims about God? The validity of these claims must be examined. Then the correlation between the missional God and the missional church must be examined. Both the notion of God as a missionary God and the correspondence between the missions of the Godhead and those of the church are not without their challenges, which we now explore.

Clarification: Is the missional God fatally flawed by subordination?
Concern has been expressed that speaking of the Son and the Spirit as sent implies their subordination to the Father. Being sent as an envoy is deemed to carry with it the notion of inferior rank. Protestant scholars such as Steve Holmes, John Flett and John Hoffmeyer have addressed this concern.[13]

---

[11]Bosch, *Transforming Mission*, p. 1.

[12]Stephen B. Bevans and Roger P. Schroeder, *Constants in Context: A Theology of Mission for Today*, American Society of Missiology Series (Maryknoll, N.Y.: Orbis, 2004), pp. 288-89.

[13]Stephen R. Holmes, "Trinitarian Missiology: Towards a Theology of God as Missionary," *International Journal of Systematic Theology* 8, no. 1 (2006): 79. John Flett comments: "This is part of Holmes' reflection on Augustine's treatment of the Trinity. Augustine was concerned to defend the divinity of the Son and Spirit against the Arian charge that sending, *eo ipso*, renders claims for the divinity of the agent impossible" (*Missio Dei: A Trinitarian Envisioning

Perichoresis. In particular, Catholic writer George F. Vicedom developed the concept that coinherence or perichoresis is a solution to this problem.[14] He insisted that God is not just sender—he is sent. As Vicedom notes, "Catholic dogmatics since Augustine speaks of sendings or the *missio* within the Triune God . . . [yet] . . . every sending of One Person results in the presence of the Other." So God is not only the one sent but is the one sending "for in every Person of the Deity, God works in his entirety."[15] The Son was with the Father and the Spirit in the willing of the incarnation, and the Father was with the Son in his incarnate sentness.

The assigning of specific missions to the persons of the Trinity is an illustration of classical trinitarian doctrine, which allows for the appropriation of certain roles to each of the persons and the concomitant dogma that each is at work in the work of the other (the doctrine of the indivisibility of the works of the divine persons, *opera extra sunt indivisa*). Thus it is clearly legitimate for the Son to appropriate to the role of sentness and yet to know that the Father and the Spirit are with the Son in that sentness.

No one has surpassed the Cappadocian Fathers' expression of this. Overcoming "the servitude of personhood to substance, a servitude which applies only to created existence," the Cappadocians were able to establish that "Being is simultaneously relational and hypostatic."[16] Thus God's self-revelation that leads to saving knowledge of God in humans and their eternal communion with him is emphasized in the Cappadocian tradition as being an expression of *the common will and action* of the three divine hypostases. This will is an expression of the love that unites the three persons within the Godhead—a love

---

of a Non-trinitarian Theme," *American Society of Missiology*, June 20, 2008), p. 6. Then he cites Holmes, "All talk of a 'missionary God' would be merely oxymoronic: one who is a missionary, and so is sent by another, is necessarily not Lord of all, and so not God; conversely, it is a necessary perfection of God's being that he is not sent" (Holmes, "Trinitarian Missiology," p. 77). See also John F. Hoffmeyer, "The Missional Trinity," *Dialogue: A Journal of Theology* 40, no. 2 (2001): 108-11.

[14]George F. Vicedom, *The Mission of God: An Introduction to a Theology of Mission*, trans. Gilbert E. Thiele and Dennis Hidgendorf (St. Louis: Concordia, 1965).

[15]Ibid., p. 7.

[16]John D. Zizioulas, *Being As Communion* (Crestwood, N.Y.: St. Vladimir's Seminary Press, 1985), p. 50.

stemming from the Father but shared within the Trinity (and not reduced as in Augustine and Edwards to a *nexus amoris* in the hypostasis of the Spirit[17]). That united love in its "inexhaustible depth and intensity . . . overflows and surpasses the boundless limits of divine being in order to embrace, save, and transfigure the object of its affection."[18] Crucial to this understanding that overcomes subordinationism was the doctrine of coinherence or perichoresis. They are mutually internal.

Personal roles, equal glory. A further consideration in this matter is that subordination, which relates to essential rank or worth, is not the same as submission within certain roles among equals. Mutual submission does not imply inferiority of essence or being. We insist on this in the context of husband-wife relationships in Ephesians 5:21-33, but this is already modeled within the Trinity. It is quite clear that on earth, Jesus was gladly in submission to the Father as the sent One ("the Father is greater than I" [Jn 14:28], understood with respect to role; see Jn 3:30) and yet without compromise to his essential equality with the Father ("I and my Father are one" [Jn 10:30]; "making himself equal with God" [Jn 5:18]). He assumed the servanthood (Phil 2:7) required for the accomplishment of God's redemptive mission. This is sometimes spoken of as his kenosis, his self-emptying. But is such a relationship true only in his earthly sojourn? Is kenosis not God's way? The willing and act of creation by God was an act of kenosis, involving the necessary mediation of the Son and the Spirit in that act, and ultimately entailing the suffering that the fall of that creation would bring. The suffering of the Son to reconcile that creation was not an afterthought with God, as passages such as Acts 2:23 and Revelation 13:8 indicate.

In this matter we must be consistent in the assertion that there is a correspondence between the economic and the immanent Trinity. It is interesting that in both the Eastern and the Western traditions of trinitarian thought, the Father is logically (not chronologically) the font or

---

[17]Literally the "bond of love," this term refers to the locatedness and hypostatizing of the love of God in the person of the Spirit as the connectedness or union of the Trinity.

[18]J. Breck, "Divine Initiative: Salvation in Orthodox Theology," in *Salvation in Christ: A Lutheran-Orthodox Dialogue*, ed. John Meyendorff and Robert Tobias (Minneapolis: Augsburg Fortress, 1992), p. 108.

source of the Trinity. This is true for the Augustinian psychological model of the Trinity as well as the social Cappadocian model. It is true that Athanasius conceived of the font as the perichoretic communion of the three persons, and this has become the preferred model for recent and contemporary social trinitarians (Torrance, Moltmann, Volf). However, even within this latter model it has to be conceded that the language of the economy gives role priority to the Father as initiator, elector and, importantly for our purposes here, sender. Furthermore, because these roles are premundane, this must in some way reflect roles within who God really is *in se* (a cherished conviction of trinitarian theology). The New Testament is unflinching in its assertions that Jesus is the sent one and that he and the Father share equality of essence as fully divine. This sending therefore must be understood as voluntary submission rather than subordination.

In his "On the Equality of the Persons of the Trinity," Jonathan Edwards's desire to honor the Spirit as equal within the Trinity despite seemingly subservient roles leads him to the conclusion that each person has superiority in different but equivalent ways that add up to equality of personal glory, not just equality with respect to deity.[19] On all these grounds we can lay to rest the notion that sentness assumes subordination.

Consequences for the missional church. Arising from the concept of perichoresis and the different role-equal glory principle, by analogy the missional church will be known as the servant of the kingdom without concerns about subordination. It will have kenotic, submissive character reflective of the King. Missional churches will therefore not understand themselves to be in competition with other local churches, but as interdependent communities.

The individual persons of a missional church will also have a servant or kenotic character. We can never truly live in perichoretic relationships with one another, in that this term implies that the divine persons are mutually internal to one another. We can however reflect in a cor-

---

[19]This work has been published in Jonathan Edwards, "On the Equality of the Persons of the Trinity," *Writings on the Trinity, Grace, and Faith*, The Works of Jonathan Edwards (New Haven, Conn.: Yale University Press, 2003), 21:146-48.

responding manner the interdependence that those in Christ can discover. They will be persons in community who find team to be the best form of leadership, reflecting in some measure the perichoresis of the Godhead. Every person in the church will be valued, and each will value themselves to the extent that they are secure enough to validate the other as they work together. The priesthood of all believers will be more than a theoretical concept. Individualistic, consumerist churchgoers will transform into "being the church" in a life together beyond gatherings, some even living out a vocation in missional, monastic communities.[20] The church will not hoard its privileges but have an openness to all humanity. It will be where lonely people find friendship, grieving people are comforted, single mothers receive the care of mechanics in the church who can change the oil in their cars, people with various addictions can find help in twelve-step communities, and so on.

Being an ecclesial person of this kind will also mean extending servant love to all humans, if we take seriously their destiny as desired by God. This will mean humble deeds of solidarity and care for the poor, identification with the marginalized, and gospel declaration no matter the ridicule received. It involves bringing beauty to communities by participation in the arts. It involves participation in the sciences in ways that explore creation and yet exercise stewardship over it. It involves sharing resources among the community.

Clarification: Is the missio Dei *really the* missio trinitatis? *(Is the God of mission the real God?).* A second area of concern has been the matter of which Trinity is in mind. The notion of the *missio Dei* is only a biblical concept if the God referred to is the biblically revealed triune God, one derived in the Christologically uttered sentiments of our Jo-

---

[20]Old monastic and "new monastic" communities are a case in point. The name of the latter movement was coined by Jonathan Wilson in his 1998 book, *Living Faithfully in a Fragmented World*. He was influenced by the desire expressed in Alasdair MacIntyre's *After Virtue* for a new Benedict in our times who could lead a renewal of morality and civility sustained in community (see Jonathan R. Wilson, *Living Faithfully in a Fragmented World: Lessons for the Church from MacIntyre's After Virtue* (Harrisburg, Penn.: Trinity Press International, 1998), pp. 69-75). The inaugural community was formed in Durham, N.C., in 2004 around the "12 marks of New Monasticism" (see Rutba House, *School(s) for Conversion: 12 Marks of a New Monasticism* [Eugene, Ore.: Cascade Books, 2005], pp. xii-xiii. See also Rob Moll, "The New Monasticism," *Christianity Today*, April 24, 2008).

hannine text, "as the Father has sent me, I am sending you." And it only has validity if there is a correspondence between the processions within the immanent Trinity and the sendings of the economy.

John Flett has written that at the Willingen Conference (1952), where the concept of the *missio Dei* was articulated in response to the resurgence of the doctrine of the Trinity, there was a serious division of thought.[21] Some separated the being and act of God and sought to derive mission in an unchristological and uneccesial way from God's generic triune nature in the immanent Godhead apart from the revelation of his being through his act in sending the incarnate Son and the Spirit to reveal him. This led to a preferential choice of God in himself over God in his redemptive act in history. On this account, missional agendas that are pluralistic, unevangelical and directly associated with political movements could be justified and evangelical preaching of Christ nullified. Flett's assertion that Barth's influence had nothing to do with the development of the concept of the *missio Dei* (via Karl Hartenstein [1933] and Tambaram conference [1938]) may slightly overstate the case, for it seems there were others at this conference who did ground the concept in a robust trinitarian theology that did not divide God's being and act.[22] Irrespective, the *missio Dei* as the revealed *missio trinitatis* should be redeemed and given its proper understanding (as Flett in fact does). The true *missio Dei* acknowledges that the distance between God and humanity has already been bridged in Christ by the Spirit and through his participating church, not that mission bridges the gap between God and humanity.

Keeping the immanent and the economic trinities in close relation (Barth)[23] and yet not identical (contra Rahner, LaCugna) is important

---

[21]John Flett, "Missio Dei, the Doctrine of the Trinity and Karl Barth," Ph.D. diss., Princeton Theological Seminary, 2007. See also John G. Flett, *The Witness of God: The Trinity, Missio Dei, Karl Barth and the Nature of Christian Community* (Grand Rapids: Eerdmans, 2010). See also Hoffmeyer, "The Missional Trinity."

[22]Flett's disparagement of the social Trinity is a red herring. The real issue here is the disconnection between the real and the revealed Trinity.

[23]Bromiley reflects Barth's thought when he asserts, "God does not just become Father to be our Father, or Son to be the incarnate Son, or Spirit to be the Spirit poured out on the church. He is Father, Son, and Spirit in his dealings with us because He is already Father, Son, and Spirit eternally and antecedently in Himself" (Bromiley, *Introduction to the Theology of Karl Barth*, p. 21).

for a proper understanding of the *missio Dei*. Among a number of Protestant dogmaticians who sought to clarify the relationship between the trinities in the seventeenth century was Lutheran theologian Johann Quenstedt, who proposed a causal connection between the eternal processions of God and the temporal missions of God. For example, the mission of the Spirit in time was proposed to be a *manifestation and consequence* of the eternal procession of the Spirit from the Father (and the Son, in Western tradition). Rahner in the twentieth century proposed that the missions are *identical with* the processions. On both accounts, the relatedness and the coalesced view, God's being is clearly in mission. Karl Barth's interesting proposal that the Son is eternally *incarnandus*, that is, that humanity has been in the Godhead purposively, eternally, is an alternative manner by which the immanent and economic trinities might be kept as closely related, but not identical, and it certainly portrays the missional essence of the Godhead.

Consequences for the missional church. The consequences of the *missio Dei* are profound in that we can understand mission first and foremost as God's mission to the world, and, amazingly, that we as the church can participate in it as we live in communion with this missional God. Furthermore, the *missio Dei* grounded in the existence and relatedness of both God's being and act will, by analogy, cause the church to have *both* an inner life that is conscious of its missional identity *and* an outer life that flows from a rich inner life and has an orientation toward gathering others into that inner life.

Thus it will not be a community of deep theological, spiritual, liturgical, catechetical and moral formation with no awareness of or intentional influence on the world of humanity and creation. This approach contains a hint of remnant theology. Flett raises such a concern with respect to the Anabaptist "communion ecclesiologies" of Yoder, Hauerwas and even Miroslav Volf, whom he accuses of focusing "mainly inside, at the inner nature of the church," while sidelining "the outside world and the church's mission" to his "peripheral vision."[24] Though this is a misconstrual of Volf's thought, Flett is rightly anxious to

---

[24]Flett, *Missio Dei: A Trinitarian Envisioning of a Non-trinitarian Theme,* p. 8 n. 25.

maintain the correspondence between the missional life of God as an overflow of his prior intratrinitarian relationships and the church's witness that "emerges as a *gestalt*—a natural overflow—of internally orientated practices that build up the community into a corresponding fellowship."[25] The church will have an awareness that modeling a loving community as the sign of the new humanity and kingdom of God is essential but not enough. It will be always aware of its missional identity. It will know that its holy priesthood within has a representative and intercessory dimension, and it will also be aware of its kingly priesthood toward the world and in regency with Christ over creation.

This will not, however, degenerate into an activism disconnected from deep spirituality; rather missional acts will be carried out in participation in what God has done and is doing in the world. As such mission will be rediscovered as the "easy yoke" of walking with Christ, through life in the Spirit, into what he is doing. The way most Christians think about mission is Christians filling in the gaps between God and the world in activism and often with guilt-driven motivation. Those gaps have already been filled by the incarnation and they continue to be filled by the church *as one with Christ by the Spirit* in participation with the mission of God. This removes tension between depth and width, between the church gathered around sacrament and Word in community and the church scattered in multiple vocations in the wider community.

Thus we can redeem the notion of the triune *missio Dei* such that being and act will be kept together. The church in its missional acts cannot be separated from its missional being. Mission is not a department or an "outreach wing" of the church. It is what the church as gathered *and* as scattered is.

Engagement in the public square *will* therefore be an important aspect of mission, and *how* it occurs will be tempered by relationship with the Trinity.[26] It will reflect the humble nature of Christ; it will be

---

[25]Ibid., p. 7 n. 21, which references Stanley Hauerwas, "Worship, Evangelism, Ethics: On Eliminating the 'And,'" in *A Better Hope, Resources for a Church Confronting Capitalism, Democracy, and Postmodernity* (Grand Rapids: Brazos, 2000), pp. 155-61; and Reinhard Hütter, "The Church as 'Public': Dogma, Practices and Holy Spirit," *Pro Ecclesia* 3, no. 3 (1994): 334-61.

[26]True to the concerns of Lesslie Newbigin, the church needs to engage in the public square not

consonant with the nature of God's people as kings *and* priests, as servant kings who serve the world in love by wooing, persuasion and even martyrdom, but never by oppression and politicking and coercion.[27] How do king-priests bring in the kingdom of God? The answer offered by Paul Stevens is that

> We do this through the mission of the church. . . . We also do this in all the fields of service in the world: home, neighborhood, civil society, politics and the environment management, grappling with the powers, proclaiming the gospel, participating creatively in the structures of society and in parachurch mission structures, witnessing through suffering powerlessness, working to change evil systems and in extreme situations by laying down lives in martyrdom. The idea that believers are royalty opens up one of the most neglected areas of New Testament discipleship.[28]

Without the royal dimension of witness, especially as expressed through the ecclesial yet scattered people of God, the church reverts to the new forms of pietism I see in some communal ecclesiologies: "the *laos* of God must be both priestly and kingly. Together it salts the earth."[29] When the church fails to be in the public square, it can, like many pietistic Christians in pre-apartheid South Africa, give tacit support to unjust regimes.

A further incentive for engagement in the world and overcoming rigid "two-realms thinking" is, as Hoffmeyer argues, a "pneumatological deficiency," by which he means a diminishing of our appreciation of the *diversity* of the presence of the Word in the world by the Spirit's work ahead of the church. Citing Rowan Williams, "The Son is manifest in a single, paradigmatic figure, the Spirit is manifest in the

---

on behalf of a monadic God but on behalf of the specifically triune God, whose primary way of being for us was in love and not in capricious power! See Lesslie Newbigin, "The Trinity as Public Truth," in *The Trinity in a Pluralistic Age*, ed. Kevin Vanhoozer (Grand Rapids: Eerdmans, 1997), pp. 3ff.

[27]As Congar notes, "Martyrdom is the supreme achievement of spiritual kingship resisting worldly power, just as it is the supreme achievement of the spiritual-real priesthood of willingness." Congar, *Lay People in the Church: A Study for a Theology of Laity* (London: Chapman, 1965), p. 241.

[28]Stevens, *The Other Six Days*, pp. 185-86.

[29]Ibid., p. 187.

'translatability' of that into the contingent diversity of history," Hoffmeyer then adds, "We fix on a centering location of the Word (in Galilee 2,000 years ago, in the church's sacraments), without corresponding clarity about the Spirit's role in extending the 'resonance' of the incarnate Word."[30] Hoffmeyer is here reflecting the thought of Michael Welker, who expressed the concept of the Spirit as Christ's "domain of resonance."[31]

Clarification: Is the sending of the missional God unidirectional? A third concern is that sentness in the Godhead and therefore in the church should not be considered unidirectional in its orientation. Does God send without bringing? And does the church send without bringing? This leads me to affirm the bipolarity of the missional nature and acts of God, and therefore of his church.

God is indeed the sending God, but he sends his Son and Spirit that he might bring them within the sphere of his communion. We cannot understand mission without understanding that "the perichoresis, or interpenetration, among the persons of the Trinity reveals that the nature of God is communion."[32] This communion is not limited within the Trinity, but "overflows into an involvement with history that aims at drawing humanity and creation in general into this communion with God's (His) very life."[33] The love within that communion spilled over in creation and the covenant to reconcile it and draw it into intimate relationship with himself but in a manner that preserves the agency of humans and the creation's ontological distinctness.

Mission is a natural extension of the Trinity's communal nature. Consequently, mission "is not primarily about the propagation or transmission of intellectual convictions, doctrines, or moral commands, but rather about the inclusion of all creation in God's overflowing, superabundant life of communion."[34] This inclusion was made possible by

---

[30]Hoffmeyer, "The Missional Trinity," pp. 110-11.
[31]See Michael Welker, *God the Spirit*, trans. John F. Hoffmeyer (Minneapolis: Fortress, 1994), pp. 312-15, cited in Hoffmeyer, "The Missional Trinity," p. 111. Welker in turn gives credit to Niklas Luhmann for this application of this resonance concept.
[32]Darrell Guder, ed., *Missional Church* (Grand Rapids: Eerdmans, 1998), p. 82.
[33]Bevans and Schroeder, *Constants in Context*, pp. 288-89.
[34]Ibid.

the work of Jesus through the Holy Spirit as directed by the Father.

If mission is God's massive story of redemption by which he creates and reconciles the world to himself, then mission is not a certain set of activities but a way of life that has God at the center. Colin Gunton states that "From this point of view, the church is learning that it is called to be a 'finite echo or bodying forth of the divine personal dynamics,' a temporal echo of the eternal community that God is."[35] As such, the missional church begins with the *missio Dei* truly conceived, God's mission for infinite communion and redemption of the world. Mission is therefore participation with God in his mission, not just something the church *does*; mission *is* the essence of the church, "for the calling and sending action of God forms its identity."[36] This is true also of the persons who make up the church. All are missional people, not just the few sent overseas. The mission-shaped church is therefore also sent as community and as persons, but in order to bring. Sending and bringing! Ecclesial evangels who are evangel ecclesials!

At one point in *Transforming Mission*, Bosch expresses this key notion of the church's bipolarity:

> Luke regards the life of Jesus and the story of the church as being united in one era of the Spirit. . . . Luke's church may be said to have a *bipolar orientation*, " inward" and "outward" (cf. Flender 1967:166; LaVerdiere and Thompson 1976:590). First, it is a community which devotes itself "to the apostles teaching, fellowship, the breaking of bread, and the prayers" (Acts 2:42). . . . All this is accomplished in the power of the Spirit: "The Church is the place where the exalted one manifests his presence and where the Holy Spirit creates anew." . . .
>
> Secondly, the community also has an outward orientation. It refuses to understand itself as a sectarian group. It is actively engaged in a mission to those still outside the pale of the gospel. And the inner life of the church is connected to its outer life (cf. LaVerdiere and Thompson 1976:590).[37]

If Elton Trueblood's dictum that the most important word in the-

---

[35]Colin E. Gunton, *The Promise of Trinitarian Theology* (Edinburgh: T & T Clark, 1991), p. 79, quoted in Guder, *Missional Church*, p. 82.

[36]Guder, *Missional Church*, p. 82.

[37]Bosch, *Transforming Mission*, pp. 119-20.

ology is *and* is to be trusted, no truer word could be said of the church's nature as the icon of the missional God, who both sends out of the depth of his inner being and also brings humanity into that inner relational life and love. What undergirds the two poles of the bipolar church and keeps them together? It is awareness of the bidirectional nature of the one God with respect to who he is in himself and how he works in the economy of salvation in the following crucial ways:

1. The bidirectional nature of God's mission is seen first in the mutuality of the processions of his inner relations, which correspond to the bidrectional orientation of his missions in the economy. The same Son who is generated eternally by the Father filiates the Father in turn (there is no Father apart from the Son and no Son apart from the Father). The Spirit proceeds from the Father as the Spirit spirates the Father. Correspondingly, as the communion of the eternal God goes out in the giving of the Son and Spirit for creation and in redemption, each in turn has in mind a remanation, a uniting of humanity with the Father, in Christ and by the Spirit.

2. In the life of the Son there is a second great unifying movement of the Trinity in mission. The Western conception has tended to focus the sending on the Son and the uniting on the Spirit. However, there is actually a uniting and bringing dimension in a full-orbed Christology, including both the *anhypostatic* or God-humanward movement and the corresponding *enhypostatic* movement entailing the presentation of the incarnate Son as our *fellow human* of humanity to the Father. This finds its locus in the much-neglected ascension of Jesus as man, our great High Priest. As Ray Anderson puts it, "This twofold mediation can be expressed as the humanity of God and the humanizing of humanity in the image and likeness of God. These two aspects of the mediation of Christ are interrelated and interdependent."[38] This suggests that Jesus' purpose was not merely to put away sin, but through his vicarious humanity to restore within humans the image of God and give them life.[39] Christian mission is thus participation in the incarnation (going) and in his ascension (bringing). Participation in his ascension involves

---

[38]Ray S. Anderson, *The Soul of Ministry* (Louisville: Westminster John Knox, 1997), pp. 73-74.
[39]Bosch, *Transforming Mission*, p. 209.

our priestly function, even in the inner life of the church, including the Eucharist, for as Costas notes, "through her worship the church acts as the representative of the world."[40]

3. The Spirit, understood within the Western tradition, is the uniting member of the Trinity, the holy love of the Father and the Son. Orlando Costas suggests that the Spirit "unites the community of faith with the Son and has made possible the unity of the world with God."[41] The Spirit, then, is not understood in the categories of sending and sent, but rather as uniting both the Son to the Father and the world to God. Costas understands the trinitarian movement as "a twofold movement: from God to the world, and from the world to God."[42] This means then that the church in which God lives by his Spirit is to be *both* a sent and a uniting organism.

4. The fact that the kingdom of God has both inner and outer dimensions keeps the church, which is the harbinger and messenger of God's kingdom on earth, bidirectional. Jesus spoke of the kingdom of God that is within or among you, leading us constantly to submit ourselves to his reign. There is a powerful call in kingdom theology for us to have undivided hearts. In the life of the church and its ecclesial persons there is a call to break the power of idols and to invite Jesus again and again to rule as King. It is as he reigns as Head of the church and King that we can hear his call and move outward in response to those places and people where his reign is being established.

Consequences for the church's mission. Because the outer missional life is connected to its inner life, the church will be both deep and wide. Deep in its communion with God as the gathered people of God. That means it will be a *drawing* community. A community that draws people inexorably into the presence of Christ, as that is made real through an intentionally Christocentric focus. A community that draws them to the hospitality of the Lord's Supper, where they may feed on Jesus. A community that draws them into the wonder of the Word of God as it

---

[40]Costas, *The Church and Its Mission: A Shattering Critique from the Third World* (Carol Stream, Ill.: Tyndale, 1974), p. 50.
[41]Orlando Costas, *Liberating News* (Grand Rapids: Eerdmans, 1989), p. 76.
[42]Ibid., p. 73.

is taught and preached. A community that draws the people of God around the essentials of the historic orthodox creeds and refuses to major on minors. A community that draws through its thoughtful liturgy as representative of all humanity, recognizing that architecture and symbols are never neutral and that we worship as cognitive and sensual beings. A community that draws by valuing all members and gifts and ministry. A community that draws by the richness of charismatic breadth experienced in the church's gatherings. A community that draws because it is a community of love!

But the church will also be wide in manner nurtured by its depth. Wide in that it is aware the church always gathers with the world in mind and scatters into every vocation to fulfill the creation mandate, the Great Commandment and the Great Commission, scatters to engage in the public square on behalf of justice and peace, and yet as scattered is just that—the church.

Mission has in mind the story of God involving creation, the Fall, redemption and consummation of whole persons in a renewed creation. God not only creates in *ekstasis*, he draws an alienated creation back into his communion. This he does through the people of the last Adam. The church is not merely a sent community with respect to humans, therefore, but a drawing community for all creation. If the goal of God's reconciling activity is a renewed creation, and its reconciliation and liberation is tied inexorably to that of the church (Rom 8:21-30), then Christians will take seriously the stewarding of creation as its vice-regents or subcreators, giving creation a voice.

The goal, then, of the church is to be sent but also to bring in. Its depth must be matched by its width, and *vice versa*.

THE NATURE OF THE MISSIONAL CHURCH

This is the response to the question, In light, then, of the *missio Dei*, what is the nature of the missional church? This in sum is the response to this question that has emerged in this chapter:

- It will have a servant or kenotic and communal character; its inner and outer life are distinct but inseparable.

- Its identity as missional will not be separated from its acts in mission.

- It will be bidirectional in its focus: deep and wide.

Carl Braaten's theocentric and trinitarian sentiments confirm that the missional church is deep as well as wide.

> This Trinitarian grounding of mission should make clear that God and not the church is the primary subject and source of mission. Advocacy is what the church is about, being God's advocate in the world. The church must therefore begin its mission with doxology, otherwise everything peters out into social activism and aimless programs.[43]

The notion that church must get dumbed down and shallow is a real fear for many who hear the term *missional*. The use of the term *deep church* by Walker and Bretherton and Belcher is unfortunate. It necessitates a counter name—*deep* was needed to correct the notion that *missional* must be shallow. But *deep* could mean "unmissional." The necessity for an outward orientation of the church has been well expressed in John Stott's comment that "our static, inflexible, self-centerd structures are 'heretical structures' because they embody a heretical doctrine of the church." He adds that if "our structure has become an end in itself, not a means of saving the world," it is "a heretical structure."[44] Thus I wish to retain the name *missional* for church, use it with a small letter, and by that term to intend "deep and wide church"! So here's hoping we're going to see some deep, wide, missional churches emerging! Deepening is needed in many Western churches to help people see church as an identity. Widening is needed also to help people see that the church as the community of Christ on earth is God's primary missioner, not individuals, and that therefore the church does not exist for itself.

In anticipation of chapter ten concerning the person and work of the Spirit, we may also now say that fully trinitarian mission, in addition to being incarnational, will also be pneumatic in its nature. Keeping the "two hands of God," as Irenaeus expressed it metaphorically, together is crucial for correct trinitarian theology and therefore also for mission.

---

[43]Carl E. Braaten, "The Mission of the Gospel to the Nations," *Dialog* 30 (1991): 127.
[44]John Stott, quoted in Tim Chester and Steve Timmis, *Total Church: A Radical Reshaping Around Gospel and Community* (Wheaton, Ill.: Crossway, 2008), p. 18.

The following is a summation of the past chapters and an anticipation of the next two:

1. If God is the incarnational, missional God, his church will be incarnationally missional. This means:

- the church will be bipolar just as Christ who became incarnate as the sent One has gathered the new humanity into the fellowship of the triune God.

- the church will see itself as the corporate Christ and will preserve or recover its catholicity; that is, local churches will value and pursue unity within their membership, between themselves and other churches, and work in collaborative and not competitive ways with sister churches.

- the soteriological mission of the church will seek the recovery of persons in the fullness of their personhood, not merely the salvation of souls. This also means that the church will feed the hungry, care for the body through health care, educate the mind, encourage community transformation, validate work in all its forms and so on.

2. If God is pneumatologically missional, his church will be pneumatically missional. This means:

- the church will see itself as bipolar in that the Spirit who has been sent and who indwells the church is the Spirit who draws human persons to God, regenerates them and incorporates them into the church.

- the missional church will be sensitive to the work of the Spirit in his ever-renewing and reviving work (*semper reformanda*), and that it will not despise the charismata given by the Spirit to each believer.

- the church and its members will work missionally in response to the leading and in participation with the preceding work of the Spirit in the world ahead of them.

- the church, filled with the power of the Spirit, will be engaged in evangelism and seeking kingdom justice in light of the Spirit's work in the world.

10

Mission as Theosis

■ ■ ■

"As the Father has sent me, I am sending you." And with that
he breathed on them and said, "Receive the Holy Spirit."

JOHN 20:21-22

For the Welsh Anglican hymn-writer William Williams (1719-1791),
as for other teachers of theosis, "the doctrines of Trinity, incarnation
and deification belong together in an indissoluble knot."

A. M. ALLCHIN, *Participation in God*

The face of [the] Spirit is the assembly of redeemed
human faces in their infinite diversity. Human persons grown to the
fullness of their particular identities but sharing in the common divine
gift of reconciled life in faith, these are the Spirit's manifestation.

VLADIMIR LOSSKY, *The Mystical Theology of the Eastern Church*

THE SIGNIFICANCE OF THE BREATHING ACT by which Jesus prefigured Pentecost is captured well by F. F. Bruce: "as the Son received
the Spirit in unrestricted fullness for the discharge of his own mission
(John 1:32-34; 3:34), so they now receive the Spirit for the discharge of

theirs."[1] The participatory nature of the mission of the church will receive emphasis in this chapter. It is the Spirit's indwelling of the church and human persons that helps us understand that the church's mission is the continuance of Christ's mission. He is in heaven, and yet by perichoresis he is also on earth, by the Spirit's indwelling and activity within and through the church, his body. Mission as participation in the life of God is the key tenet of this whole passage.

Whether one adopts the view that this event is indeed proleptic and symbolic of the outpouring of the Spirit in the Day of Pentecost or alternative views that the true Pentecost occurred here,[2] or that there were two Pentecosts,[3] or that the relationship with the Spirit was a gradually growing one for the disciples,[4] this should not detract in any way from the event's significance. My own opinion is that John's event is proleptic. Perhaps this first breathing act of Jesus was recorded to affirm that Jesus as the Son has the right to give the Spirit, and that this visible (and symbolic) event was necessary in light of the fact that when the Spirit came manifestly on the Day of Pentecost, he was not then visible as the source of the Spirit's outpouring. Athanasius in his defense against Arius makes much of this authority of the Son to give the Spirit in his consideration of this passage. It is an act of someone who must be God.[5]

The "blowing in" is in the Old Testament and Apocrypha associated with the giving of life (Gen 2:7; 1 Kings 17:21; Ezek 37:9; Wis 15:11), and, says Schnackenburg, "so here, the bestowal of a share in

---

[1]F. F. Bruce, *The Gospels and Epistles of John* (Grand Rapids: Eerdmans, 1983), pp. 391-92.

[2]Rudolf Schnackenburg, *The Gospel According to St. John*, trans. David Smith and G. A. Kon (New York: Crossroad, 1982), 3:325-26.

[3]Augustine believed there needed to be one outpouring on earth (Jn 20) to empower the love of neighbor, and one from heaven (Acts 2) to inspire love for God (Augustine, *On the Trinity* 15.26.46, cited in Joel C. Elowsky, *John 11–21*, Ancient Christian Commentary on Scripture IVb [Downers Grove, Ill.: InterVarsity Press, 2007], p. 361).

[4]As in Gregory of Nazianzus and Chrysostom, *Homilies on the Gospel of John* 86.3, *Nicene and Post-Nicene Fathers* 14:325, cited in Elowsky, *John 11–21*, p. 362.

[5]The uniqueness of the event is signaled by the fact that the verb ἐμφυσάω (lit. "blowing in") is a *hapax legomena*, that is, it occurs only here in the New Testament. The article is missing in Jesus' utterance here also, which is also unusual in his references to the Spirit, as is his use of the adjective "holy" (only 2x elsewhere in John's account (1:33; 14:26). Most often he uses the term *Spirit* in an unqualified sense or with other qualifiers (e.g., "Spirit of truth").

the life of the risen one who himself possesses the Spirit and now transfers it to the disciples."[6] However, he adds that the idea of cleansing from sins comes along also with the eschatological out-pouring of the Spirit (cf. Ezek 36:25-27), and that this may account for Jesus' unusual use (in John) of the term *holy* for the Spirit.[7] Our focus here is on the richness of the meaning of the Spirit utterance and the concomitant breathing action as that emerges from consideration of related Spirit sayings of Jesus, which John's Gospel records earlier. The relationship between the commission and the action of Jesus reveals that there is a vital correspondence between "the sentness of Jesus and his people" and the coming of the Spirit to dwell within and among them. This connection was made by Jesus in his passion ministry con-cerning the coming of the Spirit.

In this chapter we will first examine the elucidatory passage in John 14 to discover that our sentness is imparted to us through rela-tional participation with Christ, or theosis, which is enacted by the indwelling of the Spirit. The Son entered into our humanity to become one with humanity. However, in conversion, the Spirit awakens and draws us into the reality of that union with Christ by faith. By the Spirit's presence in us, Christ is present in us by coin-herence. The believing person is baptized by the Spirit into Christ to be in his church, his body. As church and as ecclesial persons we fulfill the ongoing mission of Jesus as those who are one with him. Strictly speaking we do not do mission for him but *with* him. This will reveal to us the *spirituality* of Christian mission (a *pneumatic* spirituality).

Second, in order to really grasp what "sentness" means we will ex-plore this concept as it applied to Jesus in order that we may know what this means for us. This will keep our missional spirituality grounded or *incarnational*. In light of the tendency for various traditions within church and parachurch to pursue missional spiritualities on either of the extremes of the pneumatic or the incarnational, I will suggest ways of keeping these together.

---

[6]Schnackenburg, *Gospel According to St. John*, p. 324.
[7]Ibid.

PARTICIPATION IN THE SON'S SENTNESS *BY THE SPIRIT*

What Jesus said concerning the correspondence between his sending by the Father and the disciples' sending by him is explicated by his breathing the Spirit on them. They would be able to understand this in light of what Jesus had told them about the Spirit in his prepassion discourse to them about the Spirit's coming. The key passage that illuminates John 20:21-22 is John 14:20 and its context (Jn 14:11-27): "On that day [of the Spirit's coming] you will *realize that I am in my Father, and you are in me, and I am in you*" (emphasis added). This verse expresses what the Spirit's coming, which Jesus announces clearly in verses 16-17 ("I will ask the Father, and he will give you another advocate to help you and be with you forever—the Spirit of truth") would mean. It is a profound statement by Jesus that reveals the three principal unions of Christian theology and the gospel.

When the Spirit came, they would begin to understand, first, the coinherent union of the Son with the Father; second, the union of the Son with his people ("you are in me [you in Christ]" by his incarnation to become one with humanity), and third, the union of his people with the Son ("Christ in you," union by the indwelling of the Spirit). Each union is achieved by the Spirit: the trinitarian union of the Father and the Son is in the Spirit; the incarnational hypostatic union of humanity and deity in Christ was achieved by the Spirit; and the union of the believer with Christ is accomplished by the Spirit's indwelling. This informs John 20:21-22 to suggest that the correspondence between the Son's sending and his people's sending is a consequence of his loving union with the Father, a union into which they are enabled to participate by the gospel. This had happened ontically through the union of the Son with their humanity, and they would enter that reality by their participation with him by the Spirit's indwelling.

These associations of the three unions in John are breathtaking. John's version of the gospel is first and foremost about the filial rather than the forensic. God's first thoughts in reaching out to fallen humanity were to draw them into the fellowship of his triune love and life. Justification and sanctification result from this union, but the crucial point here is that these unions which Jesus describes in verse 20 come within a context that has some important connections with mission. The antecedent context (vv. 11-19) reveals that the Spirit's coming to be *in* rather than just *with* his people, and to impart the life of Jesus in a way so real they would not even feel his absence, was given to explain how the works of Jesus would become their works, just as his works had been his Father's. They would be working with him, not just for him. By his Spirit in them Jesus and his Father would continue to be on mission—through them. Judas' question in the middle of this discourse suggests also a connection with mission: "But, Lord, why do you intend to show yourself to us, and not to the world?" This reflects the narrowing-for-expansion principle of mission. Jesus' answer drives home the point that their usefulness in this expansion (width) was dependent on the extent to which they lived into the depth of the triune communion of love by the Spirit (vv. 23-31). Furthermore, in verses 25-27 there is a double reference to the peace that would become theirs for enjoyment and then impartation in mission, in a manner that evokes the double peace benedictions of John 20:19-23.

At the heart of the passage however is the perspective that illumines what the Spirit's breathing on the disciples in John 20 meant. By way of elucidating what he has said in John 14:20, Jesus expresses that the Spirit's coming would mean the coming of the triune Godhead to inhabit the hearts of his people: "Jesus replied, 'Anyone who loves me will obey my teaching. My Father will love them, and we will come to them and make our home with them'" (Jn 20:23). This would ensure mission as outflow of intimacy with God and in response to his promptings by his power. Fecundity in John is always a product of communion.

This emphasis on participation of God's people with Christ, corporately and individually, may be new to many Western Christians. It may sound like mysticism or even monism, the confusion of human and divine persons, or maybe even like Mormonism! Yet the theology of union or participation or theosis has been present in both the Western and Eastern traditions of Christianity since the church fathers (and, indeed, in Jesus and the apostles!). Care does need to be taken when using the concept. The trinitarian foundations I have laid in chapters three and eight now come together to clarify and qualify what is meant by human participation in or union with the triune God. Participation in God is to be in relationship with the persons in the Godhead, in Christ, by the Spirit, experiencing the acts of God, that is, his life and love. It is relationality between human and divine persons that constitutes participation of humans in God, and in which human persons remain human and divine persons divine. It is not "essential participation," which is monism or pantheism. The following are some key qualifying concepts for properly understanding participation or theosis.

Trinitarian underpinnings of theosis.

1. The union of human persons and the church with God is analogous (with some limitations) to the union of persons within the Trinity conceived socially as in the economic Trinity (and therefore the immanent Trinity). That is, it is a *relational* union in which persons of irreducible identity mutually indwell one another in an interpenetrated way without loss of personal identity. I believe that theosis is only possible if the Trinity is conceived in a social manner. The inadequate theology of the divine persons' hypostatic uniqueness within the psychological model of the Trinity that has dominated Western Catholic and Protestant theology for centuries leads to some real challenges for the union of human persons with God. Because divine "persons" are viewed as "relations" within the Godhead (Pope Benedict XVI) or "modes of being" (Barth), when it comes to the union of human persons with God there is a blurring of boundaries. This is why Benedict's concept of the church and Christ together as the *totus Christus* runs into the charge of monism. Similarly, in the eighteenth century Jonathan Edwards had to answer this charge concerning his view of Spirit theosis, that the believer when infused by the Spirit at conversion was thereby brought into union with the immanent Godhead. His opponent accused him of teaching a "Godded with God" theology.[8]

Keeping the distinctiveness and the relationality of divine and human persons together keeps "participation" theology relational rather

---

[8]Edwards responded that he did not mean the "essence" of God but a moral relationship (Jonathan Edwards, "Unpublished Letter on Assurance and Participation in the Divine Nature," *Dissertation I*, pp. 636-40).

than monistic or mystical.[9] Miroslav Volf has helpfully expressed the union within the Trinity as a union based in perichoresis: the "mutually internal abiding and interpenetration of the trinitarian persons, which since Pseudo-Cyril has been called *perichōrēsis*, determines the character both of the divine persons and of their unity." It is this clear articulation of the hypostatic uniqueness yet profound relationality of the divine persons that leads, when the inclusion of human persons within the love and life of that Trinity is considered, to a view of that inclusion as a relational one, in which humans remain human. Volf is also careful to say *that human persons do not indwell divine persons in the same way that divine persons do*. There is a difference between how we indwell God and he indwells us: "The Spirit indwells human persons, whereas human beings by contrast indwell *the life-giving ambience of the Spirit*—not the person of the Spirit."[10] Only God, he maintains, can truly indwell other persons.

2. It is important to keep together the union of the Son with humanity in the incarnation with the union of humans with the Son by the Spirit in conversion. It is important to emphasize the incarnational dimension in participation, that Christ has participated in humanity by the incarnation and that we participate in him by the Spirit as humans. The coinherence between the human and divine natures of Christ, such that he was both truly human and truly divine as one person, "without confusion," provides a model for understanding human union with God such that humans stay human. Karl Barth's understanding of participation is particularly helpful. He insisted that the appropriate order for the strands that make up the knot of trinitarian salvation is Trinity, incarnation and then, and only on the basis of incarnation, deification. Barth starts with the Spirit's role as mediator of communion in the man Christ Jesus rather than with the saints.[11]

---

[9]Whereas so much Western thinking is undergirded by Plato's theory of *methexis*, the concept of participation presented in the New Testament as *koinōnia* should, as Torrance tells us, "commit us to an irreducibly relational conceptuality denoting a radically interpersonal overlapping or interpenetration of being, where this is conceived in such a way that personal hypostases are fully realized in this and not in any way subsumed by it" (Alan J. Torrance, *Persons in Communion* [Edinburgh: T & T Clark, 1996], p. 256).

[10]Miroslav Volf, *After Our Likeness* (Grand Rapids: Eerdmans, 1998), pp. 208-9.

[11]See George Hunsinger, "The Mediator of Communion: Karl Barth's Doctrine of the Holy

The Christocentricity of Barth's pneumatology and his pneumato-logical concept of participation preserves a doctrine of participation from being open to the accusation of monism. Barth clarifies that human participation in God's self-knowledge is always an "indirect participation" (CD II/1, 59), indirect because "it is mediated in and through Jesus Christ"[12] and through his humanity, in particular. It is as the fully human Jesus, through the incarnation, that his human knowing of God is, by its coinherence with his knowing as the eternal Son, "the appointed vehicle of mediation through which we come to take part in the truth of God's self-knowledge (CD II/1, p. 252)."[13] We as humans have fellowship in Christ's knowledge of God as we are 'taken up into fellowship with the life of the Son of God."[14]

3. Participation is not necessarily synergistic. Although Eastern versions of theosis tend to be synergistic, the Reformed-Barthian model of participation is not. Synergism implies that he does his part and we contribute our portion. Rather, in a model of participation that is dialectical in the sense that God does not cease to be God and neither does the human cease to be human, in a correspondingly dialectical sense we act only because he acts and in his acting we act (Barth). Humans remain human as they participate in the love, life and mission of God. This is participation by grace from start to finish. Referring to the monergism-synergism categories, Julie Canlis comments,

> Synergism is cooperation—like a bargain. (At least, in my theological term books it is). Participation is more of an overlapping, an ensconcing, a vine-and-branches kind of thing. Part of the reason we don't go for it

Spirit," *The Cambridge Companion to Karl Barth*, ed. John Webster (Cambridge: Cambridge University Press, 2000), p. 179.

[12]Hunsinger, "The Mediator of Communion," p. 190.

[13]Ibid.

[14]Karl Barth, *Church Dogmatics* II/1, ed. G. W. Bromiley and T. F. Torrance (Edinburgh: T & T Clark, 1975), 162. For more on a trinitarian conception of participation developed by contemporary trinitarian theologians, see John D. Zizioulas, *Being as Communion* (Crestwood, N.Y.: St. Vladimir's Seminary Press, 1985); Zizioulas, chap. 2 in Christoph Schwöbel, ed., *Trinitarian Theology Today* (Edinburgh: T & T Clark, 1995); C. E. Gunton, *The Promise of Trinitarian Theology*, 2nd ed. (Edinburgh: T & T Clark, 1997); C. Schwöbel and C. Gunton, eds., *Persons Divine and Human* (Edinburgh: T & T Clark, 1991); Catherine Mowry LaCugna, *God for Us* (San Francisco: HarperSanFrancisco, 1991); Volf, *After Our Likeness*; Torrance, *Persons in Communion*; and Moltmann, *The Trinity and the Kingdom of God* (San Francisco: Harper & Row, 1981).

is that we have a modern, atomistic anthropology that doesn't make room for this kind of "in"-ness. So we call it synergism, and know we don't like it![15]

This concept of participation has profound consequences for the spirituality of believers and the church. Participation in the mission of God depends on the practice of union with Christ by the Spirit. This presses the would-be missional church to be the deep church. Intimacy with God is crucial to missional participation with God of the kind that enables the church to respond to what God is about in his mission. The Nicene marks of the church do not become mission verbals without this Spirit-enabled communion enabled.

PARTICIPATION IN THE *SON'S SENTNESS*, BY THE SPIRIT

We now turn to the manner in which the Son lived out his sentness. This will provide further insight into the spirituality of mission. It will reveal the goal of the Spirit's work in our lives by unveiling what the sentness of Jesus meant for his mission. If the Spirit brings about the union we have with Christ (*unio Christi*) and imparts the power for imitation of Christ (*imitatio Christi*), it will benefit us to know what it is about him we are seeking to imitate.

We will do this by looking at what "sentness" meant for Jesus as the Gospel of John presents it, given that, by virtue of our union with Christ by the Spirit, it is a *continuation* of his sentness. This commission in John 20 is the Greatest Commission because it contains the power of our sending, which is our union with God—in Christ, by the Spirit, from and to the Father. But what does the incarnate life of Jesus tell us about what the missional life looks like? In this section we will explore the identity of Jesus as the sent One as the paradigm in which we can and must live.

The identity of Jesus as the sent One is arguably the most emphatic theme in John's Gospel. It is referred to forty-three times, mostly by Jesus himself. John, having depicted Jesus as the sent One of the Father

---

[15]Julie wrote this in an email communication to Clement Wen on February 18, 2009, in the course of our cosupervision of his MCS thesis comparing participation in Calvin and Maximus.

throughout, now brings that theme to its climax in John 20, through his record of Jesus' last words, by the passing on of this identity to Jesus' community. The following is a brief exposition of some of the most significant passages that elucidate what it meant that Jesus was the sent One of the Father.

Speaking what the sending Father says. There are a number of passages that record the claim of Jesus that, as One sent by the Father, he spoke the words of the Father. The first of these is John 3:34-35: "For the one *whom God has sent speaks the words of God*, for God gives the Spirit without limit. The Father loves the Son and has placed everything in his hands" (emphasis added). It is of interest that Jesus, unique Son of God that he is, speaks on earth in complete dependence on the Spirit and in response to the words of the Father. Such is the nature of their perichoretic relationship in teaching! There is a distinction John wished to make between Jesus and his disciples here, in that he is given the Spirit without limit and thus is in perfect intimacy with the Father and able to hear the words he is to say with perfect hearing. However, John's purpose here is not to place what Jesus modeled out of reach for us. His incarnational Jesus is also the inspirational Jesus (as key passages like John 14:12, and even the "as . . . so" nature of the John 20 commission reveals). Jesus spoke the Father's words by the gift of the Spirit and therefore so can we.

Here is the paradigm, then, for effective missional speaking! It is a consequence of a sentness from the Father derived from our union with Christ by the Spirit, and a consequence of being able to listen by the Spirit for the Father's words, and being able to utter them by the Spirit's power. This is what mission by theosis through the Spirit means. This is why Jesus breathed the Spirit on his disciples as he commissioned them for mission. Despite the downturn in popularity of personal evangelism and the deemphasis on preaching in some missional circles, I want to put a word in for the power of words uttered from the Father by the Spirit! We would be more missionally effective if we taught as an outflow of Spirit-led contemplative Bible reading, study of Scripture and utterance by the same Spirit. This devotional and submissive way of reading is anticipated in another passage in John: "Jesus replied, 'If anyone loves me, he will obey my teaching. My Father will love them, and we will come to them and make our home with them. Anyone who does not love me will not obey my teaching. These words you hear are not my own; they belong to the Father who sent me" (Jn 14:23-25). Obedience to the teaching we receive from this sent One enables the fostering and deepening of that intimate relationship with the Father and the Son that enables us to hear that we might speak as he speaks.

The coming together of a statement about Jesus' sentness and his teaching is evident again in John 12:49-50: "I did not speak of my own accord, but the Father who *sent* me commanded me what to say and *how to say it*" (NIV, emphasis added). Such is the intimacy between the Father and the Son that the Father's instruction to the Son included even the detail of how to say it! Such speaking will astound people with wisdom that is beyond the realm of mere study or human accomplishment, bringing about spiritual life (1 Pet 1:25).

Doing what the sending Father does. In John 4, Jesus spoke of his sentness by the Father in order that he might finish the work of preparing the harvest for mission:

> Then his disciples said to each other, "Could someone have brought him food?"
>
> "My food," said Jesus, "is to do the will of him *who sent me* and to finish his work. Don't you have a saying, 'It's still four months until the harvest'? I tell you, open your eyes and look at the fields! They are ripe for harvest." (Jn 4:33-35, emphasis added)

For Jesus, this harvest was the fruit of his atoning work, the "much fruit" that follows his falling into the ground which he speaks of in John 12, bringing "many sons and daughters to glory," part of what constituted the "joy set before him" (Heb 2:10; 12:2). Our task is to reap that harvest, participating in finishing the work he has given us, recognizing it may also be painful work, for in this harvesting we fill up what is lacking in his sufferings.

In John 5 there are a cluster of references to the connection between Jesus' sentness and various aspects of his work in the economy of redemption:

Jesus said to them, "My Father is always at his work to this very day, and I too am working." . . .

Jesus gave them this answer: "I tell you the truth, the *Son can do nothing by himself; he can do only what he sees his Father doing, because whatever the Father does the Son also does.* For the Father *loves the Son* and shows him all he does." (Jn 5:17, 19-20, emphasis added)

From the antecedent context we know that Jesus is referring to the work of healing. Our work as those sent in Jesus is also to do the Father's work of healing as we discern what the Father is doing. The last piece is crucial. Jesus did not heal everybody, nor can we. Of course Jesus did heal everybody he tried to heal, although even he was hindered in an ethos of unbelief. Our discerning who the Father may wish to heal through healing prayer is never perfect, nor are our prayers. On this side of the eschaton the kingdom has come, but not yet fully, so not all we pray for are healed. However, I am convinced that the reason more people are not healed in our churches has more to do with our low expectancy, which arises from our scientism (as opposed to scientific), our rationalist Enlightenment worldviews. Our effectiveness in mission is hampered by the weakness of our faith and discernment of what the Father may be doing. We need to pray for breakthroughs in this area of healing, so we may point not to the healers but to the divine Healer who came to "take up our diseases and bore our diseases" (Is 53:4; see Mt 10:17).

Later in John 5, Jesus' work of resurrection as the sent One of the Father is included. "Yes, and *he will show him even greater works than these*, so that you will be amazed. *For just as the Father* raises the dead and gives them life, even *so* the Son gives life to whom he is pleased to give it" (Jn 5:20-21). The phrase *even greater works than these* is repeated by Jesus in John 14:12: "Very truly I tell you, all who have faith in me will do the works I have been doing, and they will do even greater things than these, because I am going to the Father." Part of the work of participating by the Spirit in Christ's ongoing work on earth is to participate in the work of resurrection. Jesus is anticipating the miracles of regeneration that would happen again and again as his disciples, working in union with him by the Spirit, shared the life-giving words of the gospel! There are cases of bodily resurrection sprinkled across the face of church history. However, this is not the primary force of this text. Rather it is the equally miraculous business of the agency of human words being used by God to effect regeneration now in the hearts of believing humans, so that, in the age to come, their permanent resurrection will occur. They will not, like resurrected Lazarus, ever die again.

But notice again the missional spirituality upon which such participation in regeneration is contingent. John 14:13-14 speaks of asking in the name of Jesus, which entails a participation in the Son and his glorifying of the Father. This assumes a life of prayer seen as participation in the communion already active in the Godhead. We are brought back to the touchstone of effective mission, which is prayerful intimacy with God that entails bold supplication. For those who have worried that John 14 seems dishonoring to Jesus, the context is one of asking the Father in the Son's name for the "greater things," so it is not a question of eclipsing the Son. Rather he is glorified in requests in his name for bold things! What's more, Christian prayer is participation in the prayer of Jesus to the Father by the Spirit, so all supplication ultimately involves his gracious intercession on our behalf and the glory of the triune God. Barth spoke of the Lord's Prayer as being prayed by Jesus as the representative of all and of Jesus as the true subject of prayer, the great suppliant and petitioner.[16] It was in Christ that Barth found resolution of the tension between divine sovereignty and human agency in prayer, for all Christians pray only in Christ.

Doing the work of judgment. John 5:22-30 and John 8:16 speak of the specific work of judgment which has been given to the Son as the sent One. As his sent ones, therefore, in union with him, the church has the privilege of doing what Jesus does and what he will do. In the present age of the kingdom of God, we have the privilege of pronouncing justification in Christ (on the basis of the words of Jesus in Jn 5:24, for example: "I tell you the truth, whoever hears my word and believes him who *sent* me has eternal life and will not be judged but has

---

[16]Karl Barth, *Evangelical Theology: An Introduction* (Grand Rapids: Eerdmans, 1979), p. 143.

crossed over from death to life") over those who believe (reflected in the intent of Jn 20:23), and also of discerning and seeking justice (humbly, proleptically and provisionally to be sure) in this world. Paul makes the point in 1 Corinthians 6:2-3 that in the day of the kingdom fully come, Christians will judge the world of people and even angels. But he does so as an ethical appeal to the saints to administer justice now, within church on matters of conflict resolution and morality, rather than going to the courts. But if the kingdom has already come, then as kingdom people who have the privilege of hearing the Father, because we are in the Son and he is in us by the Spirit, then we need to be modeling good conflict resolution and justice within the church and be at the forefront of the justice issues in the wider community. The church has all too often lost its credibility in evangelism because it has been absent from issues of justice and liberation. At best the church has been absent as a voice seeking justice for the oppressed, and at worst it has been complicit with the perpetrators of injustice.

Doing what the sending Father does to completion: Servanthood and sacrifice. In John 4–5 there are references to Jesus' sentness as involving the completion of the work his Father had given him. In John 4:34, he tells his disciples, "My food . . . is to do the will of him *who sent me* and to finish his work" and in John 5:36, in dialogue with the Jewish religious leaders, he says: "I have testimony weightier than that of John. For the works that the Father has given me to finish—the very works that I am doing, testify that the Father has *sent* me." This language of "finishing" in John usually conveys the notion that Jesus' mission involves the cross. This evokes for the missional people of God in union with Christ that finishing our work must also involve sacrifice. This is borne out by what Jesus said in his passion ministry later in the Gospel: "Remember what I told you: 'Servants are not greater than their master.' If they persecuted me, they will persecute you also. If they obeyed my teaching, they will obey yours also. They will treat you this way because of my name, for they do not know the one who *sent* me" (Jn 15:20-21). Union with Jesus is not all smooth sailing.

Living in intimate communion with the Father. "Just as the living Father sent me and I live because of the Father, so the one who feeds on me will live because of me" (Jn 6:57). This describes the trinitarian life cycle of the missional person and the missional church. Jesus as the sent One lived and lives in the Father eternally and experientially as a man on earth and now in heaven. We as sent ones participate in that life shared between the Father and the Son. We give evidence that we do by feeding on Christ. We are sustained for mission only as we feed on the sent One and live in his life. This is experiential communion that lives out of the real union we have with Christ, and given the long tradition that John 6 is a eucharistic passage, this means that we must feed regularly on Christ in the Eucharist. This feeding on Christ in a spiritual way, as an act of communion with the Son and with the triune Godhead, constantly renews our missional participation in Christ, by the Spirit.

Reflecting the likeness of the Sender: For us this involves contemplation and imitation through communion. "Then Jesus cried out, 'Those who believe in me do not believe in me only, but in the one who *sent* me. *When they look at me, they see the one who sent me*'" (Jn 12:44-45, emphasis added). Jesus' comment in verse 45 conveys that the mission of Jesus to reveal the Father was guaranteed by his oneness with the Father. The notion that we too as his missional people might also be a revelation of the Father as we contemplate and imitate the Son, such that "when they look at us, they see the one who sent him," is not beyond the scope of New Testament truth. Paul speaks of such contemplation resulting in transformation into the image of Christ in 2 Corinthians 3:18. Notably, it is by the Spirit that such transformation occurs: "And we all, who with unveiled faces contemplate the Lord's glory, are being transformed into his image with ever-increasing glory, which comes from the Lord, who is the Spirit." The word translated "contemplate" here can also be rendered "reflect," but there is a mutuality of relationship between contemplation and reflection. This envisions a dynamic process by which the contemplator of the irridescent glory of the Lord Jesus becomes the reflector of reflected glory. The agent at work is the Spirit, who brings the presence of Christ to us by perichoresis. Paul picks up on the missional repercussion of this transforming contemplation in the next chapter:

For what we preach is not ourselves, but Jesus Christ as Lord, and ourselves as your servants for Jesus' sake. For God, who said, "Let light shine out of darkness," made his light shine in our hearts to give us the light of the knowledge of God's glory displayed in the face of Christ.

But we have this treasure in jars of clay to show that this all-surpassing power is from God and not from us. (2 Cor 4:5-7)

The essence of mission is the reflection of Christ's glorious face in the lives and words of people who are broken jars of clay. Here is the ultimate proof that deep church is the secret to wide church, that deeply contemplative people are the people God uses to accomplish his mission, and that they do this as they participate in the life and glory of Christ by the Spirit. Mission is not frenetic activism but contemplative action.

While I am supportive of good psychotherapy, it seems to me that North American Christians spend much more time gazing into themselves in this therapeutic age than away from themselves to the glory of Christ. Church gatherings need to make space for contemplative gazing on the face of Christ. With respect to personal devotion, Hans Urs von Balthasar has written these striking words in regard to the relationship between personal and communal contemplation:

Whatever the contemplative perceives and understands in his solitary encounter with the word will be incorporated in the Church's understanding. And whatever is greater, whatever exceeds his understanding and causes him to adore the received word and to respect its mystery, enters as a living reality into the Church's attitude of worship, bringing forth fruit in others. . . . Contemplatives are like vast underground rivers, at times causing springs to gush forth where least expected, or revealing their presence simply by the vegetation which is secretly nourished by them.[17]

These rivers springing up to produce missional fruit are the work of the Spirit (Jn 7:37-39) as the Christian contemplates Christ through meditation on the Word, prayer, silence and solitude. This is missional spirituality, depth giving rise to wide influence.

---

[17]Hans Urs von Balthasar, *Prayer*, trans. Graham Harrison (1955; reprint, San Francisco: Ignatius Press, 1986), p. 89.

Being sanctified. "Sanctify them by the truth; your word is truth. As you *sent* me into the world, I have *sent* them into the world. For them I sanctify myself, that they too may be truly sanctified" (Jn 17:17-19). Jesus' utterance here in his high priestly prayer contains the gist of the phrase he repeats in the John 20 commission: "as the Father has sent me, I am sending you." In John 17 the correspondence between his sending and ours is related to correspondence of the sanctification that Christ, and those in Christ, undergo in him. In John 17:19, sanctification as it applies to Jesus conveys the meaning that Jesus set himself apart to fulfill God's mission, which involved the cross, now imminent for him as he prays this prayer. How were his disciples to be correspondingly sanctified? By his cross they would not merely be saved from sin and its consequences—they would be set apart to God, consecrated to God's service. And that would involve for them a cross also. The idea of holiness is not absent from this term however. Just as the Son sanctified himself in perfect holiness in going to the cross, in Christ, his people also are set apart for God and his mission, granted the grace of imparted holiness. They are both holy and being made holy, as Hebrews 10:14 indicates: "For by one sacrifice he has made perfect forever those who are being made holy." This because they are participants in his holiness (Heb 12:10). The mission of the people of God is wrapped up in their embodied possession and progress in holiness.[18]

Being one: For us being one with the Father and with each other.

> My prayer is not for them alone. I pray also for *those who will believe* in me through their message, that all of them may be one, Father, just as you are in me and I am in you. May they also be in us so that the world may believe that you have *sent* me. I have given them the glory that you gave me, *that they may be one as we are one*—I in them and you in me—so that they may be brought to complete unity. Then the world will know that you *sent* me and *have loved them even as you have loved me*. (Jn 17:20-23, emphasis added)

This passage contains the New Testament's most neglected evangelistic

---

[18]Charles Van Engen, *God's Missionary People* (Grand Rapids: Baker, 1991).

strategy. How is the church to be missional? By being the church, the *one*, holy, catholic, apostolic church. The very essence of the church's union with Christ in the Father, that is, its inclusion in the Trinity relationally, is expressed more fully here than in any other biblical passage. They are the words of Jesus himself, expressing that as a consequence of his mission, his church would be included in the union between himself and his Father ("in us" [v. 21]), and that as such they would also be one as a community, with this purpose in view: "so that the world may believe that you have *sent* me" (v. 21). This theme is repeated with the additional nuance that theosis involves imparted glory in verses 22-23. This imparted glory will enable the church to reflect a oneness modeled in the Godhead. But it is not merely a oneness that is modeled, as verse 23 indicates. It is a oneness grounded in and enabled by actual union in Christ (Christ and his church as the *totus Christus*, understood relationally, not essentially), who is in the Father. The goal of trinitarian modeling for the church together with trinitarian participation of the church is once again expressed as missional: "so that they may be brought to complete unity. Then the world will know that you sent me and have loved them even as you have loved me" (v. 23). The work of mission as theosis translates very much into the mundane, incarnational work of pursuing unity and its reparation in the church's life.

We turn now to the implications of incarnational and pneumatic theosis for the church's mission.

IMPLICATIONS OF INCARNATIONAL AND PNEUMATIC THEOSIS FOR THE CHURCH'S MISSION

In that theosis is corporate and ecclesial, not merely experiential and individual, the missional church will lay emphasis on both the personal and ecclesial aspects of conversion. The church will be characterized by a theology of personal conversion and robust faith *and* by a deep sense of ecclesial identity. It will understand faith as personal and volitional and as mediated by the church. The primary distinctive of the Western evangelical tradition has been its narrative of individual conversion and lively spirituality. What has not been emphasized as much is the ecclesially mediated nature of faith and the ecclesial dynamic of conversion. Preaching by evangelicals has focused much on forensic issues and little on the fact that the gospel at its core is about filial issues, the desire and design of God to bring lost humans into union with his Son and therefore into a family, a church which is one with Christ as the body to the Head and the bride to the Bridegroom. Baptism and addition to the church have been avoided usually because of differing views of the timing and mode of baptism or of the embarrassing array of church polities.

Conversion as theosis implies, however, a union with Christ by the Spirit and therefore conversion as an ecclesial event that should be signified in baptism and embracing the convert into the church. The failure of many evangelicals to have an ecclesial identity and communal character begins with the individualistic language of conversion. Those who will believe are promised eternal salvation from sin's consequences and power, but there are often no words about joining with the other followers of Jesus. This is contrary to the apostles' language in Acts, where they repeatedly call converts to be baptized as the sign and sacrament of faith. It was clearly the convert's initiation rite, a rite of passage into being "added to the church" (Acts 2:38-47; 5:13-14). Converts in New Testament times knew from how the message was presented that coming to Christ was coming in to "the Christ," that is, the church in Christ, and that baptism signaled this.

Furthermore, when Paul in his epistles explained baptism, he did so on every occasion in the language of union (theosis). In Romans 6 and Colossians 2 it is explained as participation in Jesus' death and resurrection, and the implications of this union with Christ are worked out into sanctification in mortification and vivification. In Romans 6 Paul is answering the question about the transformation that can be expected for people who by faith have come into union with Jesus and been justified by grace (Rom 1–5). Paul's answer is that growth can happen, and this lies in living into union in Christ in communion with his people. This involves disciplines of abstinence and engagement as community, and as persons. The missional church will therefore preach a gospel that includes conversion's ecclesial dynamic. It will consider conversion not just a crisis of belief but a process of belonging. It will also engage new converts in serious catechizing, as is evident in the early church, in the devotion given to the apostles' teaching (Acts 2:42). Large sections of the epistles give the kind of catechetical teaching that should surround preparation for baptism (e.g., Col 2:12–3:4) and it has been suggested that Peter's first epistle is largely catechetical instruction for baptizing converts.[19]

2. In that theosis is ecclesial as well as personal, the church will understand itself in its gathered capacity as a community intimate with and intoxicated by the risen Christ, by the Spirit. It will not in its primary gatherings be about seekers but about intimacy with Christ, participating in the life and love of God through Communion, Word and participatory fellowship. Its gatherings will be celebrative yet restful, not frenetic; worshipful and contemplative, not given to performance and spectatorship. In this way it will maintain the tension found in Acts 5, where seekers "didn't dare join them," yet could not help but join them as they were irresistibly attracted by the presence of God among them.

The saying "mission is the mother of theology and theology is the mother of mission" represents for me the belief that what ails the church is a failure to be intoxicated with the triune God. Michael McClymond has aptly described Jonathan Edwards's approach to theology as "God-intoxicated," and Hans Frei speaks of Barth's "God-in-Christ intoxicated imagination."[20] When the church recovers a trinitarian theocentricity, it will recover its health and its mission.

3. In that theosis is union with the God who is bidirectional in his mission, both the Sender and the Gatherer, the church will be characterized in its mission by both incarnational sentness and pneumatic gathering. Much has been said in chapter nine about the bidirectional nature of God's mission, expressed most eloquently in sending the Son to bring humanity in union with him into the communion of God, and in the gathering or incorporating work of the Spirit. If the church and

---

[19]See for example, E. G. Selwyn, *The First Epistle of St. Peter*, 2nd ed. (London: Macmillan, 1947), pp. 363-466; and I. Howard Marshall, *1 Peter*, IVP New Testament Commentary (Downers Grove, Ill.: InterVarsity Press, 2011).

[20]Michael McClymond, *Encounters with God* (Oxford and New York: Oxford University Press, 1998), p. 29. Hans Frei, "Karl Barth: Theologian," in *Theology and Narrative: Selected Essays* (Oxford: Oxford University Press, 1993), p. 171.

its members are one with Christ and the Spirit, they will understand their mission also as incarnational sending and as pneumatic gathering. The whole people of God will see themselves as missional in both senses—as incarnationally sent, going where the people are to be in solidarity with them, and as pneumatically gathering those who are drawn by the Spirit to come to faith and to the church (in either order, as many will belong before they believe).

4. In that theosis is both incarnational participation of and in the Son and pneumatic participation in the Spirit, mission will involve creational, relational and evangelistic concerns. That is, it will be mission to the whole person, to whole communities for bringing in the shalom God intended for the whole creation. Participational mission involves the pursuit of justice, compassion and evangelism. The church in Christ as last Adam calls humanity toward its destiny. Therefore it takes seriously the claims and command of the sovereign Lord on every human being, and defends the human rights of all, and brings the gospel to bear on all of life. The task of the church as the *sign* of the kingdom is to provide a model of justice through addressing poverty within its own community. But it is also the *servant* of that kingdom to come, meaning it not only models just community but reaches beyond that community and calls the world to compassion and justice as servant. This is crucial in a day when North American evangelicals have become a significant lobby group in the halls of power. The words of the Latin American theologian René Padilla are timely:

> The church is not an otherworldly religious club that organizes forays into the world in order to gain followers through persuasive techniques. It is the sign of the Kingdom of God; it lives and proclaims the gospel here and now, *among men*, and waits for the consummation of God's plan to place all things under the rule of Christ. It has been free *from* the world, but it is *in* the world; it has been sent by Christ into the world just as Christ was sent by the Father (John 17:11-18).[21]

What follows is a way to summarize a coinherent trinitarian way of seeing mission:

---

[21]René Padilla, *Mission Between the Times: Essays on the Kingdom* (Grand Rapids: Eerdmans, 1985), pp. 25-26.

Incarnational Christology without pneumatology leads to:

- lack of concern for evangelism and total concern for social justice concerns

- adherence to merely inspirational Christology (neglecting incarnational Christology) with no power for imitation and no power for ministry and communal transformation

- preoccupation with Word, leading to bibliolatry and legalism

- preoccupation with the mundane, which leads to a lack of awareness and inspiration from hope perspectives which the Spirit represents concerning new creation—the body of humiliation will be transformed; the body prone to sin will be glorified

- churches so focused on incarnational continuity, liturgy and tradition that they become idolatrous of the past and spiritually lukewarm or even dead

Pneumatology without incarnational Christology leads to

- a dualistic and individualistic view of salvation that focuses merely on the salvation of the soul and its escape one day to heaven, and the avoidance of a future hell, which buttresses the endurance of present hellish conditions

- continual fracturing of the church due to a sense of catholicity that is only future and ahistorical and due to highly subjective leadership planning that often characterizes charismatic settings

- denial of physicality or theology locatedness; naiveté about truth and its contextualization

5. In that mission is in fact participation or communion with a holy God, the importance of holiness in the mission of the one, holy, catholic, apostolic church cannot be overstressed. Holiness is connected to mission, as indicated previously. Peter's comment in his first epistle illustrates that the holiness of avoidance and of engagement have a missional influence: "Dear friends, I urge you, as foreigners and exiles, to abstain from sinful desires, which war against your soul. Live such good lives among the pagans that, though they accuse you of doing wrong, they may see your good deeds and glorify God on the day he visits us" (1 Pet 2:11-12). There is a fascinating dialectical tension here concerning the disconnectedness yet connectedness of the Christian with the world. On the one hand, what draws the attention of the pagans is a slight disconnectedness that betrays a vision of a world to come and motivates abstinence for this world's illegitimate pleasures. On the other hand, a profound level of engagement, suggested by their good lives and good deeds, has evangelistic influence. As the passage continues, the context for living good lives becomes clear—it is the arena of the treatment of all people, including governmental authorities. This is summed up in 1 Peter 2:17, where Peter exhorts them to "Show proper respect to everyone, love your fellow believers, fear God, honor the emperor." This passage brings together creational, relational and evangelistic mission. Holiness is key, however, and it is, as suggested by the abstinence-engagement paradigm so typical of epistolary literature, a holiness experienced in living in and out of union with Christ in death (disciplines of abstinence) and in resurrection (disciplines of engagement).

The church today seems far from this kind of experiential union and concomitant holiness. Of course, the church is not a place for perfect people, and nothing hinders mission more than self-righteous Christians who parade their good deeds and lifestyles. Holiness is pursued in the cradle of grace, and it is enabled only as we experience repentance and forgiveness again and again. Theosis must lead to transformation. And that transformation is missionally contagious. It is the journey toward greater wholeness, toward the exocentricity that characterized Jesus and the persons of the triune God, and it is the disposition toward reconciliation that begins to characterize the people of God in union with him—it is this goodness that has influence.

Sanctification is a troublesome topic theologically that goes beyond the scope of this book. Luther's delight in justification led him to relative neglect of sanctification, leading Calvin to deal with this before justification in his *Institutes*. Edwards so stressed sanctification by the Spirit that justification in Christ played second fiddle. Barth has some similarities with Luther in his emphasis on justification in Christ and would have us look away from ourselves to the One who was holy for us.[22] In today's churches there are strands of Augustinian realism alongside Wesleyan triumphalism. There are crisis views and process views, and crises within process views. Such is our evangelical heritage. I take refuge where Calvin and Barth agree, that the key to justification and sanctification is union with Christ, and it seems fairly clear that this accurately reflects the hortatory sections of the epistles, which repeatedly influence the Christian toward living out that union with Christ in his death and resurrection. The practices required for this to be a living reality are the "road less traveled" in evangelicalism today, and until the church lives in union and communion with Christ, and until Christians engage in intimacy with Christ through the ecclesial and personal practices of abstinence and engagement (as recommended by Dallas Willard, Richard Foster and the desert fathers), mission will continue to be at a standstill.

This chapter has established that mission is a consequence of the mission of God and the sharing in it of the whole people of God by theosis, that is, relational union with God, in the Son, by the Spirit. As Paul Stevens has aptly stated, "*Laos* ministry is participation in the 'ingoing' ministry of God (relationally among God the Father, Son and Holy Spirit), and simultaneously participation in the 'out-going' (sending) ministry of God."[23] We participate in the *ad intra* life of God, Father as lover, Son as beloved, Spirit as love itself, by the indwelling of the Spirit, who has brought us into the love of the Father for the Son. The Spirit's intercession and that of the Son enable us to pray in participation with the communion of God, and work as and where he works. The *ad extra*—Father as sender, Son as sent, Spirit as sending, means that we as church participate in the mission of God as the sent One lives in us, in our sending by the Spirit!

We have established that the Spirit enabled the union of God's people with Christ so that Jesus' mission could continue even though he was in heaven. Chapter eleven will reveal that the Spirit is himself a

---

[22]Barth resonates in some respects with Calvin, however, with respect to the law-gospel dialectic and the relationship between justification and sanctification (Barth, *Church Dogmatics* IV/2, pp. 228ff.). See Jesse Couenhoven, "Grace as Pardon and Power: Pictures of the Christian Life in Luther, Calvin and Barth," *Journal of Religious Ethics* 28, no. 1 (2000): 63-88.
[23]Stevens, *Other Six Days*, p. 57.

missionary Spirit and that the community of Jesus on earth was a community of the Spirit who always works in perfect perichoretic harmony with the Son and the Father, and who yet has an irreducibly distinct function in making that community one characterized by the Spirit.

11

Communities of the Spirit

Gathered and Scattered

■ ■ ■

He breathed on them and said,
"Receive the Holy Spirit."

JOHN 20:22

The end result of this increasing isolation
[of the evangelical church in North America] is that
a spiritual culture now surrounds a secular church.

EDDIE GIBBS AND RYAN K. BOLGER, *Emerging Churches*

THE MESSAGE RENDERING OF JOHN 20:22 is particularly evocative: "He took a deep breath and breathed into them. 'Receive the Holy Spirit,' he said." This was, as I have insisted, a symbolic act by which Jesus anticipated what would happen to his disciples on the day of Pentecost, and he, along with the Father, sent his Spirit to be upon and *in* his people. It was the act by which he constituted the church and gave it missional power. These words of Jesus near the end of his time on earth accord with Jesus' last words in Luke before he ascended: "You will receive power when the Holy Spirit comes on you; and you will be my witnesses" (Acts 1:8). Here we give attention to the particular work of the Spirit in his own right, coinherent though all roles of trinitarian persons always are. As Orlando Costas suggested, the work of the Spirit must be fully embraced, for his "work in the world finds its goal precisely in the reconciliation of all created things under the Lordship of the Son and for the glory of the Father."[1]

There are certain sectors of the church who pay lip service to the doctrine of the Trinity but in particular neglect the person and work of the third person of the Trinity. Discomfort with the work of the Spirit leads them to embrace what is experientially a binitarian Christian life, and this leads to an experientially barren Christian life and missional impotence. David Bosch's outstanding missional text has been critiqued by Veli-Matti Kärkkäinen as underplaying the missiological role of the Spirit, which he sees as illustrative of a trend of disinterest within contemporary missiological studies in articulating a "pneumatological outlook in modern missiology."[2]

This chapter provides an incentive for life in the Spirit at a personal level, but it is primarily an encouragement toward greater expectancy of the renewing, empowering work of the Spirit in churches. Whereas pneumatically emphatic Christians can neglect the incarnational and catholic realities of mission, likewise can the heavily incarnational emphasis in emerging and missional churches lead to neglect of the possibility of the extraordinary work of the Spirit in awakenings. These often come in the darkest days of the church. Reasons for hope that renewal can be sustained come through the maintaining of confessional depth, catholic liturgy and ecclesial practices.

This chapter aims toward encouraging the church *gathered* to be missional by being a community fraught with the Spirit's breath, a community always invoking the Spirit in its act of worship in epiclesis, a community of the Word taught in the power of the Spirit, a community led and empowered by the Spirit with the fullness of the charismatic gifts in a manner that releases the church from human control and Western cultural formality, and yet which, governed by the "rule of

---

[1]Orlando Costas, *Christ Outside the Gate* (Maryknoll, N.Y.: Orbis, 1983), pp. 89-90.
[2]Veli-Matti Kärkkäinen, "'Truth on Fire': Pentecostal Theology of Mission and the Challenges of a New Millennium," *Asian Journal of Pentecostal Studies* 3, no. 1 (2000): 38.

community edification" does not degenerate into pneumatic anarchy. The gathered community will be a witness to the seeker that "God is really among" them (1 Cor 14:25). It will stress the importance of Spirit-gifted and Spirit-led leadership.

Second, this chapter will stress the importance of the *character* and *ethics* that undergird the charisms. Isolation of the fruit of the Spirit from the gifts is what has given rise to the cynicism around spiritual renewal. Thus the Spirit's work of spiritual formation in ecclesial people whose lives cry out for an explanation will receive brief attention.

It will, third, be an encouragement for the church as *scattered* to seek empowerment for proclaiming the gospel in a manner that explains the miracle of the church's community life in the Spirit and the character of its members, and to be attentive to what the Spirit of God is doing ahead of any missional efforts, and to cooperate with how the Spirit is at work in culture and communities. The greater freedom of the Spirit within the Eastern view of the Trinity is particularly interesting in this connection.

THE SPIRIT IN THE
MISSIONAL CHURCH GATHERED

The work of the Spirit is foundational to the establishment of the church, just as it was for the ministry of Jesus. The outpouring of the Spirit inaugurates his ministry at his baptism in Luke 3:21-23, and as acknowledged by Jesus himself in his inaugural sermon, quoting Isaiah 61:

> The Spirit of the Lord is on me,
> because he has anointed me
> to proclaim good news to the poor. (Lk 4:18-19)

Likewise, the church originates through the Spirit. The grand motif of Acts is that the church is able to have a missionary witness because it is baptized in the Spirit, endued with the Spirit's power, and led and sometimes nudged forcefully by the restless, missional Spirit. The church's pneumatic saturation and orientation is undeniably evident: it exists and continues because of the Holy Spirit's work. It is the Spirit who gathers new converts and incorporates them into new church communities. As Lesslie Newbigin states in his *Open Secret*, "Mission is not just something that the church does; it is something that is done by the Spirit, who is himself the witness, who changes the world and the church, who always goes before the church in its missionary journey."[3]

Specifically, it is by Spirit baptism that the church is birthed, and it is by the Spirit that the new community is constituted with its marks—the apostles' teaching, the fellowship, the breaking of the bread and the prayers (Acts 2:42). Though not explicitly mentioned in Acts, it is by the invocation of the Spirit in the most definitive mark of the church, the breaking of the bread (Acts 20:7), that the bread and the wine become spiritual food for the people of God, which in turn could be shared with the world. The many sermons preached in Acts under the evident influence of the Spirit, always containing the kerygmatic core of the gospel, and often explaining the extraordinary life of the church, give evidence that the Spirit is also crucial to the Word taught or preached in the gatherings of the missional church. Costas spoke a great deal about the work of the Spirit and with respect to proclamation in particular. He said that it "is not a matter of words or deeds, but of words and deeds *empowered* by the liberating presence of the Spirit."[4] The preaching and teaching of the gathered missional church in the power of the Spirit will expound the Scriptures and will always have a gospel orientation, no matter which text is being preached.

Most critical to the effectiveness of the church on mission by the Spirit is that it stays true to its nature as the community of the Spirit, with *all* of the charismata at work in every member ministry, in a community that is organism first and organization second. The words of Christopher Cocksworth express articulately the coinherence of the incarnational and the pneumatic in the life of the church:

> But I am looking for more than this. I'm searching for a form of evangelicalism that is not only self-consciously catholic but also charismatic—gifted by the Holy Spirit. In fact, strictly speaking this is an-

---

[3]Lesslie Newbigin, *The Open Secret*, rev. ed. (Grand Rapids: Eerdmans, 1995), p. 56.
[4]Costas, *Christ Outside the Gate*, p. 92.

other tautology. There is no church without the Spirit. Ignatius' Christological definition of the church needs to be held together with Irenaeus' pneumatological version, "Where the Spirit of God is, there is the church and all grace." And of course there is no gospel without the Spirit. Christ and his gospel come to us by the Spirit.[5]

Whereas the teaching of the pastor-teacher is dominant in many evangelical churches, room will be made in missional churches for the other three strategic leadership gifts of apostle, prophet and evangelist (Eph 4:11), as was evident in Acts. But all the gifts of all the priests in church will also be evident as a result of the wise and empowering operation of the leadership gifts (Eph 4:12-16; 1 Cor 12; 14; Rom 12; 1 Pet 4). Whereas some churches neglect leadership, others become anemic because the strategic leadership gifts become almost the only gifts operating (bringing the body into maturity, and mission happens only "as each part does its work" [Eph 4:16]). The fat Christian syndrome emerges in churches that have great teachers who feed well but do not stimulate and empower God's people to exercise. I am convinced that the new reformation that arises when the church discovers the giftedness of the whole people of God, in and out of the church, still awaits us. Greg Ogden has provided excellent material on how this might work, but I believe we pay lip service to this in most churches.[6] Pastor control stemming from insecurity often prevents it.

Every member ministry, of course, is easier said than done because of the especially modern fixation with control and having church be "safe." The routinization of charismata happens so easily when the church becomes institutionalized. The spectacularizing of charismata is what can happen when the church has no proper leadership and quality control on the exercising of gifts. The church should be relationally and procedurally safe (Paul outlines a rule of community edification to be effected by "the others" who "judge" in 1 Corinthians 14, designed to sift out the authentic expressions of the gifts), but not safe

---

[5]Christopher Cocksworth, "Holding Together: Catholic Evangelical Worship in the Spirit," in *Remembering Our Future*, ed. Andrew Walker and Luke Bretherton (Colorado Springs: Paternoster, 2007), p. 132. The Irenaeus quote is from Irenaeus, *Against the Heresies* 3.24.1.
[6]Greg Ogden, *The New Reformation: Returning the Ministry to the People of God* (Grand Rapids: Zondervan, 1990).

in the sense that there is no room for divine intervention (Paul's idea of order envisioned in 1 Cor 14 is much less orderly than many Western churches with their rows of pews and pastor-dominated services).

A renewed theological understanding of the church as a Holy Spirit-gathered, Holy Spirit-sent community is essential. Miroslav Volf outlines the relational shape of the church in light of the social Trinity in the following way:

> The symmetrical reciprocity of the relations of the trinitarian persons finds its correspondence in the image of the church in which *all* members serve one another with their specific gifts of the Spirit in imitation of the Lord and through the power of the Father. Like the divine persons, they all stand in a relation of mutual giving and receiving.[7]

This giftedness of all believers and ministry in mutuality is what the contemporary church needs to recover to combat consumerism. Perhaps a renewed understanding is the easier part. How this works out into the practices and life of the modern church seems to be more difficult. Proper contexts for the operation of the charismata can be found in church life such that order pertains, but the stranglehold of the control-oriented cultures of many Western churches will need to be broken, nevertheless.[8] This does not mean the loss of all structure or institutions.

Putting together structure and the work of the Spirit is difficult because Spirit and structure are assumed to be antithetical. Some churches stifle the charismata, and other churches, especially of the emerging variety, overreact to the institutional church. These churches soon discover that structure becomes necessary fairly quickly and that not too far down the track they too will be an institution! Miroslav Volf is not unaware of the tensions that the freedom and reciprocity of ministry bring, and specifically the wrestling between human control and Spirit control within the church's institutions. He recognizes that a common Protestant view is that "the Spirit of God

---

[7]Miroslav Volf, *After Our Likeness* (Grand Rapids: Eerdmans, 1998), p. 219.

[8]The "pastorates" or house churches approach of Holy Trinity Brompton have much to commend in this regard. The charisms of each person are developed in these under trained lay leaders, and this alongside the larger worship services and the smaller cell groups creates a healthy way of being the church.

and church institutions stand in contradiction."[9] To some, it seems, a sort of "pneumatic anarchy" would be the only acceptable form for a pneumatic church.[10] However, this is too simple of a view. It fails to account for the human character that exists as people are gathered together by the Spirit.

In other words, even though we must define the essence of the church through the doctrine of God and the work of the Spirit, specifically, we must not forget that it is a human community. Obviously, this is the source of tension: the divine essence and human composition of the church. In the midst of this tension it is clear that the nature of God must always drive the nature of the church. The forms (or institutions—Volf's language) of the church, then, must follow the essence of the church, which follows after the nature of God the Spirit. If the Spirit establishes the kingdom through the church and not the other way around, this both calls the church to shape its life in light of the kingdom and yet allows for structures and institutions that do indeed serve the kingdom.[11]

This does entail a vigilant role for leadership of the church, a reality also consonant with life in the Spirit, not contrary to it—if it is Spirit-raised (Acts 20:28) and Spirit-led leadership (Acts 13:1-4). In *Catch the Wind: A Precursor to the Emergent Church*, Charles Ringma states that "While God is responsible for the church's essence, we are significantly responsible for its form."[12] To be "significantly responsible" does not mean that we "take control." Rather, it means church leaders must confirm that every form lines up with the essence of the church. For instance,

> If the essence of the church is the sharing of life together through Christ's reconciliation, then that reality must be reflected in the

---

[9]Volf, *After Our Likeness*, p. 234.

[10]Ibid.

[11]See Darrell Guder, ed., *Missional Church* (Grand Rapids: Eerdmans, 1998), pp. 93ff. The primacy of the Spirit over the church serves to qualify the incarnational concreteness of the church. The church can be concrete only as its life, mission and practices are dynamically led by the Spirit. See Theodora Hawksley, "The Freedom of the Spirit: The Pneumatological Point of Barth's Ecclesiological Minimalism," *Scottish Journal Theology* 64, no. 2 (2011): 180-94.

[12]Charles Ringma, *Catch the Wind: A Precursor to the Emergent Church* (Sutherland, Australia: Albatross, 1994), p. 71.

church's structures and programs. If the essence of the church is based on an equality that Christ brings so that women and men, black and white, poor and rich have equal status by his grace, then such a reality should be reflected in the leadership structures and forms of the Christian community.[13]

Therefore, as Ringma goes on to suggest, the church's concern should be about the *process* of people empowerment rather than maintaining particular structures.[14] The leader's role, then, is not to take control of the church's growth but rather to equip the church (its present reality) to be the church (its future hope). The concern should be to empower people to be who they are—representatives of the kingdom of God.[15]

This is similar to what Jacques Ellul communicates in *The Presence of the Kingdom*. What really matters is not so much the form of the church but the people who are the church. According to Ellul, "we, within ourselves, have to carry the objective for which the world has been created by God."[16] We do not work toward external objectives of the kingdom of God, but, rather, we are the means of the kingdom of God—we *are* the foretaste, the beginning of the presence of his kingdom. We should not make plans to build the kingdom and include God as an appended blessing. Rather, we must "see that God establishes his end and that it is this which is represented by our means."[17] Again, this focus is on the church becoming more fully the people of God, empowered to *be* the church.

The modern world has told us to trust in our techniques, to take control in order to achieve success. However, in the church the opposite is true: the church can only be the church when it *submits* control to the

---

[13]Ibid.

[14]"The priority is not a particular model of being together—the hallmark is not necessarily a house church, an intentional community or a deinstitutionalized traditional church structure. The hallmark of the church is rather that it is people empowering" (ibid., p. 164).

[15]This is also what Van Engen is getting at: church leaders should "move the congregation to create plans, make decisions, and resolve internal conflicts always with the objective of mobilizing God's missionary people" (Charles Van Engen, *God's Missionary People* [Grand Rapids: Baker, 1991], p. 186).

[16]Jacques Ellul, *The Presence of the Kingdom*, trans. Olive Wyon (New York: Seabury, 1967), p. 80.

[17]Ibid., p. 81.

Spirit. This is what the kingdom of God is about—submission to God's perfect reign. And this is the only position from where the church can truly represent the reign of God. Therefore, the church must confirm that in submission to the Holy Spirit the forms of the church match its essence.[18] It is not a once-for-all change but, as Guder describes, is a "continuing conversion." This is crucial because "in some way [the church] is always conforming to this world and needs to be transformed by the renewal of its mind (Rom 12:2)."[19] The church must continue to evaluate itself and, if need be, change its structures to help the people more fully become the church, who they are.[20] Mercifully, as the church strives to harmonize its form with its essence, the Holy Spirit is actively involved. As Ringma states,

> Thus change in the church is not simply God's prerogative; it is also ours. But there can be no doubt that when we acknowledge that essence and form belong together and that God's intention and our structures should harmonize—and then work for change accordingly—that God's Spirit will be actively involved in such a process.[21]

Acts 6:1-7 is just such a case. Spirit-led structure facilitated social justice and evangelistic growth of a multiplication (v. 7; cf. v. 1, addition) variety.

THE SPIRIT IN MISSIONAL CHURCH MORAL FORMATION

We now must speak of the spiritual character that the Spirit forms in God's people. The failure of some spiritual renewals to take root in the life of the church has often been the result of a preoccupation with the Spirit's gifts and manifestations and a decided lack of emphasis on the character that should undergird the charisms and make for credible mission. Disconnections often occur between the ethical life,

---

[18]Van Engen, *God's Missionary People*, p. 190.
[19]Guder, *Missional Church*, p. 230. "One of the most important tangible forms of that conversion is the church's willingness to change its visible structures in order to become more faithful to its mission" (ibid., p. 231).
[20]Van Engen, *God's Missionary People*, p. 191.
[21]Ringma, *Catch the Wind*, pp. 73-74.

on the one hand, and spiritual gifts, of especially an ecstatic variety, on the other.

Disjunction of spiritual charisms and character, of course, affects the mission of the church in devastating ways. I am not here speaking of legalism and holier-than-thou do-goodism that has sometimes characterized overly pneumatic communities. I am speaking of formation by the Spirit in a gospel-based and grace-saturated manner. This kind of formation is characterized by profound humility and a lifelong spirit of repentance. It is this kind of life with integrity, this kind of evangelical moral formation and living that has missional impact of the kind referred to in a number of New Testament passages (e.g., 1 Pet 2:12; 3:1, 15).

Spiritual formation will therefore be a central concern in a missional church. As Paul Stevens writes, "Evangelism has as its goal the restoration of the whole person in relation to God, to neighbour, and to environment."[22] If it is true that Christian salvation is not merely a private transaction between an individual and God, "but a social reality of transformed relationships," then, as Guder asserts, "The cultivating of missional communities through ecclesial practices is not simply an instrumental means to a desired end, but manifests in itself the very mission of the church."[23] The strategy of Jesus' mission was to invest heavily in the transformation of a few. If our sentness is to reflect his, we will follow this strategy. Robert Coleman said this well when he suggested that "everything that is done with the few is for the salvation of the multitudes."[24]

Moral formation is lacking in many Christians in our contemporary culture due to the hegemony of popular ethics as conveyed by the dominance of media exposure. (This is ethics as determined by what is being done, rather than what on the basis of biblical revelation should be done.) This is true especially in the realm of sexual ethics. How can we hope to be morally formed by exposure to one hour of church when

---

[22]R. Paul Stevens, *Liberating the Laity* (Downers Grove, Ill.: InterVarsity Press, 1985), p. 94.
[23]Guder, *Missional Church*, p. 82.
[24]Robert E. Coleman, *The Master Plan of Evangelism*, Study Guide ed. (Grand Rapids: Baker, 1972), p. 30.

the bulk of leisure time is immersed in popular culture? Despair in this regard can lead pastors to deal with ethics legally rather than evangelically, and to promote an outside-in pharisaism. Ethical living is inside-out, the consequence of transformed religious affections, living into the shalom of being in Christ by the Spirit. It is relational wholeness and overflowing love. This is the fruit of the Spirit manifested over the long haul as Christian people live into their union with Christ, in death to the old habits, and in resurrection into the graces. This kind of formation necessitates a profound commitment to living in intentional community. The one-hour attendance at church won't do it. We must *be* the church.

This communal formation is in keeping with the fact that the essence and pinnacle of the spiritual life is love (1 Cor 13; Gal 5:22). If all spiritual disciplines have as their aim learning to love—God and neighbor—then they must be practiced in community. Loving is easier when we are surrounded by love. We have by the gospel been drawn into the circle of trinitarian love, and as we live in his love we experience the outpouring of love back to God and to others. It goes even further. We have by the grace of God been brought into union with God by the Son's incarnation and the Spirit's indwelling. God's love is shed abroad in our hearts by the Spirit (Rom 5:5). By Spirit indwelling we enter into filial relationship with God and so are able to cry out "Abba" (Rom 8:15-16), and we find the power to love people (Gal 5:22). Spiritual disciplines facilitate the fullness of the Spirit, which enables the Christian to live not in the mere profession of union with God but in actual communion with God. Only he can satisfy our deepest hungers and cure our addictions.

Helping one another learn to pray in the Spirit is, it seems to me, the most crucial of these forming practices, for the Spirit brings us into the experience of the triune love. Recognizing that prayer is the praying of the Trinity within us, as the Spirit presents our feeble groanings to the Son who in turn expresses them to the Father, exhorts us toward listening prayer and silence. Moral formation happens slowly as we become conscious of the reality of God's love through daily periods of silent meditation. The fourteenth-century anchoress Julian of Norwich

(1342-1416), who had a series of visions after contemplating the cross during a serious illness and dedicated her life to prayer and penance in a hut attached to the church in Norwich, became one of the greatest experiential trinitarians of church history. She describes her experience of the Trinity in contemplative prayer:

> At the same moment the Trinity filled me full of heartfelt joy, and I knew that all eternity was like this for those who attain heaven. For this Trinity is God, and God the Trinity; the Trinity is our Maker and Keeper, our eternal Lover, joy and bliss—all through our Lord Jesus Christ. This was shown me in the first revelation, and, indeed, in them all; for where Jesus is spoken of, the blessed Trinity is always to be understood as I see it.[25]

Much more could be said concerning formation in participation with the Spirit in the life of the triune God, but suffice it to say that it begets an intimacy with God that transforms the missional church and its missioners. In such Spirit-directed mission, it will not be surprising that powerful acts and words emerge, and that they will follow what the Spirit has already begun to do in communities and in individuals before we encounter them.

THE SPIRIT IN THE
MISSIONAL CHURCH SCATTERED

"The fields are white for harvesting," Jesus said. Jesus did not say "pray for a harvest"—it is a given, because the Spirit is already at work ahead of the church! The Eastern Orthodox tradition, in that it disavowed the *filioque* clause (the Spirit proceeds from the Father alone, not the Father and the Son), has tended to assign a greater freedom to the Spirit's work in the economic Trinity and specifically in the work of mission. The church is the Spirit's primary means for mission, but there are abundant examples in church history of the Spirit's work ahead of the church's missional efforts. This involves creating windows for gospel concepts in the cultures of people groups and or-

---

[25]Julian of Norwich, *Revelations of Divine Love*, trans. Clifton Wolters (London: Anthony Clarke, 1973), p. 66.

chestrating circumstances in the lives of individuals and whole communities that create a receptivity to the gospel, even redeeming tragedies that permit Christian relief workers to care for victims. In every case of conversion the Spirit works prior to and through the proclaimer of the gospel, awakening responsiveness and faith in the regeneration process, which is specifically attributed to the Spirit in the New Testament (Jn 3:5; Tit 3:5-6).

One example of the Spirit's work through the traditions of a people group was discovered during the first visit made by Brethren missionaries (R. C. Allison and George Wiseman) to people in the Camaxilo area of Angola. The natives quickly gained an awareness of a God who has a Son who suffered. Furthermore, the missionaries came across an event in which women were being baptized. They inquired as to whether these folks were perhaps Christian. The answer was no, but when a woman's husband had died and she was to be remarried, the elders would immerse her in water to signify that her old life with the first husband was gone and this was now to be a new life with her new husband! In these ways God had been at work by his Spirit in their culture preparing them for the gospel, and when they heard the gospel, thousands came to faith in a very short time. There are windows for the gospel in every culture.

The Spirit is not only at work ahead of us, however. He is at work in us so that we are the hands and feet of Jesus, the presence of God in the world. He gives us the power to do as well as to teach (Acts 1:1). I am concerned that we evangelicals have stressed the teaching but not the doing. That doing is the vocational, the justice seeking, and the compassionate doing. Of course, we cannot miss the fact that many of the deeds in Acts were "supernatural." The distinction between supernatural and natural is a tenuous one at best. God is always at work in creation and providence, providing healing constantly. Yet there are undeniable moments of God's special intervention to subvert normal processes. Such supernatural deeds characterized the people of God in Acts, and I believe they are still intended as a powerful instrument in mission as signs that the kingdom has already come. Their frequency is inscrutable in the sovereignty of God, but they are often hindered in their manifestation by rationalism and scientism. In a world where spirituality is in vogue we need to offer authentic and powerful spirituality of the Spirit. Signs and wonders which seem to be the norm at the front edges of the kingdom in the Third World are needed also in our reductionistic and dualistic and deistic Western societies. Proclamation is easy when such power erupts. In the ordinary and extraordinary seasons of the church, however, the Spirit is at work in the whole people of God, where they live and play. He is at work through these en-churched persons as they gather and scatter again and again.

12

Communities of Forgiveness

Mission of Absolution and Freedom

■ ■ ■

If you forgive the sins of anyone, their sins are forgiven;
if you do not forgive them, they are not forgiven.

JOHN 20:23

THE BRIEF SENTENCE ABOVE OF John 20:23 is code for the heart of the gospel of forgiveness and reconciliation, which elsewhere occupies whole chapters in Paul. This is the message entrusted to the missional church. This is what its hospitality means: That God is for humanity. That God has entrusted to his church the capacity, in participation with Christ by the Spirit, the privilege, of pronouncing forgiveness over repentant, broken people, when they come for the first time and when they come again and again and again. This cryptic phrase communicates the reality that the church is a community not for the healthy but for the sick, not for the "all together" people but for the rebellious yet needy who come as the prodigal came, bidden by a prodigal Father. I explore this theme of remission by recognizing first that the heart of the gospel is expressed here. I will then seek to clarify how this remission operates in the human community of the church. Following that I will clarify what is meant by *remission*. Finally, I will examine the missional consequences for humanity and creation in light of the fact that the church is, as a community of reconciliation, the new humanity and the sign of the kingdom. There will inevitably be some overlap in the themes, for they are braided together as in a rope.

REMISSION AT THE HEART OF THE GOSPEL

Christians from different traditions have disagreed about what this passage and others like it mean.[1] At minimum it means that a Christian can, on the basis of what Christ has done, pronounce to people that when they have exercised repentance and faith in Jesus, their sins are forgiven! This is the heart of the gospel.

The element of forgiveness in this whole narrative in John 20 should not be underemphasized. Rowan Williams, in his exposition of the various stories of resurrection encounters, notes,

> Taken overall, the resurrection stories, as stories, seem to be exploring various aspects of how the risen-ness of Jesus has to do with the sense of absolution by God, how the resurrection creates forgiven persons, whose relation with God and, derivatively, with each other, is transformed. They are stories that belong in a community which identifies and understands itself as forgiven, and traces its establishment as that sort of a community to the Easter event.[2]

In the same vein N. T. Wright comes at this whole story in reverse order in his commentary on John to stress the wonder of the impossibility of forgiving the sins of others: "'How do you feel about that? Are you up to the job? Of course not! But worse is to come,' he adds. 'If you retain anyone's sins, they are retained! If anyone imagines they are ready and willing to take on *that* task,' he suggests, 'they need to go back to school for a few strong lessons in humility.'"[3] Jesus' belief in his disciples' ability to do this is a consequence of what has preceded the commission to this great task, and so Wright works his way back from this into all the great empowering realities reflected in Jesus' presence and his words to them.

[1]See Derek Tidball, *Ministry by the Book* (Downers Grove, Ill.: IVP Academic, 2009), p. 24.
[2]Rowan Williams, *Resurrection* (London: Darton, Longman & Todd, 1982), p. 2.
[3]N. T. Wright, *John for Everyone, Part 2* (London: SPCK, 2002), p. 148.

The critical piece in all this is the disciples' union with Christ by the Spirit's indwelling. Clearly, part of the impossibility of this task is that only God can forgive sins. The only way through this "impossibility" is that God was going to forgive sins *through* his people, and that was only possible because of the fact that the Spirit once breathed upon them, would bring them into relational oneness with God. This union, experienced through communion with Christ by the Spirit's fullness, would impart the discernment needed to distinguish true repentance and faith from mere professions of the latter. It would also enable the authority that pronouncements of absolution need when the Christian evangel pronounces the penitent seeker forgiven, or when the Christian pronounces his or her fellow Christian clean upon hearing his or her authentic confession.

On this passage Calvin says, "Here without doubt our Lord has briefly summed up the Gospel. For we must not separate this power of forgiving sins from the teaching office . . . with which it is connected in this passage."[4] This explicates the purpose of the sending Jesus has just spoken of. For Calvin says, "He now declares what this embassy means and demands, only He put in what is necessary, that He gave them his Holy Spirit, so that they might do nothing of themselves."[5] The sequence for Calvin is important—the granting of forgiveness as the heart of the gospel is the goal of the trinitarian mission given, but this granting is not an inherent right of the apostles and their new apostolic communities. Rather, it was as the Spirit empowered them that they could pronounce the penitent, believing sinner forgiven. They were acting on a higher authority, that of Christ, and for this they needed the power of the Spirit. They would act in dependence on that same Spirit to discern the authenticity of the repentance and faith of the confessor. In anticipation of our next strand of the rope, we conclude therefore that the acts of remission and retention are *participational*.

---

[4]John Calvin, *John 11–21 and 1 John*, Calvin's New Testament Commentaries, trans. T. H. L. Parker, ed. David W. Torrance and Thomas F. Torrance (Grand Rapids: Eerdmans, 1959), p. 206.
[5]Ibid.

REMISSION EXPRESSED IN PARTICIPATION
WITH CHRIST BY THE SPIRIT

In Mark 2, when Jesus forgave the sins of the lame man and incurred the wrath of the Pharisees and the charge of blasphemy, it is interesting to note how he refers to himself. In responding to the charge of his opponents who asked, "Who can forgive sins but God alone?" Jesus responded surprisingly by using the title "Son of Man," when we might have expected "Son of God" instead. He responded by saying, "But I want you to know that the Son of Man has authority on earth to forgive sins" (Mk 2:10). Jesus is not just referring to himself as Messiah in light of the use of "Son of Man" in the book of Daniel, which implies deity. Rather, he is communicating that he is the prototypical man and that he is fulfilling God's design for humanity as God's coworker, vice regent. This begins to make sense when in John 20 Jesus conveys on his disciples the authority to forgive sins! As a community of forgivers of sin, in the God-man, humanity reaches its designed goal. Not surprising given that resurrection Sunday is the first day of the new creation!

It is important to clarify what Jesus intended by these words. F. F. Bruce observed that "the two passives—'they are remitted' and 'they are retained'—imply *divine agency*," and he concludes that "the preacher's role is *declaratory*." He goes on to assert that the "servants of Christ are given no authority independent of his, nor is any assurance of infallibility given to them."[6] The acts of remission and retention by the apostles are acts done only *in participation with God by the Spirit*. This is a derived authority, one conditioned by the authenticity and spiritual state of the spiritual leader. It is an authority given to the apostles in John 20 that must be linked to the prior breathing of the Spirit into them. This is reflected widely in patristic and Reformed writing. Chrysostom reflects the fact that Christ "prepares the apostles for being sent by breathing his Spirit on them, giving them the spiritual power to forgive sins. . . . The Father, Son and Holy Spirit do it all while the pastor only furnishes the tongue and the hand."[7] Origen confirms the

---

[6]F. F. Bruce, *The Gospels and Epistles of John* (Grand Rapids: Eerdmans, 1983), p. 392, emphasis added.

[7]John Chrysostom, *Homilies on the Gospel of John*, 86.4, Nicene and Post-Nicene Fathers 1,

legitimacy of the confession-absolution practice, but only when this is enacted by "the person inspired by Jesus as the apostles were and who can be known by his fruits as someone who has received the Holy Spirit and become spiritual by being led by the Spirit."[8] However, he is clear that "They only forgive what God forgives."[9] Calvin also is explicit that the authority to forgive sins is an honor peculiar to Christ himself and that his apostles would do so only "in his name" and in order that he might reconcile them to God through them.[10] When asking why the disciples are nevertheless so honored in being granted this participatory function (my words), Calvin responds "that He did so to confirm our faith." Christ "magnificently commends and adorns" this forgiveness-pronouncing ministry of the apostles, he explains, "so that believers may be fully convinced that what they hear about the forgiveness of sins is ratified, and may not think less of the reconciliation offered by men's voices than if God Himself had stretched out His hand from heaven."[11]

This is a *participation specifically in the judgment committed by the Father to the Son*. This recalls a theme introduced by Jesus in John 5:22-47 and reflected in the writings of a number of the church fathers. Theodore of Mopsuestia states, "If you, who are human, after receiving the gift of the Spirit, will be able to do all those things that are of God—indeed, only he has the power to judge—I leave to you to consider what the effectiveness of the Spirit is."[12] In a similar vein, Chrysostom quotes John 5:21, where Jesus stated that "the Father has given all judgment to the Son" and follows this with "But I see that the Son has placed it all in their hands. For they have been raised to this prerogative, as though they were already translated to heaven and had

---

14:326; *Patrologiae cursus completus*. Series Graeca 59:471-2, cited in Joel C. Elowsky, *John 11–21*, Ancient Christian Commentary on Scripture IVb (Downers Grove, Ill.: InterVarsity Press, 2007), p. 365.

[8]Origen, "On Prayer," in *Origen: An Exhortation to Martyrdom, Prayer and Selected Writings*, 150-51, cited in Elowsky, *John 11–21*, p. 364.

[9]Origen, *Commentary on the Gospel of John* 12.1, A Library of Fathers of the Holy Catholic Church 48:671-73, cited in Elowsky, *John 11–21*, p. 365.

[10]Calvin, *John 11–21 and 1 John*, p. 206. Cf. 2 Cor 5:20: "We are therefore Christ's ambassadors, as though God were making his appeal through us."

[11]Ibid., p. 207.

[12]Theodore of Mopsuestia, *Commentary on John* 7.20.22, Corpus Scriptorum Christianorum Orientalium 4, 3:354-55, cited in Elowsky, *John 11–21*, p. 362.

transcended human nature and were freed from our passions."[13]

All of this brings into bold relief what I have maintained, that the wide church is the deep church. Communion with God is crucial to the capacity to offer the absolution of sins when people we are leading to Christ have reached the place of expressing saving faith and repentance. Discerning their authenticity is important. Pronouncing that they are forgiven people cannot be taken lightly. In the ongoing confession practiced by committed disciples, great discernment is again required. Confession is never offered in isolation from the complexities of the human soul and styles of relating. The discernment of people's souls when they bring confession of acts like adultery in marriage or pornography or rages, and probing with them the roots of their behavior so that they may find healing and also repent at levels they had no prior insight into is the work of wisdom that the Spirit gives. Resetting dislocated soul joints like this requires the work of the Spirit, in which we participate.

There is a great need for the church to offer counseling from people who are expert in soul care and who will participate in what the Spirit is doing as he transforms dislocated, individualistic souls into being the persons in relation he designed them to be. The extent of family breakdown in our culture is frightening, and we as the church need to be there for this crisis. While I have maintained that society is overly psychologized, I insist that the route to Christ for many will be through the journey toward wholeness that is communal in its counseling experience and its result. A great deal has been written in recent years on the importance of community in counseling, including the relationship between the therapist and the client, but beyond that into the role that the church plays in healing.[14]

---

[13]John Chrysostom, "On the Priesthood 3-5," *St. John Chrysostom: Six Books on the Priesthood* 71-73, cited in Elowsky, *John 11–21*, pp. 363-64.

[14]See Rod Wilson, *Counseling in Community: Using Church Relationships to Reinforce Counseling* (Vancouver: Regent College Publishing, 2003); Larry Crabb, *Connecting: Healing Ourselves and Our Relationships* (Nashville: Word, 2005); and Larry Crabb, *Becoming a True Spiritual Community: A Profound Vision of What the Church Can Be* (Nashville: Thomas Nelson, 2007). See also the work of Daniel J. Price, *Karl Barth's Anthropology in Light of Modern Thought* (Grand Rapids: Eerdmans, 2002).

REMISSION AS AN INITIAL AND PERMANENT SAVING ACT AND AS AN ONGOING RELATIONAL PRACTICE

The language in John 20:23 is similar to that in Matthew 16:19 and Matthew 18:18 where "retaining" and "remitting" correspond to "binding" and "loosing." Bruce suggests all these passages reflect a "common Semitic original" in Isaiah 22:22—"I will place on his shoulder the key to the house of David; what he opens no one can shut, and what he shuts no one can open."[15] He notices, however, that whereas the Matthean passages relate to church discipline, "the present context is related to the disciples' mission to the world."[16] There may be a connection between these realities that lessens the gap between discipleship and mission. A community that embraces converts over whom they pronounce remission of sins continues in confessional practice as a way of being. Whereas in the first instance forgiveness of a judicial kind is pronounced in response to the person's saving faith and repentance, in the second instance forgiveness is granted when confession of sin is made, as in 1 John 1–2, which relates to restoration of fellowship rather than impartation of justification.

Jesus appears to make this distinction on two occasions in this Gospel. The first is the washing of the disciples' feet in John 13, where Peter's double faux pas evokes from Jesus the response that he didn't need a bath again, simply a footwashing. He was already and permanently clean from being a disciple of Jesus, unlike Judas who was not clean in that way, as Jesus indicates. Peter simply needed ongoing confession to stay clean relationally with God. Jesus again uses this "clean" analogy in John 15 when he speaks about permanent branches in the Vine. Suffice it to say that repentance is not merely an initial saving experience but the Christian's lifestyle and therefore a prominent feature in communal worship, which sends the message loud and clear that the church is not a place for the "together people" but for those who know they are not "together" and are always in need of forgiveness.

Schnackenburg suggests that some of the controversies that have

---

[15]Bruce, *Gospels and Epistles of John*, p. 392. Bruce references also J. A. Emerton, "Binding and Loosing—Forgiving and Retaining," *Journal of Theological Studies*, n.s. 13 (1962): 325-31.
[16]Ibid.

raged around the church's exegesis of the forgiveness saying in this passage are a consequence of asking questions this text was not intended to answer.[17] He suggests that one of these was the timing of the forgiveness. Was Jesus' intent to speak of the full and final forgiveness offered at the time of the saving faith/repentance and baptism of converts, or was it intended to reflect the ongoing confession of believers, leading to the restoration of fellowship with the Father? If the latter, was this grounds for the sacrament of penance, which has featured heavily in the history of Roman Catholicism?

Schnackenburg notes that for the first three centuries the prevailing interpretation was that it was the forgiveness granted in the conversion event that was in mind.[18] It is only after the patristic period that "later theologians assert, taking the sacrament of penance into account, that sins committed after baptism are intended." He goes on to suggest that in fact "John 20:23 will embrace baptism *and* later forgiveness of sins."[19] The Reformers tended to stress, in reaction to the penitential system's abuses, that John 20:23 has to do with the response to the proclamation of the gospel, and therefore has to do with initial justification of the believer and not the matter of the ongoing confession of sins to God (1 Jn 1:9) and to one another (Jas 5:16). In a less charged context now, it is easy to agree with Schnackenburg and suggest that it is the qualitative reality of forgiveness (without reference to and therefore including both initial and ongoing) that is being bequeathed to the church in this resurrection moment, and also to say that in both situations human assurance of the forgiveness of sincere penitent people is a critical component in the assurance of salvation or restoration of fellowship. Our failure as evangelicals to acknowledge the human instruments of forgiveness is a consequence of the way in which Western individualism has made salvation a "Jesus and me" experience.

As to whether the sacrament of penance has a foundation in this passage, Schnackenburg is less certain. He suggests that the Council of

---

[17]Rudolf Schnackenburg, *The Gospel According to St. John*, trans. David Smith and G. A. Kon (New York: Crossroad, 1982), 3:326.
[18]Ibid.
[19]Ibid.

Trent wrongly invoked it but that there are wider grounds for validating the sacrament.[20] While this moves beyond the comfort of my own Protestant sensibilities, I want to plead for a more ecclesial understanding of salvation and ongoing filial confession. The salvation moment/process is always mediated by the church. Furthermore, there is something about our communal orientation as persons made in the image of a triune relational God that makes us experience forgiveness psychologically only as we confess to another and receive words of absolution from another. This authority is what Jesus gave to his apostles for the church they were birthing.

This anticipates another question this passage does not answer directly. Who is given this authority? Is it just the initial ten apostles? Is it those who can claim physical apostolic succession from them? Is it all spiritual leaders who are in apostolic succession because they adhere to apostolic doctrine? Is it all believers? The first option is unlikely given the finite lives of these men. The second is untenable, and if the third option involving officeholders is reasonable, there is nothing in the text per se to suggest it (despite the tradition suggesting that this passage depicts the ordination of the apostles and that all ordained after them are intended to have the privilege of pronouncing absolution/retention, or that this event marked a growing tradition thereafter that the one presiding over the Eucharist is in mind for this privilege [Schnackenburg]).[21] It seems best to say that Jesus meant this for the *fellowship* of the apostles, defined by Christ's presence (and wherever two or three are gathered in his name [Mt 18:20]). This is the grace of the gospel, that within any fellowship of believers, any who hears a sincere confession of faith and repentance may pronounce forgiveness, because every believer is indwelt by the Spirit, as the apostles were, and every believer is a sent one from Jesus, as Jesus was sent from the Father. We cannot have an interpretation that does not limit the trinitarian sending and the Spirit impartation to the apostles and then suddenly limit the privilege of the pronunciation of forgiveness to the apostles or officeholders.

---

[20]Ibid.
[21]Ibid., p. 327.

Of course, this is not the only passage that deals with this matter. Other passages in the New Testament and church tradition and common sense suggest that trustworthy, confidential persons who are filled with the Spirit would seem to be most appropriate for the bringing of confession. James 5:16 seems to depict confession of sins to elders, for example. However, it seems in the spirit of the priesthood of all believers that the privilege of bringing assurance to penitent people is granted to all, especially where leading them to Christ is concerned, and indeed when they make postconversion confessions. We are built psychologically not to feel forgiven until we verbalize our sins out loud (not too loud!) to another in the fellowship of the apostles. Participation in the life of the triune God by the Spirit is the privilege of all priests, and so is absolution!

It seems, then, that both aspects of confession—the initial confession of saving repentance, as well as the ongoing confession of lifestyle repentance—are in view in this passage, simply because the two are inseparable. Just as saving faith has continuance in the Christian's life of faith, so saving repentance has a lifestyle component. In fact, what new converts become upon profession of faith is organic members in a *community of forgiveness*. For a church to be safe enough to be this kind of community it must be a *community deeply characterized by committed love*—the kind of love that exists between the Father and the Son. This is evident in another of the "as . . . so" passages in John, a profoundly missional passage: "A new command I give you: Love one another. As I have loved you, so you must love one another. By this everyone will know that you are my disciples, if you love one another" (Jn 13:34-35). The primary marker of the alternative, new creational, kingdom community is—love. This is its power in mission. John 15:9 illumines the nature of Christ's love for his disciples: "As the Father has loved me, so have I loved you. Now remain in my love." It is the intratrinitarian love poured into the saints! Notice again the deep-wide nature of the missional church. It cannot experience and demonstrate the love of Christ missionally if it does not "remain" or, better, "abide" in the love of the Father and the Son for each other.

It is important to stress that both saving repentance and lifestyle repentance are *evangelical* as opposed to legal, and that both saving repentance and lifestyle repentance have one divine Mediator in one sense, Christ, and yet for the sake of the assurance of the convert (in the broadest sense) the human pronouncer—the person in the Spirit, who is a member of Christ.

First, then, and this will be critical in discerning true repentance, true repentance is evangelical and not legal. There is a significant body of Protestant literature on distinguishing evangelical and legal repentance. The latter is brought on by fear of punishment or preacher manipulation. If the avoidance of the pain of hellfire is all that motivates a convert's faith profession, we could well argue that this is a hedonistic response unworthy of true saving faith and repentance. For Jonathan Edwards evangelical repentance is motivated by a new sight or sense of things, to coin an Edwardsean phrase. It is a response to a new awareness of God's love and of the glory of God and his Son Jesus. The change of mind is the result of a change of heart effected by the regenerating Spirit, who gives a new sense of the beauty of divine persons and things, and a love for them. For Karl Barth it is a response to what God has already accomplished for all humans in Christ. It does not require any additions, including that of my repentance and faith. It has been effected prior to my repentance.

Second, however, repentance has both a divine mediator and a secondary human conveyor. Clearly God alone forgives sins, and it is him that we are to confess (1 Jn 1:9). Furthermore, God the Son restores the broken communion when confession occurs on the basis of his atoning work on the cross and his ongoing work as our mediator or *paraclete* (1 Jn 1:7, 9; 2:1). Therefore, the act of confession in the presence of another human being is not so much a confession *to* that fellow human as it is to God in the presence of or *with* that fellow human. This qualification does not obviate the fact that God chooses to use human agents in union with himself to impart forgiveness. They do not so much forgive the sins as they convey the forgiveness of the Father. The extent to which the human pronouncer acts in harmony with the divine mediator Christ is measured by the extent to which that person is acting in and by the Spirit.

The practice of confession in the pre-Reformation church has, within the Protestant tradition, been thrown out with the proverbial bathwater. It seems that there is an important psychological component to the *experience* of forgiveness that is tied up in speaking out the sins in the presence of another and hearing words of absolution in return.

REMISSION AND RECONCILIATION AS
A SIGN OF THE KINGDOM

The impossibility of imparting and withholding forgiveness is, as we have stressed, understandable only in light of the action that preceded the privilege—the giving of the Spirit. That breathing of the Spirit into the proleptic community of faith is what constituted it the church of Christ, and only as such could it be a community of forgiveness granted and withheld. It is, as Williams notes, "the Spirit in whose power sins are to be forgiven."[22] This immense privilege of the church contained within it a concomitant responsibility to be a community of forgiveness for all humanity, the responsibility to be a community of justice as well as justification!

The notion that the church as the recipient of forgiveness must also with that privilege bear the responsibility of exercising a judgment role in the world is also associated and only possible if the Spirit is at work in the church. The Spirit is spoken of by Jesus is this manner, that he would convict the world of judgment to come (Jn 16:8-11). As Williams suggests, "In the Spirit, judgement is *constantly* to be pronounced upon 'the prince of this world,' the dominant destructiveness in unredeemed human relations."[23] Tellingly, Williams goes on to indicate that this prophetic function of the church is the task of the church community, which lives in the truth and under the discernment of the Spirit, the kind of community that speaks through the shared life it experiences and "which trusts God and itself enough to live in honesty and acceptance."[24]

In summing up the forgiveness imparted by the resurrection of Jesus,

---

[22]Rowan Williams, *Resurrection* (London: Darton, Longman & Todd, 1982), p. 52.
[23]Ibid., p. 53.
[24]Ibid., p. 54.

Rowan Williams speaks of this as both gift and a responsibility. It is "vocation and commission." On the one hand, he notes "We have learned to live by gift; to us is entrusted the vision of a humanity liberated from fear and shame by the gift of God's presence in the risen Jesus." On the other hand,

> So to live a "forgiven" life is not simply to live in a happy consciousness of having been absolved. Forgiven-ness is precisely the deep and abiding sense of what relation—with God or with other human beings—can and should be; and so is itself a stimulus, an irritant, necessarily provoking protest at impoverished versions of social and personal relations. Once we grasp that forgiveness occurs not by a word of acquittal but by a transformation of the world of persons, we are not likely to regard it as something which merely refers backwards.[25]

Two conditions are critical to the prophetic functioning of the community of forgiveness. The first is that there comes with this role the necessary integrity of the church to its own profession as such a community, for as Williams states, "The Church's role of judgement, its critical role in the world, is a nonsense (and worse) if criticism is not built into its own life and structures. Only a penitent Church can manifest forgiven-ness—a tautology, perhaps, but worth saying."[26] The church has often failed on one of two extremes when it comes to exercising discipline within its own bounds as a community, and at both ends rendered itself mute when it comes to speaking with any gravitas into the injustices and abuses of societal and international relations. The second condition has to do with the evangelical nature of such prophetic speech or action. The prophetic "word" is contained within and arises out of the "speech" of forgiveness. It is not a hammer with which to bludgeon with guilt in order to further alienate the offending person, community or nation. It convicts by its wooing, and its telos is reconciliation. The two conditions in fact coalesce into one. The most evangelical prophetic speech is the authentically holy and truly repentant life of the church community.

---

[25]Ibid., p. 52.
[26]Ibid., p. 53.

In sum, Jesus' act of breathing the Spirit into his disciples signified their becoming one with him, and the continuation of his sentness on earth was reflected in their commission—the remission of sins, leading to life, and retaining of sins, leading to judgment. Jesus had demonstrated this as his work on a number of occasions. For example, the same Jesus who absolves a blind man of guilt (Jn 9:3) and pronounces spiritual sight and life upon him (Jn 9:35-39) pronounces over the unbelieving Pharisees that their guilt remains (Jn 9:41). The assignation of both life and "all judgment" to the Son in John 5:20-23 confirms this. Now as a community in Christ by the Spirit's indwelling, the church continues his work of granting forgiveness and absolution to persons, as well as being his voice for justice in the world at large.

With respect to the first arena, in our age of relativizing ethics and casting off morality in many areas with the concomitant wreckage of human life, there is a need for folks to find pardon, and being able to pronounce it upon their confession is a sacred privilege of the gospel community and a source of great healing for humanity. The freedom for confession for Christians in our churches will go a long way to overcoming the pharisaic feel that many evangelical churches have. In most churches the ethos is such that it does look like we all have it all together, and there is a subtle pressure to keep that image up. Until we can be a community of authenticity about our sinfulness, I doubt that we can really be an attractive community of grace! And confession, with pronounced absolutions, both in public prayers and in private, will help toward that end.

However, the privilege of pronouncing forgiveness imparted to the community of faith as the presence of Jesus in the world is meant to be for the world. A deeply confessional community will be a wide community, not hoarding forgiveness but extending it to all in the world who believe. The permission to forgive and withhold forgiveness is not merely a privilege however. It assumes a community of discernment of justice and of insight into the reconciliation of human persons with God and each other. The community of Jesus' presence as the sign of the kingdom and the new humanity has responsibility to communicate forgiveness when appropriate but also to relate evangelically to all humanity with regard to issues of reconciliation and justice.

In conclusion, just as Jesus came not only to proclaim the kingdom of God but to be the physical embodiment of God's presence, so the church as the ongoing embodiment of Christ by the Spirit's indwelling is given its mission directly from Christ in this the greatest of the commissions. As Newbigin says, "His mission is to be their mission. And so also his Spirit is to be theirs. . . . [T]hey are entrusted with that authority which lies at the heart of Jesus' mission—the authority to forgive sins." Newbigin concludes that the church "is sent, therefore, not only to proclaim the Kingdom, but to bear in its own life the presence of the kingdom."[27] This authority is given as a commission to the church to bring God's forgiveness to people in every situation, through word and action, thereby enabling the shalom of God, his gift of peace. The church's ability to spread this shalom is contingent on its receptivity to that shalom as it practices the presence of the crucified and risen Christ, thereby living into and out of the triune missional God, as the deep and wide missional church.

---

[27]Newbigin, *Open Secret*, pp. 48-49.

Bibliography

Anderson, Ray S. *An Emergent Theology for the Emerging Church.* Downers Grove, Ill.: InterVarsity Press, 2006.

Barth, Karl. *Church Dogmatics*, Vols. I-V. Edited by G. W. Bromiley and T. F. Torrance. 2nd ed. Edinburgh: T & T Clark, 1975.

Bakke, Ray, and J. Hart. *The Urban Christian: Ministry in Today's Urban World.* Downers Grove, Ill.: InterVarsity Press, 1987.

Bauckham, Richard. *The Bible and Mission: Christian Witness in a Postmodern World.* Grand Rapids: Baker Academic, 2003.

Bender, Kimlyn J. *Karl Barth's Christological Ecclesiology.* Barth Study Series. Burlington, Vt.: Ashgate, 2005.

Belcher, Jim. *Deep Church: A Third Way Beyond Emerging and Traditional.* Downers Grove, Ill.: InterVarsity Press, 2009.

Bosch, David J. *Transforming Mission: Paradigm Shifts in Theology of Mission.* Maryknoll, N.Y.: Orbis, 1991.

Bonhoeffer, Dietrich. *Life Together.* San Francisco: Harper, 1954.

Braaten, Carl E. *That All May Believe: A Theology of the Gospel and the Mission of the Church.* Grand Rapids: Eerdmans, 2008.

Brueggemann, Walter. *Biblical Perspectives on Evangelism: Living in a Three-Storied Universe.* Nashville: Abingdon, 1993.

Chester, Tim, and Steve Timmis. *Total Church: A Radical Reshaping Around Gospel and Community.* Wheaton, Ill.: Crossway, 2008.

Clapp, Rodney. *A Peculiar People: The Church as Culture in a Post-Christian Society.* Downers Grove, Ill.: InterVarsity Press, 1996.

Collins, Phil, and R. Paul Stevens. *The Equipping Pastor.* Washington, D.C.: Alban Institute, 1993.

Costas, Orlando. *Christ Outside the Gate: Mission Beyond Christendom.* Maryknoll, N.Y.: Orbis, 1983.

Crouch, Andy. *Culture Making: Recovering Our Creative Calling.* Downers Grove, Ill.: InterVarsity Press, 2009.

Dulles, Avery. *Models of the Church*. Expanded ed. New York: Image, 1987.

Dyrness, William A. *Learning About Theology from the Third World*. Grand Rapids: Zondervan, 1990.

Flemming, Dean. *Contextualization in the New Testament: Patterns for Theology and Mission*. Downers Grove, Ill: InterVarsity Press, 2005.

Flett, John G. *The Witness of God: The Trinity, Missio Dei, Karl Barth and the Nature of Christian Community*. Grand Rapids: Eerdmans, 2010.

Frost, Michael, and Alan Hirsch. *The Shaping of Things to Come: Innovation and Mission for the 21st-Century Church*. Peabody, Mass.: Hendrickson, 2003.

Goheen, Michael W., and Craig G. Bartholomew. *Living at the Crossroads: An Introduction to Christian Worldview*. Grand Rapids: Baker Academic, 2009.

Guder, Darrell, ed. *Missional Church: A Vision for the Sending of the Church in North America*. Grand Rapids: Eerdmans, 1998.

———. *The Continuing Conversion of the Church*. Grand Rapids: Eerdmans, 2000.

Gunton, Colin E. *The Promise of Trinitarian Theology*. Edinburgh: T & T Clark, 1990.

Hauerwas, Stanley. *After Christendom? How the Church Is to Behave If Freedom, Justice, and a Christian Nation Are Bad Ideas*. Nashville: Abingdon, 1991.

Hauerwas, Stanley, and William H. Willimon, *Resident Aliens: Life in the Christian Colony*. Nashville: Abingdon, 1989.

Hirsch, Alan. *The Forgotten Ways: Reactivating the Missional Church*. Grand Rapids: Brazos, 2007.

Keck, Leander. *The Church Confident: Christianity Can Repent but It Must Not Whimper*. Nashville: Abingdon, 1993.

Keifert, Patrick R. *Welcoming the Stranger: A Public Theology of Worship and Evangelism*. Minneapolis: Augsburg Fortress, 1992.

Kimball, Dan. *The Emerging Church: Vintage Christianity for New Generations*. Grand Rapids: Zondervan, 2003.

Lindbeck, George. *The Nature of Doctrine: Religion and Theology in a Post-liberal Age*. Louisville: Westminster John Knox, 1984.

Moltmann, Jürgen. *The Church in the Power of the Spirit*. London: SCM Press, 1977.

———. *The Trinity and the Kingdom of God*. London: SCM Press, 1981.

Newbigin, Lesslie. *The Gospel in a Pluralistic Society*. Grand Rapids: Eerdmans, 1989.

————. *One Body, One Gospel, One World*. London: International Missionary Council, 1958.

————. *The Open Secret*. Grand Rapids: Eerdmans,1995.

Raschke, Carl. *GloboChrist: The Great Commission Takes a Postmodern Turn*. Grand Rapids: Baker Academic, 2008.

Roxburgh, Alan J. *The Missionary Congregation, Leadership and Liminality*. Harrisburg, Penn.: Trinity Press International, 1997.

Schwöbel, Christoph, ed., *Trinitarian Theology Today*. Edinburgh: T & T Clark, 1995.

Smith, James K. A. *Desiring the Kingdom: Worship, Worldview, and Cultural Formation*. Grand Rapids: Baker Academic, 2009.

————. *Introducing Radical Orthodoxy: Mapping a post-Secular Theology*. Grand Rapids: Baker Academic, 2004.

Stetzer, Ed. *Planting Missional Churches*. Nashville: Broadman & Holman, 2006.

Van Engen, Charles. *God's Missionary People: Rethinking the Purpose of the Local Church*. Grand Rapids: Baker, 1991.

Van Gelder, Craig. *The Essence of the Church: A Community Created by the Spirit*. Grand Rapids: Baker, 2000.

Volf, Miroslav, *After Our Likeness: The Church as the Image of the Trinity*. Grand Rapids: Eerdmans, 1998.

Waldron, Scott. *Karl Barth's Theology of Mission*. Downers Grove, Ill.: Inter-Varsity Press, 1978.

Walker, Andrew, and Luke Bretherton, eds. *Remembering Our Future: Explorations in Deep Church*. Colorado Springs: Paternoster, 2007.

Walls, Andrew F. *The Missionary Movement in Christian History: Studies in the Transmission of Faith*. Maryknoll, N.Y.: Orbis, 1996.

Webber, Robert E. *Ancient-Future Faith: Rethinking Evangelicalism for a Postmodern World*. Grand Rapids: Baker, 1999.

Wright, Christopher J. H. *The Mission of God: Unlocking the Bible's Grand Narrative*. Downers Grove, Ill.: IVP Academic, 2006.

Wright, N. T. *Bringing the Church to the World*. Minneapolis: Bethany House, 1992.

Zizioulas, John D. *Being as Communion: Studies in Personhood and the Church*. Crestwood, N.Y.: St. Vladimir's Seminary Press, 1985.

Name and Subject Index

Adam, last Adam, 23, 30-31, 33, 41, 108, 110, 148-49, 151, 153, 161-62, 189, 265, 288

analogia entis, 44, 75, 97

analogia relationis, 75, 96-97

Alpha course, 146, 345

Anselm, 54, 193n5

apostles, 21, 33, 79, 86, 99, 126, 131, 133, 137-38, 143, 166, 190n1, 191-92, 231, 250, 262, 272, 286-87, 296, 309-11, 315-16

apostolic leadership, 143

atonement, 85, 170, 191, 193n5, 195, 197, 223-26, 236

Augustine, 67, 94-95, 103, 150, 153, 187, 190n1, 194, 196n11, 252-54, 269n3

baptism, 105, 133-34, 146, 198-200, 202, 207-10, 286-87, 295-96, 314

Barth, Karl, 32, 44nn11, 12, 50n23, 54-55, 61, 75-76, 84, 86, 96, 109, 112-14, 129, 144, 150, 163, 178, 193n4n6, 196, 198, 226-29, 251, 257-58, 274-75, 280, 287, 312, 317, 323-25

Begbie, Jeremy, 140, 147

Belcher, Jim, 11, 14, 266

Benedict XVI, 44n10, 95, 196n11, 273

Boersma, Hans, 236-38

Bonhoeffer, Dietrich, 45, 130, 134, 145, 161, 323

Bosch, David, 12, 19, 32, 35n29, 44n11, 49, 50n23, 67, 77, 252n11, 262, 263n39, 294

Bretherton, Luke, 11, 32, 34n28, 48n14, 71, 72nn21, 23, 73, 137n18, 138n23, 139n24, 146n38, 232n15, 266, 297n5, 325

Calvin, John, 24, 29, 42, 44n12, 45, 75-76, 93n26,

108-10, 122n1, 149-50, 161, 174, 190n1, 196n11, 201n14, 208, 225-26, 229, 247, 276n16, 290-91, 309, 311

Cappadocians, 94-95, 253

catechesis, 11, 105, 138, 146

catholicity, 11, 16, 34, 71, 73, 82, 106, 115-16, 135-36, 142, 267, 289

Christ, Jesus Christ, 11-15, 20-30, 32-33, 35-37, 40-47, 52, 55, 59, 66, 69-71, 73, 75-78, 80-82, 84-99, 101-2, 105-15, 117, 121-33, 135-37, 140-46, 148-52, 155-56, 158, 160, 162-66, 168-72, 174-79, 182, 184-86, 189-200, 202-7, 209-13, 215-37, 239, 243-49, 251-52, 254, 256-57, 259-61, 263-64, 266-67, 269-94, 296-97, 299-300, 303-4, 307-12, 315-18, 320-21

Christendom, Constantinianism, 73, 89, 143, 164n4, 165, 220-21, 235

clergy/laity, 143, 184

coinherence, 32, 98-100, 175, 230, 237, 253-54

community, communities, 11-14, 20, 22-23, 25-28, 31, 33-40, 42, 47, 48n14, 50, 57, 60-61, 66-68, 70-71, 74, 77, 79, 82, 86, 89, 98-99, 104, 106-7, 109n58, 111-15, 121ff., 149-50, 157, 161, 164-66, 168, 177-78, 181-82, 184-85, 190ff., 222, 224, 232ff., 243ff., 277, 281, 285, 287-88, 292, 293ff.

consumerism, 62, 64, 125, 298

contextualization, 50, 56n45, 57, 62, 136, 146, 148, 164, 166-68, 289

Costas, Orlando, 32, 87n14,

148n2, 149, 235, 264, 294, 296, 323

covenant, 23, 28, 43, 70, 89, 100, 108, 109n58, 110-11, 113, 137, 153, 156, 161, 179, 181, 203-4, 206, 226-27, 229, 261

creation, 14-15, 20, 22n4, 23n7, 27, 30-33, 38, 40-43, 45-46, 63, 74-76, 81, 85n9, 86-87, 89, 91, 93, 98n40, 99-101, 106ff., 121-22, 128, 132, 137-38, 140, 142-43, 147-48, 149ff., 163-64, 165n15, 169ff., 179, 182-86, 188-89, 193-97, 203-4, 208, 210, 215, 219, 222, 225-28, 246, 252, 254, 256, 258-59, 261, 263, 265, 288-90, 305, 308, 310, 316

Creed, Nicene, 91, 141

cross, 20, 59, 101, 110-11, 115, 126-27, 136, 142, 166, 193-98, 200, 205, 213, 216-18, 219ff., 281, 284, 304, 317

cruciform, 191, 198ff., 210-11, 215-18, 221-22, 234

cultural mandate, 12, 31, 33, 42, 46, 106, 108, 155-57, 159, 166, 183-84, 189, 209, 215

culture, 11, 13-15, 31, 33-34, 37ff., 59ff., 130, 138n22, 139-40, 148, 150, 159, 164-69, 173, 176, 178, 181, 195, 221-24, 250, 293, 295, 298, 302-5, 312

deconstruction, 57, 237n27

Deddo, Gary, 97n38

dualism, 63, 65, 84, 100, 106, 183

Edwards, Jonathan, 85, 93, 95, 116, 162, 196, 226, 228-29, 254-55, 273, 275, 287, 290, 317

election, 45, 50n23, 88,

108-12, 115, 130n9, 196, 226, 230
Ellul, Jacques, 66, 67n12, 134n13, 300
emergent, emergent church, 14, 46, 61, 69, 71, 72, 73, 74, 124, 136, 139, 299
enculturation, 34, 37ff., 59ff., 124, 148, 164
ethics, 68, 134n15, 141, 158, 161, 171, 173, 179, 184, 198, 206, 237, 259n25, 291, 295, 302-3, 320
ethnocentrism, 63, 65, 69
Eucharist, Lord's Supper, 23, 70, 88, 105, 116, 125, 192, 199, 200ff., 264, 282, 315
evangelism, 14, 21, 31, 33, 46, 48, 65, 68, 83, 99, 105-6, 108, 116, 149, 151, 155-56, 163, 167, 168, 184, 211, 220, 232, 238, 259, 267, 277, 281, 288-89, 302, 323-24
exclusivism, 88, 91
Fiddes, Paul, 83, 86
Flett, John, 114, 251n10, 252, 257-59
Gay, Craig, 51n26, 52n28
gender, 63, 150, 153-54, 160-61, 171-73, 178ff., 186, 213
gospel, 13, 20, 22-24, 26, 28, 29n17, 34, 38-40, 47, 50-58, 61-62, 64-69, 73, 78-79, 81-82, 86, 88-90, 92n24, 93, 96, 98-99, 101, 103-4, 107, 109-10, 125, 131, 137-38, 141, 143, 146, 148-49, 161, 164, 166-72, 183-86, 199-200, 203, 205, 213, 216, 219, 221-25, 231-33, 235-36, 238-39, 245, 247, 249-50, 252, 256, 260, 262, 270-71, 276-77, 280-81, 286-88, 291n23, 295-97, 302-5, 307, 308ff., 315, 320
globalization, 91

Great Commandment, 46, 154-58, 163, 210, 265
Great Commission, 23, 46, 78n37, 108, 155-57, 248, 265
Green, Brad, 103n50, 194
Guder, Darrell, 32, 35n29, 39, 64, 78, 126n3, 143, 261n32, 262nn35, 36, 299n11, 301, 302
Hart, Trevor, 61, 62n2, 109n57, 194n9, 226n4, 227n5, 228n10, 229n12
Hauerwas, Stanley, 14, 48n14, 55, 56n42, 259n25
hermeneutics, 28, 55-56
high priesthood of Christ, 136, 212-15
Hoffmeyer, John, 87nn13, 15, 88, 252, 253n13, 257n21, 260-61
holiness, 61, 141-42, 178, 182, 284, 289-90
Holmes, Stephen R., 193, 252, 253n13
Holy Spirit, 19, 21, 25, 66, 77, 84-85, 92, 100, 102, 105, 110, 128, 131, 140, 158, 208, 213, 230, 241, 250, 262, 268, 291, 293ff., 309-11
hospitality, 48, 116, 128, 169, 181-82, 205, 236-39, 264, 307
humanity, 15, 22n4, 23-24, 31, 33, 39-42, 44-48, 57, 61, 70, 86-88, 91-92, 96-98, 101, 106-8, 113, 122, 124, 128-31, 141-42, 148-51, 155-56, 160-63, 164n3, 168-71, 175, 178-79, 183, 189, 190n1, 195-97, 206, 213, 222-25, 227-28, 239, 244, 246-47, 256-59, 261, 263, 265, 267, 270-71, 274, 288, 307-8, 310, 318-20
humanity of Christ, 15, 40-41, 54, 91-92, 96-98, 106, 109-13, 121-22, 124, 130-31, 136, 148, 151, 156, 162-63, 168-71, 175,

178, 182-83, 189-90, 194-95, 197, 206, 224-26, 244-45, 247, 263, 270-71, 274-75, 310
hypostases, 44, 94-96
hypostatic union, 91, 113, 170, 245, 271
image of God, imago Dei, imago trinitatis, 38-39, 45, 60-61, 95, 149-54, 157, 160-62, 164, 166, 170-71, 173, 178-80, 183-86, 215, 263
incarnation, 13-14, 31-32, 28, 50, 55, 56n45, 65, 73, 87, 91, 102, 106, 109-13, 129-31, 133, 135-36, 147ff., 194n9, 198, 206, 213, 225-27, 234-35, 245, 250, 253, 259, 263, 266-68, 270-71, 274-75, 277, 285, 287-89, 294, 296, 303
inclusivism, 91-92
inculturation, 32, 37ff., 137, 148
individualism, 67-70, 133-34, 175, 314
institution, institutionalism, 68, 71, 73, 115, 133, 139, 199, 220, 297ff.
Irenaeus, 13, 23n7, 44n12, 98n40, 110n59, 150, 160, 162, 266, 297
joy, 19, 22n4, 24, 25n10, 46, 76, 91, 125-26, 162, 190-92, 197, 208, 220, 229, 278, 304
Jüngel, Eberhard, 103
justice, 12, 14, 31, 33, 42, 48, 65, 69, 106, 128, 143, 149, 156, 161, 163, 166, 184, 186, 195, 210, 227, 233, 265, 267, 281, 288-89, 301, 305, 318, 320-21
justification, 15, 28, 40, 65, 93-94, 98, 109, 110n60, 114, 197, 225-26
kingdom, kingdom of God, 14-15, 20-22, 25, 31, 33-34, 46, 48, 60, 65-67,

69-70, 73, 87-90, 106,
113, 115, 126-27, 134,
144, 148, 151, 162,
164n15, 165n15, 166, 170,
186, 191, 204, 210, 215,
222, 228, 231-34, 255,
259-60, 264, 267, 279-81,
288, 299-301, 305-6, 308,
316, 318, 320-21
Küng, Hans, 54, 229
leadership, 88, 125, 143,
256, 289, 295, 297,
299-300
Lewis, C. S., 11n2, 59, 85
Lord's Prayer, 198, 280
Lyotard, François, 54, 56
MacIntyre, Alasdair, 53,
256n20
marketplace, 84, 158-59
Martland, T. R., 95
modern, modernity, 13, 28,
34, 51ff., 60ff., 74-75, 81,
83, 88, 90, 105, 108, 124,
167, 172, 178, 195, 202,
222, 226, 234, 237, 276,
294, 297-98, 300
new creation, 20, 23, 27, 30,
33, 76, 106, 122, 138, 140,
147-49, 152, 156, 160,
165n15, 169-70, 183-86,
188-89, 194, 210, 219,
265, 289, 310
new monastic communities,
48n14, 256n20
Newbigin, Lesslie, 12, 32,
34, 43, 48, 53, 62, 67-68,
77, 83-84, 103-4, 111-12,
130, 219, 232-34, 260,
296, 321
Niebuhr, H. Richard,
164-65
O'Donovan, Oliver, 149n4,
163
participation, 15-16, 21,
26-27, 32-33, 42, 44-45,
71, 74-78, 80, 114, 117,
125, 129, 150-51, 155,
161-62, 165n15, 175, 178,
185-86, 193n6, 198,
203-4, 206-7, 209, 211-12,
214, 222, 231-32, 244-45,
247, 249, 251-52, 256,

262-64, 267, 268ff., 280,
282, 285-86, 288ff., 304,
307, 309-11
pastors, 47, 174, 144, 158,
174, 183, 205, 214,
297-98, 303, 310
peace, 19, 24-26, 28n15,
30n24, 46, 76, 119, 121,
126-28, 135, 144, 147,
208, 210, 216, 233-34,
241, 244, 265, 272
perichoresis, 98-99, 175, 237,
253-56, 261, 274
personhood, 56, 90, 93-94,
96-99, 101, 149, 152, 162,
171-73, 188, 253, 267
Polanyi, Michael, 53
postmodernity, 43, 51-58,
60, 62-65, 69, 72, 81, 83,
88, 90-91, 113, 124, 168,
222, 236-37, 239
prayer, 50-51, 105, 114-15,
124, 134, 141, 174-77,
198, 201-2, 204, 213-15,
262, 279-80, 284, 296,
303-4, 320
preaching, 47, 68, 108, 125,
134, 138, 142, 144-45,
211, 215-16, 222-25, 233,
257, 277, 286, 296
priesthood, 13, 15, 31-32,
40-41, 133, 141-42,
212-15, 256, 259, 260n27,
316
prophetic, 39, 51-52, 114,
318-19
public square, 15, 45, 52, 74,
76, 166, 259-60, 265
Radical Orthodoxy, 43, 52,
53n30, 55-56, 58, 74-76,
81
Raschke, Carl, 90-91
reconciliation, 14, 27, 46,
48, 82, 105, 112-14,
128-29, 142-43, 152, 156,
161, 193, 195-96, 198,
225, 230-31, 236, 238,
247-48, 265, 290, 294,
299, 307ff.
reign of God, 31, 67, 126,
152-53, 170, 232-33, 301
relations, relationality, 45,

81, 84, 86-93, 96-101,
103n49, 110n60, 114-15,
151-55, 157, 160-61,
169-71, 173, 175-77,
178ff., 193n6, 245, 263,
273-74, 298
resurrection, 15, 17, 20, 22,
29-30, 60, 65, 76, 78-79,
106, 110-11, 122, 136,
140, 147ff., 190n1,
197-98, 200, 206-7, 210,
218-19, 225-26, 232, 236,
279-80, 286, 290-91, 303,
308, 318
resurrection of Christ, 27,
65, 106, 110, 126, 148,
210, 218, 225-26, 291, 318
Roxburgh, Alan J., 72
sacrament, 16, 32, 71n20,
72, 88, 116, 128, 137,
144-45, 198, 201-2, 206,
213, 215-17, 259, 261,
314-15
sanctification, 85, 96, 109,
114, 152, 170, 229, 247,
271, 284, 290-91
Scriptures, 89, 112, 145,
216, 222, 296
sexuality, 178ff.
shalom, 13, 21-22, 24-27,
33, 42, 46, 123, 126-28,
142, 144, 146, 152,
155-57, 160-62, 166,
183-84, 190, 198, 209,
216, 241, 245-46, 288,
303, 321
Smail, Tom, 54-55, 231,
232n15
Smith, James F. K., 42,
43n5, 47, 48, 52-53, 55,
56n44, 58, 74, 75n29, 81
social gospel, 99, 149
Stackhouse, John G., 92n24
Stark, Rodney, 21
Stevens, Paul, 35n29, 48-49,
100, 143, 184, 251, 260,
291, 302
Stott, John R. W., 179,
180n30, 184, 266
theosis, 78, 82, 131, 132n10,
245, 268ff.
Torrance, Alan, 44n12,

96n33, 194n9, 274n9, 275n15

Torrance, James, 32, 137n17, 194n9, 212, 113, 255

Torrance, Thomas F., 29n18, 32, 44n12, 76n30, 110n60, 122n1, 190n1, 309n4

trinitarian, 13-14, 16, 24, 26, 32-33, 36, 44n12, 46, 55, 68, 77-78, 80, 83-84, 91ff., 125, 131, 141, 146, 168, 171n24, 172, 174, 185, 194-96, 208, 212-13, 230, 243ff., 248, 251-53, 255, 257, 258n24, 264, 266, 271ff., 282, 285, 287, 289, 294, 298, 303-4, 309, 315-16

Trinity, 14-15, 26-27, 32, 44, 54, 69, 77, 79, 80ff., 133, 137, 153, 157, 163, 171, 176, 178, 185, 194, 201, 206-7, 231, 248ff., 260-61, 263-64, 268-69, 273-74, 285, 294-95, 298, 303-4

Van Engen, Charles, 48,

141-42, 213, 284n19, 300n15, 301nn18, 20

vicarious humanity of Christ, 15, 91, 110, 170, 224-26, 263

Vickers, Jason, 102, 104-5

vocation, 12, 46-47, 68, 112-14, 148, 157-59, 161, 163, 171, 173, 178, 184-85, 256, 259, 265, 319

Volf, Miroslav, 116n68, 123n2, 133, 135, 139, 237, 255, 258-59, 274, 275n15, 298-99

Walker, Andrew, 11, 32, 34n28, 48n14, 70n18, 71n20, 72, 73n24, 137n18, 138n23, 139n24, 146, 231, 232n15, 266, 297n5

Ward, Graham, 51, 53, 56

Walls, Andrew F., 166

Webster, John, 64n6, 145, 275n11

Wesley, Charles, 104-5

Williams, Rowan, 86n12, 261, 308, 318-19

Willimon, William, 14, 48n14, 55-56

Wilson, Jonathan R., 48n14, 256n20

Word, Word of God, 47, 72, 88, 98, 98n40, 101, 144, 146, 150n5, 168, 200, 215-16, 224, 227, 230, 259-61, 263, 265, 277-78, 284, 287, 289, 294, 296

work, 33, 45, 47, 148, 150, 152, 155-60, 162, 166, 171, 173, 183ff., 215, 218, 278ff.

worship, 12, 40, 61, 64-66, 70-71, 87, 97, 104-5, 116, 124-26, 136-40, 172, 184, 191, 193-94, 198, 200, 211ff., 217, 221, 238, 246, 264-65, 283, 287, 294, 297-98, 313

Wright, Christopher, 56-57, 166n17, 188, 244, 245n1, 246-47, 251n10

Wright, N. T., 30, 43, 147n1, 188, 229, 308

Yoder, John Howard, 14, 48n14, 165, 258

Zimmerman, Jens, 51n26

Zizioulas, John, 32, 94, 95n33, 153n8, 253n16, 275n15

Scripture Index

Genesis
1, *106, 107, 150, 159*
1–2, *12, 46, 106, 155, 215*
1:26, *154*
1:26-27, *150, 170, 178*
2, *30, 155*
2:7, *23, 30, 269*
2:24, *30*
3, *160*
3:5, *161*
4:2, *159*
4:17-22, *159*
9:6, *150, 154*

Leviticus
4–6, *197*

1 Kings
17:21, *269*

Psalms
122, *30*

Isaiah
22:22, *313*
53:4, *279*
61, *295*

Ezekiel
36:25-27, *270*
37:9, *269*

Matthew
1:20, *195*
9:37-38, *50*
10:17, *279*
16, *59*
16:19, *313*
18:18, *313*
18:20, *123, 131, 315*
22, *155*
26:29, *210*
28, *155*
28:18, *126*
28:18-20, *226*

Mark
2, *310*
2:10, *310*
16, *12*

Luke
3:21-23, *295*
4:18-19, *295*
24:49, *29*

John
1:1-14, *107*
1:32-34, *268*
3:5, *305*
3:16, *195, 223*
3:30, *254*
3:34, *268*
3:34-35, *277*
4, *181, 278*
4–5, *281*
4:14, *72*
4:33-35, *278*
4:34, *185, 281*
5, *278, 279*
5:17, *279*
5:18, *254*
5:19, *101*
5:19-20, *279*
5:20-21, *279*
5:20-23, *320*
5:21, *244, 311*
5:22-30, *280*
5:22-47, *311*
5:24, *280*
5:25-26, *244*
5:36, *281*
6, *199, 220, 282*
6:13, *199*
6:57, *199, 282*
7, *311*
7:37-39, *283*
7:39, *29*
8:16, *280*
9:3, *320*
9:35-39, *320*
9:41, *320*
10:30, *254*
11–21, *20, 25, 29, 122, 187, 190, 191, 269, 309, 311, 312*
12, *25, 50, 223, 278, 311*
12:23-26, *223*
12:44-45, *282*
12:49-50, *278*
13, *174, 313*

13:34, *244*
13:34-35, *132, 316*
14, *98, 270, 280*
14–16, *131*
14:9, *101*
14:10, *101*
14:11-27, *271*
14:12, *277, 279*
14:13-14, *280*
14:17, *29*
14:18, *28*
14:20, *28, 132, 244, 248, 271, 272*
14:21, *244*
14:23, *132, 244*
14:23-25, *278*
14:27, *24, 28*
14:28, *101, 254*
15, *313*
15:9, *244, 316*
15:20-21, *281*
16:8-11, *318*
16:22, *191*
16:33, *28*
17, *114, 284*
17:11-18, *288*
17:17-19, *284*
17:18, *244, 251*
17:19, *284*
17:20-23, *284*
17:20, *114-15*
17:21, *115, 135*
17:22-23, *115*
20, *12, 22, 23, 24, 27, 30, 35, 60, 68, 69, 76, 77, 79, 83, 86, 99, 125, 130, 131, 132, 135, 136, 141, 142, 143, 144, 152, 155, 156, 169, 171, 174, 175, 177, 186, 190, 197, 200, 204, 220, 229, 232, 236, 269, 272, 276, 277, 284, 308, 310*
20:17, *245*
20:19, *20, 28, 30, 121, 122, 124, 126, 131, 147*
20:19-20, *119, 136*
20:19-21, *135, 144*
20:19-23, *16, 19, 22, 28, 32, 59, 65, 143, 198, 214, 243, 272*

20:20, *125, 144, 190, 219*
20:20-23, *20*
20:21, *15, 28, 78, 80, 82,
    114, 140, 199, 243, 244*
20:21-22, *268, 271*
20:21-23, *128, 241*
20:22, *28, 293*
20:22-23, *131*
20:23, *272, 281, 307, 313,
    314*
21, *142*

Acts
1:1, *15, 78, 305*
1:5-8, *29*
1:8, *78, 293*
1:14, *141*
2, *22, 28, 38, 116, 123, 217,
    269*
2:1, *141*
2:11, *116*
2:23, *162, 194, 254*
2:36, *174*
2:38-47, *286*
2:41, *202*
2:42, *125, 201, 262, 287, 296*
2:42-47, *47, 216*
2:46, *125, 217*
2:46-47, *126*
4, *21*
4:28, *162*
5, *287*
5:13-14, *86, 286*
6:1-7, *301*
13:1-4, *299*
14:14, *143*
17, *38, 223*
17:25-28, *90*
18:10, *226*
20:7, *125, 201, 202, 296*
20:28, *299*

Romans
1–5, *286*
1:4, *174*
3:24-26, *197*
4:25, *171, 186, 197*
5:1, *24*
5:5, *303*
6, *286*
8:9-10, *248*
8:15-16, *303*

8:21-30, *265*
8:30, *151*
12, *297*
12:1-2, *37*
12:2, *301*
16:7, *143*

1 Corinthians
1:23, *194, 222*
2:2, *222*
2:4, *51*
2:4-5, *144*
2:10, *51*
2:14-16, *154*
3:6, *51*
3:9, *51*
3:21-23, *243*
6:2-3, *281*
8:1, *154*
9:16, *222*
9:20-21, *37*
10, *206*
10:16-17, *200*
10:25-27, *206*
11, *205*
11:18, *202*
11:20, *125, 202*
11:26, *203, 210*
11:28, *204*
12, *297*
12:13, *198*
13, *303*
13:1-2, *154*
14, *47, 297, 298*
14:24-25, *86*
14:25, *295*
14:26, *214*
15:3-4, *222*
15:35-50, *187*
15:42-44, *122, 187*
15:45, *31*

2 Corinthians
3:18, *209, 282*
4:3-6, *154*
4:5-7, *283*
4:6, *209*
4:10, *220*
5, *230*
5:1-10, *189*
5:11-21, *82*
5:18, *24*

5:18-20, *248*
5:19, *142, 230*
5:20, *311*

Galatians
5:22, *303*
6:14, *222*
6:17, *220*

Ephesians
1, *111*
1:3, *109*
1:4, *110*
1:6, *174*
2:1-10, *154*
3, *174, 175, 176, 177*
3:16-17, *175*
3:17-18, *177*
4, *143, 207*
4:11, *297*
4:12-16, *297*
4:16, *297*
5:1-2, *195*
5:21-33, *254*

Philippians
1:21-24, *189*
2:7, *254*
3:10, *232*

Colossians
1:15, *151, 170*
1:15-20, *107, 197*
1:19-20, *24*
1:20, *24, 142*
1:27, *248*
2, *286*
2:9-10, *248*
2:12–3:4, *287*
2:13-15, *197*
3:2, *248*

1 Timothy
2:5-6, *92*
6:16, *102*

2 Timothy
3:12, *220*

Titus
3:5, *170*
3:5-6, *305*

Hebrews
1:5, *174*
2, *170, 197*
2:10, *278*
2:14-15, *197*
3:1, *245*
5, *162*
7, *197*
8:2, *125*
9:14, *195*
10:14, *284*
12:2, *278*
12:10, *284*
13:2, *238*
13:11-14, *234*
13:15, *214*

James
5:16, *205, 314, 316*

1 Peter
1:25, *278*
2, *142, 214*
2:4-10, *142*
2:5, *215*
2:9, *215*
2:11, *40*
2:11-12, *290*
2:11-17, *142*
2:12, *302*
2:17, *290*
3:1, *302*
3:15, *302*
4, *297*
4:11, *144, 224*

2 Peter
1:4, *245, 247*
1:8, *247*

1 John
1–2, *313*
1:7, *317*
1:9, *205, 314, 317*
2:1, *317*
2:15-17, *61*
3:1-2, *151, 189*
5:8, *195*
5:19, *61*

Revelation
2, *124*
2:4, *124*
5:6, *190, 194*
13:8, *162, 194, 254*
21, *189*